Alaska For Dummies,® 1st Edition

Cheat Sheet

Date Due →

Making Your Way around Alaska

To get from town to town in Alaska, you'll likely need more than just a rental car. Some communities in Alaska are isolated enough that you can get to them only by plane or by boat. This table shows which mode of transportation you need to get to particular Alaska towns.

City	Air	Ferry	Rail	Road
Anchorage	Jet		x	x
Barrow	Jet			
Denali National Park			x	x
Girdwood				x
Homer	Prop	x		x
Juneau	Jet	x		
Katmai National Park	Prop			
Kenai	Prop			x
Kodiak Island	Jet	x		
Mat-Su				x
Nome	Jet			
Seward (Kenai Fjords National Park)	Prop	x	x	x
Sitka	Jet	x		
Skagway	Prop	x		x
Whittier		x	x	x

Alaska Mileage Chart

	Anchorage	Fairbanks	Homer	Kenai	Seward	Skagway
Anchorage		358	226	157	126	832
Fairbanks	358		584	513	484	710
Homer	226	584		83	173	1058
Kenai	157	513	83		105	967
Seward	126	484	173	105		958
Skagway	832	710	1058	967	958	

JUL 2 7 2007

For Dummies: Bestselling Book Series for Beginners

Alaska For Dummies®, 1st Edition

Cheat Sheet

Spotting Alaska's Wildlife

What It Is	What to Look For	Where to Find It
Bald eagle	6- to 7½-foot wing span; a distinctive white head (though younger birds have mottled brown plumage)	Common in coastal towns of Southeast and South Central Alaska, such as Seward, Homer, Juneau, and Sitka
Black bear	5 feet tall and not necessarily black; smoother back, bigger ears, and longer, straighter nose than brown bear	Locals in coastal communities often know salmon-spawning streams where bears congregate
Brown bear (or grizzly bear)	Up to 9 feet tall when standing; humped back; smaller ears than black bear	Denali National Park; Katmai National Park; Kodiak Island; Admiralty Island near Juneau
Caribou	4½ to 8 feet in height; like open country; travel in groups	On broad, wide-open tundra (for example, along northern Interior highways); Denali National Park; the Arctic
Dall sheep	4 to 5 feet tall; curled horns; less shaggy than mountain goats	High, craggy mountains; on the cliffs along the Seward Highway near Anchorage
Humpback whales	50 feet in length; white fins up to 14 feet long that they use to slap the water	Icy Strait near Gustavus, accessible by tour boat from Juneau or as part of a trip to Glacier Bay National Park; Sitka Sound near Sitka; in Resurrection Bay and Kenai Fjords National Park near Seward; in Prince William Sound near Whittier
Moose	7 to 10 feet tall; brown, shaggy hides, bulbous noses, and heavy antlers	Much of Alaska; most reliably in Interior and South Central regions, especially along roads in wet, brushy country
Musk ox	4 to 5 feet high; big, shaggy mop, curved horns	Tundra roads from Nome
Orca whale (or killer whale)	23 to 27 feet in length; tall, black dorsal fin	Resurrection Bay from Seward; Prince William Sound from Whittier; waters near Juneau
Polar bear	8 to 10 feet tall; unmistakable	Point Barrow, on the Arctic Ocean shore, north of Barrow
Puffin	14 inches tall; horned puffins are the most familiar (think Toucan Sam); tufted puffins have tufts of feathers curling back from their heads	Kenai Fjords National Park; Homer; Sitka

For Dummies: Bestselling Book Series for Beginners

Alaska
FOR
DUMMIES®
1ST EDITION

by Charles Wohlforth

WILEY

Wiley Publishing, Inc.

Alaska For Dummies®, 1st Edition

Published by
Wiley Publishing, Inc.
909 Third Avenue
New York, NY 10022
www.wiley.com

Copyright © 2003 by Wiley Publishing, Inc., Indianapolis, Indiana

Published simultaneously in Canada

For general information on our other products and services or to obtain technical support, please contact our Customer Care Department within the U.S. at 800-762-2974, outside the U.S. at 317-572-3993, or fax 317-572-4002.

Wiley also publishes its books in a variety of electronic formats. Some content that appears in print may not be available in electronic books.

Library of Congress Cataloging-in-Publication Data:

Library of Congress Control Number: 2003101853

ISBN: 0-7645-1761-9

ISSN: 1541-633X

Manufactured in the United States of America

10 9 8 7 6 5 4 3 2 1

About the Author

Charles Wohlforth, a lifelong Alaskan, began his career in 1986 as a writer and journalist. His two other books for Wiley are *Frommer's Alaska* and *Frommer's Family Vacations in the National Parks,* the latter of which covers parks across the United States and is based on insights from the Wohlforth family's own camping experiences. Wohlforth lives in Anchorage with his wife, Barbara; sons, Robin and Joseph; and daughters, Julia and Rebecca. His book about climate change and Native people in the Arctic is due out from Farrar, Straus and Giroux in 2004. He welcomes reader questions through his Web site, www.wohlforth.net, which also contains other writings and travel advice about Alaska.

Author's Acknowledgments

Although my name alone appears on the title page, many people helped create this book. My editors deserve credit, including Kelly Regan, who developed the outline with skill and flexibility, and Michael Kelly, who made many improvements in the text. Much of the information in the book is based on my other Alaska travel guide, *Frommer's Alaska,* now in its sixth edition under my authorship. I've had plenty of help gathering all that data over the years. In the most recent edition, my team included Karen Datko, Kathleen Tessaro, Tom Morphet, Kris Capps, Tom Begich, Pat Branson, Jed Smith, Andrea Senn, Kerry Wilson, and Bryan Talbott-Clark. Many other friends and family members have helped, too, and I'm grateful to all of them.

Publisher's Acknowledgments

We're proud of this book; please send us your comments through our Dummies online registration form located at www.dummies.com/register/.

Some of the people who helped bring this book to market include the following:

Editorial

Editors: Michael Kelly, Development Editor; Mike Baker, Jennifer Connolly, Project Editors

Copy Editors: Jennifer Bingham, Neil Johnson, Greg Pearson, and Chad Sievers

Cartographer: Nicholas Trotter

Editorial Manager: Jennifer Ehrlich

Editorial Assistant: Melissa Bennett

Senior Photo Editor: Richard Fox

Cover Photos: Kenai Lake: Cooper Landing, Mother and twins (front cover) © Ken Graham/Accent Alaska, Cruise Ship in Bay (back cover) © Ken Graham/Accent Alaska

Cartoons: Rich Tennant, www.the5thwave.com

Production

Project Coordinator: Nancee Reeves

Layout and Graphics: Amanda Carter, Carrie Foster, Joyce Haughey, LeAndra Johnson, Stephanie D. Jumper, Tiffany Muth, Scott Tullis, Jeremey Unger

Proofreaders: David Faust, John Greenough, Susan Moritz, TECHBOOKS Production Services

Indexer: TECHBOOKS Production Services

Publishing and Editorial for Consumer Dummies

Diane Graves Steele, Vice President and Publisher, Consumer Dummies

Joyce Pepple, Acquisitions Director, Consumer Dummies

Kristin A. Cocks, Product Development Director, Consumer Dummies

Michael Spring, Vice President and Publisher, Travel

Brice Gosnell, Publishing Director, Travel

Suzanne Jannetta, Editorial Director, Travel

Publishing for Technology Dummies

Andy Cummings, Vice President and Publisher, Dummies Technology/General User

Composition Services

Gerry Fahey, Vice President of Production Services

Debbie Stailey, Director of Composition Services

Contents at a Glance

Maps at a Glance

Table of Contents

• •

Introduction

Years ago, I was on Kodiak Island, a ten-hour ferry ride from the Alaskan mainland, when three chic Italian women walked into the visitor center, their fashionable black outfits wet, their manner confused. In beginner's English, they explained they had boarded the boat in Homer thinking it would be an afternoon lark, a short ferry ride like those at home. Instead, the ship had plunged onward through the night in the stormy North Pacific, and here they were, a day later, marooned. The folks in Kodiak took care of the visitors, and they ended up having a good visit. But before leaving, one of them asked me discreetly about what was missing: snow and ice. They had arrived looking for Jack London's Alaska, but that summer everything was green.

They could've used this book. It's an instruction manual for a place that's probably unlike anything you've ever experienced.

Alaska is a world apart from the rest of the United States, or, for that matter, most other peopled places. It, quite simply, is wild. Many stereotypes about Alaska do not hold. For example, during the summer, the weather is pleasant and short sleeves get plenty of use. But other clichés are quite accurate. Wildlife roams freely across vast spaces, unfettered by fences or roads. Grand scenery, on equal footing with the most awesome sights on earth, is within reach in every part of the state. Opportunities to experience real wilderness are plentiful.

Alaska isn't just what you expect. It's probably much better.

About This Book

Forget about traditional travel guidebooks that try to lead you through your destination like a school group trooping through a museum. This book is a handy reference, designed for you to dip in and find the one piece of information you're looking for at the moment you need it. You can refer to a single chapter on a visit to a region, jump to the section about traveling with children, or just grab the facts you need to immediately find a good restaurant. I don't expect you to end up knowing who Tagish Charlie was (if you want to know, check out the Gold Rush Primer in Chapter 21), and you won't be tested on anything after you're done reading. So, forgetting everything between these pages is okay as long as your trip to Alaska is a memorable one.

I make every effort to provide accurate advice, but remember that travel information is subject to change at any time — and that is especially true of prices. I therefore suggest that you write or call ahead for confirmation when making your travel plans. The author, editors, and publisher can't be held responsible for the experiences of readers as they travel. Your safety is important to us, however, so we provide you with tips on staying safe in the outdoors in Chapter 9 and encourage you to stay alert and be aware of your surroundings wherever you are. Keep a close eye on cameras, purses, and wallets, all favorite targets of thieves and pickpockets.

Conventions Used in This Book

I organize the book to help you quickly find the information you need without wading through bunches of extra information or options. Use the table of contents and index to go directly to the topic you want to read about. When traveling, mark the pages for the area you're visiting with sticky notes, or simply fold over the page corners.

The information that most people need from a travel book most of the time is advice about finding the right restaurant or hotel. To simplify your selection, I divide these establishments into two sets: the ones that I like best and others that are also good but not necessarily my favorites. Of course, most readers want the best, but because the best are so good at what they do, you may find them booked up when you're planning to travel. That said, don't shy away from the runners-up, which I also wholeheartedly recommend.

As I describe each hotel, restaurant, or attraction, I use abbreviations for commonly accepted credit cards, including:

AE: American Express

DC: Diners Club

DISC: Discover

MC: MasterCard

V: Visa

I also use a system of dollar signs to show a range of costs for one night in a hotel or for a meal at a restaurant. Hotel prices are for a standard room in the high season (off-season prices are as little as half of the high-season prices). For more information about high and low seasons, be sure to check out Chapter 2. Meal prices are for a dinner with the main course constituting a full meal and not including appetizers, dessert, or alcohol. Whenever the restaurant doesn't serve dinner, the prices are for lunch. The following table explains the dollar signs:

Cost	Hotel	Restaurant
$	$90 or less	$10 or less
$$	$91–$125	$11–$17
$$$	$126–$160	$18–$25
$$$$	$161–$200	$26–$35
$$$$$	$201 or more	$36 or more

Foolish Assumptions

As I wrote this book, I made some assumptions about you and what your needs are as a traveler. Here's what I assume about you:

- ✔ You may be an inexperienced traveler looking for guidance about whether to take a trip to Alaska and how to plan for it.

- ✔ You may be an experienced traveler who hasn't been to Alaska and wants expert advice when you finally get a chance to go.

- ✔ You're not looking for a book that provides all the information available about Alaska or that lists every hotel, restaurant, or attraction available to you. Instead, you're looking for a book that focuses on the places that give you the best or most unique experiences.

If you fit any of these criteria, then *Alaska For Dummies* has the information you're looking for!

How This Book Is Organized

With the straightforward organization of this book, finding what you're looking for should be intuitive. On the other hand, if you want the complete picture upfront, work your way through it from start to finish.

Part 1: Getting Started

In this part, I introduce you to what Alaska has to offer and help you decide when and where to go. I provide five great itineraries that touch on Alaska's best destinations. I also give you tips for planning a budget and saving money, and specialized information for families, seniors, travelers with disabilities, and gays and lesbians.

Part II: Ironing Out the Details

How do you get to and travel around in Alaska? It isn't as easy as it is in most other places, and that's one of the big attractions. The journey is at least half the experience in this wild land. One long chapter covers the options for visiting by cruise ship, and another provides details for going to Alaska for an outdoor adventure. Finally, this part provides you with all those less-fun details that you can't do without: booking information, money, and tying up the loose ends.

Part III: Anchorage and Environs

Aha! Now you're into the meat of it! Anchorage is the gateway to Alaska, its largest and most diverse city. It also lies at the threshold of some excellent outdoor destinations, including Girdwood (for skiing), Whittier and Prince William Sound (for sea kayaking, wildlife-watching, and glacier cruises), and the Mat-Su Valley (for fishing, hiking, dog mushing, and more).

Part IV: Road Trips from Anchorage

The easiest way for most independent travelers to see the bulk of Alaska is by flying or taking a cruise ship to Anchorage and then driving a rented car in big loops from there. On this simple premise, I cover much of Alaska as road trips from Anchorage: the Kenai Peninsula, including Seward, Kenai Fjords National Park, Kenai, and Homer; Fairbanks and its environs; Alaska's long rural highways; and Denali National Park.

Part V: Southeast Alaska

Southeast Alaska is a mountainous strip of rain forest and narrow ocean channels full of islands and quaint, historic towns. In this part, I focus on Juneau, the area's travel hub, the state capital, and an outdoor gateway; on the gold rush destinations at Skagway; and on the rich Russian and Alaska Native cultural history at Sitka.

Part VI: The End of the Road and Beyond: Bush Alaska

For those of you who are ready to go *way* out to the end of the earth, here's how to do it. I cover four remote and fascinating places in the Arctic, along with the giant bears of Kodiak Island and Katmai National Park.

Part VII: The Part of Tens

Skip the rest and jump here for the best of the best: ten Alaskan experiences not to miss, ten ways to become embroiled in an Alaskan controversy, and ten ways to look like a real Alaskan.

Quick Concierge

Look here for quick reference to facts about emergency phone numbers, odd or important laws, tipping, and so on.

At the back of the book, you also find *worksheets* to make your travel planning easier. Among other things, you can use them to draw up your travel budget, create specific itineraries, and keep a log of your favorite restaurants so that you can hit them again — the next time you're in town. Just look for the pages printed on yellow paper.

Icons Used in This Book

While skimming through these pages, the icons help attract your eyes to the information you're looking for. This section tells you what each icon means.

These little nuggets of hard-won knowledge may make your life significantly easier or more interesting — information you probably wouldn't otherwise stumble upon.

Follow these notices for potentially dangerous situations, rip-offs, or simple annoyances, such as tourist traps, unsafe neighborhoods, and other travel pitfalls.

I have four kids. Believe me, when you see this icon next to an attraction, hotel, restaurant, or activity, the place has passed a very rigorous test indeed.

These nuggets of info highlight ways and places to get more for your money: good deals, money-saving tips, and more.

Where you see this icon, be on the lookout for critters. I also use it to mark some of the best wildlife-viewing destinations.

Where to Go from Here

Be not afraid! True, you go to Alaska for adventure. True, the essence of Alaska is untamed wilderness, wild animals, and uncontrollable nature. But Alaska is a popular visitor destination with every comfort you're looking for, and no harm is likely to come to you that you wouldn't face on any other vacation.

I receive many questions from my readers on my Web site (`www.wohlforth.net`). One common thread is the fear of the unknown, a hidden expectation that heading to Alaska is like leaving the planet. Maybe it is, a little. But with too much trepidation, you may miss out on the adventure. Relax and get out into the wilderness.

My advice: Go bravely northward!

Part I
Getting Started

The 5th Wave   By Rich Tennant

"This afternoon I want everyone to go online and find all you can about Tlingit culture, history of the gold rush, and discount airfares to Alaska for the two weeks I'll be on vacation."

In this part . . .

*I*f planning a trip is like putting together a jigsaw puzzle, this part helps you get those all-important edge pieces into place so that you can start to fill in the picture of what your journey to Alaska will look like. Use these pages to find out why Alaska is such a great place to visit, when and how to get there, suggested itineraries, how to budget for the trip, and tips for special travelers.

Chapter 1

Discovering the Best of Alaska

Satellite photographs taken at night show the United States, Europe, and much of the populated part of the world as a thick network of lights. Cities and highways stand out clearly, like a map, and it's easy to imagine light from electric fixtures bleeding into every corner of the land — but this is not the case with Alaska. The same pictures of Alaska show just a couple of bright spots, with the rest of the land appearing as a vast, velvety blackness. It's as though this great subcontinent is an undiscovered country that extends beyond the web of civilization and beyond the edge of the map.

That impression isn't very far off. Alaska is completely mapped (although it only happened within my lifetime), but immense areas remain where virtually no one has ever been. Not only are thousands of mountains unclimbed, but most of them have never even been named. Alaska has 10 million lakes and 100,000 glaciers. Alaska is not only large and untouched, it's also extraordinarily scenic and diverse. As a travel writer, I have visited a majority of the nation's great, crowded national parks, yet every summer in Alaska, I see equally impressive or greater vistas that have no special designation — they are simply places you come across by chance. After a lifetime of traveling here, I'm not even close to exhausting this wonder of discovery, and I don't think I ever will be.

How can you take all this grandeur in as a first-time visitor? You can't! But neither can a lifelong resident, so that's okay. The point is that a trip to Alaska isn't like one to Paris or the San Diego Zoo. You don't come to see certain sites or objects. It's silly to focus on a particular mountain or glacier when practically an infinite number are available to see. You never know when you may encounter wildlife — these meetings can't be scheduled. Instead, you should focus on the experience. Launch your own exploration and open yourself to discovery. Get out into all that

vastness on foot, in a boat or kayak, in a small aircraft, or in a car —
doing whatever you can to experience the unlimited expanse of the
Alaska experience.

Sampling Unique Alaskan Experiences

First-time visitors often have the most extraordinary experiences. I've
observed this phenomenon at gatherings with visiting family or friends
(living in Alaska means hosting a lot of out-of-town guests — the local
tourism authorities even have an acronym for them, *VFRs,* or visiting
friends and relatives). When asked what they've seen since they've
been in Alaska, these guests of honor often answer: "Oh, we saw a polar
bear feeding in Barrow," or "We saw whales jumping out of the water at
Glacier Bay," or "We joined in an Eskimo dance." And, inevitably, an
Alaskan or two murmurs with surprise, "Hey, I've never done that."

Seeing big ice

A glacier is a strange and unfamiliar thing. It looks like land, but it flows
like water. Glaciers can be larger than a city or even a state, and yet
they move constantly, sometimes suddenly, and they can bulldoze
straight through rock mountains. Nothing else looks like a glacier. They
are white, gray, and fluorescent blue. They drape gracefully through
the mountains, but they also crack in enormous shards. And they can
drop ice chunks the size of office buildings into the ocean. Alaska's
best glacier-viewing is in Prince William Sound from Whittier (Chapter
15), Kenai Fjords National Park near Seward (Chapter 16), and Glacier
Bay National Park and Tracy Arm near Juneau (Chapter 20).

Encountering bear

Bears can turn up almost anywhere in Alaska — even in a city park.
Kincaid Park in Anchorage recently posted signs that warn "You Are
Entering Bear Country," because of the joggers and bicyclists who have
run into black bear. Alaska's black, brown (or grizzly), and polar bear
populations are all thriving. But seeing a bear is a good thing when you
expect it. You can find great brown-bear-viewing at Denali National
Park (Chapter 19), at Kodiak and Katmai National Park (Chapter 24),
and near Juneau (Chapter 20). If you want to view some polar bears,
check out Barrow (Chapter 23). See Chapter 9 for a rundown of
statewide wildlife-viewing opportunities.

Whale-watching

Imagine a whale leaping between the narrow, mountainous walls of a fjord. Imagine being close enough to feel the water spray and to feel your boat move as the wave moves past. It happens every day, many times a day, somewhere on Alaska's southern coast. I've seen people weep at the experience. The best places for reliable whale-watching, primarily for humpbacks and orcas, are near Juneau at Gustavus (Chapter 20), Sitka (Chapter 22), Prince William Sound (Chapter 15), and Kenai Fjords National Park (Chapter 16).

Meeting up with Alaska Natives

Alaska is home to many distinct peoples. The cultural heritage and ways of life of Alaska's indigenous people remain largely intact in many areas of the state, and Alaska Natives are often interested in sharing their traditions with visitors who bring needed economic support to their communities. Meet the Tlingit and see their totem poles in Sitka (Chapter 22). In Barrow, Inupiat Eskimo culture is alive and well; sometimes you can see whaling, and you can visit a fascinating cultural center any time (Chapter 23). In Anchorage, many peoples have combined to present a spectacular living museum, the Alaska Native Heritage Center (Chapter 14).

Discovering the Gold Rush

The Klondike Gold Rush of 1898, when the non-Native population arrived all at once in search of riches, is the biggest event in Alaska's short history. The scene of the wild times that followed is well preserved in Skagway, where the stampeders got off the boat (Chapter 21). The Gold Rush also impacted Nome (Chapter 23) and Fairbanks (Chapter 17); both cities have gold mining that continues today and the historical evidence of gold mining from the past.

Paddling the ocean

Alaskans invented the kayak, and paddling among the sea otters of Alaska's rocky coastline is where the sport is at its best. Virtually every small town has a sea-kayak guide ready to take beginners out to view the lovely shores and their abundant wildlife. Among the best places to go kayaking are Whittier (Chapter 15), Seward and Homer (Chapter 16), Juneau (Chapter 20), and Sitka (Chapter 22).

Venturing into deep wilderness

You don't have to be an experienced outdoor person to get into the kind of spectacular wilderness that few people ever get the chance to experience. Guides take visitors (even travelers who have never gone beyond a simple footpath) to amazingly remote and beautiful places. You can explore by sea kayak, river raft, dog sled, or on foot. Or you can settle in at a remote lodge and explore from there. Ideas for outdoor adventures are covered in Chapter 9.

Understanding Alaska's Three Histories

You can't say exactly when Alaska's history began until you figure out which history you're talking about.

Examining Alaska's Native origins

The indigenous people of North and South America arrived about 10,000 years ago (perhaps in boats, or maybe on foot). They may have walked over ground that's now the seabed beneath the Bering Sea, which was exposed at the time by the lower sea level of those Ice Age years — or maybe not. As a matter of fact, archaeologists are less sure now than they have been in years about exactly how these indigenous people arrived. New theories keep cropping up, each with an apparent claim on the evidence.

However it happened, though, communication among Native people continued long after the Ice Age. Greenlanders understand the language spoken on Alaska's North Slope, and western Alaskans can communicate with indigenous people in Siberia. Some Native legends span the entire arctic world. (Storytellers at the Alaska Native Heritage Center in Anchorage recount some of these legends for visitors; see Chapter 14.)

Exploring Alaska's European history

If you want to talk about when Europeans first came to Alaska, you have to go back to 1741, when Vitus Bering claimed the area on a mission from Czar Peter the Great. Bering crossed Asia, sailed to the Kamchatka Peninsula and crossed it, built new ships, and sailed across the North Pacific (the part now known as the Bering Sea). He made the journey twice, in fact, before he actually found Alaska and landed a man there for a few hours. Although Bering died without making it back home, Russian fur traders followed, and what became known as

Russian America survived as a sea-otter exporting colony until the czar sold Alaska to the United States in 1867. After the sale, all the Russians left, and their history in Alaska essentially stopped. (But you can still see the remains of this history in Sitka; check out Chapter 22.)

Understanding today's Alaska

The history of most of the people who live here now relates to the natural resources and government spending that still support the state economy: oil, minerals, fishing, timber, tourism, and the military. This history starts with the Klondike Gold Rush of 1898, when almost the entire non-Native population showed up overnight and took the place over. (Skagway, discussed in Chapter 21, is the best place to see gold rush history.) A series of gold rushes continued until World War I. Then came construction of the Alaska Railroad, which was ordered built by President Woodrow Wilson to open up the territory and bring out its resource wealth.

With World War II, Alaska became a key to the nation's defense. Alaska was the only place where enemy forces were able to land and seize part of the U.S. homeland; early in the war, the Japanese held two islands in the outer Aleutian Archipelago. They were dislodged only after one of the most ferocious and costly battles of the Pacific War. After the war, Alaska became a critical element of the nation's Cold War defenses, with large bases and advanced radar. And missile-defense plans may one day return Alaska to prominence in space-age warfare.

The biggest boost in Alaska's development, however, came after the territory won statehood in 1959. The discovery of the largest oil field in North America on state-owned land on Alaska's North Slope brought a new, black-gold rush of people and money. For the decades that followed, Alaska was fabulously wealthy, and development proceeded as fast as a videotape on fast forward. These were the years that made cities such as Anchorage and Fairbanks look like the grubby outskirts of any prosperous western U.S. urban area, with the same kinds of chain stores and wide highways you would find there. More than 30 years later, the ugly boomtown development has only partly been softened by more gracious cityscapes.

But that current of history has scratched only skin deep in Alaska. A few miles from the most urbanized spot in the state, nature prevails as if no one had ever come this way at all.

Chapter 2

Deciding When and Where to Go

*F*iguring out where to go in Alaska is not daunting; at least it won't be after you read this chapter. For one thing, you're not likely to go wrong with anywhere you choose to visit. For another, I lay out the options simply in this chapter, along with the best times of year to visit, the most noteworthy events in the state, and some tips I've developed from a lifetime of traveling in Alaska and advising travelers who go there.

Narrowing Your Destination Options: Places worth Going

Did I mention that Alaska is large? Well, it is. (We Alaskans put down Texans by telling them that Alaska could split in half and make Texas only the third largest state.) That being true, covering every town or even every region in the state in this book wouldn't make sense. Some parts of Alaska are so sparsely populated and rarely visited that telling each potential visitor about them, one by one, would take less time than writing about each area. Other places receive a reasonable number of visitors but don't have as much to offer as other similar places. So, this chapter spends more time on the best locations, where you'll find the range of what Alaska offers — amazing, fascinating places, but not every place.

Anchorage

They say that **Anchorage** isn't Alaska, but you can see it from there. They're wrong: Any city with moose, black bear, and eagles in its parks and neighborhoods is part of Alaska. But what they're hinting at is true. With 40% of the state's population (260,000 out of 627,000 in the state), Anchorage dwarfs all other towns, has little in common with typical remote Alaska communities, and serves as the overwhelming hub of Alaskan activities, with services and an urban feel you'd expect to find only in a much larger city.

As a visitor, taking advantage of these qualities can make your trip easier and less expensive. For example, plane fares to Anchorage are cheap because of heavy competition, but flying to many other Alaskan towns costs a fortune. Many cruises end in Anchorage, too, after docking in Seward and taking a 124-mile bus or train ride into town. Car and RV rentals are plentiful in Anchorage, and flight services fan out for day trips as far north as **Denali National Park** and as far south as **Katmai National Park.**

Anchorage was built by the federal government in 1915 on a site chosen for its location along the best route from the coast to Alaska's **Interior.** It grew because of its strategic location as an international crossroad for air travel. The city sits in South Central Alaska in a bowl of mountains at the head of **Cook Inlet,** handy to the **Kenai Peninsula** to the south and the entire **Interior** region to the north.

Because of its central location, I structure this book around the idea that your visit to the main part of the state (everything but the Southeast Panhandle) should begin and end in **Anchorage.**

The city has much to offer, indoors and out, including the state's largest museum, the most extensive Native cultural center, and several other sites of interest. **Chugach State Park,** the city's backdrop, contains some of Alaska's best day hikes and backpacking routes; and in town, you find superb bike and cross-country ski trails.

Just outside of town, **Girdwood** is a hip little skiing town with beautiful, steep slopes overlooking the waters of Turnagain Arm, a glacier-carved fjord. A bit farther, and through a tunnel, **Whittier,** an hour from Anchorage, is the jumping-off point for day trips and longer voyages into **Prince William Sound** by ship, boat, or sea kayak.

The Kenai Peninsula

The **Kenai Peninsula** is Anchorage's playground. It's a big area, a five-hour drive from one end to the other, with three distinct parts you should consider for a visit.

✔ **Seward and nearby Kenai Fjords National Park:** About 124 road miles from Anchorage, this is a prime area for sea kayaking, whale- and bird-watching, and ocean salmon fishing. Visiting the park as a day trip from Anchorage is possible, but staying a night or two is a better idea. In the fjords, you'll see some of the world's most extreme scenery: Rock mountains rise straight up from the sea a mile high.

 ✔ **Kenai and Soldotna:** An area for fishing, the king salmon in the Kenai River grow to world-record size. Silver and red salmon and enormous trout run in the river, too.

 ✔ **Homer:** Sitting on the edge of the panoramic and fish-rich **Kachemak Bay,** Homer offers some of Alaska's best opportunities for outdoor exploration, with a guide or on your own, using serv- ices that make it easy for beginners to get into the wilderness for the first time. The town and its satellite waterfront communities also are home to many of Alaska's best artists and several of its best restaurants.

Fairbanks and the Interior Highways

Long rivers and two-lane highways connect the central part of Alaska. These highways are worth exploring, when you have the time. The center of the region is **Fairbanks,** Alaska's second largest city, sitting on the banks of the muddy Chena River. It's known for its **gold rush history,** river floating, hot spring soaks, and in winter, dog mushing and the **Northern Lights** (or the Aurora Borealis — see Chapter 17).

Denali National Park

Partway between Anchorage and Fairbanks, **Denali National Park** is home to North America's tallest mountain (**Mount McKinley**) and some of its most expansive **alpine scenery.** It's also the place for the least expensive **wildlife safari** you'll ever take, a $20 bus ride that usually encounters brown bear and other animals: While riding these buses, I've seen wolves, caribou, moose, Dall sheep, beaver, and much more.

Southeast Alaska

The Panhandle, as this relatively narrow strip of land is called, is an extension of the Pacific Northwest, a region of big spruce, hemlock, and cedar trees, deep fjords, crashing glaciers, and islands full of wildlife. Almost the entire region is part of **Tongass National Forest,** and the opportunities for sea kayaking, ocean fishing, whale-watching and bear-viewing, and hiking are almost limitless.

The best hubs to visit are **Juneau** and **Sitka,** cities with interesting museums and historic sites. **Skagway** is a center of gold rush history.

In planning your trip, however, it's wise to choose to visit *either* the Southeast *or* the balance of the state, unless you have two weeks or more. No roads connect most Southeast towns, and the distances between Anchorage and other towns are so great that getting to those places costs as much as getting to Alaska in the first place.

The bush

Many people come to Alaska with an itch to see the **Arctic,** or simply to get beyond the roads into deep wilderness full of wildlife. That, however, describes most of the state, yet getting there takes extra money, planning, and time. In Part VI of this book, I discuss some of the best bush destinations and details for making the trip.

Understanding the Secret of the Seasons

Although Alaska actually spans five time zones, its residents tell time squeezed into just two of them: Alaska time for most of the state, and Hawaii-Aleutian time for a few Aleutian Islands. Similarly, Alaska has at least five distinct climates, ranging from temperate in the Southeast, with precipitation as heavy as any in the world, to the frigid Arctic, with skies as dry as any desert. (The distance north to south is the same as the distance from Bangor, Maine, to Miami, Florida — a little over 1,700 miles.) The seasons aren't simple, and another factor weighs in on the calculation: light. In the state's middle latitudes, the sun rises for only a few hours in December, but in June, the sky is light all night. In the Arctic, one winter night can last two months.

To help plan, Tables 2-1, 2-2, and 2-3 show the average temperature highs and lows (in degrees Fahrenheit) and the number of days per month with rain or snow for three major destinations. These tables also offer the hours of daylight on the 21st day of every month.

Table 2-1	Anchorage's Average Highs and Lows, Days with Precipitation, and Daylight Hours											
	Jan	*Feb*	*Mar*	*Apr*	*May*	*Jun*	*Jul*	*Aug*	*Sep*	*Oct*	*Nov*	*Dec*
Average high	21	26	33	44	55	62	65	63	55	40	28	22
Average low	8	11	17	29	39	47	51	49	41	28	16	10
Days of precipitation	8	8	8	6	7	8	11	13	14	12	10	11
Daylight hours	6:53	9:41	12:22	15:20	18:00	19:22	18:00	15:15	12:19	9:29	6:46	5:27

Table 2-2	Fairbanks' Average Highs and Lows, Days with Precipitation, and Daylight Hours											
	Jan	*Feb*	*Mar*	*Apr*	*May*	*Jun*	*Jul*	*Aug*	*Sep*	*Oct*	*Nov*	*Dec*
Average high	−2	8	24	42	60	71	73	66	55	32	11	1
Average low	−19	−15	−2	20	38	52	52	47	36	17	−5	−16
Days of precipitation	8	7	6	5	7	11	12	12	10	11	11	9
Daylight hours	5:46	9:14	12:22	15:54	19:22	21:48	19:26	15:52	12:24	9:04	5:39	3:43

Table 2-3	Juneau's Average Highs and Lows, Days with Precipitation, and Daylight Hours											
	Jan	*Feb*	*Mar*	*Apr*	*May*	*Jun*	*Jul*	*Aug*	*Sep*	*Oct*	*Nov*	*Dec*
Average high	29	34	39	48	55	62	64	63	56	47	37	32
Average low	18	23	27	32	39	45	48	48	43	37	28	23
Days of precipitation	18	17	18	17	17	15	17	17	20	24	20	21
Daylight hours	7:31	9:55	12:18	14:55	17:11	18:17	17:13	14:54	12:20	9:49	7:27	6:22

The seasons from Anchorage north

The area of the state from **Anchorage** north, including **Fairbanks, the Interior,** and **the Arctic,** is significantly drier and colder in winter than coastal areas, making it better than the state's coastal areas for winter and fall visits.

Summer is wonderful because:

- ✔ Temperatures are comfortable from mid-May through August, although fall rains usually start in mid-August.
- ✔ Salmon fishing is strong from early June through mid-September.
- ✔ The visitor season is in full swing, so you'll find plenty to do and everything open. Traditionally, in fact, this is the only time of year when visitors come to Alaska.

But keep in mind:

- ✔ Prices are highest, reservations are hardest to get, and crowds are most common from mid-June to mid-August (when weather is best).

✔ Alaska's mosquitoes are worst when the weather is best.

✔ Cool, rainy weather can occur at any time, but the driest summer months are June and July.

✔ As you travel north, the season shortens. Ice often doesn't leave the Arctic until July and hiking trails can be wet and muddy through June almost everywhere in the state. At **Denali National Park,** frosty nights and fall colors start in late August.

Winter is wonderful because:

✔ Skiing, both downhill and cross-country, peak in February and March, with plenty of light and snow.

✔ Dark winter skies mean the Northern Lights shine frequently.

✔ Sled dog racing season peaks in February and March, great times for your own dog-mushing adventures.

✔ Prices are as low as half off and reservations are easy to make.

But keep in mind:

✔ Many attractions and even some roads are closed for the season.

✔ A road trip requires special safety preparations in extreme cold conditions.

✔ Wildlife-viewing is generally impossible.

Shedding light on all the light

You may have "always wanted to know but were afraid to ask" why summer days are so long in the north and winter days are so short. The short answer is geometry. Seasons are controlled by the way the earth leans on its axis: toward the sun in summer and away from the sun in winter. (Seasons are opposite in the northern and southern hemispheres.) As the earth spins, any particular spot on the globe, such as Anchorage, travels a certain circle every day. On a globe, that circle is depicted as a line of *latitude.* When the northern hemisphere leans closer to the sun in summer, light hits more of that circle, so daylight lasts longer at any point along that line. As you travel farther north, each circular line of latitude becomes smaller but is shadowed less by the top of the earth, so summer daylight lasts longer each day.

The **Arctic Circle** is the first latitude in which the sun doesn't set at least one day of each year. During winter the reverse is true: The sun doesn't rise at least one day each year at the Arctic Circle. By comparison, every day at the equator has basically 12 hours of light (and 12 hours of darkness) all year. At the poles, which aren't affected by days, because they sit right on the earth's axis, the sky is light all summer and dark all winter. Everywhere in between, differences between light and dark change throughout the year.

Spring and **fall** are wonderful because:

✔ Prices are low and weather, although chilly, is not extreme.

✔ Fall colors are spectacular on the *Arctic tundra* of northeast Alaska and in the *boreal forests.* (*Boreal forests* refers to forest areas closest to the Arctic Circle.) Depending on latitude, colors peak from late August to early October.

✔ Spring weather can be dry and bright.

But keep in mind:

✔ Most summer and winter attractions are closed.

✔ Weather is unpredictable and can be bad; visits in April, October, and November are probably not worth the risk of potentially rotten conditions.

✔ Not much wildlife is visible in spring or late fall.

The seasons in coastal Alaska

The climate of **Southeast Alaska, Prince William Sound,** and **the Kenai Peninsula** — the entire arc of the southern Alaska coastline, in fact — is controlled by the warmth and dampness of air from the Pacific Ocean. That's why rain forests grow here, why winters stay warm and summers cool, and why a waterproof raincoat is never a bad idea.

Summer is *the* time to come because:

✔ The region comes alive with outdoor activities, attractions, events, fishing, and wildlife-viewing.

✔ Weather is never dry, but it is much drier than in fall or winter. Temperatures are comfortable.

But keep in mind:

✔ Crowds can close in; reservations are a necessity.

✔ And naturally, because of the season's popularity, prices are high.

Fall and **winter** are impractical because:

✔ Attractions close or post short hours, outdoor activities become difficult, and most fishing shuts down.

✔ Heavy precipitation and chilly temperatures prevail beginning in mid-September.

Spring is an intriguing possibility because:

✔ March, April, and May are the driest months of the year, and comfortable temperatures arrive at least a month earlier than farther north, with some nice days in late March or early April.

✔ The tourist season doesn't begin until mid-May or later, leaving more than a month of lower prices and friendly hosts eager to please; prices are low and reservations easy.

But keep in mind:

✔ Many attractions and guided outdoor activities don't start until mid-May.

✔ Salmon fishing hasn't started yet.

Alaska's Calendar of Events

Something always is going on in Alaska, but I list only the cream of the crop here — the kind of events that you can plan part of your trip around. Ironically, many of these events take place during the time of year when Alaska doesn't play host to as many visitors. In summer, when most tourists arrive, Alaskans are too busy fishing, getting outdoors, and serving visitors to be able to organize many community events. But whenever you arrive during the low season, getting involved in one of the truly local happenings can give you a special entrance into the heart of these communities. For a more exhaustive events calendar, visit the state tourism authority's Web site (www.travelalaska.com), click on the Trip Planner link, and then click on the Calendar link.

February

The **Anchorage Fur Rendezvous Winter Festival,** which takes place during a week in mid-February, is a huge, citywide winter celebration, with many community events, fireworks, craft fairs, snowshoe softball, dog-sled rides, and other fun. The main event is the **World Champion Sled Dog Race,** a three-day sprint event of about 25 miles per heat (☎ 907-274-1177; Internet: www.furrondy.net).

March

Starting the first Saturday in March, the **Iditarod Trail Sled Dog Race** is Alaska's most famous event. The 1,000-mile sled dog race starts with fanfare from Anchorage and follows the historic gold rush trail to Nome. Some animal-rights activists outside Alaska oppose the race on the grounds that it's cruel to the dogs. But race supporters maintain that sled dogs love running and thrive on cold, and they believe that decade-long reforms in dog-care rules have addressed the activists' concerns. The finish of the race, in Nome, is the biggest event of the year in the Arctic, attracting world media attention and turning Nome into a huge party for a few days with many community events, even a golf outing on the sea ice (☎ 907-376-5155; Internet: www.iditarod.com).

The **World Ice Art Championships** take place in Fairbanks in mid-March. Carvers from around the world come to sculpt immense chunks of clear ice cut from a Fairbanks pond. Among ice carvers, Fairbanks' ice is famous for its clarity and the great size of the chunks. Some spectacular ice sculptures stand as tall as a two-story building (☎ 907-451-8250; Internet: www.icealaska.com).

May

In early May, the **Kachemak Bay Shorebird Festival** in Homer celebrates the annual influx of thousands of migrating birds with guided bird-watching hikes and boat excursions, natural-history workshops, art shows and performances, a wooden-boat festival, and other events (☎ 907-235-7740; Internet: homeralaska.org/shorebird.htm).

June

The **Sitka Summer Music Festival** offers three weeks of chamber-music concerts and other musical events, presenting top performers from around the world (☎ 907-747-6774; Internet: www.sitkamusic festival.org).

July

You've never experienced a small-town Fourth of July until you've joined the throngs on the streets of Seward for its **Independence Day** celebration. Besides the parade and many other festivities, the main attraction is the **Mount Marathon Race,** an insane scramble from the middle of town straight up the rocky mountain that is the race's namesake to its 3,022-foot peak and down again in less than an hour (☎ 907-224-8051; Internet: www.sewardak.org).

August

The **Alaska State Fair** runs the 11 days before Labor Day in the Anchorage suburb of Palmer. The region's biggest event of the year, it features rides, musical performances, and country competitions. The biggest news of each year's fair is the winning cabbage; the area's good soil and long days team up to produce cabbages the size of bean-bag chairs. Mere beach ball-sized cabbages are laughed off the stage (☎ 907-745-4827; Internet: www.alaskastatefair.org).

November

In Anchorage during Thanksgiving weekend, the University of Alaska-Anchorage Seawolves play host to the **Carrs/Safeway Great Alaska Shootout.** The event features a roster of the nation's top-ranked NCAA Division I men's and women's basketball teams for a weekend-long tournament (☎ **907-786-1230;** Internet: www.goseawolves.com/shootout).

Remembering Just A Few Trip-Planning Tips

When you're planning a trip, it's easy to get lost in the details and forget the most important things — such as why you wanted to go to Alaska in the first place. You'll know when you've forgotten that all-important fact when you find yourself on a trip thinking, "What am I doing here?" Because I see too many Alaska visitors with that thought on their faces, I put together some ideas here to keep you on track:

✔ When you're visiting Alaska for scenery and wildlife, plan plenty of time outdoors, rather than in towns at museums and such.

✔ Getting out to see the wilderness takes planning and time; be sure to contact guides and tour operators in advance and allow plenty of money in your budget and time on your schedule for these activities (see Chapter 12 to find out how early you need to make reservations for each kind of activity).

✔ Schedule plenty of extra time in your itinerary, not only for the unexpected things that make travel more fun, but also for bad weather, which frequently postpones activities, flights, and boat rides in Alaska. Flexibility is a requirement.

✔ Don't try to see widely separated regions of the state unless you have plenty of money or time to spend; distances between regions are truly extraordinary, and you can see most of the same highlights in either the Southeast or South Central/Interior regions.

✔ Try not to get hung up on bagging the big name sights. Alaska has incredible experiences and scenery in many lesser-known places where you can make your own discoveries. Remember that weather sometimes won't cooperate at headline attractions you're hoping to see.

Chapter 3

Great Alaska Itineraries

*R*eality is such a drag, because it always dictates that you won't have unlimited time for a trip to Alaska. In fact, most people's reality requires negotiating with a boss or co-workers to be able to get a week or two off for a trip. (You really should consider being a travel writer!) With reality in mind, then, I've designed the itineraries here so that you can make the most of the time you'll spend in Alaska. I don't think you need to jet or drive around to the four corners of the state, the way some commission-hungry travel agents seem to think is best. Instead, these itineraries put visitors in some of the very best places, where you have a chance of seeing and doing a great deal without spending too much money or time on the road.

Please don't take my word for it, however; simply use these itineraries as a basis for putting together *your* ideal trip with *your* own interests in mind. People often ask me (on my handy-dandy Web site, www. wohlforth.net), "What's the best way to spend a week in Alaska?" I generally respond by asking whether the travelers are interested in scenery, wildlife, or cultural attractions, and whether they're athletic or disabled, adventurous or averse to discomfort. Readers can be sturdy backpackers, inquiring elders, or families with kids in diapers. Without knowing everything about you, I can still give you advice, but it's based on my own preferences and interests. I don't think I'm so much of an oddball thinking that most people probably will find something that interests them here. But we're all different, so these itineraries simply present some options to consider as you tailor your own travel plans to fit your interests.

These itineraries also show the complexity and diversity that awaits you when traveling among Alaska destinations. Alaska has trains, planes, boats, and automobiles, but not all go to each destination. Most locales in Alaska aren't even connected by roads. Even the state capital, Juneau, relies heavily on water and air transportation to link it with the rest of the world. As it happens, that isn't a bad thing, because authentic charm grows best in isolation. On the other hand, isolation makes trip planning a bit more complicated than jumping in the car. For a chart that shows the modes of transportation you can use to access each destination, see Chapter 7.

Appreciating Southeast Alaska on a One-Week Juneau Journey

Southeast Alaska is a part of the world where people travel from town to town mostly in boats rather than in cars and buses. Boating, to them, is no inconvenience, and it's what makes this itinerary so very appealing. The lack of highways continues to keep towns in this area quaint and the wild lands surrounding them remote. Everything on this itinerary is covered in Part V of this book (Chapters 20 and 22).

Day 1 begins with a flight to Juneau, where you grab a cab to your hotel in the downtown area; you have no need for a rental car unless you insist on having one. After settling in, explore the charming downtown streets on foot, stopping at the **State Museum** for an overview and orientation to Alaska's history and culture. In the evening, relax for dinner next door to the museum at the **Fiddlehead Restaurant & Bakery,** or if you have a more formal meal in mind, check out its sister restaurant, **Di Sopra,** located upstairs.

If you're blessed with good weather on **Day 2,** hike the **Perseverance Trail,** visiting the **Last Chance Mining Museum.** If your preference is for a less strenuous outing, then ride the aerial tram up **Mount Roberts** for its amazing views and nature walks you can take while up top. Consider filling out the day with a helicopter ride to the **Juneau Ice Field,** perhaps a dog-sled ride, or just a walk on the snow. In the evening (again, when the weather is good), attend the **Gold Creek Salmon Bake,** for outdoor dining and folksy entertainment, or enjoy an elegant dinner at **The Summit Restaurant** downtown, if the weather's not cooperating.

Day 3 is good for a daylong boat ride to **Tracy Arm** to see glaciers, high fjord cliffs, and wildlife. If you're more interested in whale-watching, take the **Auk Nu passenger ferry** to see humpback whales feeding near Gustavus. Those who like to plan ahead may be able to obtain one of the scarce reservations to fly to the **Pack Creek Bear-Viewing Area** on Admiralty Island to see lots of feeding brown bears. After seeing the bears, you can dine at the **Hanger** for a fun end to the day.

On **Day 4,** check out of your Juneau hotel for an early 40-minute flight to **Sitka** on Alaska Airlines. Settle in there for a couple of days of walking amid historic sites, making sure that you visit the **Sitka National Historic Park** with its Tlingit battlefield and totem poles, exquisite Native art in the **Sheldon Jackson Museum,** and Russian–American architecture and treasures at the **Russian Bishop's House** and **St. Michael's Cathedral.** In the evening, dine at the **Bayview Restaurant,** which overlooks the harbor, and attend a traditional **Sitka Tribal Dance Performance** at their community house, before turning in at your Sitka hotel.

Staying in the Sitka area for **Day 5,** you can join a sea kayaking outing to see the wildlife of **Sitka Sound,** including sea otters, sea lions, and eagles, and possibly even whales. Fishing charters are also popular, or, less active travelers can take one of the excellent boat tours offered on a variety of large or intimate vessels. Dine at the **Shee Atika Hotel.**

Day 6 starts aboard an **Alaska Marine Highway System ferry** for the spectacular 9-hour, 150-mile ride back to Juneau, where you take a cab from the docks to the airport so that you can rent a car for 24 hours and drive to your accommodations, dining along the way at one of the outlying restaurants, such as the **Douglas Café** or **Chan's Thai Kitchen.**

On **Day 7,** before your evening flight back home, use the car you rented yesterday to see the **Mendenhall Glacier,** the **Shrine of St. Therese,** and to enjoy the scenery **"Out The Road"** (which is how locals refer to the lovely 40-mile drive on the Glacier Highway).

Exploring the National Parks: Denali and Kenai Fjords in One Week

This itinerary combines the amazing scenery and abundant wildlife of two of Alaska's most popular destinations, Denali National Park and Kenai Fjords National Park, for one full week of witnessing the best of the state's outdoor highlights.

On **Day 1,** fly to Anchorage, where you spend your first night and rent a car. (Chapter 7 offers information about car rentals in Alaska.) If you arrive early enough, you can take in some of the city, with a visit to the **Anchorage Museum of History and Art** or the **Alaska Native Cultural Center.** Or, if the weather is good, rent a bike and ride along the **Tony Knowles Coastal Trail.** In the evening, eat at **Simon and Seafort's Saloon and Grill,** which overlooks the waters of Knik Arm. (Part III of this book offers much more detail about the greater Anchorage area.)

On **Day 2,** drive 124 miles south on the Seward Highway to the **Kenai Peninsula** and Seward, your overnight destination for the next couple of nights. (For details about the sights and services in this part of the itinerary, check out Chapter 16.) Fortunately this rather long drive is one of the world's most spectacular, — scope out some of the places you'd like to stop, but don't actually stop until your return trip. You need to arrive in Seward in time to board a pre-reserved tour boat into **Kenai Fjords National Park,** where you'll see mountains jutting a mile out of the water, big blue glaciers, thousands of sea birds, and many marine mammals, usually including humpback or orca whales. Dine tonight at **Ray's Waterfront.**

Remaining in Seward for **Day 3,** paddle a sea kayak into **Resurrection Bay** among sea otters and (possibly) spawning salmon, or join a fishing charter. You should still have time to see the charming downtown and visit the **Alaska SeaLife Center,** a research aquarium. If, on the other hand, you want to spend more time outdoors, make the short side trip to see **Exit Glacier,** just north of town. Try the **Apollo Restaurant** or **Resurrection Roadhouse** for dinner.

Driving back to Anchorage on the morning of **Day 4,** don't forget to stop at some of those beautiful or intriguing spots you noted on the way down along the Seward Highway, and don't miss the **Portage Glacier Visitor Center.** You can have lunch in **Girdwood** at **Chair 5** or the **Alyeska Prince Hotel,** and you may even want to take the aerial tram up to the top of **Mount Alyeska** for its mountaintop views or for a hike on one of the trails near here in **Chugach National Forest** or **Chugach State Park.** On the drive into Anchorage, keep your eyes open for **beluga whales** and **Dall sheep.** With plenty of time left, you have a good opportunity to try either the **Marx Brothers Café** or **Sacks Café** in Anchorage, two of Alaska's best restaurants, yet still turn in early in preparation for a long day on the road.

Getting an early start on **Day 5** is important for the 4½-hour drive north to **Denali National Park** (see Chapter 19). Stop in **Talkeetna** along the way for a flightseeing tour of **Mount McKinley** (preferably with a landing on the mountain itself) before continuing on to the park, where you still have time for a **hike** or **raft ride** in the park's entrance area. The best place to eat is the **Black Diamond Grill,** north of the park. Check into a hotel in **Healy** or near the park entrance for tonight and tomorrow night.

On **Day 6,** board a shuttle bus into Denali for **wildlife-viewing** and **day hiking.** You need to make your shuttle bus reservations several months in advance; choose the earliest departure time that you can stand. Arriving back at your lodging after a very long day, eat at your hotel or one of the low-key places near the park.

Reserve **Day 7** to drive back to Anchorage and catch your plane home.

Covering a Lot of (Alaskan) Ground in Two Weeks

One option for a two-week trip to Alaska is simply linking the preceding two one-week itineraries. Although that's a good trip, you may end up spending more time looking at sea otters and glaciers than you need. A better plan is padding those one-week itineraries with more days, more activities, and more side trips within the regions you're already covering. Doing so saves time and gives you a better chance to dig in and really get a better feel of the destinations. So, I've designed this two-week itinerary to show you more of the variety that Alaska offers. Some days overlap with the "Exploring the National Parks" itinerary.

For **Days 1 and 2,** follow the first two days of the "Exploring the National Parks" itinerary, earlier in this chapter.

On **Day 3,** from Seward, get back in the car and drive about four hours to **Homer.** That gives you plenty of time to visit the galleries and the **Pratt Museum** and to find out why Homer is the art center of Alaska. Dine on the water at **Land's End** (see Chapter 16).

Head outdoors on **Day 4** by paddling a sea kayak out into **Kachemak Bay** to view sea birds and otters and other marine mammals, and to land on a lovely pebble beach in the wilderness. Less active travelers can choose a wildlife boat tour through some of those same waters, or join a fishing charter. Before heading back to your hotel for your second of three nights in Homer, have dinner at **The Homestead** (see Chapter 16).

Day 5 gives you the chance to find out how adventurous you really are. Take a water taxi to **Kachemak Bay State Park** for a day of **self-guided hiking** far from any road or settlement; you have a good chance of spending a day on the beaches and in the woods without seeing another human until your water taxi picks you up in the evening. If that's too scary for you, then consider a day trip for lunch or dinner to **Halibut Cove,** a roadless arts community built on docks and board-walks with a restaurant that sells great sushi (see Chapter 16).

You leave Homer on **Day 6,** driving back toward Anchorage, stopping along the way at the places you spotted on the way down. Don't miss the **Portage Glacier Visitor Center.** Stop in **Girdwood,** a half-hour short of Anchorage, and check in at the wonderful **Alyeska Prince Hotel.** With one day left, you can ride the aerial tram to the top of **Mount Alyeska** for the mountaintop views, or hike the **Glacier Creek/Winner Creek Trail.** Eat at the hotel or at **Chair 5** (see Chapter 15).

Briefly retracing your steps on **Day 7,** drive about 15 miles back to the south to the **Whittier Tunnel,** wait your turn, and go through the 2-mile-long, single-lane tunnel to **Whittier,** where you can put your car on the **Alaska Marine Highway System ferry to Valdez,** a seven-hour passage through the sublime rain-forest scenery along **Prince William Sound.** With any time that's left, you may want to visit the **Valdez Museum** or the **Solomon Gulch Salmon Hatchery** (see Chapter 18).

On **Day 8,** drive the **Richardson Highway** to Fairbanks (364 miles). A long haul, yes, but I suggest this drive on purpose because it may be the most awesome car trip that you ever experience. For up to six hours, you pass through unpopulated wilderness, rising from tidewater steeply into rocky mountains, passing the face of a glacier, and climbing still higher into the vast, treeless country of the **Alaska Range.** The road is a paved two-lane highway, but you'll encounter little other traffic. Find your room in **Fairbanks** and then relax as you dine at **Gambardella's Italian Café** (see Chapter 17).

Day 9 is an indoor day, taking in the sights of Fairbanks, including the **University of Alaska Museum** and other on-campus sites, the **historic riverboat at Pioneer Park,** and perhaps the gold panning tour at **Gold Dredge No. 8.** Or, when the weather's right, go outside and rent a canoe to float down part of the **Chena River,** landing at the **Pump House Restaurant and Saloon** for dinner (see Chapter 17).

You head out for the Arctic on **Day 10.** Board an Alaska Airlines jet bound for **Barrow,** the northernmost community in North America, on the shores of the Arctic Ocean. Through the airline, you can join a guided tour that includes a bus tour, **Eskimo dancing,** and a visit to the **cultural center,** or you can try the self-guided approach, and in the proper season, ride a van on caterpillar tracks to the extreme northern end of Alaska to see **polar bears** (see Chapter 23). After your visit to the far reaches of Barrow, simply fly back to Fairbanks for the night or stay over in Barrow and fly back in the morning when you want more time.

By **Day 11,** you've been traveling hard, so this day's for pure relaxation. Drive an hour from Fairbanks to **Chena Hot Springs Resort** and spend the day soaking in the hot pond or indoor and outdoor pools. If you have the energy, you can enjoy a little horseback riding or one of the many other activities. Spend the night here or back in Fairbanks (see Chapter 17); it's your choice.

For **Days 12 and 13,** drive to **Denali National Park,** which is less than two hours south of Fairbanks on the George Parks Highway, and follow the suggestions for days 5 and 6 in the "Exploring the National Parks" itinerary, earlier in this chapter.

On **Day 14,** drive 4½ hours back to Anchorage to catch your plane home.

Planning a Kid-Friendly Week in Alaska

Alaska isn't an easy trip to hurry through with the kids. The distances are great ("Are we there yet?") and activities are expensive. Nevertheless, I have four children of my own, and we spend entire Alaskan summers having fun outdoors and reminding ourselves that this really *is* our life; it's often too great to believe that it's real. The key for us is discarding the idea of set goals. We hope to see wildlife, but we never plan to. We set out for a long drive, but we're always ready to stop . . . overnight if necessary. When we're outdoors, usually on the water, we usually abandon any plan at all. We give our extended family a general outline of where we are going, but after we're out there, any of the kids can say, "Let's land there," and we do. Who knows, we may even end up staying for a couple of days.

That sort of travel is much easier when you live in the place you're actually visiting (makes sense, doesn't it) and know it well; easier, that is, than when you're visiting for the first time. However, even first-timers can design a less goal-oriented trip that favors more of an experiential itinerary. Here are some suggestions for a family trip that uses Anchorage as home base.

On **Day 1,** fly in to **Anchorage.** After finding your bearings, explore the downtown area. Don't miss the **Imaginarium,** a children's science museum that's fun and explains much of what you're going to see. If you have time, rent bikes for a roll along the **Coastal Trail** (see Chapter 14). The **Downtown Deli** is kid-friendly for dinner (see Chapter 13).

Take a day trip by boat on **Day 2** to see the glaciers and wildlife of **Prince William Sound** from Whittier. The tour boat company arranges your transfer from Anchorage, or you can drive a rented car or take the train. Every kid enjoys the 2-mile-long **tunnel to Whittier** and the weird town itself, where everyone lives in one huge, concrete building. If your children are older than 10 or 12, you can instead choose a **guided sea kayaking outing** from Whittier as a day trip (see Chapter 15). Back in Anchorage, try the **Lucky Wishbone** for a zero-stress dinner (see Chapter 13).

On **Day 3,** go hiking in **Chugach State Park.** The mountains behind Anchorage comprise one of the nation's greatest alpine parks. For the easiest access to **doable mountain climbs, mountain biking above the tree line,** and **tundra rambles beyond trails,** start at the Glen Alps parking lot. The **Alaska Zoo** is right on the way there, if you have energy left for it (see Chapter 14). Eat at the **Moose's Tooth Pub and Pizzeria,** with the best pies and brews in town and a tent dining room where manners aren't required (see Chapter 13).

For **Day 4,** drive to **Talkeetna,** on the south side of **Mount McKinley.** Although it's 112 miles from Anchorage, that's nevertheless about 120 miles shorter than a trip to the mountain's main park entrance. From there you can take a flight with a real glacier pilot over the mountain and, in season, land on a glacier high on its flanks. Although expensive, the glacier flight unquestionably becomes the highlight of your trip. Eat at the **Talkeetna Alaskan Lodge,** where you also should spend the night (see Chapter 19).

Leaving Talkeetna on **Day 5,** you head for **Hatcher Pass,** exploring the old mine buildings in a high mountain valley and staying in one of the cozy A-frame cabins at the **Hatcher Pass Lodge.** It's just short of camping, and you can walk from your door across a wide expanse of tundra. The tiny lodge dining room serves good burgers (see Chapter 15).

Day 6 offers an opportunity for a **white-water raft ride.** A company called Nova invites children as young as 5 on rides that start in front of the impressive **Matanuska Glacier** (see Chapter 14), located up the Glenn Highway about two hours north of Anchorage and about 90 minutes from Hatcher Pass. After your adventure, you can spend your last evening at the **Glacier Brewhouse,** a fun place for your last dinner in Anchorage (see Chapter 13).

On **Day 7,** rent bikes to use up energy on Anchorage's paved and dirt trails before boarding a flight for home.

Experiencing Alaska in White: A Week of Real Winter

If you enjoy winter and winter sports, few places compare to Alaska. Even if you don't, winter is when the state is most beautiful. The scenery is purified by snow, and the Aurora Borealis brightly illuminates velvety skies. Travel is a bit trickier, however, and most of the attractions that pack in people during the summer are closed for the season.

Here is a weeklong itinerary that assumes you have an interest in skiing. Two of the destinations on the schedule are resorts where skiers normally spend more time than I have listed, so adjust the schedule to your liking.

On **Day 1,** arrive in **Anchorage** in February, during the **Fur Rendezvous** sled dog races and winter carnival, or in March, to see the start of the **Iditarod Trail Sled Dog Race** (see Chapter 2). **Go mushing** yourself for a full-immersion introduction to an Alaskan winter, with Birch Trails Adventures (see Chapter 14).

On **Day 2,** go to the Alyeska Resort for **downhill skiing on Mount Alyeska** and to stay in the resort's magnificent **Alyeska Prince Hotel.** You can ski 1,000 acres of mostly steep terrain right from the hotel's back door and dine on either side of the mountain or on top (see Chapter 15). If you prefer **cross-country skiing,** remember that Anchorage has trail systems that are among the nation's best at **Kincaid Park** (see Chapter 14).

Day 3 offers another day of skiing at Mount Alyeska, or you can go **backcountry skiing** or join a **snowmobile** outing into the **Chugach Mountains** from the resort.

On **Day 4,** catch the Alaska Railroad's weekly, **one-car winter train from Anchorage to Fairbanks,** a 12-hour journey through Alaska's most spectacular scenery with no sign of human activities. With any luck, you'll see plenty of moose and a stunning view of **Mount McKinley** (see Chapter 7).

In Fairbanks for **Day 5,** visit the **University of Alaska Museum** and, in March, see the ice sculptures of the **World Ice Art Championships.** Day 5 finishes up with a relaxing visit to **Chena Hot Springs Resort** (see Chapter 17).

Relax a bit more on **Day 6,** enjoying the **hot pond,** the **indoor and outdoor pools,** and the **aurora-viewing facility** on the mountain above the resort at Chena Hot Springs. Go **cross-country skiing** or explore the surrounding wilderness by snowmobile.

Day 7 offers time for one last soak or ski before you head back to the airport in Fairbanks for the trip home.

Chapter 4

Planning Your Budget

· ·

In This Chapter

▶ Estimating how much your trip will cost

▶ Keeping an eye on hidden expenses

▶ Picking up a few money-saving tips

· ·

*A*laska can be expensive: At times, hotels and meals cost more than comparable choices elsewhere in the United States, and because the peak season is short, operators charge all that the market will bear during the three or four months of active business.

However, with careful planning, you can keep a lid on costs — the trick is knowing which ones. But you can't cut the cost of getting outdoors to see and do the things that make Alaska a special place to visit. Unless you're an expert sea kayaker, you can't get out on the water cheaply. You need a guide to find out where and how to fish. And without your own wings, you can't see what Alaska looks like from above.

In this chapter, I explain when to save and when to splurge. The tips that I offer can help you reduce your costs so that you don't have to cut out any of the enjoyment that comes with vacationing in Alaska.

Adding Up the Elements

I know the impulse well. After adding up the costs in your head, you shave a figure or two here, leave out a detail there, and convince yourself that you can't afford not to go! If you want to do that, skip this section and ask your boss for a raise. However, if you want to go in with your eyes open, use these pages to make sure that you don't miss any costs in your planning. After you read this chapter, add everything up using the yellow "Making Dollars and Sense of It" worksheets in the back of the book, and then decide whether you can afford your trip or you need to cut corners. (See Chapter 8 for the costs of traveling to Alaska by cruise ship.)

Transportation

Airline competition makes getting from Seattle to Anchorage, by far, the cheapest way into the main part of the state (even cheaper than driving). Obtain current price listings by checking a travel Web site such as Travelocity.com (`travelocity.com`). A round-trip fare of $350 usually is available, and sometimes you can get a ticket for $250 or even less. Prices are about the same when flying from Seattle to Juneau. When flying within the state, however, airfares rise substantially, because Alaska Airlines is the only game in town (or the state for that matter). At times, flying from Anchorage to some Alaska bush communities costs as much as flying from Anchorage to Europe. Again, the Web is the best place to check for current prices; `www.alaskaair.com` is a good place to start. For more information on getting to Alaska, see Chapter 6.

The cheapest and most convenient way to travel the part of the state that has roads is by rental car ($200 to $250 a week in Anchorage). But in Southeast Alaska, where most towns aren't linked by highways, a car is nothing more than an inconvenience. In that part of the state, relying on the Alaska Marine Highway System ferries (cheap travel at $30 for a 9-hour, 150-mile trip) or flying short hops by jet or propeller aircraft (generally less expensive than the previously noted high intrastate fares) makes more sense. The Alaska Railroad runs from Seward, south of Anchorage, to Fairbanks. Trips along this line are beautiful, and reminiscent of the golden days of railways, but they're priced as tours, not as transportation, and as such, cost far more than any other modes of travel. For many more details and contact information about getting around Alaska, see Chapter 7.

Lodging

With the exception of some smaller towns, lodging in Alaska during the high season generally costs 25% to 50% more than is typical the rest of the year; prices in Anchorage and Fairbanks are comparable to high-priced destinations such as New York City. A comfortable place without any luxuries goes for around $165 a night, while a room in a high-rise or resort is more than $200.

You can reduce what you pay for lodging by staying in bed-and-breakfasts (B&Bs); many such accommodations have moved beyond the spare bedroom and now are like personal little inns. I prefer them anyway, because you meet real Alaskans. With a private bath, expect to pay about $130. The breakfast saves you time and money, too.

Dining

A couple can spend $100 for dinner in Alaska's best restaurants, and you need to splurge at least once so that you can sample the great regional cuisine that's based on the state's wonderful seafood trade. Most of the time, however, dining at mid-range places, where a main course is $15 or less, makes more sense. Traveling that way, a couple can budget $20 for breakfast, $25 for lunch, and $55 for dinner, or an average of $100 per day. Remember to adjust these prices downward whenever you stay at B&Bs, because breakfast is, of course, included.

Attractions and outdoor activities

Don't pinch your pennies when planning what to see and do in Alaska; otherwise, you may end up spending your time simply looking through museums or walking through towns. That's not a bad thing, but you'll miss out on some of Alaska's more impressive and unique sights, scenery, and experiences, such as soaring over glaciers or paddling among whales. For an idea of how much to budget for your Alaska adventures, check out the following activities and prices:

- ✔ Typical in-town attractions, such as visiting museums (walking through towns is generally free), are $10 to $25.

- ✔ Boat tours range from $75 to $160.

- ✔ A five-hour guided excursion by sea kayak or raft is $75 to $150.

- ✔ The best flightseeing tours are $125 to $250.

- ✔ Wilderness lodges and multiday all-inclusive outdoor adventures start at $125 a day for a rough tent experience and can go up to as much as $500 a day for the best. The typical outdoor adventure is $300 a day.

The high cost of outdoor activities is one reason why Denali National Park is such a bargain; the bus ride there is one of the state's best wildlife safaris for under $25 per person.

For more details about outdoor activities, see Chapter 9.

Shopping

Finally, a break after all those big numbers! You don't have to spend a penny shopping on your trip to Alaska. When you get home, and you meet the expectant gaze of your grandchildren or significant other, you can just tell them about all the money you saved by not buying gifts, and they'll, of course, be thrilled by your thriftiness.

If skipping the gift-buying part of the program won't work, Alaskan shops willingly accept your dollars. Here are some options:

- ✓ **T-shirt and gift shops:** Every Alaskan town has one. Full of inexpensive tourist items from Taiwan and other such places, you can find a plastic totem pole that may satisfy the less discriminating on your list, such as those ages 5 or younger.

- ✓ **Shops that have more usable stuff:** This is the next level of souvenir shopping. I mention these locations throughout the book. Expect to pay more for fabric, ceramic, or wooden crafts, but you can still find items under $100.

- ✓ **Authentic Alaska Native arts and crafts shops:** If authenticity is what you seek, be ready to spend money. Except for small items, authentic Native items, such as handmade knitted clothing, usually sell for more than $100, and larger pieces, such as masks or fine art, often are priced in the thousands of dollars. Totem poles sell for around $1,000 a foot.

You can find less expensive items that look like they were made by Alaska Natives, but they may be fakes turned out by unscrupulous operators willing to cheat visitors and to take food off the tables of the real artisans they copy (see Chapter 11 for more information about how to avoid these scams).

Nightlife

Nightlife in an Alaskan summer? Fly-casting for red salmon on the Russian River under the midnight sun! But that's certainly not *all* there is. In summer, many communities play host to tourist shows (costing around $20); they're often fun but almost always corny, and I doubt you'll want to attend more than one. Otherwise, performing arts events, movies, and nightclubs cost about the same as in the lower 48 or anywhere else.

Keeping an Eye on Hidden Expenses

How is it that a final bill can be more than the sum of its parts? It may have something to do with the little surprises that creep up on you unawares. Check out the following frequent culprits:

- ✓ **Taxes:** Most towns in Alaska (Anchorage is one notable exception) have sales taxes, and all have bed taxes designed to soak the tourists; together, these taxes can add 10% or more to the cost of your room. Car-rental taxes and airport-concession fees are 10% to 20%, so make sure that you include them when you price your reservation.

✔ **Tipping:** All the tipping rules with which you're familiar hold true in Alaska: 15% to 18% in restaurants, $1 per bag for bell service, and so on. When you get into the area of guides, fishing charters, tour boats, and wilderness lodges, tipping becomes a little trickier. As a general rule, tip guides and outfitters $10 to $20 per person per day. For outings of less than a day, adjust the tip accordingly; a $20 tip for a family of four on a half-day sea-kayaking outing is plenty. At wilderness lodges, which normally have all-inclusive rates, adding the tip to your final payment when you leave often is best, because doing so allows the proprietor to distribute the gratuity to the staff rather than you trying to do it at each meal. A blanket tip of $15 per guest per day is acceptable. Tipping isn't necessary when you're on a big tour boat with dozens of other guests, unless you want to reward a particular crew member who helped you.

✔ **Taxis and transfers:** Alaskan towns, especially the larger ones, can be expensive to get around in when you don't have your own car. Allow $10 to $20 per person for each of your airport transfers unless you pick up a car at the airport or your lodging has a courtesy van. If you plan activities out of the center of town, check ahead of time how to get there to make sure that it isn't too expensive. (The listings that I recommend in this book include descriptions on how to get to particular locations.)

Cutting Costs

With a bit of planning, plenty of options are available to help reduce the cost of your trip, often with only small sacrifices. Note the "Bargain Alert" icons scattered throughout this book. They offer hints on ways to trim the fat from your vacation budget. While you're planning a trip, keep the following in mind:

✔ **Travel at off-peak times.** Prices drop significantly during May and September, yet these months still offer plenty to do. See Chapter 2 for a discussion of what you gain and give up by traveling during each of Alaska's seasons.

✔ **Check out a package tour.** Package deals and escorted tours often include better deals on airfares, rail tickets, and hotel rates than you get when you pay for them separately. See the section on package tours in Chapter 6 for suggestions, specific companies to call, and the inevitable downside.

✔ **Consider a cruise.** When you add it all up, cruising can be less expensive than independent travel in Alaska at the same comfort level. Similarly, the all-inclusive price of a cruise protects against the budget creep that often sneaks up on you when you pay as you go. See Chapter 8 for details on cruising.

✔ **Have some meals in your room.** Some hotel rooms are equipped with kitchenettes, giving you the comfortable and cheap option of eating in. Even when you get a room with just a fridge and coffee-maker, you can save time and money on breakfast and snacks.

✔ **Always ask for discount rates.** You won't get any discounts when you don't ask for them. Don't forget to mention your membership in any clubs that can earn you a discount.

✔ **Choose rooms large enough for your entire family.** Even if you pay 50% more for a bigger room or suite, it still saves you the difference of renting two rooms (and you have more control over your kids).

✔ **Try expensive restaurants at lunch rather than dinner.** Lunch tabs are usually a fraction of what dinner costs at most restaurants. Besides, the lunch menu often offers many of the same specialties in smaller portions at less expensive prices.

✔ **Ask about hotel telephone charges up front.** Most hotels now offer free local calls from rooms, but don't count on it. Ask when you check in so that you make sure you don't get hit with big extra charges for your calls.

✔ **Take the Alaska Marine Highway System.** The ferry system is a fun and inexpensive way to travel from town to town and see the scenery in coastal Alaska. Chapter 7 includes more information about getting around Alaska by ferry.

✔ **Use pedal power.** In all but only a few Alaska towns (and during the warmer seasons, of course), bicycles are a great way to get around and are much cheaper than renting a car or using taxis.

✔ **Buy a coupon book.** Although *The Great Alaskan TourSaver* (☎ 907-278-7600; Internet: www.toursaver.com) costs $100, it nevertheless is well worth the price when you plan to travel as a couple, especially in the South Central region. Among more than 100 coupons, you'll find some freebies and many two-for-one deals on some of the best activities and tours that are valuable enough to pay for the book with only a couple of uses.

Chapter 5

Tips for Travelers with Special Needs and Interests

. . . .

In This Chapter

▶ Bringing the kids with you to Alaska

▶ Going to Alaska as senior citizens

▶ Visiting an Alaska that's accessible to people with disabilities

▶ Finding gay-friendly resources

. . . .

A lot of visitors have been going to Alaska for a long time. By now, the place is pretty much ready with services that cater to just about everyone. This chapter offers some advice on finding and using those services.

Vacationing in Alaska with Children

Even though my name appears on the title page, I think of my travel books as a family project. (We also write *Frommer's Alaska* and *Frommer's Family Vacations in the National Parks* together.) When I researched my first Alaska travel book, my son, Robin, was 3, and my daughter, Julia, was 6 months. Today, Robin is 11, Julia is 7, Joseph is 3, and Becky is 1. You may run into us at a campground or on a boat dock anywhere in Alaska or across the country as we travel to research our next travel guide. Yes, it's a great job, and bringing the family along is the best part.

Alaska's magnificent scenery is something that even young children can understand and appreciate. Also, an Alaska vacation is largely spent outdoors, which is where kids like to be. Children never get enough ferry riding, boating, or camping, and the older ones especially enjoy hiking, canoeing, sea kayaking, skiing, and dog mushing. Overall, Alaska can be a family-friendly destination as long as you do your homework. In this section, I provide you with tips to plan a vacation that everyone in your family can enjoy.

Tackling the challenges

Alaska does have a few drawbacks as a family destination, primarily, the expense. Some activities, such as flightseeing and tour-boat cruises, tend to have less-than-generous children's discounts and cost too much for most families. Hotel rooms and restaurant meals in Alaska can be expensive for an entire family (though I include some family-friendly listings for these services throughout this book). And often, bed-and-breakfast rooms are too small for a family. Although camping solves many of these problems, getting your camping gear to Alaska is a logistical challenge. For tips on doing so, see Chapter 12, and for an extended discussion on a camping vacation in Alaska, check out *Frommer's Alaska,* published by Wiley. (Need a book that covers all of Alaska's campgrounds in detail? Check out *Traveler's Guide to Alaskan Camping,* by Mike and Terri Church and published by Rolling Homes Press.)

Not only do you have to be careful when planning the necessities, such as food and lodging, you also have to be careful in choosing your itinerary and activities with children. The highways in Alaska are long, and children require a gradual approach to covering a lot of ground. They also need time to play, explore, and rest. Frankly, children often don't enjoy wildlife-watching. Searching for the animals takes a long time, and when you do find them, they're usually off in the distance. Kids younger than 8 often don't have the visual skills or patience to pick out the animals from the landscape and can get bored quickly even when they can see the animals. The upcoming section, "Keeping kids happy on the road," includes some ideas that I've picked up over years of traveling the state with my kids that may keep your kids more engaged during your trip.

Though your kids will likely love the outdoors as much as you will, don't overtax them with excessively long walks and hiking trips. Keep track of the longest hike you've managed without excessive whining, and then try to extend that record just a little bit each time out. If your kids aren't that accustomed to hiking, try taking them on a few hikes at home to help them (and you) build stamina for the trip. Short sea-kayaking excursions, on the other hand, are great for children who are old enough, riding in the front of a double-seat boat with a parent in back. In practice, the age limit depends on the outfitter and your child's level of responsibility.

If you're like most families, you'll be getting on each other's nerves after a few weeks on the road. Our family makes it through those tough moments by leaving time for low-key kid activities monitored by one adult, such as beachcombing and playing in the park, while the other grown-up splits off for a museum visit, shopping, or a special, more expensive activity. Of course, if you want to preserve your marriage, you'll have to be scrupulously fair about who gets to go flightseeing and who has to stay behind and change diapers because you won't have my all-purpose excuse (research).

Catering to families

If you're interested in a package tour for your family, most of the compa-nies in Chapter 6 take children, but research the tours carefully to make sure you'll have enough down time. A better choice is an outdoor-oriented trip specifically designed for children by an outfitter. **Alaska Wildland Adventures** (☎ **800-334-8730** or 907-783-2928; Internet: www.alaskawildland.com) has various trips for kids as young as 12, and even offers a **Family Safari** for families with children ages 6 through 11 that strings together day trips in various places with stays at wilder-ness lodges. With the Family Safari, you take a float trip on the Kenai River and spend several days in Denali National Park. The nine-day trip costs $3,895 for adults and $3,595 for kids, exclusive of air travel.

In addition, the cruise-ship industry is courting families, and many ships have several fun activities for children. Some cruise lines even have pro-grams that take the kids off your hands for a while — something that both the children and parents enjoy. See Chapter 8 for details.

Keeping kids happy on the road

We've taken trips with our children that no sane person would attempt — all over Alaska and all over the United States, for as long as seven weeks at a time; we've even spent two weeks all alone in remote wilderness with three kids and a baby. We've enjoyed all our trips. One reason, besides having great kids, is that we have learned the importance of adjusting our plans and our behavior to our children's needs. Here are some of our discoveries:

- ✔ **Keep consistent meal times.** This is the most important factor to keeping your crew happy. Carry food with you in case you can't make it to a restaurant when your regular lunch, dinner, or after-noon snack time arrives. Make no exceptions. Hungry people get grumpy and irrational, and then everything falls apart.

- ✔ **Don't compromise on nutrition when you're traveling.** If you normally eat junk all the time, okay. But if you have a healthy diet at home, don't stop now. With the stress of traveling, your kids need good food more now than ever. Pass on the burger in a box in favor of a healthy, real restaurant meal or a picnic.

- ✔ **Choose rooms with cooking facilities.** You'll go crazy if you eat three meals a day in restaurants with children for your whole trip. You can save a considerable chunk of change by staying in for breakfast and an occasional lunch or dinner.

- ✔ **Remember Alaska's long summer days.** We don't sweat bedtime in the summer, and neither do most of the Alaskan parents we know. The Alaskan sky stays light late at night and everyone is energized. Getting to bed early is hard for kids and adults.

✔ **Leave time for fun and spontaneity.** Often, when driving a high-way in Alaska, you may see a place where it's tempting to just jump out of the car and romp in the heather. What a shame if you're in a rush to get somewhere and can't stop.

✔ **Don't overdo it.** One big activity a day is enough.

✔ **Bring toys.** But just a few, and then buy more as you go. Hold back some fresh toys for tough times. New toys are a lot more fun than old ones.

✔ **And don't forget other activities.** Bring crayons, pencils, pads of paper, stickers, pipe cleaners, cards, magnetic checkers, picture books, coloring books, activity books, and maps. Also, bring little prizes to make car games more exciting. Try to limit the amount of toys and other diversions so that they fill only one additional bag.

✔ **Let the professionals entertain your kids.** Bring an inexpensive personal stereo with headphones for each child and a collection of music or stories on tape. Kids enjoy listening to something that no one else can hear. Buy some new story tapes to break out on the way when the going gets rough.

✔ **Craft a family journal.** Make a journal of your trip by buying post-cards everywhere you go (even gas stations) for your child to put in a cheap photo album or otherwise make into a book. He or she can write on the back of the postcards, or draw pictures, and put them in the album. Rearranging, editing, and showing off the book uses up a lot of time. And when you get home, it's a good souvenir.

✔ **Create a personal journal.** Our children keep journals every night when we're traveling, even the children too young to write (they draw pictures and dictate words). I let each child pick out a good bound journal that they really value. Journal time is a wonderfully quiet evening ritual and a good prelude to bedtime. We find it interesting to find out what experiences they think are important enough to mention, and keeping a journal maintains their writing skills over the summer. And they're proud when the summer is over to have made something worth keeping.

✔ **Take this time to get to know your kids again.** Talk to them, read to them, take advantage of learning about a new place together.

Traveling as Senior Citizens

People over age 65 get reduced-admission prices to many Alaska attractions, and some accommodations have special senior rates. And joining organizations such as **AARP** (☎ **800-424-3410** or 202-434-AARP; Internet: www.aarp.org) and **Mature Outlook** (☎ **800-336-6330**), if you haven't already done so, may open the door to additional travel discounts.

National parks offer free admission and special camping rates for people over 62 with a **Golden Age Passport,** which you can obtain at any of the parks for $10 and which never expires (everyone with you in the car comes in free, too). Make sure to mention your pass when making shuttle or camping reservations at Denali National Park, as park attendants automatically add the entrance fee to your bill. Also mention your age when booking your airfare; most domestic airlines offer senior discounts.

Most towns have a senior citizens center where you find activities and help with any special needs. For example, the **Anchorage Senior Center** (1300 E. 19th Ave.; ☎ **907-258-7823**) offers guidance for visitors, as well as use of the restaurant, showers, gift shop, and fitness room; a big band plays Friday nights for dancing. (You may have to pay a small fee for use of the facilities; call for advice.)

Elderhostel, 11 Avenue de Lafayette, Boston, MA 02111-1746 (☎ **877-426-8056;** TTY 877-426-2167; from overseas, ☎ **978-323-4141;** Internet: www.elderhostel.org), operates many weeklong Alaska learning vacations for groups of people 55 and older. The catalog of choices, including destinations, activities, and costs, is on the Web site.

Finding Services Accessible to People with Disabilities

The Americans with Disabilities Act and economic competition have sped the process of retrofitting hotels and even B&Bs to be accessible for people with disabilities. The result is often the best rooms in the house. Hotels without accessible facilities now are the exception; however, check when making reservations.

Several Alaska agencies cater to people with disabilities. In Anchorage, **Challenge Alaska** (☎ **907-344-7399;** Internet: www.challenge.ak.org), a nonprofit organization, offers therapeutic recreation and education, including outdoor adventures. The organization operates an adaptive ski school at its International Sports, Recreation, and Education Center at Alyeska Resort in Girdwood (☎ **907-783-2925**). Summer outings are inexpensive: A two-day sea-kayaking outing is only $115. Get on the mailing list for current listings. Challenge Alaska also welcomes inquiries and keeps track of tourism operators who are authentically accessible.

Alaska Welcomes You! Inc., P.O. Box 91333, Anchorage, AK 99509-1333 (☎ or TTY **800-349-6301** or 907-349-6301; Internet: www.accessible alaska.com), books accessible cruises, tours in South Central Alaska, and extended travel packages to Denali National Park and the Kenai Peninsula, and plans trips for independent travelers with special needs. The operator is a respected community worker for the disabled who field-checks the places he books to make sure that they're really accessible.

Discovering Resources for Gays and Lesbians

Anchorage, Juneau, and Fairbanks have active gay and lesbian communities. In Anchorage, **Identity Inc.** (☎ **907-258-4777;** Internet: www. alaska.net/~identity) offers referrals, publishes a newsletter called *Northview,* and sponsors activities throughout the year, including the **June Pridefest,** with many events, such as a parade and picnic. Their community center is at 2110 E. Northern Lights, Suite A (☎ **907-929-4528**). The **S.E. Alaska Gay/Lesbian Alliance** (SEAGLA) (☎ **907-586-4297;** Internet: www.ptialaska.net/~seagla) is a similar organization in Juneau.

Bob DeLoach is a real expert on gay and lesbian Alaska travel. His **Apollo Travel,** operating with **Whitsett Travel** (☎ **907-892-1888**), has a Web site with online booking at www.apollotravelalaska.com.

Part II
Ironing Out the Details

The 5th Wave   By Rich Tennant

"Oh Ted, this Alaskan cruise is everything I'd ever imagined! The sweeping vista of the salad bar, the breathtaking dessert tray, the majesty of the carving station..."

In this part . . .

You've planned your trip in your daydreams; now it's time to plan it on paper (or with electrons, if you use the Internet). This part covers how to reserve your trip, whether to go it alone or with a package or escorted tour, and how to get to and around Alaska. In addition, you'll find two in-depth chapters on other traveling options: one about cruising, and the other about outdoor adventures. Finally, I discuss how to book accommodations, how to best handle your money, and many other little details that are hard to remember but even harder to live without.

Chapter 6

Getting to Alaska

T he moment of putting down a credit card for a plane ticket is, to me, like the moment of leaping off a diving board. That's when I realize I really am going. Getting to the edge of the board is hard, too, just as narrowing all your choices and taking the plunge on a trip can be difficult. But delaying only means that you lose some of the best choices. When you buy the tickets, you nail down your dates. You then can start filling in all the days in between and line up all your other reservations.

I'm assuming you *will* buy a plane ticket. You can find other ways to get to Alaska, but except for travel by cruise ship or possibly ferry, they're not practical for a typical one- or two-week vacation. (For more information on cruising to Alaska, check out Chapter 8.) The real questions for you to examine, then, are how and from whom you should buy your plane ticket, and whether you want it as part of a package or escorted tour.

Enlisting the Help of a Good Travel Agent

Finding a *good* travel agent can really be a feat. If you find one, tell everyone you know. They're as rare as trustworthy auto mechanics. The problem is, the job is a very tough one, and the incentives — commissions on the trip's price — reward agents who make the trip cost *more,* not less. At the same time, agents working on commission are struggling as the airlines steadily clamp down on what they pay them. So planning a trip and getting a good price has become quite complex. Add in the need to be universally knowledgeable about every place in the world that your client may want to go, and you have a virtually impossible job.

I've seen the result of some well-off travelers simply calling a local travel agent and asking for the perfect Alaska vacation. They end up flying back and forth across the state going to expensive places in quick succession, with little consideration of their true interests. So if you do use a travel agent, make sure that he or she has your best travel interests at heart.

If you already have a good agent, use his or her resources. But first, know where you want to go and what you want to do. Unless your agent is an Alaska expert, he or she likely won't know much beyond the biggest, best-advertised options. However, if you can do some research beforehand — based on this book — a good agent can take your preferences, shop for the best prices, and make your reservations, saving you a good deal of work and sometimes finding you bargains you'd be hard-pressed to find on your own.

Do keep in mind that some businesses in Alaska don't pay agents any commission, especially small operators such as bed-and-breakfasts and outdoors guides. Moreover, even some big operations have cut agency commissions to the breaking point. So, it's probably unreasonable to expect an agent, especially an Alaska expert, to work without charging you a fee these days. Some of the best Alaska experts — the ones you really can trust to plan your whole itinerary — charge clients $100 or more per person, on top of the commissions they receive from service providers. You get what you pay for, and if you're spending several thousand dollars on a trip, a couple of hundred more to ensure the best trip is probably a good investment.

The following lists a handful of agencies that are especially helpful with planning those uniquely Alaska experiences:

✔ **Alaska Bound,** 434 E. Lake St., Petoskey, MI 49770 (☎ 888-ALASKA-7 or 231-439-3000; Internet: www.alaskabound.com), a Michigan-based agency, is the only one I know of in the Lower 48 that specializes in Alaska. The company started as a cruise planner, working primarily with Holland America, but now plans many independent trips, too, charging $100 per person.

✔ **Fantasia Travel,** 290 N. Yenlo, L-2, Wasilla, AK 99654 (☎ 800-478-2622 or 907-376-2622; Internet: www.alaskaflights.com), offers travel packages (fee inclusive) that gladly put clients in B&Bs and cabins, not just the high-priced places most agents prefer to use. Sign up for notification of airfare sales by e-mail on their Web site.

✔ **Sport Fishing Alaska,** 9310 Shorecrest Dr., Anchorage, AK 99502 (☎ **907-344-8674;** Internet: www.alaskatripplanners.com), is a good choice for a fishing vacation. The owners, former guides and float, charter, and air-taxi operators, Larry and Sheary Suiter, know where the fish are from week to week. They also can book the balance of your trip at fun and interesting places. They charge a $95 upfront fee plus commissions.

✔ **Viking Travel,** P.O. Box 787, Petersburg, AK 99833 (☎ **800-327-2571** or 907-772-3818; Internet: www.alaska-ala-carte.com), an agency started by an entrepreneur in the small Southeast Alaska town of Petersburg, initially specialized in independent outdoor trips in its own area but now plans trips for the whole state. Instead of a fee or percentage, Viking Travel charges a package price for an itinerary you help design. Sample itineraries are on the Web site. The firm also books Alaska and B.C. ferries without a surcharge (Internet: www.alaskaferry.com). Get on the list, and the agency books your cabins and vehicle reservations on the first day the system makes them available.

Choosing the Right Package

You can often save money on airfare, hotels, and activities by buying an all-inclusive package tour. *Package tours* often include some combination of airfare, accommodations, transportation, and activities. You can purchase escorted or on-your-own packages, although the escorted version is by far the more prevalent flavor in Alaska. I cover unescorted package tours in the next section, and then I discuss the more common escorted tours in the "Checking out escorted package tours" section that follows.

Tour operators buy some tour packages in bulk and then resell them to travelers. Sometimes, a package that includes airfare, hotel, and transportation can cost you less than just the hotel alone that you book yourself. Some packages offer a better class of hotels than others. Some offer the same hotels for lower prices. Some offer flights on scheduled airlines, while others book charters. The packages vary, so work closely with your tour operator, covering all the specific details and options. Keep in mind with some packages that your choice of accommodations and travel days may be limited.

Checking out unescorted package tours

Though most Alaska visitors who are inclined to purchase a packaged vacation do so with escorted tour providers, you can find some unescorted tour providers. Unescorted package tours offer you some of the security of knowing that you have a place to lay your head each night, as well as some of the cost-saving benefits that you find in an escorted tour package. However, you also get a certain level of independence to plan your own sightseeing based on your own interests and at your own pace.

Finding out the basics

With unescorted package tours, you generally pay for your airfare, hotel, and sometimes transportation — all in a neat, inclusive bundle, often at prices that are lower than you'd pay for airfare or lodging on its own when you book everything separately. Make sure that you do some comparison shopping before you commit to one of these packages, however. You may be able to undercut all package-tour prices using my money-saving tips about airfare (see "Booking on Your Own," later in this chapter) and lodging (see Chapter 10).

Shopping for unescorted package tours

Airlines often package their flights with accommodations. To find a bargain, you may need to be flexible. Prices vary significantly depending on the time you travel and the kinds of hotels you pick.

Within Alaska, certain hotels and even destinations that are priced reasonably as package tours cost much more if you book them separately. If you go to Barrow, Nome, or Katmai National Park, the package tour price offered by **Alaska Airlines Vacations** (☎ **800-468-2248;** Internet: www.alaskaair.com) is sometimes less than the cost of the plane ticket by itself. (Compare current prices on the Web site.) This pricing doesn't make much sense, but you may as well take advantage of it. These packages are for day trips with a tour, or for the tour and an overnight stay. If you're not the escorted-tour type, you can still take advantage of the bargain, stick around for as much of the tour as you want, and then do your own thing.

Traveling on the **Alaska Railroad** (☎ **800-544-0552** or 907-265-2494; Internet: www.alaskarailroad.com) is also cheaper as a package. The railroad sells its own packages from Anchorage to Denali and Kenai Fjords national parks on its Web site, as well as full vacation packages covering the part of the state that the railroad services, from Fairbanks to Seward. You may call these partly escorted tours — they're pretty full of guided activities — but you don't get your hand held every minute as with Alaska's major tour companies. Prices are reasonable, too.

Try the following resources to research package tours:

- ✔ Any of the Alaska expert travel agencies that I list in this chapter — some of those outfits put together their own packages.

- ✔ Your local Sunday newspaper's travel section.

- ✔ The ads in the back of national travel magazines.

- ✔ The Web site, www.vacationpackager.com, where you can link up with many different operators, dozens of which are in Alaska. Note that most of these are escorted tours, not simply packages.

Checking out escorted package tours

Hundreds of thousands of visitors come to Alaska each year on escorted package tours, leaving virtually all their travel arrangements in the hands of a single company that takes responsibility for ushering them through the state for a single, lump-sum fee. But more and more visitors are cutting the apron strings and exploring Alaska on their own, and in the process discovering a more relaxed, spontaneous experience. Each approach has advantages and disadvantages, of course, and which way you choose to visit depends on how you value those pros and cons.

Finding out the basics

An escorted package tour does provide security. If you can't relax and enjoy a trip knowing unforeseen difficulties could happen, then take an escorted package tour. You'll know in advance how much everything costs, you don't have to worry about making hotel and ground-transportation reservations, you're guaranteed to see the highlights of each town you visit, and you'll always have a guide. If you experience weather delays or other travel problems, it's the tour company's problem, not yours. Everything happens on schedule, and you never have to touch your baggage other than to unpack when it magically shows up in your room. Though you may sometimes feel like you're a member of a herd on an escorted tour, you'll also meet new people — a big advantage if you're traveling on your own. Many passengers on these trips are retired, over age 65.

But escorted packages have their disadvantages, too. They often travel at an exhausting pace. Passengers get up early and cover a lot of ground, with sights and activities scheduled solidly through the day. Not necessarily a negative, especially if you're short on time, except that stops last only long enough to get a taste of what the sight is about. You typically don't have time to dig in and learn about a place you're especially interested in.

Also, on an escorted trip, you meet few, if any, Alaska residents, because most tour companies hire college students from "Outside" (a term Alaskans use to refer to anyplace that's not in Alaska) to fill summer jobs. You stay in only the largest hotels and eat in the largest, tourist-oriented restaurants — no small, quaint places loaded with local character. For visiting the wilderness, such as Denali National Park, the quick and superficial approach can spoil the whole point of going to a destination that's about an experience, not just seeing a particular object or place.

Unfortunately, some people choose an escorted tour based on expectations that aren't valid. Make sure you really know what you're getting into when traveling to Alaska. Studies by Alaska tourism experts have found that visitors choose escorted packages to avoid risks that don't really exist. Alaska may still be untamed, but that doesn't mean it's a dangerous or uncomfortable place to travel. Visitors who sign up for a tour to avoid having to spend the night in an igloo or use an outhouse may wish they'd been a bit more adventurous when they arrive and find that Alaska has the same facilities found in any other state. Except for tiny bush villages that you're unlikely to visit anyway, you'll come across the standard American hotel room almost anywhere you go. The tourism infrastructure is well developed, even in small towns — you're never far from help unless you want to be.

Shopping for an escorted package

When researching an escorted tour, ask about the following details:

- ✔ **Cancellation policy:** How large is the required deposit? When and under what circumstances can you get your deposit back if you're unable to go? (I strongly recommend trip cancellation insurance; see Chapter 12.)

- ✔ **Schedule:** Make sure that the tour's pace matches your idea of a vacation. Tour companies make more money by packing in more activities during the day, but I sometimes see visitors sleeping through spectacular scenery because they're exhausted from early departures and jam-packed days.

- ✔ **Group size:** Generally, you want to be in as small a group as possible to minimize the time you spend waiting and crowding in and out of attractions. Typically, the big companies carry full buses. Expect to pay more for a van tour with a smaller group. When you shop, ask roughly how many people will be on the tour with you.

- ✔ **Hidden costs:** Make the tour operator list any and all costs that aren't included in the quoted price. You may have to pay to get yourself to and from the airport, for example. Calculate the cost of meals "on your own" that are included in the itinerary.

- ✔ **Flexibility:** Can you ditch the group at times and do your own thing? Often, the answer is no, because a big group with a fast pace has to stick together. But you can look for a tour with more "on your own" time.

Selecting a tour company

A few major tour and cruise-ship companies dominate the Alaska package-tour market with operations that allow them to take care of everything you do while in Alaska with tight quality control. Each also offers tours as short as a couple of hours for independent travelers who want to combine their own exploring with a more structured experience. You can book all tours through any travel agent.

- ✔ **Holland America Tours,** 300 Elliot Ave. W, Seattle, WA 98119 (☎ 800-544-2206; Internet: www.graylineofalaska.com or www.hollandamerica.com), affiliated with the Holland America cruise line, became the giant of Alaska tourism by buying local tour companies, such as Gray Line and Westours, to carry visitors in buses, trains, and boats, and the Westmark hotel chain to put them up for the night. Today, the Alaska/Yukon operation employs more than 2,500 workers operating 184 buses, 13 railcars, and 2 day boats. Most clients arrive in the state on one of the company's ships (see Chapter 8). Even within Alaska, chances are good that your tour will put you on a Gray Line coach and exclusively in Westmark hotels. The quality of the Westmark chain is inconsistent. Other than the classy Baranof in Juneau, the hotels tend to have standard to small rooms with typical amenities, although on a group tour, you don't spend much time in the room, as schedules generally are tightly planned and daily departures are early. Gray Line coaches and the company's Denali National Park railcars are first-rate. And the company goes more places than any other, with a catalog that covers just about anything in the state that you can possibly do with a group. Prices depend on a variety of factors, but in general, a week-long tour costs about $1,600 per person.

✔ **Princess Cruises and Tours,** 2815 Second Ave., Ste. 400, Seattle, WA 98121-1299 (☎ **800-426-0442;** Internet: www.princesslodges. com), has built its land-tour operation from the ground up instead of buying it (as Holland America did), and the result is a smaller but consistently top-quality collection of properties. The five Princess hotels are all among Alaska's best. Princess operates its own coaches and has superb railcars on the Alaska Railroad route to Denali. Most people on the tours come to Alaska on a cruise ship, but tours are for sale separately, too. The company's network of tours is less extensive than Holland America's, but the tours do visit the places most people want to go.

✔ **Goldbelt Tourism,** 9097 Glacier Hwy., Ste. 100, Juneau, AK 99801 (☎ **800-478-3610** or 907-789-4183; Internet: www.goldbelttours. com), a Juneau Native corporation, bought and built some of the best tours and cruises Southeast Alaska has to offer, including the Glacier Bay National Park concession, an excellent small-ship cruise line, the Misty Fjords National Monument tour, and some of the most popular Juneau activities. Besides selling these tours to independent travelers and helping them plan trips, Goldbelt Tourism offers packages that take guests to the very best of the region, as well as provide a few departures to other parts of the state.

Booking on Your Own

Armed with this book and an Internet connection, you can find just about everything that you need to know to get a good deal on your flights.

Knowing who flies to Alaska

Several major carriers serve Anchorage as the main entry hub from the rest of the United States and Canada and a smattering of flights from Germany, Japan, and Korea. You can also fly into Fairbanks or Southeast Alaska. With plenty of competition on flights from Seattle to Anchorage, prices are usually reasonable and sometimes, when price wars break out, really good ($350 is good, $250 is excellent). Nonstop flights from various other U.S. cities to Anchorage are also available, generally with less competition and higher prices. But many travelers are willing to pay more for a direct flight: It takes a long time to get to Alaska, and avoiding a change of plane in Seattle can save three hours, though you won't find many nonstop options from the East Coast. Summer offers far more choices than winter, but planes fill up and cheap seats are harder to snag.

Alaska Airlines (☎ 800-252-7522; Internet: www.alaskaair.com) has more flights than all other airlines combined, with 20 a day to Seattle in summer and nonstop summer flights to various other cities, including Los Angeles, San Francisco, Chicago, Detroit, Minneapolis, and Dallas. The other airlines with significant Anchorage coverage are **Northwest** (☎ 800-225-2525; Internet: www.nwa.com) to Minneapolis and Dallas; **Continental** (☎ 800-525-0280; Internet: www.continental.com) to Seattle, Newark, Phoenix, and Houston; **United** (☎ 800-241-6522; Internet: www.ual.com) to Seattle, Chicago, San Francisco, and Denver; and **Air Canada** (☎ 888-247-2262; Internet: www.aircanada.ca) to Vancouver. Several other airlines have a few flights. *Note:* This flight information is subject to frequent and radical change.

You can fly by jet to Alaska cities other than Anchorage, but keep in mind that, with a few minor exceptions, **Alaska Airlines** is the only choice of carrier. It's a terrific airline, but the lack of competition and expensive operating conditions make prices higher. Fares from Seattle to Juneau are roughly the same as from Seattle to Anchorage, even with the extra hour of flight time needed to get to Anchorage. And getting most anywhere else in Alaska by jet from Anchorage costs as much or more as fares to Seattle. You'll have a difficult time saving on fares to smaller communities. The only ways to save are to buy your ticket well ahead of your trip, possibly catch a last-minute bargain on the Alaska Airlines Web site, or buy a package from Alaska Airlines Vacations. (See "Shopping for unescorted package tours," earlier in this chapter.)

The balance of the advice I have in this section is for purchasing your ticket from where you live to Anchorage. To help you with your comparison shopping, check out the worksheet at the end of this book entitled, "Fare Game: Choosing an Airline."

Catching sales

With airfare, you pay for flexibility. If you buy a ticket at the last minute or choose to fly on premium days, such as Friday, you often have to pay full fare. However, if you book your ticket far in advance, stay over Saturday night, or travel on a Tuesday, Wednesday, or Thursday, you may pay only a fraction of the full fare. Can you imagine if they sold paint this way? "If you paint on Tuesday, it's $10 a gallon, but on Friday, paint is $20 a gallon. You can have the paint for $5 a gallon if you agree to paint after midnight."

Airlines serving Anchorage get embroiled in fare wars every year. Alaskans travel a lot — plenty of people travel to Seattle or San Francisco just for concerts or sporting events — and the airlines are the only practical connection to the outside world. So when a fare war hits, it often makes front-page news here. The wars for summer travel usually break out in the spring, perhaps in April, and they can save you a lot of money, as much as half, if you book quickly and go along with the sometimes weird restrictions about when you can fly and how long you have to stay. Wait for these fare wars and then act fast before the airlines change their prices (within a day or two for the best fares). One way to find out about these sales is to sign up for an e-mail alert service; various travel Web sites have them. Alaska-based Fantasia Travel has one at `www.alaskaflights.com`.

Buying from a consolidator or charter

Consolidators, also known as *bucket shops,* often offer lower prices than you can get from a travel agent or by yourself. Consolidators buy seats in bulk from the airlines and then sell them back to the public at prices usually below even the airlines' discounted rates. At times, consolidators and charter operators offer discounts to Alaska, but they're few and often aren't available at all. Ask your travel agent to check when you're in the planning stages, but don't count on beating the system this way.

Before you pay a consolidator, request a confirmation number and then call the airline to confirm your seat. Be aware that consolidator tickets are usually nonrefundable or rigged with stiff cancellation penalties, often as high as 50 to 75 percent of the ticket price. Protect yourself by paying with a credit card rather than cash. And keep in mind that if an airline sale is going on, or if it's high season, you often can get the same or better rates from the airlines directly.

You often can find consolidators' advertisements in the Sunday travel section of big-city newspapers. TravelHUB is a Web site (`www.travelhub.com`) listing consolidators and packages.

Buying your ticket online

For a simple, point-to-point ticket, the Internet is hard to beat. Shopping online sometimes takes longer than having a professional travel agent find you a deal, but you have more control and avoid agent fees. Scores of travel sites populate the Web. Most sites allow you to enter your dates of travel and destination, and then the site produces a list of flights and fares from which you can choose.

Unless you really know what you're doing, don't use the Internet if you have a complicated itinerary or special circumstances. Using the Internet is tough to manage all the variables in a multiple layover or open-jaw itinerary. For example, a good travel agent may figure out how you can buy the tickets as pairs of round trips and save money rather than putting all your stops on the same ticket. You can spend hours on the Internet figuring out something like that, but a good agent already knows. Likewise, if you're traveling with children or using a combination of frequent-flier and paid-for tickets, you may miss companion fares or other tricks you don't know about. A skilled travel agent can beat the system in these circumstances in ways that just aren't obvious.

When I buy airline tickets or make rental-car reservations on the Web, I usually search using an agency site that covers many companies' offerings, and then I go directly to the sites of the top two or three on the list. Often, you can get extra bargains or bonus frequent-flier miles by using an airline or rental-car company's own Web site, and you avoid any agency fees.

Finally, you can easily spend a lot of time on the Internet without ever knowing whether you received the best deal. At some point, you have to accept that someone else on the plane may be paying a few dollars less than you are. Remember that going on vacation is supposed to be fun. If you end up happy, why sweat what someone else paid?

Finding the online travel agents

Two of the most respected and most complete online travel agents are **Travelocity** (Internet: www.travelocity.com) and **Expedia** (Internet: www.expedia.com). Each site offers an excellent range of options for booking flights and package tours as well as reserving hotels and car rentals. **Orbitz** (Internet: www.orbitz.com), a popular site launched by United, Delta, Northwest, American, and Continental airlines, often offers special deals that are unavailable on other sites. **Qixo** (Internet: www.qixo.com) is another powerful search engine that enables you to search for flights and accommodations from some 20 airline and travel-planning sites (such as Travelocity) at once.

Alaska Air online for Alaska air (travel)

Alaska Airlines, the dominant carrier serving Alaska, is a leader in using electronic tickets and check-in. The airline makes it worth your while to use the Internet, both when you buy your ticket (Internet: www.alaskaair.com) and when you get to the airport. Especially in Anchorage, the lines for a human ticket agent can be hideous, while you'll usually not wait at all for the electronic kiosks and the baggage check agent that takes luggage from those who check in electronically. You can save an hour this way.

Keep in mind that because several airlines no longer pay commissions on tickets sold by online travel agencies, these Web sites may add a $5 or $10 surcharge to your bill if you book on one of those carriers, or may simply exclude those carriers' flights from their listings. And the excluded carriers may have the best fare. Check several sites to compare the best prices before you book any tickets.

Using an opaque-fare service

Another category of online travel agencies is the *opaque-fare service,* so called because some details of your flight remain hidden until you purchase your ticket. When you book an opaque fare, you give up control of your flight times and your choice of airline (although you're guaranteed to fly a full-service, large-scale carrier). You also give up frequent-flier miles and lock yourself into a nonchangeable, nonrefundable ticket. You *can* specify the days you travel, whether you're willing to take "off-peak" flights (those that leave before 6 a.m. or after 10 p.m.), and how many connections you will accept (with a minimum of one). You also get to pick the airports you fly into and out of. Only after you pay for your ticket with a credit card do you get the full details of your flight.

The most popular opaque-fare sites are **Priceline** (Internet: www.priceline.com) and **Hotwire** (Internet: www.hotwire.com), although Expedia and Travelocity now offer similar services as well. Priceline allows you to "name your price" for airline tickets, hotel rooms, and rental cars; Hotwire, Expedia, and Travelocity offer fixed-price deals on unnamed airlines (at least, unnamed until you purchase the ticket).

Opaque-fare sites are undoubtedly the source of the cheapest domestic fares around. But you need to be flexible. Opaque fares are a *bad choice* for people who fall into one of these categories:

- ✔ Can't stomach 6 a.m. departures

- ✔ May need to change their tickets

- ✔ Demand nonstop flights or more complex itineraries

Understanding the new air-travel security measures

The airline industry began stricter security measures in airports after the terrorist attacks of September 11, 2001. Expect a lengthy check-in process and extensive delays. Although regulations vary from airline to airline and are still being revised, you can make the process of traveling smoother by taking the following steps:

✔ **Arrive early.** Arrive at the airport at least two hours before your flight is scheduled to depart.

✔ **Try not to drive your car to the airport.** Parking and curbside access to the terminal may be limited. Call ahead and check.

✔ **Don't count on curbside check-in.** At press time, curbside check-in no longer exists in any Alaska airport.

✔ **Be sure to carry plenty of documentation.** A government-issued photo ID (federal, state, or local) is now required. You may need to show your ID at various checkpoints. With an electronic ticket, the airline may require that you have a printed confirmation of purchase, and perhaps even the credit card with which you bought your ticket. This policy varies from airline to airline, so call ahead to make sure that you have the proper documentation. And *be sure that your ID is up-to-date:* An expired driver's license, for example, may keep you from boarding the plane.

✔ **Know what you can carry on and what you can't.** Travelers in the United States are now limited to one carry-on bag plus one personal item (such as a purse or briefcase). The Transportation Security Administration (TSA) also has issued a list of newly restricted carry-on items, but the list changes frequently. Consult the TSA Web site at www.tsa.gov for the latest information.

✔ **Prepare to be searched.** Expect spot checks. Remove electronic items, such as laptops and wireless phones, from your carry-on bags and hand them over for additional screening. Limit the metal items you wear so that you're less likely to set off the metal detector. Don't complain about being searched; the security people have the power to ruin your day on a whim if you irritate them.

✔ **Prepare to have your checked bags searched.** Airlines are now screening all checked baggage, sometimes resorting to hand searches. If you prefer to lock your checked bags, you may consider using cable ties that can be easily cut and then replaced.

✔ **Don't joke around.** A physician who made a stupid joke at one Alaska airport after September 11 was barred permanently from flying on Alaska Airlines. Because no other airline flies to the town he was in, he was stuck there for some time and humiliated in the media to boot.

✔ **Don't try to get to the gate unless you have a ticket.** Only ticketed passengers are allowed beyond the screener checkpoints, except for those people with specific medical or parental needs.

Finding last-minute specials online

Airlines regularly offer last-minute specials, such as weekend deals or Internet-only fares, to fill empty seats. Airlines announce most of these specials on Tuesday or Wednesday and require that you purchase the tickets online. The tickets are often valid for travel only that upcoming weekend, but you can book some tickets weeks or even months in advance. Check one of the sites that compile comprehensive lists of last-minute specials, such as **Smarter Living** (Internet: www.smarter living.com) and **WebFlyer** (Internet: www.webflyer.com), or sign up for weekly e-mail alerts at individual airline Web sites. (Refer to the Quick Concierge appendix at the back of this book for a complete list of airline Web sites.)

Getting to Alaska by Land, Water, or Rail

You can get to Alaska via ground or sea, and cruises are the most popular way (see Chapter 8). However, you need extra time and money for these options. Neither of these options beats the least expensive way into the state: a competitive plane fare to Anchorage.

Wheeling it to Alaska

You need to understand the distances involved in driving to Alaska. Driving from Seattle to Anchorage is 2,250 miles on two-lane highway. That's about 200 miles farther than Seattle to Chicago. You'll put a lot of wear on your car and yourself, you'll spend a lot of money on gas and lodgings, and you'll burn up a lot of vacation time: up to two weeks to go both ways, depending on your starting point. Get a mile-by-mile road guide, such as *The Milepost* (Morris Communications, $25; ☎ 800-726-4707; Internet: www.themilepost.com).

Also, bring photo ID *and* a passport or birth certificate (including your children's) to get across the Canadian border. If you plan to cross the border with firearms, pets, or items made from wildlife, especially ivory or marine mammal products, research customs requirements. The local contacts for the customs services of the two nations are the **Canada Customs and Revenue Agency** in Whitehorse (☎ 867-667-3943; Internet: www.ccra-adrc.gc.ca) or the **U.S. Customs Service** in Anchorage (☎ 907-271-2675; Internet: www.customs.ustreas.gov).

Taking the ferry to Alaska

You can shorten your drive to Alaska and add interest to the trip by taking the **Alaska Marine Highway** ferry part of the way (☎ **800-642-0066;** TTY 800-764-3779; Internet: www.alaska.gov/ferry). From the south, embark at Bellingham, Washington, or Prince Rupert, British Columbia. This option is best only if you plan to tour Southeast Alaska. Riding the ferry is fun and you can stop over anywhere along the way without paying much extra for your tickets.

You're better off not bringing a car. These small towns are easy to tour on foot or by bicycle; you can rent a car for a day when you want to go farther inland. I include car-rental agency suggestions in the appropriate city chapters later in this book. If you do bring your car, you need to reserve your ferry space at least several months ahead. The fare for your car will probably be more than renting one in Alaska for a week or two.

If you're headed beyond Southeast Alaska, disembark the ferry in **Haines** or **Skagway.** Here, you need a car (or need to board a bus) to get to the rest of the state. You still have a lot of road ahead of you; Skagway to Anchorage is 832 miles. You can take the bus from Skagway (see Chapter 7), or rent a car in Haines and drive it one-way to Anchorage. The local **Avis** franchise (☎ **800-230-4898** or 907-766-2733; Internet: www.avis.com) offers this service with a $300 drop-off charge plus the rental cost.

No, you can't take the train to Alaska

No railroad tracks link Alaska to the rest of the world. The closest you can get is to take **Amtrak** (☎ **800-USA-RAIL;** Internet: www.amtrak.com) to Bellingham, Washington. From there, you can catch the Alaska ferry north (see the preceding section). Or from the east, catch the ferry in Prince Rupert, British Columbia, getting there on Canada's **Via Rail** (☎ **888-VIA-RAIL;** Internet: www.viarail.ca); you change from the transcontinental route in Jasper, Alberta. A few times a year you can take a ferry all the way to Seward and catch an **Alaska Railroad** train (☎ **800-544-0552,** 907-265-2494, or TTY 907-265-2620; Internet: www.alaskarailroad.com) north to Anchorage and Fairbanks.

Chapter 7

Getting Around Alaska

● ●

In This Chapter

▶ Flying around Alaska

▶ Traveling by train, ferry, or bus

▶ Driving around Alaska

● ●

A s I may have mentioned elsewhere, Alaska is big. And it's rugged and sparsely developed. So even in this modern age, you can't get everywhere you want to go any way you choose to get there. Airplanes are the only vehicles that go everywhere (although, in some cases, it makes no sense to fly); you can only get to the capital city of Juneau by boat or air; and trains serve only a narrow region.

So, to put it positively, you have an opportunity for an adventure by traveling in a variety of ways. Almost everyone will need to combine at least two modes of transportation, with air and car being the most common. But in Southeast Alaska, you're likely to need three: air, boat, and car. Adding a little rail is a tasty seasoning to the mixture, because Alaska's only railroad is quite luxurious. And don't overlook the attractions of connecting small towns by propeller-driven aircraft. Flying in one of these little planes is as Alaskan as dog mushing and gives you a vivid, bird's-eye perspective of the countryside that you can't get any other way.

Table 7-1 lists the places I cover in this book and the practical modes of transportation to get there. I leave off choices that are possible but not advisable. The rest of this chapter provides you with the details of getting from here to there in Alaska.

Table 7-1   Planes, Trains, and Automobiles May Not Cut It

City	Air	Ferry	Rail	Road
Anchorage	Jet		X	X
Barrow	Jet			
Denali National Park			X	X
Girdwood				X
Homer	Prop	X		X
Juneau	Jet	X		
Katmai National Park	Prop			
Kenai	Prop			X
Kodiak Island	Jet	X		
Mat-Su				X
Nome	Jet			
Seward (Kenai Fjords National Park)	Prop	X	X	X
Sitka	Jet	X		
Skagway	Prop	X		X
Whittier		X	X	X

Soaring over the State

You'll discover three levels of scheduled air service around Alaska, which are:

- **Alaska Airlines jets:** The airline (☎ 800-252-7522; Internet: www.alaskaair.com) serves most communities of 1,000 residents or more, including most towns in Southeast Alaska, hubs around the Alaska bush, and towns that you can't reach by road.

- **Commuter-class airlines:** Operating frequently scheduled service with larger propeller-driven planes to towns that may or may not have roads, these services fan out from Anchorage, Fairbanks, and Juneau to smaller communities.

- **Bush air services:** Operating planes that may hold as few as three passengers, these services fly from hubs to tiny communities and wilderness lodges that you can't get to any other way. This mode of transportation serves more than 200 communities in Alaska.

Bush planes are scheduled, but operators don't get hung up on strict definitions of time. I remember the surprise of some tourists who walked into a flight service for the 4 p.m. flight. A guy reading the newspaper behind the desk got up and said, "Okay, let's find a plane." He eventually found one and flew them where they were going.

I list the air services that go to each community in the appropriate chapters in this book, with sample airfares. Fares change frequently, so use these listings only as guidelines. Also, shop both the jet and the prop options, if both exist — either one may be cheaper. Usually, taking a prop saves time on security. Sometimes, the larger commuter carriers have specials that you can find on their Web sites, as does Alaska Airlines. These specials are usually last-minute deals, and they turn up infrequently in the high tourist season. Otherwise, you rarely can save much money over the regular, quoted fare on flying between Alaska communities.

Anyone who comes to Alaska should take at least one flight in a small plane. Only then can you see for yourself how little civilization exists in this vast place. Every part of the state has beautiful scenery, but the very best flights go around Denali National Park from Talkeetna or Anchorage, or fly over the glaciers and islands of Southeast Alaska from Skagway or Juneau. If a flightseeing outing doesn't fit into your budget, maybe you can plan to travel between two towns on a small plane.

Roaming around Southeast Alaska

The best (but not speediest) way around Southeast Alaska is by ferry, but if you're on a tight schedule, you can combine the ferry with air travel to make the most of your trip. For example, a ferry ride to Sitka from Juneau takes a whole day and the adult fare is $30. For less than $100, you can fly back and save a day of your trip that you would otherwise spend taking the same boat ride back.

Flying around South Central Alaska and the Interior

Driving makes the most sense for this highway-connected portion of the state, because you get to see so much between towns and because driving is less expensive. But for wintertime trips, or to save time, you can hop from town to town by plane and rent a car when you arrive. (I don't recommend long wintertime highway drives for folks not used to driving on ice; Alaska roads are icy all winter, help is often far away, and temperatures can be very cold.) Instead, flying from, for example, Anchorage to Fairbanks can cost under $200 round-trip, and often as low as $100. You can also fly to towns such as Homer, Kenai, or Seward to save time and take fishing or sightseeing trips as day trips from Anchorage rather than spend the minimum of two days if you drive or take the train.

Touring the bush

The only way to the great mass of Alaska is by air. Alaska Airlines flies jets to larger bush hubs, such as Nome, Barrow, and Kodiak. Expect to pay $350 or more to Barrow or Nome, and more than $250 to Kodiak. After you arrive in the bush communities, small flight services carry passengers and cargo to the surrounding Alaska Native villages in prop-driven planes. Taking one of these planes, for a fare of $75 to $200, gets you into very remote areas where you can see how Native people live; but don't go in bad weather.

Riding the Rails

Alaska has only one full-service rail line, running from Seward about 500 miles north, through Anchorage and Denali National Park and ending in Fairbanks. The **Alaska Railroad** (☎ **800-544-0552** or 907-265-2494; Internet: www.alaskarailroad.com) runs through unbelievably beautiful country. The trains are well appointed, recalling the golden days of rail. On-board guides provide commentary, and you can ride in dome cars to soak in the views.

The train is quite expensive and slow. For example, to get from Anchorage to Denali National Park takes 7½ hours each way and costs $250 round-trip. (For the same money, you can rent a car for a week, and the drive is only 4½ hours.) And, after you arrive by train, you still need to find a way to get around. For these reasons, I advise most parties to drive; but if you're traveling alone, or traveling as a couple and you don't like to drive, consider using the railroad. Also, check out the Alaska Railroad's package tours, on its Web site (see Chapter 6 for information on package tours).

The state's other railroad, the gold rush–era **White Pass and Yukon Route,** is primarily an excursion train, as opposed to a dedicated people-moving service. It takes sightseeing runs from Skagway into the pass and back (see Chapter 21).

Sailing the Alaskan Coast

The state-run **Alaska Marine Highway System** (☎ **800-642-0066** or 907-465-3941; Internet: www.alaska.gov/ferry) is a subsidized fleet of big, blue-hulled ferries whose mission is to connect the roadless coastal towns of Alaska for roughly the same kind of cost you'd pay if the area had roads to drive on. Call for a free schedule or download it from the Web site.

The system's strengths are its low cost, frequent summer sailings, inexpensive stopovers, exceptional safety, and the fact that kids love it. In the summer, Forest Service guides offer interpretive talks onboard. The system's weaknesses are crowds during July peak season, occasional lengthy delays, and a shortage of cabins, which means that most people camp on deck or in chairs during overnight passages.

You can ride the ferry to Alaska, starting off in Bellingham, Washington, or Prince Rupert, British Columbia, but you're going to need to add a couple of days to your itinerary. For most travelers, however, it makes more sense to fly to your starting point somewhere in the middle of Southeast Alaska. Flying saves time and reduces the chance of having to spend the night sleeping in a chair onboard. *Long hauls* on the ferry can be uncomfortable and don't save much money compared to flying, but the ferry is much less expensive and more appealing for *connecting towns* within the Southeast region. Fly into Juneau or Sitka and plan a ferry trip from there, stopping at various places before returning to catch your plane home. During the summer, the larger ships among the nine-ship fleet stop at least daily (although sometimes in the middle of the night) in Ketchikan, Wrangell, Petersburg, Juneau, Haines, and Skagway. Check out the map on the inside back cover of this book to find out where the Alaska ferries travel.

The ferry is quite economical. For example, the nine-hour run from Juneau to Sitka is $32, plus an extra $36 if you bring your car along (though you have more flexibility and freedom if you don't — see the upcoming section, "Making your ferry ride more enjoyable"). Fares for children 11 and under are half price, rounded up to the next dollar, and children 2 and under ride free. And you'll pay a few dollars extra for a private cabin. Off-season, October through April, fares go down; during that time only, the driver of a vehicle doesn't need a separate walk-on ticket, and kids 4 and under ride free.

Reserving ferry passage

The **Alaska Marine Highway's** statewide toll-free number (☎ **800-642-0066**) can be understaffed and have long waits, but you can get around that problem. You can make online reservations at www.alaska.gov/ferry, which also allows you to check availability. (You can't use the site to change reservations.) Or if you need to talk to someone, call the staff at the office in Anchorage (☎ **907-272-7116**). The office in the Alaska Public Lands Information Center, at Fourth and F streets in Anchorage, allows walk-ins, too. In addition, the contractors who operate ferry terminals in Kodiak (☎ **800-526-6731**; Internet: www.akferry.com) and Homer (☎ **800-382-9229** or 907-235-8449; Internet: www.akmhs.com) maintain toll-free numbers and Web sites where you can reach an agent quickly, receive detailed advice, and make reservations for anywhere in the system. **Viking Travel,** in Petersburg

(☎ **800-327-2571** or 907-772-3818; Internet: www.alaskaferry.com), holds your early booking until the first day it becomes available on the system, making sure you're the first in line.

Making your ferry ride more enjoyable

You won't find anything difficult about riding the ferry — in fact, it's the most relaxing mode of transportation I know. But a few insider tips help make it as relaxing as possible for you.

✔ Buying ahead or booking round-trip tickets saves you nothing on the ferry, and stopovers of any length add little to the cost of your passage. Use the ferry system to explore the towns along the route, grabbing the next ferry through to continue your journey.

✔ If you travel without a vehicle, you generally don't need reservations (with the possible exceptions of the Bellingham sailings and passages across the Gulf of Alaska from Juneau to Valdez or Seward).

✔ Bring along a bike, or even a sea kayak, to have total freedom in exploring Southeast Alaska. You can carry these "alternate means of conveyance" quite inexpensively.

✔ Don't count on port calls to be long enough to see the towns. If the boat is running late, the staff may not let you off at all. Instead, get off (if you can) and catch the next ferry through.

✔ In the summer, you need a reservation for any real chance of taking a vehicle on the ferry, and you often need it several months ahead. It's expensive, too. Renting a car at your destination will probably save money and enhance your trip by allowing you more flexibility in your stopovers.

✔ If you can, bring at least some of your own food on the ferry. Ferry food can get boring after several meals in a row, and during peak season, lines are sometimes unreasonably long. We usually bring a cooler or picnic basket. Even if you're traveling light, you can pick up some bagels and deli sandwiches on a stopover or long port call.

✔ You can avoid some crowds on the boats by scheduling around them. Ferries are crowded northbound in June and southbound in August and both ways in July. If you're planning to fly one way and take the ferry the other, go against the flow (southbound in June and northbound in August).

Experiencing the Land by Bus

If you don't want to rent a car or pay the outrageous fares on the Alaska Railroad, you can get around by bus or van. If you're traveling alone, the bus is a good way to meet other adventurous travelers.

Many of the buses run only in the summer and mainly serve visitors. No single large bus company serves the entire state. Instead, mom-and-pop operations cover certain home routes (sometimes with a wireless phone onboard to take orders from their neighbors who may need something from a store in Anchorage). I list some of the larger operations with the places they serve:

- ✔ **Alaska Trails** (☎ **888-600-6001;** Internet: www.alaskashuttle. com), a van and bus service, operates three routes: on the Parks Highway from Fairbanks to Anchorage, on the Richardson Highway from Fairbanks to Valdez, and on the Alaska and Top of the World highways from Fairbanks to Dawson City. You can start or stop anywhere in between. The Anchorage to Denali fare is $54, a third of the train fare.

- ✔ **The Alaska Park Connection Motorcoach Service** (☎ **800-266-8625** or 907-245-0200; Internet: www.alaskacoach.com) connects Seward with Anchorage and Denali National Park daily in summer in each direction. Fares are comparable with Alaska Trails.

- ✔ **Homer Stage Line** (☎ **907-235-7009,** Homer; 907-868-3914, Anchorage; or 907-399-1847, on the van; Internet: www.homer stageline.com) runs from Homer to Anchorage and from Homer to Seward. The Anchorage to Homer fare is $48 one-way.

- ✔ **Alaska Direct Busline** (☎ **800-770-6652** or 907-277-6652) operates year-round from Skagway to Anchorage and Fairbanks, and at this writing was experimenting with a bus running all the way up the Alaska Highway from the Lower 48. The fare from Skagway is $215 one-way to Anchorage, $190 to Fairbanks.

Wheeling around Alaska by Car

In the summer, driving is the most practical way to see the part of Alaska away from the Southeast or the remote bush: the Interior and South Central Alaska. The road network is simple, with just a few two-lane highways connecting Anchorage, Fairbanks, and the towns in their orbits. But even though few roads exist, after you get on them, you encounter little traffic. The drive can be a highlight of your trip; you pass stunning, undeveloped scenery on nearly any road you choose. Details on the best driving routes are in Chapter 18.

Renting a car

Because I don't recommend driving to Alaska (unless you have lots of time on your hands), you should rent a car after you get here. You can find all the major car-rental companies based at the Anchorage airport, including Alamo, Avis, Budget, Dollar, Hertz, National, Payless, and Thrifty (national reservation numbers and Web addresses are listed in the appendix). In Fairbanks, you can rent from Avis, Dollar, Hertz, National, Payless, and Thrifty. I don't recommend renting a car in Southeast Alaska towns, except perhaps for a day to see the edges of town.

Some of Alaska's greatest drives are on gravel roads, but nearly every rental agency prohibits taking their cars off pavement. (Cars can get damaged on gravel highways.) But if you're willing to pay more and drive a sports-utility vehicle, the downtown Fairbanks location of **National Car Rental,** 1249 Noble St., Fairbanks, AK 99701 (☎ **800-227-7368** or 907-451-7368), rents for people driving even the wild Dalton Highway (which leads to the Arctic Ocean; see Chapter 18).

Finding the best deal

Car-rental rates vary widely and you can save a lot of money if you keep some of the following details in mind when you book.

- ✔ Weekend rates may be lower than weekday rates. Weekly rates usually amount to the daily rate for five days. Check if the rate is the same for pickup Friday morning as it is Thursday night.

- ✔ Some companies may assess a drop-off charge, often quite a high one, if you don't return the car to the same rental location; others, notably National, don't.

- ✔ Picking up your car is usually cheaper (but not nearly as convenient) at a location in town other than the airport, because airports charge concession fees. Renting at a site away from the airport makes sense if your hotel has a courtesy van. But if you have to take a cab both ways, it probably wipes out the savings.

- ✔ Always check the taxes and fees. In Anchorage, you pay an 8% tax and an 11% airport concession fee. In Fairbanks, you don't pay tax, just a 9.5% concession fee. However, rental rates are higher in Fairbanks and it costs more to fly there, so you're unlikely to save by making it your base.

- ✔ Many car-rental companies add on a fee for drivers under 25; some don't rent to them at all.

- ✔ If you see an advertised price, ask for that specific rate. Don't forget to mention membership in AAA, AARP, and trade unions, which usually entitle you to discounts ranging from 5 to 30%.

- ✔ Check your frequent-flier accounts. Not only are your most-used airlines likely to have sent you discount coupons, but also most car rentals add at least 500 miles to your account.

- ✔ As with other aspects of planning your trip, using the Internet can make comparison-shopping for a car rental much easier. Major booking sites, such as **Frommer's** (Internet: www.frommers.com), **Travelocity** (Internet: www.travelocity.com), **Expedia** (Internet: www.expedia.com), **Orbitz** (Internet: www.orbitz.com), and

Smarter Living (Internet: www.smarterliving.com), have search engines that dig up discounted car-rental rates. After finding the companies with the best rates, go to their own sites and find out whether they have additional discounts or incentives available only to direct customers.

Knowing what to initial on the rental contract

In addition to the standard rental prices, taxes, and airport fees, optional charges apply to most car rentals. If you're not careful, you can lose all the savings you gained by shopping around if you impulsively initial the rental contract for one of these extras. Here are some key items:

✔ The car-rental contract generally makes you responsible for damage to the car and the company's associated costs in case of an accident, which may go well beyond the car's replacement cost. The car-rental companies let you out of that obligation, however, if you buy the Collision Damage Waiver when you rent the car. The waiver is essentially insurance, but it's very unreasonable at the price of as much as $20 a day. To get an idea how bad a deal that is, imagine paying $7,000 a year for collision insurance on your own car. Your own car insurance or your credit card probably covers you for most of this risk. Check before you leave home.

✔ The car-rental companies also offer additional liability insurance (if you harm others in an accident), personal accident insurance (if you harm yourself or your passengers), and personal effects insurance (if someone steals your luggage from your car). Your insurance policy on your car at home probably covers most of these unlikely occurrences. However, if your own insurance doesn't cover you for rentals or if you don't have auto insurance, the rental company's liability coverage is a wise choice.

✔ How should you bet on the refueling gamble? Some companies try to sell you an initial full tank of gas with the agreement that you don't have to return it full. Then you spend the trip trying to run the car on empty to avoid giving gas back to the rental company, for which you get no credit. The better option is to buy the gas yourself and fill up the car before you return it, so you pay for only the gas you use. But if you're running late and don't fill up, the rental company zings you with astronomical refueling charges of up to $4 a gallon. If you often run late and a refueling stop may make you miss your plane, go ahead and buy the agency's gas; otherwise, buy your own. (Check out the location of a gas station when you leave the airport at the start of your trip so that you can refuel quickly before you drop off your car.)

Driving safely in Alaska

Driving in Alaska is definitely different than driving in other states. You don't have to worry about carjacking or purse snatching, but you do need to be ready for immense distances between services and even, in winter, survival in extreme conditions.

Here are a few tips for **summer driving on paved highways:**

✔ Keep your headlights on all the time for safety on these two-lane highways.

✔ The law requires that you pull over at the next pullout whenever five or more cars are trailing you on a two-lane highway, regardless of how fast you're going. Pulling over saves the lives of people who otherwise will try to pass.

✔ Driving fast on an empty highway is tempting, but remember that these roads sometimes have violent dips and humps called *frost heaves.* Hitting a frost heave at high speed isn't fun and can be dangerous. Also, wildlife, such as moose, caribou, or bear, sometimes wanders onto the road.

✔ Bring along sweaters and jackets, a picnic or some snacks, water or other beverages, CDs and tapes for the stereo, and mosquito repellent.

✔ Check your jack and spare tire before you leave.

✔ Bring a wireless phone if you have one; you'll find coverage available in most of the state's populated regions.

✔ You can usually use a credit card wherever you go, but bring along at least $100 in cash just in case.

✔ Don't let your gas tank get low, because it may be a couple of hours between gas stations — even on the paved highways.

But not all Alaska roads are paved. Here are few tips for **summer driving on gravel highways:**

✔ When passing a vehicle going the other way, slow down or stop and pull as far as possible to the side of the road to avoid losing your windshield to a flying rock. Always think about the path of rocks that you're kicking up toward other vehicles.

✔ Make sure that you have a good, full-size spare tire and jack.

✔ Bring along a first-aid kit, emergency food, a towrope, and jumper cables, and keep your gas tank full. On some rural roads, it's a tank of gas between gas stations.

In **winter,** Alaska's roads are always icy, and dark most of the time. Moose stand or run in the road in the dark, causing potentially fatal accidents for the people in the car as well as the moose. Long periods of time go by between each car, long enough for frostbite in extreme cold if you have a breakdown and don't plan ahead. For many people, flying makes more sense for long trips than driving, but if you choose to drive rural Alaska highways in winter, take precautions.

✔ Be prepared for cold-weather emergencies far from help. Take all the items previously listed for summer driving on gravel roads, plus a flashlight, matches and materials to light a fire, chains, a shovel, and an ice scraper. A camp stove to make hot beverages is also a good idea.

✔ If you're driving a remote highway (such as the Alaska Highway) between December and March, take along gear adequate to keep you safe from the cold in case you if you have to wait overnight with a dead car at –40°F. (See the list of heavy winter gear in Chapter 12, and add warm sleeping bags.)

✔ Never drive a road marked "Closed" or "Unmaintained in Winter."

✔ Studded tires are a necessity; nonstudded snow tires or so-called "all-weather" tires aren't adequate.

✔ Never leave your car's engine stopped for more than four hours in temperatures of –10°F or colder. Alaskans generally have electrical head-bolt heaters installed to keep the engine warm overnight. You can find electrical outlets everywhere you might park in cold, Interior Alaska areas.

Checking road conditions

In winter, always check highway conditions before heading out of town. In summer, checking the road conditions is less critical, but making a call can save you from drastic construction delays. Road workers can close highways for certain times — say, midnight to 8 a.m. — which you can plan around if you know. The **Alaska Department of Transportation** updates road-condition hotlines frequently in winter and as needed in summer. Call ☎ **800-478-7675** or check out www. dot.state.ak.us. For conditions on the Alaska Highway in Canada, call the **Yukon Department of Infrastructure** at ☎ **867-456-7623** or check www.gov.yk.ca/roadreport.

Chapter 8

Cruising Alaska's Coast

· ·

In This Chapter

▶ Sorting out when and where to cruise in Alaska

▶ Choosing a big or small ship

▶ Finding the best cruise bargains

▶ Profiling Alaska's best cruise lines

· ·

As you may expect from a state that offers a number of varied options for getting into and around its communities, cruising in and out of Alaska's coastal towns is big business. This chapter offers the details you need to help you decide whether cruising is the option for you to take to arrive in Alaska. You can also find information that helps you choose which type of cruise is best for you and what you can expect to pay for traveling to Alaska via cruise ship.

Waterway transportation is so critical to Alaskans that the state has its own ferry system, the Alaska Marine Highway System, which you can use to travel to and around Alaska. However, to make this option work, you must be willing to invest more time — for actual travel and for planning — and be willing to give up the comforts and diversions that a cruise ship offers. I cover the Alaska State ferry system in more detail in Chapter 7. I devote this chapter to the cruise ship, focusing primarily on those cruise options that give a real in-depth experience. (If you want more information about cruising in Alaska, pick up a copy of *Frommer's Alaska Cruises & Ports of Call,* published by Wiley.)

Contemplating Your Cruise Options

More than half a million people cruise Alaska's Southeast coast every year, attracted by the prospects of seeing towering glaciers, charming small towns, and all manner of wildlife. The sheer ease of cruise travel is one reason for its popularity. You take in the scenery from your boat, disembarking to visit ports of call or to engage in sports activities. The dearth of roads between towns in the Southeast makes the waters of the Inside Passage the region's de facto highway.

The three main questions to ask yourself when choosing a cruise in Alaska are, "When should I go?" "Where do I want to go?" and "How big a ship should I travel on?" I help you answer those questions in this section and provide some tips and tricks for matching a cruise line to your particular (or peculiar) interests.

Deciding when to go

Alaska is a seasonal, as opposed to year-round, cruise destination. The season generally runs from May through September, although some smaller ships start up in April. May and September are considered the shoulder seasons, and lower rates and more aggressive discounts are offered then.

Cruising in May is extremely pleasant; crowds have yet to arrive, and locals are friendlier than they are later in the season, when they're pretty much ready to see the tourists go home for the winter. Statistically, May is also the driest month of the season for the Inside Passage ports. Late September, on the other hand, offers the advantage of fewer fellow tourists clogging the ports.

The warmest months are June, July, and August, with temperatures generally around 50°F to 80°F (10°C to 27°C) during the day, and cooler at night. You may not need a parka, but you definitely need to bring along some outerwear. June 21 is the longest day of the year, with the sky lit virtually all night. June tends to be drier than July and August. It isn't uncommon for an Alaska vacation in July to include rain nearly every day. April and May are drier than September, although in early May you may encounter freezing rain and other vestiges of winter.

If you're considering travel in Alaska during a shoulder month, keep in mind that some shops don't open until Memorial Day, and visitor season generally ends on Labor Day (although cruise lines operate well into September).

Knowing where to go

Many Alaskan cruises, particularly of the smaller-ship variety, combine transportation with activities after you arrive. This section offers the lowdown on your primary options.

✔ **Inside Passage cruises:** One of two basic weeklong itineraries offered by the major cruise lines, Inside Passage cruises generally sail round-trip from Vancouver, British Columbia, visiting three or four port towns (typically Juneau, Skagway, Ketchikan, and either Sitka, Haines, or Victoria, British Columbia) along the Inside Passage, spending a day in Glacier Bay or one of the other glacier areas, and spending two days at sea, meaning they just cruise along, enabling you to relax and enjoy the scenery.

✔ **Gulf of Alaska cruises:** The second most popular cruise choice is a Gulf of Alaska cruise, which generally sails northbound and southbound between Vancouver and Seward (the port for Anchorage) in alternating weeks. These cruises visit many of the same towns and attractions that the Inside Passage cruises hit, but because they don't have to turn around and sail back to Vancouver, they tack on visits to Valdez, Hubbard Glacier, College Fjord, or other gulf towns and natural attractions.

✔ **Small-ship cruises:** Although most of the major cruise operators stick pretty closely to these two basic routes, the small-ship cruise lines tend to offer more **small-port and wilderness-oriented itineraries,** some sailing round-trip from Juneau or Sitka, some sailing between Juneau and Ketchikan, and one even sailing between Juneau and Glacier Bay. Although many of these ships visit major ports of call, they may also include visits to small ports that aren't accessible to the bigger ships — towns such as Petersburg, Wrangell, Gustavus, Elfin Cove, and possibly the Native village of Metlakatla. Some ships have itineraries that enable passengers to explore waterways by kayak or hike inland trails.

✔ **Cruise tours:** Combining a cruise with a land tour, either before or after the cruise, typical cruise-tour packages link a cruise with a three- to five-day Anchorage to Denali to Fairbanks tour, a seven-day Yukon tour (which visits Anchorage, Denali, and Fairbanks on the way), or a five- to seven-day tour of the Canadian Rockies. Holland America, Princess, and Cruise West are the three leaders in the cruise-tour market (Cruise West is a distant third). Even when you book with another cruise line, chances are your land tour will be through one of these operators.

Choosing between a big and small ship

Imagine an elephant. Now imagine your pet beagle, Sparky. That's the kind of size difference you can expect between your options in the Alaska cruise market: behemoth modern ships and small, more exploratory coastal vessels.

But your choice is more than just deciding between a bunch of or a little extra room for stowing your bags, although, truth be told, cabin size is pretty minimal in most cases, even on the largest ships. Your interest in the variety of activities and amenities also needs to play a role in your choice of which cruise ship to sail.

Cruising on bigger ships

The **big ships** in the Alaska market fall generally into two categories: mid-sized ships and megaships.

Carrying as many as 2,670 passengers, the **megaships** look and feel like floating resorts. Big on glitz, they offer loads of activities, attract many families and (especially in Alaska) seniors, offer many public rooms (including fancy casinos and fully equipped gyms), and provide a wide variety of meal and entertainment options. And although they may feature one or two formal nights per trip, the ambience is generally casual. The Alaska vessels of the Carnival, Celebrity, Princess, and Royal Caribbean fleets all fit this category, and so do Norwegian Cruise Line's *Norwegian Sky* and *Norwegian Sun*.

Mid-sized ships in Alaska fall into three categories, ranging from luxurious to classical: the ultra-luxurious ships of the Crystal and Radisson Seven Seas fleets; ships featuring a more modern décor and atmosphere, such as the *Veendam, Ryndam, Volendam, Amsterdam, Maasdam, Zaandam,* and *Statendam* of Holland America Line and *Norwegian Wind* of Norwegian Cruise Line; and the older, education-oriented *Universe Explorer* of World Explorer Cruises.

In general, the sizes of these bigger ships are less significant than the general onboard atmosphere created by the companies that run them; therein lie the **advantages** of big-ship cruising:

- ✔ **You have lots of opportunities to meet and greet (and meet and greet).** With the many and varied meal and entertainment options, combined with the diversity of activities, you're bound to meet a passenger or ten who share your interests.

- ✔ **The cruise ship is your oyster.** Mid-sized ships and megaships offer a great range of facilities for passengers. You won't lack things to do and places to go on these ships.

- ✔ **Big ships have a room for every need, with or without a view.** Cabins on these ships range from cubbyholes to large suites, depending on the ship and the type of cabin you book.

- ✔ **You *will* eat well.** Big dining rooms and a tremendous variety of cuisines are the norm.

The sizes of these big ships also come with **four major drawbacks** for passengers:

- ✔ **You have lots of opportunities to meet and greet (and meet and greet).** These bigger ships carry many people and, as such, can at times feel crowded.

- ✔ **Size limits access.** The big ships just can't sail into narrow passages or shallow-water ports, limiting your in-port and sailing options.

- ✔ **Size limits opportunity.** The size and inflexible schedules of bigger ships limit their ability to stop or even slow down when wildlife is spotted.

- ✔ **Alaska becomes lost in the crowd.** When passengers on a big ship disembark in a town, they tend to overwhelm that town, thus limiting your ability to see the real Alaska. (For more info on the relationship between Alaska towns and the cruise industry, see the "Where there are ships, there are crowds" sidebar in this chapter.)

Where there are ships, there are crowds

Now for the bad news: All those cruise ships aren't necessarily good for Alaska and its residents. Alaskans, who are known for their hospitality, all have their limits. Imagine living in a coastal settlement and having the equivalent of an entire town full of new people arriving all at once — doubling the population, and then some. These one-day visitors crowd your streets and hiking trails, and their ships spew pollution into the air and water. Imagine this deluge happening every day, all summer. Suppose also that tacky souvenir stands and seasonal gift shops have driven out the old, community businesses on the waterfront!

For years, the cruise-ship industry exploited the hospitality of Southeast Alaska as if it were an inexhaustible resource. Local residents took a stand, however, when two lines, Royal Caribbean and Holland America, were convicted of felonies for dumping pollution such as dry-cleaning fluid, photo chemicals, and used oil in the pristine waters of the Inside Passage, and then lying about it. A series of environmental scandals followed, leading to new state laws and a commitment by the cruise industry to clean up its act. Alaska now has the toughest cruise-ship legislation of any state.

Protecting the environment is easier, however, than restoring the experience of living in or visiting a small town. The presence of too many cruise passengers has spoiled some of these quaint places. Once-charming streets are transformed into carnival midways jammed wall-to-wall with people from ships landing simultaneously. Some communities think the income generated by these "floating cities" isn't worth what they must sacrifice in their quality of life, and thus place limits on the number of ships that can dock or levy new taxes based on the number of people each ship carries.

After years of fast growth, the industry also began talking of a *carrying capacity,* that is, determining just how much tourism is too much. And yet still more ships come, bringing ever more visitors. The terrorist attacks of September 11 aggravated the situation further, because cruise lines withdrew ships from certain foreign routes and brought them to Alaska. Although the increase in capacity produced some extraordinary bargains for cruise passengers, whether that continues is anyone's guess.

Cruising on smaller ships

In the same way that big cruise ships are mostly for people who want every resort amenity, **small** or **alternative ships** are best suited for people who prefer a casual, crowd-free cruise experience that offers passengers a chance to get up close and personal with Alaska's natural surroundings and wildlife.

Smaller ships have a number of what I consider to be pretty important benefits on the plus side of the ledger:

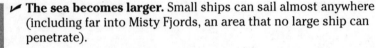

✔ **The sea becomes larger.** Small ships can sail almost anywhere (including far into Misty Fjords, an area that no large ship can penetrate).

✔ **You can take more time to smell the roses — or whatever may be swimming your way.** Small ships tend to have more flexibility in their schedules than the large ships, and usually take time to linger whenever whales or other wildlife are sighted nearby.

✔ **Everything looks bigger.** Smaller watercraft don't scare off wildlife as easily as the big ships, and the fact that you're at or near the waterline (as opposed to ten stories up on the large ships) means you get a more close-up view.

✔ **Land-based activities truly are land-based.** Many smaller cruise companies compensate for a lack of onboard activities by offering more active off-ship opportunities, such as hiking or kayaking.

✔ **You can discover Alaska's depth.** The alternative ships are also more likely to feature expert lectures on Alaska-specific topics, such as marine biology, history, and Native culture.

But, as with everything in life, small ships also have their drawbacks:

✔ **Small ships are, well, small.** Small ships usually have small cabins, only one lounge-bar and dining room, and no exercise facilities, entertainment, or onboard organized activities. They just don't have room for all the amenities.

✔ **Don't expect a smooth ride.** Most of these smaller ships have no stabilizers, so the ride can be bumpy in open water — which isn't much of a problem on Inside Passage itineraries, because most of the areas in which small ships cruise are protected from sea waves.

✔ **Accessibility is not always a given.** Smaller ships are also difficult for travelers with disabilities. The three exceptions are Cruise West's *Spirit of '98* and *Spirit of Oceanus* and Clipper's *Clipper Odyssey,* which are equipped with elevators.

✔ **Face it — you'll pay more.** Despite all the disadvantages — at least from an amenity and activity standpoint — smaller ships are universally more expensive than their bigger counterparts, and the small-ship cruise lines offer fewer discounts.

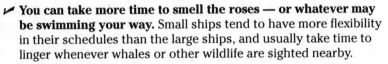

Visitors aboard large ships may physically be in Alaska, but unless they're reminded of it, they may never know it — such is the disjunction between the glitzy modern ships and the real world outside. The experiences of visitors aboard small ships, however, are many times more intimate, which enables them to get in touch with the places they've come to see. For these reasons, my advice to anyone who wants to experience Alaska (rather than receive just a mere postcard impression of it) is to spend the extra money for a small-ship cruise.

As is true of any product, you get what you pay for, and by paying extra in the short term for a more intimate cruise, you're almost always guaranteed of having an Alaska experience that you can fondly recall for the rest of your life.

Finding the cruise ship for you

Cruise lines are in the business of providing a good time for their guests, so they all have something going for them. This section provides a brief rundown of some of Alaska's best, in a few different categories (with more details near the end of this chapter under the individual cruise listings).

Defining luxury

So you think any type of cruise ship offers a certain measure of luxury? Well, although you're probably correct, these lines really know how to serve up the extravagance:

- Crystal Cruises' 940-passenger *Crystal Harmony* is *the* big luxury ship in the Alaska market. Think superb cuisine, elegant service, lovely surroundings, great cabins, and sparkling entertainment.

- If a more casual kind of luxury (a nice ship with a no-tie-required policy) is in your cards, Radisson Seven Seas Cruises' *Seven Seas Mariner* offers just that, including plush all-suite cabins (most with private balconies) and excellent cuisine (plus you receive complimentary wines with dinner).

- For the ultimate Alaska small-ship experience, check out the yachts of *American Safari Cruises,* where soft adventure comes with luxury accoutrements.

If you're looking for beauty in a boat, every line's most recent ships are beautiful, but Celebrity's *Infinity* is a stunner, and so is its sister ship, *Summit.* These modern vessels, with their extensive art collections, cushy public rooms, and expanded spa areas, give Celebrity a formidable presence in Alaska.

Being pampered in style

The following ships offer the crème de la crème of indulgences:

- Celebrity's *Infinity* and *Summit* offer wonderful AquaSpas complete with thalassotherapy pools and a wealth of soothing and beautifying treatments.

- The solariums on Royal Caribbean's *Vision of the Seas, Legend of the Seas,* and new *Radiance of the Seas* offer relaxing indoor pool retreats.

- And the *Crystal Harmony* pampers you all-around.

Finding the best meal

Radisson and **Crystal** (in that order) are tops among the luxury lines, but among the mainstream lines, **Celebrity** is the best. Renowned French chef Michel Roux oversees its cuisine. And signs of a new and rather surprising challenger for the cuisine award are appearing in the **Carnival** camp, which has upgraded its main dining room and buffet offerings.

Bringing the family along

All the major lines have well-established kids' programs. However, **Holland America** and **Norwegian Cruise Line** win points in Alaska for their special shore excursions for youngsters and teens, and **Carnival** offers special shore excursions for teens.

Participating in the best onboard activities

The ships operated by **Carnival** and **Royal Caribbean** offer full rosters of onboard activities, ranging from the sublime (such as lectures) to the ridiculous (such as contests designed to get passengers to do or say crazy things).

Setting the bar for the small-ship market

Clipper Cruise Line's newest vessel, the *Clipper Odyssey,* is a really stunning little ship, offering a higher level of comfort than most of the other small ships in this category.

For the most adventurous small-ship itinerary in Alaska, check out Glacier Bay Cruiseline, whose *Wilderness Adventurer* and *Wilderness Explorer* concentrate on kayaking, hiking, and wildlife-viewing, hardly visiting any ports at all.

Experiencing whale-watching at its best

When they come close enough, you can see whales from all the ships in Alaska. Smaller ships, however — such as those operated by **Glacier Bay Cruiseline** and **Cruise West** — may actually change course and follow a whale. Get your cameras ready!

Exploring with the best itinerary

World Explorer Cruises' *Universe Explorer* is unmatched with its 14-day, round-trip itineraries from Vancouver, which visit all the major ports of call and then some, including an extended visit to Metlakatla, a stop at a Tsimshian Indian village on Annette Island, and a visit to Kodiak Island, famous for its bear population. No other cruise ships regularly visit Kodiak Island.

Booking the best cruise tours

Princess and **Holland America** are the entrenched market leaders in getting you into the Interior either before or after your cruise. Some of the other lines actually buy their cruise-tour products from them.

The strength of Holland America's cruise tour is its three- and four-night cruises combined with an Alaska-Yukon land package. Princess arguably is stronger in seven-day Gulf of Alaska cruises in conjunction with Denali-Fairbanks or Kenai Peninsula land arrangements.

Stopping at the best ports

Juneau and **Skagway** are perennial favorites, but **Haines** also is a winner.

✔ Juneau is one of the most visually pleasing small cities anywhere and certainly the prettiest capital city in America.

✔ As for Skagway, no town in Alaska is more historically significant, and the old buildings are so perfect you may think that you've stepped into a Disney version of what a gold rush town looks like.

✔ For a more low-key Alaska experience, take the ferry from Skagway to Haines, which may remind you more of the low-key Alaska as depicted on the TV show *Northern Exposure*. It's also a great place to spot eagles and other wildlife. Some ships stop at Haines as a port of call.

Discovering the best shore excursions

Most cruise lines offer some great shore excursion options to include with your trip. Here are a few of the most recommended activities to ask about when booking your cruise:

✔ Flightseeing and helicopter trips in Alaska are unforgettable ways to check out the scenery if you can afford them. (They're pretty pricey.) A helicopter trip to a dog-sled camp at the top of a glacier (usually the priciest of the offerings) affords you incredibly pretty views and a chance to try your hand at the truly Alaskan sport of dog sledding (earning you great bragging rights with the folks back home).

✔ For a less extravagant excursion, nothing beats a ride (on a clear day) on the White Pass and Yukon Route railway out of Skagway.

✔ Active excursions, such as kayaking and mountain biking, afford not only an opportunity for working off those shipboard calories, but also optimum opportunities for spotting eagles, bears, seals, and other wildlife.

Witnessing the best natural sights seen from onboard

Communing with nature, regardless of whether from up close or afar, is a category that no cruise line can corner the market on; that market belongs to the region. And there are so many regions of Alaska that choosing what you want to see is difficult. However, Glacier Bay, Hubbard Glacier, College Fjord, and Misty Fjords National Monument (into which big ships can only travel a short distance) are likely to appear on virtually everyone's top-ten list.

Booking Your Cruise

Almost every cruise line publishes brochure prices that are the travel equivalent of a new car's sticker price: wildly inflated, hoping that someone, somewhere, might take them at face value. In reality — especially as sailings grow near and it looks as if the line will get stuck with unsold space — cruise lines almost universally are willing to let their cabins go for much, much less. Note, however, that small-ship lines tend to be the exception to this rule, primarily because they have less space to sell, and they appeal to a more specific market niche. As a result, smaller ships can often hold firm to their initial asking prices.

You have more ways than ever to book a cruise and find the best discounts. In the United States, 90% to 95% of all cruise bookings are arranged through **travel agents.** But instead of using the services of a traditional travel agent, these days you can also head for your computer and check out what the **online cruise agencies and discounters** are offering; a handful even allow you to submit your credit card online and make a reservation without talking to a soul. And some cruise lines, such as Carnival, Norwegian Cruise Line, Royal Caribbean, and Celebrity, even have their own booking Web sites (although, so far, they haven't proven particularly user-friendly).

In this section, I cover the details for booking cruises on large and small ships. So, regardless of whether you're a veteran cruiser or a first-timer, the details and money-saving tips I provide below can help you book an enjoyable and affordable cruise.

Shopping for shore tours

Most cruise-ship passengers sign up for on-shore activities and excursions when they arrive on board. It's easy and convenient, and you can be sure that the outing will be timed to your port of call.

On the downside, these excursions tend to be the most superficial and highest-priced choices in town and almost always involve large groups. For outdoor activities, trooping down a trail or paddling a sea kayak in a big mob can spoil the experience. You do have an alternative.

A large part of the high shipboard price for shore tours is the cut that's taken by the cruise line. You can get a much better deal (as much as half off) by arranging your own activities in advance. Most guides are happy to tailor an outing to your limited time, and you'll probably encounter a far more intimate experience in the bargain. It only takes a little advance prep work: Study your ports of call, the activities and operators in those locations (for which this book will be an invaluable guide), and the amount of time you'll be ashore, and then make your reservations before you leave, putting down the appropriate deposits and getting directions for making transfers.

Reserving a small-ship cruise

The small-ship companies in Alaska — **Glacier Bay Cruiseline, American Safari Cruises, Clipper, Cruise West,** and **Lindblad Expeditions** — offer real niche-oriented cruise experiences, attracting passengers who have a very good idea of the kind of experiences they want (usually educational and/or adventurous, and always casual and small-scale). In many cases, a large percentage of passengers on any given cruise have sailed with the line before. Because of all this, and because the passenger capacity of these small ships is so low (roughly between 12 and 138), you won't likely find the kind of deep discounts you do with the large ships.

Nevertheless, for the most part, these lines rely on agents to handle their bookings, taking very few reservations directly. (Clipper is the exception. It takes most of its Alaska bookings directly, rather than through agents.) All the lines have a list of agents with whom they do considerable business and can hook you up with one of them whenever you call (or e-mail) and ask for an agent near you.

Finding an agent who specializes in mainstream cruises

The following full-service and cruise-only agencies have solid reputations in selling mainstream cruise bookings such as with Princess, Carnival, Royal Caribbean, Celebrity, Holland America, and Norwegian Cruise Line, and they operate a combination of walk-in and 800-number telephone-based business:

- ✔ **Admiral of the Fleet Cruise Center,** 12920 Bluemound Rd., Elm Grove, WI 53122 (☎ **800-462-3371** or 262-784-2628); or 3430 Pacific Ave. SE, Suite A-5, Olympia, WA 98501 (☎ **800-877-7447** or 360-866-7447)

- ✔ **Cruises By Brennco,** 508 E. 112th St., Kansas City, MO 64131 (☎ **800-955-1909** or 816-942-1000)

- ✔ **The Cruise Company,** 10760 Q St., Omaha, NE 68127 (☎ **800-289-5505** or 402-339-6800; Internet: www.thecruisecompany.com)

- ✔ **Cruise Value Centers,** 6 Edgeboro Rd., East Brunswick, NJ 08816 (☎ **800-231-7447;** Internet: www.mycruisevalue.com)

- ✔ **Hartford Holidays,** 129 Hillside Ave., Williston Park, NY 11596 (☎ **800-828-4813** or 516-746-6670)

- ✔ **Just Cruisin' Plus,** 5640 Nolensville Rd., Nashville, TN 37211 (☎ **800-888-0922** or 615-833-0922; Internet: www.justcruisin plus.vacation.com)

✔ **Kelly Cruises,** 1315 W. 22nd St., Suite 105, Oak Brook, IL 60523
(☎ **800-837-7447** or 630-990-1111; Internet: www.kelly
cruises.com)

✔ **Mann Travel & Cruises American Express,** 4400 Park Rd., Charlotte,
NC 28209 (☎ **866-591-8129;** Internet: www.manntravels.com)

✔ **National Leisure Group,** 100 Sylvan Rd., Suite 600, Wobrun, MA
01801 (☎ **800-435-7683** or 617-424-7990; Internet: www.nlg.com)

✔ **The Travel Company,** 220 Congress Park Dr., Delray Beach, FL
33445 (☎ **800-242-9000;** Internet: www.mytravelco.com)

Figuring out what's included in the cost

No matter how you arrange to buy your cruise vacation, what you basically have in hand at the end is a contract for transportation, lodging,
dining, entertainment, housekeeping, and assorted other miscellaneous
services that are provided for you during the course of your vacation.
Remembering what extras are *not* included in your cruise fare, however,
is just as important. Aside from **airfare,** which usually isn't included in
your cruise fare (see "Booking air travel through the cruise line," later in
this chapter), the most pricey additions to your cruise fare, particularly
in Alaska, are likely to be **shore excursions.** Ranging from about $29 for
a bus tour to $250 or more for a helicopter or fixed-wing flightseeing
excursion, these sightseeing tours are designed to help cruise passengers make the most of their time at the ports that their ship visits, but
they do add a hefty sum to your vacation costs.

Another item you'll want to add to your calculations is the amount of
tips you need to reserve for the ship's crew. Tips are given at the end of
the cruise. Count on tipping at least $9 for each passenger in your party,
per day ($63 per passenger for the week). That figure takes care of the
room steward, waiter, and busperson. (In practice, most people tend to
give a little more.) Additional tips to other personnel, such as the head-
waiter or maître d', are given at your discretion. On the small ships, all
tips often go into one pot, which the crew divides up after the cruise.

All but only a few ships charge extra for **alcoholic beverages** (including
wine at dinner) and for soda. Prices are comparable to what you'd pay
at a bar or restaurant on shore. Nonbubbly soft drinks, such as lemonade and iced tea, are included in your cruise fare.

Port charges, taxes, and other fees are usually included in your cruise
fare but not always, and these charges can add as much as $175 per
person onto the price of a seven-day Alaska cruise. Make sure that
you know whether these fees are included in the cruise fare when you
compare rates.

Of course, the same as at a hotel, you also pay extra for such items as ship-to-shore phone calls or faxes, e-mails, spa treatments, and so on.

Keeping in mind some money-saving strategies

Cruise pricing, like airfare costs, can be extremely relative. And you can employ a number of strategies to save money off the booking price.

Late versus early booking

More than ever, no steadfast rules exist about pricing — policies differ from line to line, and from week to week, depending on supply and demand. When a ship has empty space as the sailing date nears, lines would rather sell a cabin for a lower fare than let it stay empty. Although booking early still means as much as a 50% discount off the brochure rates (not to mention a better choice of cabins), booking late (just a few weeks or a month or two before sailing) often means an even better rate.

When booking at the last minute, you must consider that if you're flying to the port of embarkation, you may end up paying an airfare so high that it cancels out your savings on the cruise.

You can find last-minute deals advertised online and in the travel section of your Sunday newspaper. You should also check with a travel agent or an agency or discounter that specializes in cruises to find out whether they know of any last-minute deals.

Shoulder season discounts

Think of the Alaska cruise season as three distinct periods: **peak season** (late June, July, and early to mid-August), **value-standard season** (early June and late August), and **budget season** (May and September). You can save by booking a cruise during this last period, during the shoulder months of May or September. That's when cruise pricing is lower. Although the weather may be a little chillier — and September is known for rain — fewer people visit during those months, thus enabling your experience of Alaska to be a bit more pristine, especially when you're sailing on a small ship. A friend who recently took an early May sailing with Glacier Bay Cruiseline reports that he felt like he had the state all to himself.

Discounts for third and fourth passengers (and groups)

Most ships offer highly discounted rates for third and fourth passengers sharing a cabin with two "full-fare" passengers (even when those two have booked at a discounted rate). Although doing so may mean a tight squeeze, it nevertheless saves you a bundle. Some lines offer **special rates for kids,** usually on a seasonal or select-sailings basis that may include free or discounted airfare. Those younger than age 2 generally cruise free.

One of the best ways to obtain a cruise deal is booking as a **group** of at least 16 people in at least eight cabins. The savings include a discounted rate, and at least the cruise portion of the 16th ticket is free. A *group* in this instance can be a real group of friends, relatives, and so on, or simply a block of passengers booked by a travel agency on the same cruise. You don't even have to pretend that you know the other people — the savings are the same. Ask about any group deals your travel agent may offer.

Senior discounts

Seniors may be able to get extra savings on their cruise. Some lines will take 5% off the top for those 55 and up, and the senior rate applies even if the second person in the cabin is younger. Membership in groups such as AARP is not required, but such membership may bring additional savings.

Booking air travel through the cruise line

Except during special promotions, airfare to the port of embarkation rarely is included in cruise rates, so you have to purchase airfare on your own or buy it as a package with your cruise through your travel agent or online cruise site. You can usually find information about these *air-sea programs* in the back of cruise-line brochures, along with prices.

The benefits of booking through the cruise line are that round-trip transfers between the airport and the ship usually are included, and the cruise line knows your airline schedule, so that in the event of delayed flights and other unavoidable snafus, it can do more to make sure that you and other people on your flight board the ship. When you book your air transportation separately, you're on your own.

On the downside, air add-ons may not be the best deals and booking your own airfare may be cheaper. Furthermore, you probably won't be able to use any frequent-flier miles that you've accumulated.

Choosing your cabin

Cruise-ship cabins run from tiny boxes with accordion doors and bunk beds to palatial multi-room suites with hot tubs on the balcony. Cabins are either **inside** (without a window or porthole) or **outside** (with). Rooms with windows or portholes are more expensive. On big ships, the more deluxe outside cabins may also come with **private verandas.** Which is right for you?

Price is often a big factor, but think about the vacation style you prefer. If, for instance, you plan to spend a bunch of quiet time in your cabin, you probably need to consider booking the biggest room you can afford. Conversely, if you plan to be out on the deck all the time checking out the glaciers and wildlife, you may be just as happy with a smaller (and cheaper) cabin to crash in at the end of the day.

Speaking up about special health concerns

The cruise line needs to be informed about any special dietary requests you may have when you make your reservations. Some lines offer kosher menus, and all have vegetarian, low-fat, low-salt, and sugar-free options available.

Every summer, hundreds of cruise-ship passengers come down with an illness caused by a bug known as a Norwalk virus. The bug's rarely serious symptoms, vomiting and diarrhea, last a day or two, although some passengers do end up in the hospital. The virus can be transmitted quickly through the close quarters onboard ships. Sometimes it can be carried over from one cruise to the next. In 2002, passengers of Holland America, Princess, and Glacier Bay Cruiseline all experienced outbreaks; Holland America even cancelled a cruise by the *Ryndam* in an attempt to rid the ship of the virus. The U.S. Centers for Disease Control and Prevention (CDC) suggests washing your hands frequently, drinking bottled water, and avoiding eating shellfish to minimize your chances of contracting the virus while on board. In 1998, the CDC also advised passengers ages 65 and older and those with chronic illnesses to check with their doctors before taking a cruise. The CDC Web site (Internet: www.cdc.gov/nceh/vsp) posts sanitation inspection scores for each ship.

The Small-Ship Cruise Lines

Small ships enable you to see Alaska from sea level, without the kind of distractions that you encounter aboard the big ships — no glitzy interiors, no big shows or loud music, no casinos, no spas, and no crowds, because the largest of these ships carries only 138 passengers. You're immersed in the 49th state from the minute you wake up to the minute you fall asleep, and for the most part, you're left alone to form your own opinions. These types of cruises usually cost more, but by far, they provide the better cruise experience for anyone who really wants to get the feel of Alaska.

Small-ship itineraries can be placed into one of the following categories:

- ✔ **Port-to-port:** These itineraries mimic larger ships by simply sailing between port towns.

- ✔ **Soft-adventure:** These itineraries provide some outdoor experiences such as hiking and kayaking, but they don't require participants to be trained athletes.

- ✔ **Active-adventure:** For the true adventurer, the hiking and kayaking are the focus of the trip, and the experience may be strenuous.

On each of these types of cruises, the small-ship experience tends toward the educational rather than the glitzy. You'll likely listen to **informal lectures** and sometimes watch video presentations about Alaska wildlife, history, and Native culture. Meals are served in open seatings, so you can sit where and with whom you like, and time spent huddled on the outside decks scanning for whales fosters great camaraderie among passengers.

Cabins on these ships don't generally offer TVs or telephones and tend to be small and sometimes spartan (see the individual reviews for exceptions). Cruise West's *Spirit of '98* and *Spirit of Oceanus* and Clipper Cruise Line's *Clipper Odyssey* have elevators, but in general, the small ships aren't good choices for travelers who require the use of wheelchairs or have other mobility problems.

American Safari Cruises

Directed to the slightly jaded high-end traveler, American Safari Cruises promises an intimate, all-inclusive yacht cruise to some of the more out-of-the-way stretches of the Inside Passage. The company books only 12 to 22 people per cruise, guaranteeing unparalleled flexibility and privacy. Black-bear aficionados can chug off in a Zodiac boat for a better look; active adventurers can explore the shoreline in one of the yacht's four kayaks; and lazier travelers can relax aboard ship. Another big plus: All off-ship excursions — including flightseeing and trips to boardwalked cannery villages and Tlingit villages — are included in the cruise fare, and so are drinks. The price is considerable, but, again, so is the pampering.

Passengers, almost always couples, tend to be more than comfortably wealthy and range from 45 to 65 years of age. Most hope to get close to nature without sacrificing luxury.

American Safari's vessels feel more like private yachts than cruise ships. The 22-passenger *Safari Quest,* the 12-passenger *Safari Spirit,* and the newest vessel, the 12-passenger *Safari Escape* look like Ferraris, all sleek, contoured lines and dark glass. Cabins are comfortable, and sitting rooms are intimate and luxurious, almost as if they were transported from a spacious suburban home. A big-screen TV in the main lounge forms a natural center for impromptu lectures during the day and movie-watching at night.

A shipboard chef barters with nearby fishing boats for the catch of the day, and raids local markets for the freshest fruits and vegetables — say, strawberries the size of a cub's paw and potent strains of basil and cilantro.

19101 36th Ave. W., Suite 201, Lynnwood, WA 98036. ☎ *888-862-8881. Fax: 425-776-8889. Internet:* www.amsafari.com. *Sample rates per person: Lowest-price outside cabins $3,995 for a 7-night cruise; no inside cabins or suites.*

Clipper Cruise Line

Clipper's down-to-earth, comfortable small ships focus on offbeat ports of call, learning, and mingling with your fellow passengers. It's the ideal small-ship cruise for people who've tried Holland America or Princess but want a more intimate cruise experience. Its ships sail port-to-port itineraries, and as is true aboard Alaska's other small-ship lines, the onboard atmosphere is casual; what lies out there beyond the ship's rail is the focus of most passengers. Lectures and videos about Alaska make up the bulk of the entertainment program, and a nightly social hour encourages passengers to mix and mingle. Motorized landing craft, carried aboard the ship, ferry passengers to remote beaches, pristine forests, small villages, and wildlife refuges, where naturalists and/or historians and other experts may conduct walking tours.

Passengers generally are older than 55, educated, and financially sound, with relatively high expectations when it comes to food, comfort, and overall experience. Although they want to experience Alaska's natural wonders — whales, glaciers, woodlands — they're not necessarily run-the-rapids types.

Along with Alaska Sightseeing's *Spirit of Endeavor* and *Spirit of Oceanus* and Glacier Bay's *Executive Explorer,* the 128-passenger **Clipper Odyssey** and 138-passenger **Yorktown Clipper** are two of the best choices in Alaska for someone who wants small-ship intimacy and flexibility but doesn't want to skimp on comfort. Their public rooms are larger and more appealing than those aboard competing ships, and all cabins are outside. Except for those at the lowest level, all have picture windows, and the top suite on the *Odyssey* offers a private veranda.

11969 Westline Industrial Dr., St. Louis, MO 63146. ☎ *800-325-0010 or 314-655-6700. Fax: 314-655-6670. Internet:* www.clippercruise.com. *Sample rates per person: Lowest-price outside cabins on Yorktown Clipper: $2,410 for 7-night cruise; on Odyssey: $5,850. Neither ship has inside cabins.*

Cruise West

Cruise West is the largest operator of small ships in Alaska, offering port-to-port itineraries, friendly service, and a casual onboard atmosphere. Similar to the Clipper Cruise Line, Cruise West's ships are for people who want to visit Alaska's port towns and see its wilderness areas up close but in a relaxed, small-scale environment without big-ship distractions; they're not for people who want to spend their days hiking and kayaking. The line's friendly, enthusiastic staffs are a big, big plus, making guests feel right at home. A cheerful and knowledgeable cruise coordinator accompanies each trip to answer passengers' questions about Alaska's flora, fauna, geology, and history, and Forest Service rangers, local fishermen, and Native Alaskans sometimes come aboard to present informal talks about the culture and industry of the state.

Cruise West passengers tend to be older (typically around 60 to 75 years of age), financially stable, well-educated, and independent-minded folks who want to visit Alaska's ports and see its natural wonders in a relaxed, dress-down atmosphere.

The 96-passenger *Spirit of '98,* a replica of a 19th-century steamship, carries its Victorian flavor so well that fully two-thirds of the people I met onboard thought the ship had been a private yacht at the turn of the 20th century. If you use a wheelchair or otherwise have mobility problems, note that the *Spirit of '98* is one of only three small ships in Alaska that has an elevator. (The line's *Spirit of Oceanus* and Clipper's *Clipper Odyssey* are the others.) The 78-passenger *Spirit of Alaska* and *Spirit of Columbia,* and 84-passenger *Spirit of Discovery* are all spartan ships designed to get passengers into small ports and allow them to see the state up close. The 102-passenger *Spirit of Endeavour,* on the other hand, offers among the highest levels of small-ship comfort of any small ship in Alaska, comparable to Clipper's *Yorktown Clipper* and Glacier Bay's *Executive Explorer.* The line's new, 114-passenger *Spirit of Oceanus,* the former *Renaissance V* of Renaissance Cruises, is the line's most luxurious ship, capable of sailing more far-flung itineraries.

2401 4th Ave., Suite 700, Seattle, WA 98121. ☎ *800-426-7702 or 206-441-8687. Fax: 206-441-4757. Internet:* www.cruisewest.com. *Sample rates per person: Lowest-price inside cabins $1,099, lowest outside $2,599.*

Glacier Bay Cruiseline

Glacier Bay Cruiseline — the only Native-owned cruise line in Alaska — offers three types of cruises: soft-adventure aboard the *Wilderness Explorer,* active-adventure aboard the *Wilderness Adventurer,* and port-to-port aboard the slightly more luxurious *Executive Explorer.* The *Wilderness Discoverer* is a hybrid, with itineraries that mix three days of adventure activities with three days spent visiting popular ports of call.

The adventure sailings are for a particular type of traveler, one interested in exploring Alaska's wilds rather than its towns. On the *Wilderness Explorer*'s soft-adventure cruises, for example, the biggest town you're likely to encounter after departing Juneau is tiny little Elfin Cove, population around 30 to 35 (at least in the summer). Otherwise, days are spent hiking in remote regions, exploring the glaciers, cruising the waterways looking for whales and other wildlife, and **kayaking** — the *Wilderness Adventurer, Wilderness Explorer,* and *Wilderness Discoverer* carry fleets of stable two-person sea kayaks that are launched from dry platforms at the ships' sterns. A weeklong sailing typically includes three kayak treks. **Naturalists** sail with every cruise to point out natural features and lead off-ship expeditions, all of which are included in the cruise price. On board, the atmosphere is casual and friendly; the staff provides just enough informal attention while leaving you the space to enjoy your vacation. Entertainment facilities on all ships are minimal: board games, books, and a TV/VCR in the lounge, on which passengers can view tapes about wildlife, Alaska history, Native culture, and a few feature films. Cabins are basic and quite small.

On the *Wilderness Explorer, Adventurer,* and *Discoverer,* passengers tend to be on the youngish side, with as many couples in their 40s and 50s as are in their 60s and 70s, and a scattering of 30-somethings (and a few 80- or 90-somethings) filling out the list. Whatever their ages, passengers tend to be active and interested in nature and wildlife. On the *Executive Explorer,* passengers tend to be older (60 and up) and less active and adventurous, but they still enjoy the same informality as aboard the line's other vessels.

The 49-passenger *Executive Explorer,* the line's fanciest vessel, won't be in service in 2003, and whether she will be relaunched in 2004 is unclear (check with the cruise line). The spartan, 74-passenger **Wilderness Adventurer** and almost identical 86-passenger **Wilderness Discoverer** are the line's soft-adventure ships, outfitted with sea kayaks and kayak dry-launch platforms in their sterns. The 36-passenger **Wilderness Explorer** is the line's most basic ship, with tiny cabins and bunk-style beds. She visits no ports, instead offering the most active cruise experience available in Alaska, with cruises structured so passengers are out kayaking and hiking most of each day and using the vessel only for eating, sleeping, and getting from place to place.

226 2nd Ave. W., Seattle, WA 98119. ☎ 800-451-5952 or 206-623-2417. Fax: 206-623-7809. Internet: www.glacierbaycruiseline.com. Sample rates per person: Lowest-price inside cabins $2,295 (on the Adventurer and Discoverer), lowest outside $1,380 (on the Explorer) for a 7-night cruise.

Lindblad Expeditions

Lindblad Expeditions specializes in environmentally sensitive, soft-adventure vacations that are explorative and informal in nature, designed to appeal to the intellectually curious traveler seeking a cruise that's educational and relaxing. Days aboard ship are spent finding out about the Alaskan outdoors from high-caliber expedition leaders trained in botany, anthropology, biology, and geology, and observing the world around you either from the ship or on shore excursions, which are included in the cruise package. Educational films and slide presentations aboard ship precede nature hikes and quick jaunts aboard Zodiac boats.

Not too small, not too big: A one-of-a-kind educational cruise

With World Explorer Cruises, you have the chance for a real Alaska cruise experience that combines a relatively large ship (the dowdy, 731-passenger *Universe Explorer*) with an education-oriented approach more typical of a small-ship line. The ship offers an incredible itinerary (a 14-night round-trip cruise out of Vancouver that visits all the popular ports of call along with Haines, Wrangell, Valdez, and Seward), an educational lecture series, an atmosphere of friendly informality, and some truly high-caliber shore excursions. Likewise, the ship is equipped with a library stocked with 16,000 volumes (many on Alaska nature, history, and culture), a 150-seat cinema for movie-watching, and a 16-terminal computer learning center operated by a company called SeniorNet. Entertainment-wise, one night may feature a string quartet and the next a cello soloist, a classical pianist, or an operatic soprano, cabaret singer, or ballad singer. The ship's **lecture circuit** includes talks on ecology and the cultures of Alaska, presented by experts in their subject.

The *Universe Explorer* tends to attract an older clientele, but the average age of its passengers is declining, mostly because of bike-hike-and-cruise options that allow passengers to bike or hike their way through the ports of call. These more active shore excursions appeal to a family market. Sailing with between, say, 15 and 30 teens and preteens on board is not unusual for this ship, which has a youth program and a team of counselors.

The 731-passenger *Universe Explorer* has nice but not spectacular public spaces and adequate if not palatial cabins. The bulk of the ship is taken up with double-occupancy rooms with twin beds (convertible to queen-size). Some also are capable of accommodating third passengers in foldaway sofa beds. Public areas are fairly spartan. The ship has a functional reception area, lounge-bar facilities, a comfortable but not glamorous show room, and a huge library, with many selections on nature and wildlife.

For more information, contact World Explorer Cruises at 555 Montgomery St., Suite 1400, San Francisco, CA 94111-2544 (☎ 800-854-3835 or 415-393-1565. Fax: 415-391-1145. Internet: www.wecruise.com). Sample rates per person: Lowest-price inside cabins $1,995, lowest outside $2,651 for a 14-night cruise (no suites).

Passengers tend to be older than 55, educated, relatively well off, and physically active (even so, the ships become very quiet not long after dinner; everyone crashes early to store up energy for the next day).

The shallow-draft, 70-passenger **Sea Lion** and **Sea Bird** are identical twins. With only two public rooms and utilitarian cabins, they're similar to other *expedition style* small ships, such as Glacier Bay's *Wilderness Adventurer* and Cruise West's *Spirit of Alaska* (as a matter of fact, the *Spirit of Alaska* and the two Lindblad Expedition ships all sailed at one time for the now-defunct Exploration Cruise Lines). Cabins are small and functional, and public space is limited to the open sun deck and bow areas, the dining room, and an observation lounge that serves as the nerve center for activities.

720 Fifth Ave., New York, NY 10019. ☎ *800-397-3348 or 212-765-7740. Fax: 212-265-3770. Internet:* www.expeditions.com. *Sample rates per person: Lowest-price outside cabins $3,690 for a 7-night cruise; no inside cabins or suites.*

The Big-Ship Cruise Lines

The ships featured in this section vary in size, age, and offerings, but share the common thread of having more activities and entertainment options than any one person can possibly take in during the course of a cruise. You'll find swimming pools, health clubs, spas, nightclubs, movie theaters, shops, casinos, multiple restaurants, bars, and special kids' playrooms, and in some cases sports decks, virtual golf, computer rooms, cigar clubs, and even quiet spaces where you can get away from it all. In most cases, you'll find an abundance of onboard activities, including games, contests, classes, and lectures, plus a variety of entertainment options and show productions, some very sophisticated.

Carnival Cruise Lines

Carnival is the big kahuna of the cruise industry, but translating the line's warm-weather "24-hour orgy of good times" philosophy to Alaska's "Look at the bears and whales!" temperament isn't an easy trick. In one of its Alaska brochures, the line says that, like the prospectors, you may find yourself shouting "Eureka" — but in the ship's casino, not at a gold rush site. Kinda makes you wonder why you aren't just going to Vegas.

On the plus side, entertainment is among the industry's best, with each ship boasting a dozen dancers, a 12-piece orchestra, comedians, jugglers, numerous live bands, and a big casino. Activity is nonstop. Cocktails begin to flow before lunch, and through the course of the day you can learn to country line-dance or ballroom dance, take cooking lessons, learn to play bridge, watch first-run movies, practice your golf swing by smashing balls into a net, join in a knobby-knee contest, or just eat, drink, shop, and then eat again. Alaska-specific naturalist lectures are delivered daily. In port, Carnival offers nearly 100 **shore excursions,** divided into categories of easy, moderate, and adventure. For kids, the line offers Camp Carnival, an expertly run children's program with activities that include Native arts and crafts sessions, lectures conducted by wildlife experts, and special shore excursions for teens.

Overall, Carnival has some of the youngest demographics in the industry: mostly younger than 50, including couples, lots of singles, and a good share of families. It's the same Middle America crowd that can be found in Las Vegas and Atlantic City and at Florida's megaresorts. Even though passengers on the Alaska sailings may be older than on Caribbean sailings, they tend to be young at heart. They're not a sedate, bird-watching crowd. They may want to see whales and icebergs, but they also dance the Macarena on cue. And single travelers take note: Carnival officials estimate that their ships attract more of you than any other line.

The 2,124-passenger, 84,000-ton *Carnival Spirit* is big, new, and impressive, with four swimming pools, a wedding chapel, a conference center, and, in addition to the formal dining room and casual buffet restaurant, an alternative restaurant sitting high up by the ship's smokestack. The ship also has more of what makes Carnival tick, including a two-level oceanview gym, balconies on more than half the cabins, a large children's center (complete with beepers for parents who want to stay in touch), and two consecutive decks of bars, lounges, and nightspots, one with an outdoor wraparound promenade.

3655 NW 87th Ave., Miami, FL 33178-2428. ☎ *800-CARNIVAL. Fax: 305-471-4740. Internet:* www.carnival.com. *Sample rates per person: Lowest-price inside cabins $1,579, lowest outside $1,879, lowest suite $2,929 for a 7-night cruise.*

Celebrity Cruises

Celebrity Cruises offers a great combination: a classy, tasteful, and luxurious cruise experience at a moderate price — it's definitely the best in the midpriced category. The line's ships are real works of art; its cuisine — guided by Michel Roux, one of the top French chefs in Britain — is outstanding; its service first-class, friendly, and unobtrusive; and its spa facilities among the best in the business.

A typical day may offer bridge, darts, a culinary art demonstration, a trap-shooting competition, a fitness fashion show, an art auction, a volleyball tournament, and a none-too-shabby stage show. Lectures on the various ports of call, the Alaskan environment, glaciers, and Alaskan culture are given by resident experts. Among the cruise tour options is a three-night stay in Denali National Park. For children, Celebrity ships employ a group of counselors who direct and supervise a camp-style children's program. Activities are geared toward different age groups. An impressive kids' play area and a separate lounge area for teens also are provided.

The typical Celebrity guest is sophisticated and more independent-minded, preferring to pursue his or her R&R at a relatively relaxed pace, with a minimum of aggressively promoted group activities. The overall impression leans more toward sophistication and less to the kind of orgiastic Technicolor whoopee that you'll find, say, aboard a Carnival ship. You'll find everyone from kids to retirees.

Sleek, modern, and stunningly designed, the 1,870-passenger *Mercury* and the larger, 1,950-passenger *Infinity* and *Summit* have plenty of open deck space and large windows that provide access to the wide skies and the grand Alaskan vistas. Overall, none of the cabins on these ships is bad — inside cabins are about par with industry standard, outside cabins are larger than usual, and suites (which come with butler service) are particularly spacious. Startlingly modern art — by the likes of Robert Rauschenberg, Jasper Johns, David Hockney, Pablo Picasso, Andy Warhol, and Richard Serra — is scattered throughout both vessels. Both ships (but especially *Infinity*) feature incredible spas with hydrotherapy pools, steam rooms, and saunas, plus health and beauty services and exceptionally large fitness areas.

1050 Caribbean Way, Miami, FL 33132. ☎ *800-437-3111 or 305-262-8322. Fax: 800-437-5111. Internet:* www.celebritycruises.com. *Sample rates per person: Lowest-price inside cabins $850, lowest outside $1,150, lowest suite $1,800 for a 7-night cruise.*

Crystal Cruises

Crystal Cruises are luxury all the way, offering all the amenities of much bigger ships, but in a more luxurious and intimate atmosphere with only 940 passengers. Everything on the **Crystal Harmony** is first-class, with fine attention paid to detail and to making guests feel comfortable. Service on the ship is nothing short of superb. The ship carries a battery of Alaska naturalists, environmentalists, and National Park Service rangers to educate and entertain passengers in the wilderness areas of the 49th state. The line's food-and-wine series presents well-known chefs and wine experts who put on food preparation demonstrations, lecture on the art of cookery, and prepare dinner one night during the cruise. A PGA-approved golf pro accompanies practically every *Harmony* cruise, conducting clinics along the way. The *Harmony* also has a flourishing computer room on board, with training for the uninitiated. Dazzling show-lounge entertainment, first-run movies, and a Caesar's Palace at Sea casino also are featured.

Passengers aboard Crystal tend to be successful businesspeople who can afford to pay for the best. In years past, the average age was probably closer to 60 than 70. But that average age is dropping fast — probably thanks to Crystal's excellent shore-excursion program, its casino, and its entertainment package. Whatever their ages, Crystal passengers tend to be people who like to dress up rather than down. "Casual night" doesn't mean the same thing to Crystal guests as it means to other people.

A handsome ship by any standard, the **Harmony** has one of the highest passenger-space ratios of any cruise ship. Its cabins are large, well appointed, and tastefully decorated with quality fittings and agreeable color tones. Almost half of them have private verandas. One small criticism is that space to hang clothes is a little tight in some of the lower cabin categories. Public rooms are classy throughout. Two alternative restaurants, Prego (Italian, mostly northern) and Kyoto (Asian-Japanese), introduce variety to the dining experience.

2049 Century Park E, Suite 1400, Los Angeles, CA 90067. ☎ **800-446-6620** or 310-785-9300. Fax: 310-785-3891. Internet: www.crystalcruises.com. Sample rates per person: Lowest-price inside cabins $4,115, lowest outside $4,485, lowest suite $9,575 for a 12-night cruise.

Holland America Line

Holland America can be summed up in one word: *tradition*. The company was formed way back in 1873 as the Netherlands-America Steamship Company, and its ships today strive to present an aura of history and dignity, like a European hotel where they never let rock stars register. And thanks to its acquisition, through the years, of numerous land-based tour operators, Holland America has positioned itself as Alaska's most experienced and comprehensive cruise company (a position that's being challenged by Princess Cruises).

Although most of the line's Alaskan fleet is relatively young, the ships are designed with a decidedly "classic" feel — no flashing neon lights here. Similarly, Holland America's ships are heavy on more mature, less frenetic kinds of activities. You'll find good bridge programs and music to dance (or just listen) to in the bars and lounges, plus health spas and the other amenities found on most large ships. The line has improved its nightly show-lounge entertainment, which was once, frankly, not so hot. Each week includes a crew talent show in which the Indonesian and Filipino staff members perform their countries' songs and dances. In 2003, the line continues its Artists in Residence Program, arranged through the Alaska Native Heritage Center in Anchorage, with Alaska Native artists accompanying all seven-night cruises and demonstrating traditional art forms such as ivory and soapstone carving, basket weaving, and mask making. Club HAL is one of the industry's more creative children's programs, although the children's playrooms (often no more than a meeting room stocked with toys) are no match for what you find on the latest Princess or Celebrity megaships.

Although Holland still caters mostly to the older crowd that's long been its bread and butter, the average age is dropping, thanks to a revamping of onboard entertainment and an increased emphasis on its children's program.

The 1,266-passenger *Maasdam, Ryndam, Statendam,* and *Veendam* are more or less identical. All cabins have a sitting area and plenty of closet and drawer space, and even the least expensive inside cabins run almost 190 square feet — quite large by industry standards. Outside doubles have either picture windows or verandas. The striking dining rooms, two-tiered showrooms, and Crow's Nest forward bar-lounges are among these ships' best features. The newer, 1,440-passenger *Volendam* and *Zaandam* are larger and fancier, with triple-decked oval atriums, 197 suites and deluxe staterooms with private verandas, five showrooms and lounges, and an alternative restaurant designed as an artist's bistro, featuring drawings and etchings. The smallest cabin is a comfortable 190 square feet. The 1,380-passenger **Amsterdam** is an attractive, midsize ship that combines classic styling with innovation. The centerpiece of the foyer atrium is an enormous, elaborate astrolabe that chimes tunes at certain hours of the day. Strategically located in public areas around the ship are sculptures of big ol' Alaskan grizzly bears, created by British artist Susanna Holt. Accommodations are warm, comfortable, low-key, and totally functional.

300 Elliott Ave. W., Seattle, WA 98119. ☎ *800-426-0327 or 206-281-3535. Fax: 206-286-7110. Internet:* www.hollandamerica.com. *Sample rates per person: Lowest-price inside cabins $1,879, lowest outside $2,379, lowest suite $3,399.*

Norwegian Cruise Line

Norwegian Cruise Line (NCL) offers an informal and upbeat onboard atmosphere on the medium-sized *Norwegian Wind,* sailing from Vancouver, and the megaships *Norwegian Sky* and *Norwegian Sun,* sailing from Seattle. The line excels at activities, and its recreational and fitness programs are among the best in the industry. Though the onboard food has been described as unmemorable, NCL recently inaugurated what has become a popular casual-dining policy that allows passengers to dine whenever they want within a certain time frame, with whomever they want, dressed however they want.

In Alaska, NCL offers an Alaskan lecturer, wine tastings, art auctions, trap shooting, cooking demonstrations, craft and dance classes, an incentive fitness program, and bingo, among other activities. Passengers can choose from a good selection of soft-adventure shore excursions, including hiking, biking, and kayaking. Entertainment is generally strong, and includes Vegas-style musical productions. The top-notch kids' program includes an activity room, video games, an ice-cream bar, and guaranteed babysitting aboard, plus sessions with park rangers and escorted shore excursions.

In Alaska, the demographic tends more toward retirees than on the line's warmer-climate sailings, but you'll also find families, including grand-parents bringing along the grandkids.

The new 1,936-passenger **Norwegian Sun** is the first ship built with NCL's new *freestyle dining policy* in mind, as evidenced by the nine separate onboard restaurants. An airy, eight-story glass atrium welcomes visitors in the lobby. More than two-thirds of the guest rooms (about 650 in all) have ocean views, and closet space is more generous than on other NCL ships. The 2,002-passenger **Norwegian Sky** has an Internet cafe, a huge sun deck (complete with a driver in a golf cart delivering drinks), a basketball court and batting cage, and a wedding chapel (for in-port ceremonies only). In contrast to its large public spaces, standard cabins are small at 154 square feet and have little storage space. The smaller, less fancy, 1,700-passenger *Norwegian Wind* has three main dining rooms, an alternative restaurant, and the typical range of lounges, bars, and entertainment facilities. Closet and drawer space in cabins is quite limited, so pack lightly.

7665 Corporate Center Dr., Miami, FL 33126. ☎ *800-327-7030. Fax: 305-448-7936. Internet:* www.ncl.com. *Sample rates per person: Lowest-price inside cabins $1,099, lowest outside $1,269, lowest suite $3,299 for a 7-night cruise.*

Princess Cruises

Consistency is Princess's strength. With new ships joining its fleet like so many cars off a Detroit assembly line, you'd think that maintaining acceptable service standards could be a problem. All things considered, though, Princess accomplishes this rather well. Throughout the fleet, the service in all areas — dining room, lounge, cabin maintenance, and so on — tends to be of consistently high quality. Although its ships serve every corner of the globe, nowhere is the Princess presence more visible than in Alaska. Through its affiliate, Princess Tours, it owns wilderness lodges, motor coaches, and railcars in the 49th state, making it one of the major players in the Alaska cruise market, alongside Holland America.

Princess passengers can expect enough onboard activities to keep them going morning to night, if they've a mind to, and enough nooks and crannies to allow them to do absolutely nothing, if that's their thing. Kids are well taken care of, with especially large children's playrooms. On shore, the line's shore-excursion staffs get big points for efficiency.

Typical Princess passengers are likely to be between, say, 50 and 65. Recent additional emphasis on its youth and children's facilities is attracting a bigger share of the **family market,** resulting in the passenger list becoming more active overall.

The most interesting addition to the Alaska fleet is the *Pacific Princess,* a smaller ship that Princess bought from the now defunct Renaissance Cruises less than a year ago. Its arrival in the fleet enables Princess to operate an itinerary that it has not operated in some time — an 11-night Inside Passage round-trip out of San Francisco. The *Dawn, Sun, Coral,* and *Island Princess* ships are virtually indistinguishable from one another except for cosmetics. Each carries an estimated 1,950 passengers, but despite their size, you'll probably never feel crowded. Decks, buffet dining areas, and lounges feel spacious. Beautiful libraries, patisseries for pastries and cappuccino, and pizzerias for good made-to-order Italian fast food are featured. The ships have extensive children's playrooms with castles, computer games, puppet theaters, and more. As for cabins, even the smallest is a spacious 175 square feet, and more than 80% of rooms have private verandas. The 2,670-passenger *Diamond Princess* and the 2,600-passenger *Star Princess* are the largest ships ever to sail Alaska's waters. Their offerings are similarly large scale; for example, on the *Star Princess* you'll find four pools, nine hot tubs, 12 bars and lounges, restaurants too numerous to count, and a futuristic nightclub-disco located 15 decks above the sea and reachable by a moving sidewalk.

24305 Town Center Dr., Santa Clarita, CA 91355. ☎ *800-LOVE-BOAT (568-3262) or 661-753-4999. Fax: 310-277-6175. Internet:* www.princess.com. *Sample rates per person: Lowest-price inside cabins $1,469, lowest outside $1,869, lowest suite $2,779 for a 7-night cruise.*

Radisson Seven Seas Cruises

Radisson offers the best in food, service, and accommodations in an environment that's a little more casual and small-shiplike than Crystal's more determined luxury. The line assumes for the most part that passengers want to entertain themselves on board, so organized activities are limited, but they do include lectures by local experts, well-known authors, and the like, plus facilities for card and board games and the occasional dance lesson. Three computers in the library enable guests to send e-mail and use CD-ROMs. Entertainment includes production shows, cabaret acts, and local acts that come on board at ports. The library stocks books and movies that guests can play on their in-cabin VCRs. The line has a no-tipping policy, and offers creative shore excursions. Room service is about the best you'll find on a ship.

Radisson tends to attract high-income, low-key passengers ages 50 and up. The typical passenger is well educated, well traveled, and inquisitive.

Cabins on the 700-passenger **Seven Seas Mariner** are all oceanview suites, all with private verandas. The standard suite is a large 301 square feet; some suites can interconnect if you want to book two for additional space. In the public areas, the show lounge is designed to resemble a 1930s nightclub. Two additional lounges plus a casino and the Connoisseur Club, a cushy venue for predinner drinks and after-dinner fine brandy and cigars, provide additional comforts for passengers. The ship's spa offers Judith Jackson European spa treatments using a variety of herbal- and water-based therapies.

600 Corporate Dr., Suite 410, Fort Lauderdale, FL 33334. ☎ *800-285-1835. Internet:* www.rssc.com. *Sample rates per person: Lowest-price suite $2,515 for 7-night cruise; no inside or standard outside cabins.*

Royal Caribbean International

Royal Caribbean sells a mass-market style of cruising that's reasonably priced and offered aboard casual, well-run ships with plenty of the standard cruise-line fare — craft classes, horse racing, bingo, shuffleboard, deck games, line-dancing lessons, wine-and-cheese tastings, cooking demonstrations, art auctions, and the like — plus elaborate health clubs and spas, covered swimming pools, large open sun deck areas, and innumerable bars, lounges, and other entertainment centers. The Viking Crown Lounge and other glassed-in areas make excellent observation rooms from which to see the Alaska sights. Royal Caribbean spends big bucks on entertainment, which includes high-tech show productions. Headliners are often featured. Port lectures are offered on topics such as Alaska wildlife, and the line offers some 65 shore excursions. The line's children's activities are some of the most extensive afloat.

The crowd on Royal Caribbean ships, like the decor, rates pretty high on the whoopee scale, although not quite at the Carnival level. Passengers represent an age mix from 30 to 60, and the line's well-established and fine-tuned kids' programs attract a good number of families. In Alaska, Royal Caribbean is focusing more on international sales than the entrenched market leaders, Princess and Holland America, which has resulted in sailings populated by a good many international passengers, including travelers from Canada, Asia, and Europe.

The 1,800-passenger *Legend of the Seas* and the 2,000-passenger *Vision of the Seas* are almost identical, and offer plenty of nice touches that give them the feel of top-flight shore resorts. You'll find sumptuous, big-windowed health club-spas and loads of fine shopping, dining, and entertainment options. Cabins are not large but they have small sitting areas. All outside cabins on both ships' Bridge and Commodore decks have balconies and can sleep up to four quite comfortably. The 2,100-passenger *Radiance of the Seas* is slightly more upscale than the line's other vessels and is designed to remind guests they are at sea — walls of glass everywhere you go enable you to view the passing Alaska scenery. Even the 12-story lobby elevators and Internet cafe have water views. Cabins are larger than on the *Vision* and *Legend* — the smallest is 170 square feet — and more come with verandas. And here's a nice touch: The pool tables have built-in self-leveling mechanisms in case waves get too high.

*1050 Caribbean Way, Miami, FL 33132. ☎ **800-327-6700** or 305-379-4731. Internet:* www.rccl.com. *Sample rates per person: Lowest-price inside cabins $1,579, lowest outside $2,179, lowest suite $3,229 for a 7-night cruise.*

Chapter 9

Planning an Outdoor Adventure

●●

●●

*Y*ou wouldn't go to Paris and view the Louvre only by driving by it on a bus. But many visitors to Alaska see the wilderness only through glass. They miss the detail in the flowers, the scent of the forest, the feeling of the air on their skin, and the tundra under their feet. They miss the irreplaceable feeling of being a small part of the overwhelming power of nature.

For some very elderly or frail travelers, surveying the scenery from a vehicle is better than missing out on all things wild. But most visitors, even those with disabilities, can get outdoors in Alaska in some way. Experienced hikers, anglers, sea kayakers, canoeists, and other nature lovers will be in heaven. But you don't have to know anything or have any experience in the great outdoors; someone is always available to help and to introduce you to Alaska's outdoors at your own level.

The Seven Deadly Warning Signs: Ways to Get Killed in Alaska's Outdoors

 Violent death is the first thing that some urbanites think of when they contemplate going out into nature. As it happens, some rural Alaskans share the same thoughts when they contemplate going to a big city. (I remember as a child being told by friends, and believing, that New York City had "blocks of death" — normal looking blocks where, if you set foot there, immediate assassination was virtually guaranteed.)

In Alaska, we have no blocks of death, or trails of death (or whatever your version would be). Some activities are inherently hazardous, such as white-water rafting or snowmobiling. (Any time you have to sign a release, it probably means you're taking a risk.) Other than those obvious exceptions, however, you encounter danger mainly if you behave foolishly or get in over your head. Consider this safety rule number one: If you don't know what you're doing, you need to be with someone who does, such as the experienced guides that I recommend later in this chapter.

I feel safer in the Alaska wilderness than anywhere else, but I know some folks get nervous, so I arrange tips here according to the worst fantasies of disaster that anyone can imagine.

Getting eaten by a bear (and such)

Bear mauling is probably the least likely way for your vacation to end. Deaths from dog bites are much more common, for example. (Don't worry: It's an example. I'm almost certain you won't die from a dog bite either.) But you still need to be prepared for bears and know how to avoid being trampled by moose.

The first rule of defense is simple: *Don't attract bears.* And I just happen to have a few tips to keep in mind to avoid attracting bears:

- ✔ Keep all your food and trash in airtight containers when you're camping. (When car camping, the vehicle's trunk works.)

- ✔ When possible, avoid cooking foods with particularly pungent odors, and make sure your cleanup prevents food odors from spreading. (For example, pour liquids down available drains or keep them in airtight containers until you can properly dispose of them.)

- ✔ Never keep food, pungent items, or clothing that smells like fish in your tent.

- ✔ Clean fish away from your campsite.

When walking through brush or thick trees, make lots of noise to avoid surprising a bear or moose. Bells you can hang on your belt are for sale at sporting-goods shops, or you can sing or carry on a loud conversation. At all costs, avoid coming between a bear and its cubs or a bear and food. Here's one safety tip that's the same in New York as in Alaska: If a mugger wants your wallet, give it to him; if a bear wants the fish you just caught, consider it his. Moose also are strongly defensive of their young and can attack if they feel you're getting too close.

If you see a bear, stop, wave your arms, and make noise. If you're with others, group together so that you look larger to the bear. Don't run, tempting the bear to chase; depart by slowly backing away, at an angle if possible so that you can see peripherally where you're going. If the bear follows, stop and begin making noise again. Many Alaskans carry a gun for protection in bear country, but that's not practical for most visitors. A good alternative is a bear-deterrent spray. You can find the spray in a canister at most sporting goods stores for about $50. You shoot the spray to produce a burning fog of capsaicin pepper between you and a threatening bear. While less effective than a gun, especially in wind or rain, the sprays are legal in national parks and okay to carry across the Canadian border — big advantages over firearms. You also can order pepper spray direct from **Counter Assault** (☎ **800-695-3394**; Internet: www.counterassault.com).

Drowning in freezing water

Because of the cool temperatures, unpredictable weather, and cold water, going out on the ocean or floating down a fast river is more hazardous in Alaska than in most other places. You should go only with an experienced, licensed operator unless you really know what you're doing. With little margin for error if you fall into the water or capsize, you have only minutes to get out and get warm before hypothermia and death. A life jacket can keep you afloat, but it won't keep you alive in 40°F water. If you're sea kayaking or canoeing, stay close to shore and take plastic dry bags (also called *float bags*) with everything you need to quickly warm a person who gets wet (see the next section).

Succumbing to exposure

Hypothermia, also called exposure, is a potentially fatal lowering of core body temperature. It's most dangerous when it sneaks up on you, perhaps in 50-degree weather on a damp mountain hike or rainy boating trip. Dress in material (whether wool or synthetic) that keeps its warmth when wet, choosing layers to avoid chilling perspiration. Make sure you eat well and avoid exhaustion. Keep chocolates or other fatty energy foods in reserve. Hypothermia's symptoms include:

- Having cold extremities
- Being uncommunicative
- Displaying poor judgment or coordination
- Fighting sleepiness

A shivering victim still has the ability to warm up if better dressed. A lack of shivering means the body has gone beyond that point and you need to add warmth from the outside or from warm drinks. Get indoors, force hot liquids (except in cases of shock), and, if shelter is unavailable, apply body heat from another person, skin on skin, in a sleeping bag.

Getting eaten alive by bugs

Actually, you can't die this way. Alaska has no snakes or poisonous spiders or, at this writing, West Nile virus. But you may wish you were dead when the mosquitoes or black flies swarm during warmer weather. The bugs can be too intense for anyone to stand. As a reporter, I once covered the story of a man who threw a rock through a bank's plate glass window so that he could get arrested and get away from the mosquitoes. Effective insect repellent is a necessity, as is having a refuge from the bugs, such as a tent or cabin. In the Interior and Arctic, where mosquitoes are worst, we use jackets of tightly woven fabric with net hoods, which you can buy in Alaska. Mosquitoes can bite through light fabric. Benadryl tablets or other antihistamines often relieve swelling caused by mosquito bites.

Drowning while crossing a river

Hiking off trails in Alaska's backcountry, such as at Denali, can require crossing rivers without bridges. Little streams are safe, but use great caution in substantial flows: You can easily get in trouble. Often, the water is glacial melt, barely above freezing and heavy with silt that makes it opaque. The silt can fill your pockets and drag you down. If in doubt, don't do it. If you do decide to cross, unbuckle your pack, keep your shoes on, face upstream, use a heavy walking stick if possible, and rig a safety line. Carry children or have them follow behind an adult.

Keeling over from bad clams

Don't eat mussels, clams, or scallops you pick or dig from the seashore unless you know they're safe. To find out, call the **Alaska Department of Environmental Conservation (☎ 907-269-7501)**, which tests the beaches. Most of Alaska's remote beaches aren't tested, so they aren't safe. The risk is paralytic shellfish poisoning, a potentially fatal malady caused by a naturally occurring toxin. It causes total paralysis, including your breathing. You can keep a victim alive with mouth-to-mouth resuscitation until you obtain medical help.

Drinking tainted water

Unpurified river or lake water may not be safe to drink (although it won't kill you). Hand-held filters available from sporting-goods stores for about $75 are the most practical way of dealing with the problem on long backcountry trips. Iodine kits and boiling also work. The danger is a protozoan cyst called *giardia lamblia,* which causes diarrhea and has been spread to thousands of water bodies all over the United States by dog feces. You may not notice the side effects for a couple of weeks after exposure, and then it could become chronic. If symptoms show up after you get home, tell your doctor you may have been exposed so that he or she can test and treat you.

Getting Active Outdoors in the Alaska Summer

Summer in Alaska is a time to get outside; on a sunny weekend, you're hard pressed to find an Alaskan in town. Here's a mini-directory to help you figure out which activities are for you, where you can do them, and who you can get to take you. I also provide information to help you decide whether to participate in these activities on your own or with a guide. I suggest a few guides here to get you started; the destination chapters in this book include alternative guides, as well as information on renting equipment.

Backpacking

I can't imagine a more beautiful or exciting place for a backpacking expedition than Alaska, where you can have immense swaths of tundra or mountain to yourself, seeing far more wildlife than people.

- ✔ **Difficulty level:** Take an overnight hike near home, before you invest in a backpacking trek in Alaska, to hone your skills and make sure you enjoy carrying a pack. Even Alaska's trail hikes tend to be remote, with potentially tough weather; the most dramatic hiking routes are challenging, far beyond the trails.

- ✔ **Best places:** For self-guided trail hikes, pick the pathways of Chugach National Forest and Chugach State Park near Anchorage (see Chapter 14). For self-guided, off-trail hiking, try Denali National Park (refer to Chapter 19). For guided, off-trail hikes, consider St. Elias Alpine Guides at Wrangell–St. Elias National Park (see below).

- ✔ **Guided or on-your-own:** To set up your own trip, you need to buy trail guidebooks and maps, bring or rent equipment, and arrange for transportation at your starting and ending points. You can start with the outfitters that I recommend throughout this book. You have a lot of planning, but it's doable if you're motivated. A guided trek takes out the guesswork.

- ✔ **Who to go with: St. Elias Alpine Guides** (☎ **888-933-5427** or 907-345-9048; summer 907-554-4445; Internet: www.stelias guides.com) specializes in trekking and climbing the rugged and spectacular Wrangell–St. Elias National Park, some of the most remote wilderness on the planet. A four-day trek starts at $615 per person.

Biking — off-road

Mountain biking is allowed off-road almost everywhere in Alaska. Literally thousands of miles of dirt roads and tracks reach through the coastal forests. In the cities, excellent cross-country ski trails become excellent mountain biking trails in summer.

- ✔ **Difficulty level:** Mountain biking rough terrain is a real skill, but novices can enjoy fat-tire bikes on dirt roads around many communities without difficulty.

- ✔ **Best places:** Many places in Alaska have superb mountain biking. The remote roads across Kachemak Bay from Homer may be the best: They're not connected to the highway network, they're easy to reach by boat, and the town has good bike shops (see Chapter 16).

- ✔ **Guided or on-your-own:** Some areas do have guided mountain-biking day trips, including Denali National Park, but mostly it's a self-guided activity: rent the bike and go. Plan ahead by contacting a bike shop in the area where you plan to ride (see the appropriate chapter in this book for suggestions), getting advice on the area, and reserving your equipment.

- ✔ **Who to go with:** At Denali National Park, Denali Outdoor Center (☎ 888-303-1925; Internet: www.denalioutdoorcenter.com) leads rides with views of Mount McKinley daily, $50 for 2½ hours.

Biking — on pavement

In many Alaska communities, a bicycle is a visitor's most efficient way of getting around. A bike also can take you easily into natural places, on day trips, or peddling over the state's long highways, without glass getting between you and the world.

- ✔ **Difficulty level:** Almost anyone with physical mobility can get on a bike and coast along the coastal trail in Anchorage. Highway trips are for physically fit riders who can handle traffic.

- ✔ **Best places:** The bike paths of Anchorage (see Chapter 14) allow casual rides into the woods, possibly to see moose or even eagles and beluga whales — from vantage points along the Tony Knowles Coastal Trail. The Richardson Highway from Fairbanks to Valdez is Alaska's most beautiful paved highway and carries little traffic (check out Chapter 18).

- ✔ **Guided or on-your-own:** You don't need a guide to rent a bike and explore a quaint town or wooded bike trail. But for a challenging intercity ride, most people would want support.

- ✔ **Who to go with:** Alaska Bicycle Adventures (☎ 800-770-7242 or 907-243-2329; Internet: www.alaskabike.com) provides all the arrangements for bicycle expeditions on Alaska's rural highways, including a support van that follows the group and ferries bicyclists over the dangerous or boring patches of road. Other activities and sightseeing round out the vacation. A week costs about $2,595.

Canoeing

Gliding down a gently flowing stream or across the mirror surface of a pristine lake may be the gentlest way to get into the true Alaska. Wild land unfolds around you as if you were the first person to float on the waterway.

- ✔ **Difficulty level:** Anyone can get out for a paddle on Fairbanks's gentle Chena River. Expert canoeists find a paradise of thousands of miles of little-used routes in many locations.

- ✔ **Best places:** Fairbanks is a canoeing center, with accessible river routes for every level of ability or length of journey (refer to Chapter 17). The Swan Lake Canoe Route, near Kenai, is a good self-guided backcountry trip for novices (see Chapter 16).

- ✔ **Guided or on-your-own:** If you're confident paddling a canoe, you can manage the easier routes that we mention in this section. Always check with local authorities on water levels and stream conditions. To get deeper into the wilderness, where emergency help is unavailable, go with a guide.

- ✔ **Who to go with:** River guide Karen Jettmar wrote the book on floating Alaska's rivers (*The Alaska River Guide,* Alaska Northwest Books). She leads long floats by canoe or raft on exotic wilderness rivers for small groups all summer through her firm, **Equinox Wilderness Expeditions** (☎ **907-274-9087;** Internet: `www.equinoxexpeditions.com`). A nine-day float costs $2,850.

Day hiking

Part of Alaska's magic is that no place is so urban that you can't be hiking in big, unspoiled natural places in less than an hour. Anyone who has the use of their legs should make a point of getting off on the trails that lead from every town.

- ✔ **Difficulty level:** You set the level of difficulty. Hike a half-mile up a level seaside trail or conquer a mountain on an all-day hike.

- ✔ **Best places:** You find great day hikes everywhere you go in Alaska. The best trails are near towns in coastal Alaska, including Anchorage (see Chapter 14), the Kenai Peninsula (see Chapter 16), and every town in Southeast Alaska (many of which are covered in Part V of this book). You can hike on tundra, off trails, at Denali National Park (see Chapter 19), and many other places.

✔ **Guided or on-your-own:** All you need are walking shoes and directions to the trailhead. I mention some of the best hikes throughout the book. If you're uncomfortable on your own, the national parks lead guided hikes.

✔ **Who to go with:** The best guided day hikes are at Denali National Park, where rangers lead daily Discovery Hikes off trails deep into the park (see Chapter 19).

Fishing

Alaska's legendary salmon and halibut fishing drive the rhythm of life in coastal communities. Just try not to get too excited when you haul in a fish bigger than you up from the sea floor, or hook a mass of fighting muscle in a remote stream.

The best all-around source of information about fishing in Alaska is the **Alaska Department of Fish and Game Sport Fish Division** (☎ **800-874-8202;** Internet: www.state.ak.us/adfg). The agency produces guides and fields questions from the public; the Web site offers a wealth of resources, including the capability to purchase licenses online. Nonresident sport-fishing licenses start at $10 for a one-day license and go up to $50 for a two-week license. You can also get a license from most sporting-goods stores in the state.

✔ **Difficulty level:** Just about anyone can enjoy guided fishing on a boat in the Kenai River or on the ocean in Southeast or South Central Alaska. Avid anglers can schedule time at a remote fishing lodge or on a guided or unguided floatplane fly-in, or just fish streamside on one of Alaska's highways.

✔ **Best places:** For halibut (from a boat): Homer, Juneau, and Sitka (see Chapters 16, 20, and 22); for salmon in the ocean (from a boat): Seward, Juneau, and Sitka (see Chapters 16, 20, and 22); for salmon in a stream (on a boat or the bank): Anchorage environs and Kenai (see Chapters 14 and 16).

✔ **Guided or do-it-yourself:** Fishing is easy; catching the fish is what takes some skill. Unless you have plenty of time for research and trial and error, take at least your first fishing trip with a guide to learn the unique skills required for salmon fishing. (You must have a guide for halibut, because you need a boat.)

✔ **Who to go with:** If fishing is *the* goal of your trip, contact **Sport Fishing Alaska** (☎ **907-344-8674;** Internet: www.AlaskaTrip Planners.com), a fee-based booking agency that gets anglers to where the fishing is hottest when they come to Alaska. If fishing is just one of your goals, check with the fishing resources that we list in the chapters specific to the towns you plan to visit.

Rafting

River rafting comes in different flavors: half-day white-water thrill rides or multiday journeys across great swaths of Alaska wilderness that you can't reach any other way — or a combination of the two.

✔ **Difficulty level:** Sitting in a raft is easy. But floating through violent rapids in cold water is inherently hazardous and definitely not for everyone. A guided raft expedition is the most comfortable way to see more remote wilderness, but you still must be ready to sleep in a tent and endure the bugs, and you have no way to quit before the end.

✔ **Best places:** For day trips, the Nenana Canyon outside Denali National Park (see Chapter 19) and the fast rivers around Anchorage (see Chapter 14) are among the best options. For expeditions, the rivers of the Arctic may be best for their broad scenery and wildlife-viewing (see the information about Equinox Wilderness Expeditions below).

✔ **Guided or on-your-own:** Putting together your own raft trip is probably impractical except for experts. Guided expeditions should be planned and booked at least three months in advance, just to make sure you know what you are getting into. You can take day trips on a next-day basis.

✔ **Who to go with:** For day trips near Anchorage, try **Nova** (☎ 800-746-5753 or 907-745-5753; Internet: www.novalaska.com). At Denali National Park, contact **Denali Outdoor Center** (☎ 888-303-1925; Internet: www.denalioutdoorcenter.com). For expeditions, check out **Equinox Wilderness Expeditions** (☎ 907-274-9087; Internet: www.equinoxexpeditions.com) or **Alaska Discovery** (☎ 800-586-1911 or 907-780-6226; Internet: www.akdiscovery.com).

Sea kayaking

A sea kayak is a uniquely intimate way to see the abundance of the marine world. Rich sea-floor life glides by inches below you in clear water, sea otters and birds let you approach, whales take no notice. You enter into their universe.

✔ **Difficulty level:** Almost any adult or teen can safely handle a guided sea kayaking outing, but you can get into serious danger quickly without a guide or the proper skills. People with joint or back problems may not be comfortable, and young children must be able to sit perfectly still.

✔ **Best places:** Virtually every coastal community has a sea kayaking guide and someplace beautiful to take guests for day trips. My favorites are Homer and Sitka (see Chapters 16 and 22).

Expeditions are available in many places, too; the best waters for extended paddling are in Southeast Alaska, and a superb outfitter is based in Juneau (Chapter 20).

✔ **Guided or on-your-own:** Experienced kayakers can easily rent what they need for a wonderful trip. You also find operators who rent sea kayaks to raw beginners — a life-and-death gamble I don't recommend. You're better off going with one of the excellent guides mentioned below. Reserve expeditions well in advance — for day trips, a day or two ahead.

✔ **Who to go with:** For day trips in Homer, try **True North Kayak Adventures** (☎ 907-235-0708; Internet: www.truenorthkayak.com); in Sitka, contact **Sitka Sound Ocean Adventures** (☎ 907-747-6375; Internet: www.ssoceanadventures.com). A firm in Juneau called **Alaska Discovery** (☎ 800-586-1911 or 907-780-6226; Internet: www.akdiscovery.com) offers the best catalog of sea kayaking expeditions, starting with a three-day trip that costs $495 to $595 per person.

Keeping Active in the Alaskan Winter

For people who live in Alaska, getting outdoors in winter is a matter of maintaining sanity: Winter lasts from October to April, and you can't stay inside that long. Many visitors see the outdoor experience as a magnificent opportunity. Snow that you can count on means you can confidently plan a trip based on winter sports.

The following sections discuss the variety of winter activities you can try, including their difficulty level, some suggestions for the best places to go, and whether to try them on your own or with a guide. As with the preceding summer-activities section, I also suggest a few providers for you to consider; you can find more options, as well as rental providers, in the destination chapters in this book.

Dog mushing

No one should come to Alaska in the winter and not take at least a quick spin in a dog sled. You simply can't believe the speed, joy, and intelligence of the dogs running ahead of you as you ride quietly through the trees.

✔ **Difficulty level:** Anyone can ride in a sled driven by an experienced musher, although few folks will want to do it for more than an hour or two. You can easily learn to drive a well-trained team, but you need to be confident around dogs and agile enough to handle situations that arise.

✔ **Best places:** The Anchorage and Fairbanks areas have plenty of mushers, dogs, snow, and land for running — all the necessary ingredients (see Chapters 14 and 17). The Denali National Park region may be the most beautiful mushing domain for expeditions.

✔ **Guided or on-your-own:** If you don't own a dozen trained dogs and a sled, doing it yourself isn't an option. The choice is in the basket or on the runners (riding or driving); learning to drive a sled is great, but it takes time and money. Book expeditions well in advance. You can usually arrange day-trip rides a day or two in advance, or a few weeks for peak race periods.

✔ **Who to go with:** For day trips near Anchorage, **Birch Trails Adventures** (☎ and Fax: **907-688-5713**; E-mail: birchtrails@ excite.com) is my favorite; they take you for a ride or teach you to drive. For do-it-on-your-own mush expeditions, the unrivalled best (but be prepared to pay) is **Denali West Lodge** (☎ or Fax: **888-607-5566** or 907-674-3112; Internet: www.denaliwestlodge. com). They pick up you at the landing strip with a dog team that you drive back to the lodge. A nine-day journey from the lodge to Mount McKinley is $6,050 per person.

Skiing

Alaska has outstanding downhill skiing and snow that you can count on, but because of the distance from population centers, lift lines are a rarity even at the busiest ski resorts on the busiest days of the year. Cross-country skiers find great trails and unlimited backcountry to explore.

✔ **Difficulty level:** Going all the way to Alaska to ski makes sense mostly for those who already know how, but you can find easy slopes to learn on, too. Expert skiers find no limit to challenges in the heli-skiing and other backcountry opportunities.

✔ **Best places:** Alaska's best ski resort is Alyeska Resort in Girdwood, just south of Anchorage (see Chapter 15). The best cross-country trails, more than 50 kilometers of them, are at Kincaid Park in Anchorage (see Chapter 14). Turnagain Pass, near Girdwood, is prime country for backcountry skiing.

✔ **Guided or on-your-own:** Planning a skiing vacation is relatively easy, as you only need to deal with one place. For Christmas or spring break reservations, call well ahead.

✔ **Who to go with: Alyeska Resort** offers inexpensive learn-to-ski and more advanced lesson packages; you can set up heli-skiing through them, too (☎ **800-880-3880** or 907-754-1111; Internet: www.alyeskaresort.com).

Snowmobiling

In most of Alaska, snowmobiles are like cars in other places: They're simply the most practical way to get from place to place in a frozen landscape. Recreationists also use them for thrill riding, but for visitors, their primary value lies in the ability to get to beautiful places without using more muscle than you may have.

- ✔ **Difficulty level:** Riding is easy to pick up, but you can easily get stuck or tip over in powder snow. The sport is hazardous: The machines are fast, your body is unprotected, and you can find yourself far away in cold, dangerous places in minutes. Take it easy.

- ✔ **Best places:** The snowy mountains and glaciers south of Anchorage offer plenty of room to ride and scenery to enjoy, and a well-run outfitter, based at the ski resort in Girdwood, leads groups of beginners there (Chapter 15).

- ✔ **Guided or on-your-own:** Even experienced riders should go with a guide first to get the lay of the land and learn about the special hazards of this extreme terrain before setting out on their own.

- ✔ **Who to go with: Alaska Outdoor Adventures** (☎ **888-414-7669** or 907-783-7669; Internet: www.akadventures.com), based at the Alyeska Resort in Girdwood, is a professional outfit, leading groups to play on snowmobiles for a few hours or for a half-day trip to a glacier.

Viewing Alaska's Wildlife

Ask any visitors to Alaska, "How was your trip?" and they'll probably respond by telling you what kind of animals they saw, such as "We saw two bears and a whale." This newly discovered law of nature even works for lifelong residents; Alaska's wildlife experience is *that* impressive. Of course, when the person questioned saw no animals, he or she just complains about the weather.

I'm pretty sure that you'll value your own wildlife sightings. That being the case, why not plan your trip to maximize the amount of wildlife you see? Don't count on just tripping over a moose here or there. Pick the very best places to see bears or whales and go there. Even then, you still may not see anything. Part of the electricity of encountering wild animals is the sheer unpredictability of the experience. But you stand a much better chance of giving one of those positive trip reports than when you don't plan for it.

Like so many good things in life, enhancing your chances of seeing wildlife is expensive. Wild animals stay away from highways, which are noisy and dangerous. During a one-week trip, you may see moose or caribou or some other creature from a road (or on a hike or while snowmobiling), or you may not. It's a matter of probabilities. With one very significant exception, you'll need a boat, a small plane, or some other means of traveling into large-mammal habitat. The significant exception is Denali National Park (see Chapter 19), where a bus ride on a road that's closed to the public leads to superb wildlife-viewing for a reasonable price.

Bottom line, what are your chances? I've seen every animal on the list in this section more than once, but that's after a lifetime of traveling in Alaska. On a short trip, you need to make an investment of time and money, you need luck, and you may need to be satisfied with seeing animals at a distance (binoculars are required). But if you try, you're almost certain to see some exciting wildlife in Alaska.

The following sections give you a brief introduction of the varieties of wildlife you may be lucky enough to view during your visit, including some distinguishing features, where they hang out, how easy they are to find (or not), and whether you need help to find them. For general safety tips in the event that you come too close to the most dangerous wildlife, see "Getting eaten by a bear (and such)," earlier in this chapter.

Bald eagle

The bald eagle, the symbol of America, is a huge bird of prey that has always been quite common and easy to find in Alaska.

- ✔ **Size:** 6- to 7½-foot wing span. Weight: 8 to 14 pounds.

- ✔ **Where to find them:** Bald eagles show up over most of the state, even wheeling around the high rise hotels in Anchorage. They're more common in coastal towns in Southeast and South Central Alaska, such as Seward, Homer, Juneau, and Sitka, where they feed on fish (see Chapters 16, 20, and 22).

- ✔ **Easy or hard to spot:** Easy. Go to the waterfront, and you see them.

- ✔ **Guided or on-your-own:** You can just take your binoculars to the beach. If you take a tour-boat ride to see other birds and animals, you're likely to see eagles, too.

- ✔ **ID notes:** Bald eagles take five years to mature into their distinctive white head; younger birds have mottled brown plumage.

Black bear

The smallest, most common, and least dangerous of North American bears, black bears show up in most of Alaska's coastal forests; in Southeast Alaska towns, they're often pests getting into the garbage.

✔ **Size:** 5 feet. Weight: 200 pounds.

✔ **Where to find them:** Locals in coastal communities often know salmon-spawning streams where bears congregate. The town of Wrangell has access to prime black-bear viewing; see my book, *Frommer's Alaska* (Wiley Publishing, Inc.).

✔ **Easy or hard to spot:** Hard. Without chartering a floatplane to certain spots at certain times, you can't count on finding black bear (although you have a good chance of stumbling across one).

✔ **Guided or on-your-own:** Most people don't focus on black bears. If you do, you need a knowledgeable float-plane guide to find them reliably (see the list in the section on brown bear).

✔ **ID notes:** Black bears come in many colors (even blue or white); you can distinguish them from a brown bear by the smoother back, bigger ears, and long, straight nose.

Brown bear (grizzly)

Also known as the grizzly bear when found inland, brown bears are among the largest and most ferocious of all land mammals, and among the most exciting to see. More than 98% of the U.S. brown bear population is in Alaska.

✔ **Size:** Up to 9 feet tall when standing. Weight: normally 250 to 900 pounds; maximum 1,400 pounds.

✔ **Where to find them:** Denali National Park (see Chapter 19), Katmai National Park, Kodiak Island (both in Chapter 24), near Homer (refer to Chapter 16), and Admiralty Island near Juneau (see Chapter 20).

✔ **Easy or hard to spot:** Can be easy. Certain surefire spots on salmon streams predictably gather many huge bears, but all are expensive to get to ($400 per person and up). Grizzly sightings are common but not assured on Denali National Park bus rides for much less cost; these are the smaller animals, under 500 pounds.

✔ **Guided or on-your-own:** Denali and Katmai National Parks are the on-your-own options (see Chapters 19 and 24). Other choices are with fly-in guides. From Homer, **Emerald Air Service** (☎ **907-235-6993;** Internet: www.emeraldairservice.com); in Kodiak, **Sea Hawk Air** (☎ **800-770-4295** or 907-486-8282; Internet: www.seahawkair.com); in Juneau, **Alaska Fly 'N' Fish Charters** (☎ **907-790-2120;** Internet: www.alaskabyair.com).

✔ **ID notes:** Brown bears are generally larger than black bears, and have a humped back and smaller ears.

Caribou

Alaska's barren-ground caribou are genetically identical to reindeer, but were never domesticated as reindeer were in Europe. For Inupiat and Athabaskan people, their huge herds remain an essential source of food and hides.

- ✔ **Size:** 4½ to 8 feet. Weight: 200 to 400 pounds; 700 pounds max.

- ✔ **Where to find them:** On broad tundra areas where you can see a long way, for example, along northern Interior highways, such as the Richardson, Dalton, or Denali (see Chapter 18); in Denali National Park (see Chapter 19); and in the Arctic (see Chapter 23).

- ✔ **Easy or hard to spot:** Hard. Caribou don't stand still and are shy of humans. You need some luck.

- ✔ **Guided or on-your-own:** You won't find any guided options for caribou viewing; your best chance is the Denali National Park shuttle bus ride.

- ✔ **ID notes:** Unlike other Alaska deer (including moose), caribou prefer open country and travel in groups.

Dall sheep

These sheep, which look like smaller versions of bighorn, stay in high, rocky places, where their incredible agility makes them safe from predators.

- ✔ **Size:** 4 to 5 feet. Weight: 150 to 300 pounds.

- ✔ **Where to find them:** Dall sheep live in high, craggy mountains over much of Alaska, but are usually difficult to spot. The notable exception is on the cliffs along the Seward Highway near Anchorage (Chapter 15), where they often venture near the road.

- ✔ **Easy or hard to spot:** Generally hard, but often easy on the Seward Highway near Anchorage.

- ✔ **Guided or on-your-own:** Just keep your eyes on the high cliffs and keep checking white spots you see with your binoculars; no guided option is available.

- ✔ **ID notes:** Mountain goats use the same habitat as Dall sheep; the goats have straighter horns and shaggier bodies.

Humpback whales

Behaviors, such as feeding by lunging through the surface and leaping completely out of the water for reasons unknown, make the huge humpback the most spectacular of whales to watch. I've seen leaping humpback from sea kayaks, looming above in the fog while I fish. In Alaska, you can find them reliably, in beautiful settings, and without many other boats around.

 ✔ **Size:** 50 feet. Weight: 45 tons.

 ✔ **Where to find them:** The very best, no-fail humpback watching is in Icy Strait near Gustavus, accessible by tour boat from Juneau or as part of a trip to Glacier Bay National Park. Go there also for sea kayaking among whales (see Chapter 20). Whales also usually show up in Sitka Sound near Sitka (refer to Chapter 22), in Resurrection Bay and Kenai Fjords National Park near Seward (see Chapter 16), and in Prince William Sound near Whittier (see Chapter 15).

 ✔ **Easy or hard to spot:** Easy, if you're willing to invest some time and money. For your best chance of success on any particular day, you have to spend some money on a tour-boat ride; budget $90 to $150 per person. Seeing humpbacks from a sea kayak requires a bigger commitment of time and money, plus a little of your own effort. Spotting them from shore is hit-and-miss.

 ✔ **Guided or on-your-own:** Booking a whale-watching boat ride is easy a few days ahead and even possible the day of the outing. From Juneau, take the *Auk Nu* passenger ferry (☎ **800-820-2628** or 907-586-8687; Internet: www.goldbelttours.com) to see whales in Icy Strait, near Glacier Bay. To see them from a sea kayak at Glacier Bay or Icy Strait, contact **Alaska Discovery** (☎ **800-586-1911** or 907-780-6226; Internet: www.akdiscovery.com). For tours from Whittier, Seward, or Sitka, see Chapters 15, 16, and 22.

 ✔ **ID notes:** Humpback whales have white fins up to 14 feet long that they use to slap the water.

Moose

In winter, when they move to the lowlands, Alaska's abundant moose can be a pest, blocking roadways and eating expensive shrubbery. In the summer, they're a little more elusive, often standing in forest ponds eating the weeds from the bottom or pruning willows from stream banks or disturbed roadsides.

 ✔ **Size:** 7 to 10 feet. Weight: 800 to 1,600 pounds.

 ✔ **Where to find them:** Moose live over much of Alaska, but show up most reliably in the Interior and South Central regions. Your best chance of seeing one is along a road in wet, brushy country.

 ✔ **Easy or hard to spot:** Seeing a moose by design is hard, but it's a rare month that goes by at our home in Anchorage when we don't run across at least one.

✔ **Guided or on-your-own:** You never know when you may see a moose.

✔ **ID notes:** Alaska moose can grow larger than horses, with brown, shaggy hides, bulbous noses, and heavy antlers.

Musk ox

The musk ox may be the strangest animal you'll ever see: a big, shaggy mop of a thing that seems to glide slowly over the tundra. The wool, said to be one of the earth's warmest fibers, is gathered from the tundra and knitted by Alaska Native women into exquisite garments.

✔ **Size:** 4- to 5-feet high at the shoulder. Weight: 400 to 800 pounds.

✔ **Where to find them:** Along the roads that radiate across the tundra from Nome (see Chapter 23).

✔ **Easy or hard to spot:** Getting to Nome is expensive; after you're there, a guide can find you a musk ox without much difficulty.

✔ **Guided or on-your-own:** You can rent a car in Nome and explore the surrounding roads. With less time, join a van tour with **Nome Discovery Tours** (☎ 907-443-2814; E-mail: Discover@nome.net).

✔ **ID notes:** If you see an animal that looks like it wandered out of a science fiction movie, you probably are observing a musk ox.

Orca (killer whale)

The starkly defined black-and-white patches of the orca seem painted by their creator to reflect the speed, agility, and fierceness of the ocean's top predator. You can easily feel envy when a well-organized family pod of orcas passes by your boat in calm procession.

✔ **Size:** 23 to 27 feet. Weight: 10 tons.

✔ **Where to find them:** Resurrection Bay from Seward (see Chapter 16), Prince William Sound from Whittier (see Chapter 15), and waters near Juneau (see Chapter 20).

✔ **Easy or hard to spot:** Moderate. Orcas aren't as predictable in their feeding locations as humpbacks, but good tour boat captains often know where to find the resident pod.

✔ **Guided or on-your-own:** Join a tour-boat cruise from Whittier or Seward (see Chapters 15 and 16). One marine biologist, leading tours by small boat from Whittier, is an expert at finding them: Gerry Sanger of **Sound Eco Adventures** (☎ 907-472-2312; Internet: www.soundecoadventure.com). See the "Humpback whales" section, earlier in this chapter, for a Juneau operator.

✔ **ID notes:** Look for the tall, black dorsal fin.

Polar bear

The polar bear is among the most scary and dramatic of all animals. To see one is a rare and unforgettable experience shared by few Alaskans and even fewer visitors. Polar bears, classified as marine mammals, live on the pack ice, north of Alaska, venturing ashore only at certain times.

- **Size:** 8 to 10 feet. Weight: 400 to 1,200 pounds; maximum 1,500 pounds.

- **Where to find them:** The only place for a visitor to see polar bears is at Point Barrow, on the shore of the Arctic Ocean north of Barrow (see Chapter 23), where they feed on a bone pile of leavings from an Eskimo whale hunt.

- **Easy or hard to spot:** Hard. Going to Barrow is expensive, and you must arrive at the right time (mid-October through June) and have good luck to see a bear. Moreover, regulatory changes are in progress that may limit access to Point Barrow (see Chapter 23 for details).

- **Guided or on-your-own:** You're better off hoping that you don't see a polar bear on your own! **Alaskan Arctic Adventures** (☎ 907-852-3800) is one of several companies that take Barrow visitors to the bone pile in off-road vehicles.

- **ID notes:** The polar bear is unmistakable.

Puffin (and other alcids)

The horned and tufted puffin is the most delightful of sea birds to encounter, with its large, brightly colored beak and comedic movements. When you enter their habitat of seaside cliffs, you also find many other *alcids,* fascinating sea birds that live only at sea.

- **Size:** 14 inches. Weight: 1¼ pounds.

- **Where to find them:** Kenai Fjords National Park, Homer (see Chapter 16), and Sitka (see Chapter 22).

- **Easy or hard to spot:** Easy during the summer season on a boat tour to the bird rookeries.

- **Guided or on-your-own:** For a good chance of seeing puffins, you need to get to the rocky, offshore bird rookeries on Alaska's southern coast. A tour boat is the best chance, with Kenai Fjords National Park leading the list (see Chapter 16). You can also see puffins on a sea kayaking tour (see "Sea kayaking" earlier in this chapter), with less certainty of success.

- **ID notes:** Horned puffins are the familiar kind (think Toucan Sam of Froot Loops fame); tufted puffins have tufts of feathers curling back from their heads.

Sea otter

The charming sea otter is quite common in coastal Alaska, rarely warranting a second glance from locals. Otters usually put up with close inspection as they float on their backs using their tummies as tables for shellfish or to carry their young.

- ✔ **Size:** Up to 4 feet. Weight: 40 to 90 pounds.

- ✔ **Where to find them:** All coastal waters off rocky shores; most common in Prince William Sound (see Chapter 15), and near Sitka (see Chapter 22), Juneau (refer to Chapter 20), Seward, Homer (see Chapter 16), Kodiak (refer to Chapter 24), and other shoreside communities.

- ✔ **Easy or hard to spot:** Easy. Often you don't even need to leave the dock, and you can expect a good look on a tour boat or sea kayak ride.

- ✔ **Guided or on-your-own:** Otters live in the ocean, where you need help to get to them. Any of the tour boats or sea kayaking guides in this book can get you to see them.

- ✔ **ID notes:** Tell the otter from seals and sea lions that are common in the same waters by their legs (the others have flippers); even when legs aren't showing, more of the otter shows above the surface.

Wolf

Unlike other parts of the United States, wild wolf populations in Alaska are plentiful, yet the animals are shy of humans, and sightings are a rare treat even here.

- ✔ **Size:** 3½ to 6½ feet. Weight: 75 to 145 pounds.

- ✔ **Where to find them:** Denali National Park (see Chapter 19) and other mountain tundra areas with long views, such as along the Richardson or Denali highways (see Chapter 18). Wolves live all over Alaska, but are hard to see in brush or trees.

- ✔ **Easy or hard to spot:** Very hard. Wolves don't like to show themselves. You need to be able to see a long way to have any chance of sighting a pack.

- ✔ **Guided or on-your-own:** Any wolf sightings are likely to be fleeting, lucky glimpses. Although wolf numbers are low in Denali National Park, conditions on the shuttle bus rides are good for making sightings.

- ✔ **ID notes:** I've seen wolves, yes, but I've heard them more often; listen for the howl during quiet outings in the evening, such as while hiking or cross-country skiing.

Choosing an Activity-Based Escorted Tour

If it seems intimidating to schedule an outdoor vacation in Alaska, you have an easier way. Book an outdoor escorted tour, a group exploration of some of the state's best activities and wildlife-viewing with a guide to take care of all the details. These trips are samplers of places and activities. The companies that offer them know the itineraries work and have polished the outings along the way to appeal to the majority of their guests. On the downside, you don't get to choose each stop or linger longer than the group. (For more on escorted tours, see Chapter 6.)

- **Alaska Wildland Adventures** (☎ **800-334-8730** or 907-783-2928; Internet: www.alaskawildland.com) is a leader in escorted tours, having pioneered the "Alaska safari," a highway tour from lodge to lodge, with fishing, rafting, wildlife-viewing, and the like scheduled along the way. Alaska Wildland owns an outstanding fishing lodge on the Kenai River, a wilderness lodge deep within Denali National Park, and another fly-in lodge outside the park, in addition to other high-quality facilities. Trips concentrate on Denali and South Central Alaska. Guides tend to be young and enthusiastic. Packages include choices for varying interests, and tours aimed at families with teens or younger children. It's not a cheap way to travel, however, with a ten-day safari costing about $4,200 per person.

- **Alaska Discovery** (☎ **800-586-1911** or 907-780-6226; Internet: www.akdiscovery.com) offers similar kinds of trips to Alaska wildland for comparable per-day prices, but in Southeast Alaska, and calls them "Inn-To-Inn Tours." The company is best known for more rigorous outdoor adventures and has superb guides for activities.

- **CampAlaska Tours** (☎ **800-376-9438** or 907-376-9438; Internet: www.campalaska.com), a bargain choice, offers more-affordable escorted outdoor tours by having guests sleep in tents rather than in expensive wilderness lodges or inns. CampAlaska Tours still does plenty of activities, and camping out helps the group build a sense of camaraderie. Schedules are loose so that you can pursue your own interests. Prices are about $125 a day.

Chapter 10

Booking Your Accommodations

● ●

In This Chapter

▶ Discovering your lodging options

▶ Reserving in plenty of time

▶ Getting a good rate

▶ Using the Internet

● ●

*T*he room you sleep in isn't the most important factor in determining how much you enjoy your trip, but it certainly is right up there close to the top of the list. You want to be comfortable, feel safe and clean, and have at least the amenities you're used to at home. But it also is nice when the room adds something to your vacation, giving you some insight into why living in Alaska is so worthwhile.

Alaska offers plenty of places that meet the first set of needs: Alaska has all the chain hotels you already know, with the comfort and predictability that make them reassuring. But those places are guaranteed to miss on the second criteria, so I recommend very few of them. When you want your lodging to add to your experience of Alaska and make you feel at home, you have to look a little harder.

Finding the Right Room

Authentically Alaskan accommodations come in different flavors. Wilderness lodges are the best, but they cost a lot ($300 or more per person, per night), they're often expensive to get to, and they usually have minimum stays of three days or more (which is as it should be, given the investment you put into getting to the lodge). A $5,000 stay at a wilderness lodge is probably not in the cards for you. On the other hand, many inns and bed-and-breakfasts (B&Bs) and some specialty hotels can also add to your feel for Alaska, saving you money over strictly anonymous accommodations.

Bed-and-breakfasts

If you haven't skipped over this section, you haven't discounted the idea of staying at B&Bs and small inns. I can offer some sensible reasons for using them but few reasons for avoiding them.

You don't have to worry about being stuck in junior's room in an otherwise ordinary family home; you can still find some places like that, but I don't list them in this book, and they're easy to steer clear of. Most B&Bs do have hosts who live there, but the rooms usually have the amenities (and twice the charm) of an ordinary hotel room, with a smaller bathroom and perhaps a small TV. The hosts are great assets when visiting a place like Alaska. They have stories to tell about bear and moose encounters (everyone has plenty of these), and they're full of advice for your trip. At best, they'll make you feel like you have friends in Alaska.

The other important benefit of staying at a B&B is the significant money you'll save. Rates are often $30 to $50 less than for a comparable room in a hotel, and the inclusion of breakfast saves you another $20 (for a couple). Expect to pay about $130 per night.

If you're vacationing with children or you have a disability, don't choose a B&B unless you first question the proprietor about whether you'll be comfortable in the rooms. B&Bs often have narrow stairs or small rooms that may not be suitable for you.

Hotels

Good, inexpensive hotel rooms can be found in Alaska's cities, but you won't find many of them (the good ones, that is). Instead, you'll find a variety of the standard hotel rooms (with an interior hallway and the expected amenities) with a wide range of prices. At the top of the list are the luxury hotels in the larger cities, which are often found in the town's tallest buildings. These rooms usually cost more than $200 a night. The next tier down consists of good, comfortable places that are often found in smaller buildings. Some of these establishments are operated by particular owners who keep the quality top notch. These rooms rent for $160 to $180 a night. Next are the budget lodgings, which are usually found in older buildings, with small rooms and perhaps less desirable addresses. I've found the good ones, where excellent management teams maintain decent rooms for a reasonable price. They charge $100 to $130 per night.

Wilderness lodges

Another category of hotels, which may be unique to Alaska, are hotels impersonating wilderness lodges. An Alaskan wilderness lodge, even a very expensive one, generally has plenty of rough edges but loads of authentic frontier atmosphere. Operating way out in the boonies, with difficult transportation, a short season, and a staff that has to live on-site, real wilderness lodges have to charge enough to make it. But in recent years, some beautifully built mid-sized hotels and small inns that are situated on the road system have taken on the wilderness lodge persona, with good results. They are in the upper end of the cost scale (upwards of $300 per night), but you end up feeling like you've been somewhere after staying there.

Knowing When to Reserve

With an upheaval in the travel industry, rooms have been much easier to get recently, but in general, coming to Alaska during the high season without all your rooms booked at least a month or two in advance is unwise. When you show up without a room, you'll surely find one somewhere, but you may go through plenty of trouble to find it — and it won't be anyone's first choice.

Lodgings that I recommend often book earliest because they're the best, so it makes sense to start reserving the minute you set the dates for your trip (six months should be adequate). Before June, or after August, rooms are much easier to reserve; you usually can have your choice with little advance notice. The exceptions are at a pair of winter destination resorts, Alyeska Resort and Chena Hot Springs Resort (see Chapters 15 and 17, respectively), which also have wintertime peak seasons.

Getting the Best Rate

Some hotels publish *rack rates* — the public rates that are really their maximums — without ever really meaning to charge them. I've run into hotel managers who try to keep the rack rate a secret, because they know it's outrageous and nobody pays it anyway: Everyone who comes in the door qualifies for a discount. But other lodgings, especially smaller establishments and budget places, really mean the rates they publish. Here are some tips on requesting a better rate and knowing when not to try.

Shop early for peak times

As your date nears and rooms book up, you have fewer choices, and that means you have to pay more. If you're coming to Alaska between mid-June and mid-August, January is not too early to be on the phone shopping among lodgings for the best prices and accommodations. Proprietors love early bookings and may be willing to compete for your business, especially when you let them know you're shopping around for the best price.

Travel off-peak

Rates crash like a bear stock market when the season starts winding down; big, luxury hotels often charge less than half their peak rates during the off-season, putting them in competition with the cheapest budget lodgings. Rooms stand empty, so you can show up at the desk and ask for their best deal, ready to walk next door if they don't go low enough. You can sometimes use these same tactics to get killer deals at the big, package-tour hotels at Denali and elsewhere on the day of your stay, even during high season, but that's only for gamblers.

Ask for discounts

Hotels (but not usually B&Bs and small inns) usually offer various discounts for people with travel club or other memberships, and some offer discounts just for anyone who asks. I recently told a reservationist that I wanted her hotel's AAA discount even though I don't have AAA; she laughed and said, "Sure." It never hurts to ask. Small places don't have these programs, but then you can dicker with the person reserving your room — B&Bs sometimes will knock something off the price when you stay more than one night or when you offer to pay cash. But don't count on it, and don't push it when they say no, because you can sour your relationship from the start.

Don't stop with the Internet

Using Web sites to shop for prices is great, but you need to follow up by checking out the establishments Web site or calling directly. Sometimes you can get a Web special, extra airline mileage, or other deals by contacting a hotel yourself (this works for rental cars and airline tickets, too). Check out the "Booking Rooms Online" section, later in this chapter, for more helpful info.

Book a package tour

Package tours, whether escorted or unescorted, often save you significant money over the à la carte approach to booking hotels. The big hotels at Denali National Park have set their rates to accentuate the value they give customers on their escorted packages (which makes up virtually the entire clientele). See Chapter 6 for more about booking packages.

Don't worry about it

If the thought of all this checking and calling and dickering makes you tired, don't fret over it. Some people ruin their vacations worrying about how much they've paid for things. (I know; I get letters from some of them.) The point is: Did you have a good time? Did you stay within your budget? If so, you got a good deal.

Booking Rooms Online

The Internet is a great way to find out about a hotel or B&B and to check availability and going rates. Virtually every hotel and B&B has its own Web site now, and you can discover a great deal about an establishment from what you see there (and from what you don't). I remain skeptical, however, about using Internet booking services to search for and reserve rooms. My spot checks of major Web sites have turned up huge gaps in coverage and some painfully inaccurate information (just now, on one of these booking-agency sites, I found a hotel listing that misstated the location by 111 miles). The more interesting and truly Alaskan places are the least likely to turn up on a search; mostly, standardized chains and franchises fill the lists. Besides, after you find a hotel on a search, checking its site directly to make sure that you like it and to possibly get a better deal simply makes sense.

Before discussing lodging choices in each city and region covered elsewhere in the book, I provide Web sites that link you with the local B&Bs or small inns. You can also go to Innsite.com (Internet: `www.innsite.com`), which lists these places all across the state (and around the world) and provides links to each establishment's own site. You can also start shopping and checking current prices, using national booking Web sites, including Travelocity.com or Expedia.com; the large hotels usually show up on these. If you have a favorite chain, search its site for locations and prices in Alaska.

Chapter 11

Money Matters

This chapter is about how to carry your money. Of course, you had to use something to buy this book, so you probably already have some idea of how to carry money. On a trip to Alaska, you need to carry more of it, however, and you may be tempted to change your habits. My advice: Keep it simple.

You've probably purchased gifts before, too, but perhaps not authentic Alaska Native art and crafts. You can come home from Alaska with something truly unique, but if you're not careful you can get ripped off instead, and in the process, help rip off the indigenous people of Alaska. Read on for advice about how to be part of the solution to counterfeiting and to discover some tips about the best way to handle your money while visiting Alaska.

Will That Be Cash or Credit: Ways to Pay

Alaska is as modern as any place in the United States, so you don't have to worry about relying on the barter system. Instead, pack your plastic, and keep cash on hand for emergencies or trips to wilderness lodges, some of which don't take credit cards.

ATMs and getting cash

An ATM card is by far the most convenient way to keep your wallet stocked with money. ATM machines are everywhere in Alaska. In the cities and along the road network, they're in every bank, grocery store, shopping mall, and gas station. In the bush, you can find one somewhere in every town that has jet service at the airport. ATMs are linked to national networks that almost always include your bank at home.

The two major networks in the United States are **Cirrus** (☎ 800-424-7787; Internet: www.mastercard.com) and **PLUS** (☎ 800-843-7587; Internet: www.visa.com); check the back of your ATM card to find out which network your bank belongs to. From the 800 numbers and Web site addresses for these networks, you can get the specific locations of an ATM close to where you are. Or you can just look out the window.

National banks with branches in Alaska include Wells Fargo, which is everywhere, Key Bank, and First Interstate. The latter two have far fewer branches. If your own bank doesn't have branches in Alaska, you can call to find out whether it's affiliated with a bank that does business in the state. Doing so may save you a charge of $1.50 or more for using a nonaffiliated ATM. Many banks limit the amount of money per day that you can withdraw from an ATM; before you depart, make sure that you know your bank's daily withdrawal limit. To reduce the withdrawal fees you pay, take out plenty of cash every time you use the ATM, or use your ATM card to buy something at the grocery store and get extra cash (with no extra fee).

Some credit cards let you obtain cash advances from ATMs or from a bank teller. However, interest rates and special fees for cash advances can be shocking. Remember that you start paying interest on the advance the moment that you receive the cash. Save this option for emergencies.

Traveler's checks

Traveler's checks have only one advantage: Many banks now charge a fee ranging from $1.50 to $3 whenever a nonaccount holder uses their ATMs. Your own bank may assess an additional fee for using an ATM that's not located at one of its own branches. What that means is that in some cases, you'll be charged twice just for using your ATM card while you're on vacation. In such cases, reverting to the use of traveler's checks may be a little cheaper (but certainly less convenient).

Not every merchant accepts traveler's checks, because merchants incur small fees when cashing them. Don't forget your ID — you'll need to show it every time you cash a check.

You can get traveler's checks at almost any bank. The three main companies that offer them are

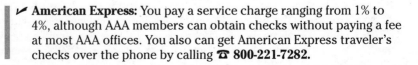

 ✔ **American Express:** You pay a service charge ranging from 1% to 4%, although AAA members can obtain checks without paying a fee at most AAA offices. You also can get American Express traveler's checks over the phone by calling ☎ 800-221-7282.

✔ **MasterCard:** Call ☎ **800-223-9920** for a location that sells these checks near you.

✔ **Visa:** These checks are available at Citibank locations across the country and at several other banks. The service charge ranges from 1.5% to 2.0%. Call ☎ **800-732-1322** for more information.

Credit cards

Credit cards are usually the best way to pay. They're a safe way to carry money, and they provide a record of all your travel expenses when you arrive home. Many credit cards give you some form of insurance against dishonest commercial behavior, and you can earn frequent-flier miles or get money back for every dollar that you spend. As long as you don't get in over your head and run up a balance that you can't pay at the end of the month, using a credit card is free.

Virtually every Alaska business accepts a variety of credit cards, even small B&Bs, convenience stores, and guys selling tourist junk from card tables on the street. Exceptions to the rule are ever-present, though, so checking is wiser than just looking at the stickers on the door or asking the waiter or clerk. Generally, you don't need cash except for taxicabs and incidentals so small that going through the credit-card signing ritual is just too much trouble.

Foreign currency exchange

When you're visiting from a foreign country, be sure to obtain some U.S. dollars before arriving in Alaska, because you won't find many places in Alaska that exchange foreign currencies. After that, you can use your credit and ATM cards whenever possible. The only dedicated foreign currency exchange desk is at the **Wells Fargo Bank** branch in the Fifth Avenue Mall in Anchorage (☎ **907-265-2093**; Internet: www.wellsfargo.com).

What to Do If You Lose Your Wallet

However you lose your wallet or purse — perhaps you misplaced it or you were a victim of a crime — it's an extremely unpleasant experience, but really nothing to panic over. Take the following simple steps:

✔ Call your credit-card company right away to report the theft. **Citicorp Visa**'s U.S. emergency number is ☎ **800-645-6556**. **American Express** cardholders and traveler's check holders need to call ☎ **800-221-7282** for all money emergencies. **MasterCard** holders need to call ☎ **800-307-7309**. Or you can call 800 information at ☎ 800-555-1212 to find out your card's 800 number. The credit-card company may be able to wire you a cash advance off your credit card immediately, and in many places, the company can get you an emergency credit card within a day or two.

✔ When you've purchased traveler's checks, call the emergency number provided with your checks and report the serial numbers of the stolen checks. Hopefully, you've kept the phone number and serial numbers in a location *other* than your wallet or purse.

✔ Call the police. Your wallet may be a lost cause, but you may need a police report number for credit-card or insurance purposes.

Help Alaska's Natives: Don't Buy Fakes

In a gift shop in Southeast Alaska, I watched as a woman who said she was an artist's assistant sanded a Tlingit-style carving. When I asked who made the carving, the artist said, "It's my work." At the time, that seemed like an odd way of putting it. Only later did I discover from one of the artist's former assistants that his "work" involved ordering the carvings from Southeast Asia and shipping them to Alaska, where he hired locals to pretend to be working on them in the shop. Journalists repeatedly document shops that fraudulently remove "Made in Taiwan" stickers, and the like, and replace them with one that reads "Made in Alaska." One journalist found an entire village in Bali carving "Alaska Native designs" out of materials sent from Alaska.

What's the scam?

Estimates vary regarding the amount of counterfeit Alaska Native art sold annually, but authorities put it at close to $100 million. That's money taken from Alaska bush villages where jobs in the cash economy are virtually nonexistent and prices for essentials such as fuel and housing are astronomical. Buying fake Alaska Native art is cultural and financial theft from subsistence hunters and fishermen who can least afford it. Besides, who wants to go home with an Eskimo mask made in Bali?

Federal enforcement has proved ineffective, which officials publicly acknowledge. Even in rare cases when dealers are caught, they go right on with the business. Some have found easy ways around the law. In one case, a Cambodian swindler spent a few months in an Alaskan village so that he could use its name when signing carvings with an Alaska Native-sounding pseudonym. The Federal Trade Commission has turned to educating the consumer as the only solution.

Eluding the scam

Avoiding the scam isn't difficult when you pay attention. A few tips include:

- ✔ **Asking questions before you buy.** Any reputable art dealer will provide you with a biography of the artist who created an expensive work.

- ✔ **Asking specifically whether that artist actually carved the piece.** Some Alaska Native artists actually have sold their names and designs to wholesalers who produce knockoffs.

- ✔ **Considering the cost.** Price is another tip-off. An authentic elaborate mask is more likely to cost $3,000 than $300.

- ✔ **Checking the material.** Another indicator is the choice of materials; most soapstone carvings, for example, are not made in Alaska. Authentic materials include ivory, bone, and animal furs and skin.

- ✔ **Making dealers stand behind their offerings.** Even craftwork that is less expensive needs to have the name of the person who made it attached, and the shop owner needs to be able to tell you how he or she acquired the item.

The **Alaska State Council on the Arts** (☎ 907-269-6610) authenticates Native arts and crafts with a **silver hand label,** which assures you that an item to which it is affixed was made by the hands of an Alaska Native with Alaskan materials. The problem: The program isn't universally used, so the absence of the label isn't necessarily proof of a fake. And yet, other labels aren't worth much: An item can legitimately say **ALASKA MADE** even when only insignificant assembly work happened here. Of course, in Bush Alaska, and in some urban shops, you can buy authentic work direct from craftspeople. Buying in Native-owned co-ops also is safe.

For gifts that don't claim to be made by Natives but nevertheless purport to originate in the state, a symbol of two bears that says **MADE IN ALASKA** (Internet: www.madeinalaska.org/mia) indicates that a state contractor has determined that the item was at least substantially made in Alaska. Non-Natives produce Alaskan crafts of ceramics, wood, or fabric, but not plastic. If it's plastic, it probably wasn't made here.

Chapter 12

Tying Up the Loose Ends

• •

In This Chapter

▶ Buying travel and medical insurance

▶ Reserving popular activities in advance

▶ Knowing what to pack — and how

▶ Getting your outdoor stuff to Alaska — without buying an extra airline seat

• •

*R*eady to go? Have you asked someone to feed the cat? I can't come over and feed your pet, but in this chapter, I discuss some important matters you need to resolve before you leave for Alaska — including what to do with the variety of insurance options, how to make sure you don't miss out on any activities, and what and how to pack for your trip.

I also solve a puzzle I've created. Throughout this book, I suggest that you do a lot outdoors in Alaska, but I also recommend that most visitors fly. So how do you get your gear to Alaska on a plane? It won't fit in the overhead bin or under the seat, but I do have some handy solutions.

Playing It Safe: Travel and Medical Insurance

Several kinds of travel insurance are available, ranging in value from essential to rip-off; I cover the differences below. Buying any sort of travel insurance is easy: Go to www.quotesmith.com and click on the Travel tab. The site allows travelers to get quotes from many insurance companies at once by providing the dates of the trip, the amount and type of coverage, and the age of the travelers. To contact a reputable firm directly, try **Access America** (☎ **800-284-8300;** Internet www.accessamerica.com), **Travel Guard International** (☎ **877-216-4885;** Internet: www.travelguard.com), or **CSA** (☎ **800-873-9855;** Internet: www.csatravelprotection.com).

Trip cancellation insurance

If you've already made many of your reservations, you've probably put down a lot of money in deposits. Alaska tour operators, guides, lodges, and bed-and-breakfasts all make this demand, and often with more rigorous refund requirements than you may be used to. These deposits are nonrefundable after a certain date. The reasons are understandable: Alaskans in the tourism industry have only two or three months to make a year's income, so they can't afford any significant number of no-shows that leave them with empty rooms or seats. But what if you get sick or bad weather intervenes and you can't get there? Or what if your airline goes bankrupt or a catastrophe prevents travel? You lose your deposits and your vacation. Trip cancellation insurance protects you against that dreadful possibility for around 8% of the cost of the trip. Given the uncertainty of Alaska travel, I think this insurance is worth the price.

Medical insurance

Medical insurance for travelers from outside the United States is a worthwhile investment, but probably doesn't make sense for most travelers from the United States, who likely are already covered under their regular health insurance. If you belong to an HMO, check to see whether you're fully covered while away from home.

Baggage and life insurance

Travel insurance that covers your baggage or covers you in the event of airplane catastrophes is unlikely to be a good deal. Your baggage is probably covered under your homeowners' policy or credit-card benefits. Besides, if the airline loses your bags, they're usually responsible for up to $2,500 per piece on domestic flights and about $640 on international flights. Don't check baggage worth more than that. Your chance of involvement in an airplane accident is so slim that selling insurance against it is a very good bet for the insurance company and a poor bet for you. Besides, ordinary life insurance covers you in these circumstances. Some credit cards (American Express and certain gold and platinum cards from Visa and MasterCard, for example) also offer automatic insurance against death or dismemberment in case of a plane crash.

Reserving Activities, Restaurants, and Shows

After you've reserved your flights, car, and rooms, you may think you're done planning your vacation. Not unless you want to spend the trip sitting in the room and the car. The highlights of an Alaska trip are the activities: fishing, wildlife-watching, flightseeing, and the like. Make reservations for most of these activities at least a few days in advance; for others (such as the Denali National Park bus tour), you should make reservations as soon as you know your vacation schedule. I let you know which activities need more advanced reservations in the destination chapters in this book. A few of the best restaurants also require advance reservations, and if you want to catch a popular performing arts event, you should check schedules before you leave home.

Booking your activities

As a general rule, the larger your party compared to the size of the entire group on the outing, the more important reservations become. If you want to fish, sea kayak, or take a bear-viewing flight on a certain day — all activities that involve four to ten people per outing — reserve a few days ahead; preferably a few weeks ahead to make sure that you get to do what you want on the day you're ready to do it. If your party is larger than three, make reservations even further in advance.

Likewise, if your vacation is short, reserve everything ahead. On a quick trip, you don't have flexibility in your schedule to adjust for booked-up activities. Besides, spending valuable vacation time on the phone trying to line things up at the last minute is a real drag.

When you call to reserve, always check for cancellation policies in case of bad weather so that you're not faced with the choice between losing a deposit and going on a seasickness-inducing or scary ride.

Set up your itinerary so that it includes an extra day after each weather-dependent activity. Even in summertime, weather often crops up to stop or disrupt outdoor activities, especially on the water. Guides, boat captains, and pilots won't put you in danger by going out in bad weather, but they may make you miserable on a tossing sea or bumpy aircraft, able to see little in driving rain. And, if the boat or plane is going out despite marginal weather, they may not want to give you your money back if you prefer to stay behind. However, if you have an extra day, most operators are more willing to reschedule than to give you a refund.

Certain activities are so difficult to book and so important to a great trip that you should, if possible, build your trip around them. Make the hard-to-get reservation first so that you have flexibility to accept any available dates. Then fill in your itinerary with that one date locked in. If you can adjust the dates of your entire vacation, you'll have an even better chance of doing the most popular activities.

Here are the main activities ranked by how quickly you need to act. I don't list activities included in package tours or multiday adventures, which are also integral to setting up your trip. (For activities without chapter references, see area-specific chapters for more information.)

- ✔ **Reserve as early as possible:**
  - Permit-limited bear-viewing hot spots, including Brooks Camp at Katmai National Park (Chapter 24) and Pack Creek on Admiralty Island in Tongass National Forest (Chapter 20)
  - Early morning Denali National Park shuttle bus rides (Chapter 19)
  - White Pass and Yukon Route rail tickets (Chapter 21)
  - Guided river fishing during run peaks (the only time you should fish for salmon)
- ✔ **Reserve a week or two ahead:**
  - Sea kayaking and ocean charter fishing
  - Fly-in fishing
  - Mount McKinley flightseeing from Talkeetna (Chapter 19)
  - Helicopter flightseeing in Juneau (Chapter 20)
  - Dog mushing and snowmobiling during peak periods (February and March)
- ✔ **Reserve a few days ahead:**
  - Whale-watching and tour-boat outings (on large boats)
  - Most flightseeing outings
  - River-rafting
  - Rental equipment such as bikes and canoes
  - Town tours and other bus tours
- ✔ **No need to reserve:**
  - Museums and other public facilities
  - Hiking and self-guided outdoor activities
  - Skiing

Reserving a table at restaurants

Just a few of the best restaurants in Anchorage fill up all reasonable dining hours on weekends several days in advance. If you plan on some special meals, read the listings in this book and call ahead to make sure that you can get a table at any that say, "Reservations recommended."

Getting the best seat in the house: Performing arts reservations

Although winter is the busy season for concerts and theater, you can catch shows in the summer also. Make your evenings more interesting by checking out what will be showing and arranging your schedule to attend a live performance. (Check Chapter 2 for happenings such as the Sitka Summer Music Festival.) The Web site or phone number of the festival itself is the best place to find event times and tickets.

 Anchorage boasts the state's most active performing arts scene. If you're planning to spend time there, you can check upcoming events on the *Anchorage Daily News* Web site at www.adn.com/weekend. You can buy tickets for most Alaska events through Tickets.com (☎ 800-478-7328).

Some events are aimed specifically at tourists, including gold rush melodramas, dramatic Robert Service poetry recitations, and films about wildlife or the aurora. You generally don't need to reserve these activities ahead, unless I note otherwise in my descriptions in each chapter.

Packing for the Hinterland (Or for Anchorage)

You'll find little use for a tie or any formal attire anywhere in Alaska, but you do need to prepare for broad swings in weather. This section helps you plan for changing weather conditions, but you should also remember to bring (or buy) the following:

- ✔ Binoculars
- ✔ Insect repellent
- ✔ Your prescription medications
- ✔ Identification and discount membership cards for organizations such as AARP or AAA
- ✔ Tickets, confirmation numbers, e-ticket confirmations, and so on
- ✔ Credit-card and ATM PIN numbers

Tips for summer clothing

You're not going to the North Pole, and in the summer, you don't need a down parka or winter boots weighing down your luggage. But you do need to be ready for a variety of weather, from sunny 80° days to windy, rainy 50° outings on the water.

The way Alaskans prepare for such a range is with layers. The content of the layers depends on what you're doing, but everyone should bring at least the following:

- ✔ Warm-weather clothes
- ✔ Heavy long-sleeved shirts and pants
- ✔ A wool sweater
- ✔ A warm jacket
- ✔ A waterproof raincoat and rain pants

Gloves and wool hats are a good idea, too, especially for boating trips. If you're camping, add synthetic thermal long underwear and wool socks to the list and make your jacket thick synthetic fleece. Combine these items, and you're ready for any summer conditions. For hiking, bring sturdy shoes or cross trainers.

Tips for winter clothing

You can be warm and comfortable no matter how cold it is. When you know how to dress, winter isn't a time of suffering, and the world of snow opens up to you. First though, what not to wear: People don't wear heavy arctic gear in town, even in the Arctic. To make the dash from car to heated building, all you need is a greatcoat, sweater, hat, gloves, wool socks, and long underwear. A pair of pants would helps too.

What you need for more active outdoor winter activities

For outdoor pursuits, what you wear depends on how active you are. The key to warmth and safety during vigorous outdoor activities is to wear layers of breathable clothing that stay warm when wet, such as wool or synthetics. With the following layers, you're ready for temperatures well below zero (at which point you won't want to ski or skate anyway). Strip off these layers for warmer temperatures:

- ✔ Synthetic thermal long underwear
- ✔ Synthetic fleece pants and coat
- ✔ Wool sweater

✔ Wind-resistant pants and jacket

✔ Wool socks and hat

✔ Warm boots with liners or covers

✔ Lined mittens

What you need for more sedate outdoor winter activities

For more sedentary outdoor activities, such as watching the aurora or riding a snowmobile or dog sled, you need warmer clothing. Likewise, drives on rural highways in winter require warm clothing in case of breakdowns. On guided trips or at cold-weather resorts, they either tell you what to bring or provide it for (or rent it to) you. A full outfit should include the following:

✔ Synthetic thermal long underwear

✔ The stoutest Sorel-style or Air Force bunny boots

✔ Insulated snow pants

✔ A heavy down parka with a hood

✔ Thick, insulated mittens (not gloves)

✔ A wool hat

✔ A face-insulating mask

✔ Ski goggles or quality sun glasses

You don't want any skin showing while riding a snowmobile or standing in a strong wind in below-zero (Fahrenheit) temperatures. Such a get-up costs more than $500. You can buy what you need in Anchorage at **Army Navy Store,** 320 W. Fourth Ave. (☎ **907-279-2401**), or in Fairbanks at **Big Ray's Store,** 507 Second Ave. (☎ **907-452-3458**).

Dressing like a local

One of the most dramatic examples of a culture clash I ever witnessed was during the *Exxon Valdez* oil spill, which I covered as a newspaper reporter. Suddenly, Texan oil executives in sharp suits flooded into little Alaskan fishing towns where, previously, a man in any kind of a business suit was enough to cause a double take. The Exxon executives took only a few days to figure out just how out of place they looked and how poorly that served their PR aims, and soon they all started wearing flannel shirts and blue jeans — crisply pressed flannel shirts and blue jeans. They stood out just as much as ever!

The uniform of coastal Alaska is simple: rubber boots, T-shirts or flannel shirts, and blue jeans or Carhart canvas pants. (Carhart brand clothes are those stiff, loose-fitting, rough-woven work clothes that you may have seen on your auto mechanic. They're for sale all over Alaska, especially at the shops listed at the end of the preceding section.) In inclement weather, add a fleece or lined Carhart canvas jacket and rubber rain gear. Fish blood on the clothing is a mark of pride. Away from the coast, the rubber boots may be replaced by hiking boots, and the Carharts become a permanent fixture: Mosquitoes can't bite through them.

If you don't really want to dress like a local, you won't go wrong with sturdy casual clothing. The great thing about Alaska is that no one really cares what you wear.

Flying with Outdoor Equipment

Backpackers already have compact equipment; they can just check the pack with the airline, and assuming the airline doesn't lose it, everything shows up on the other end. But family camping takes a lot more gear. Just the bedding for our family of six could fill the belly of a 747. Here are some tips for getting to Alaska with outdoor equipment:

- ✔ **Start with a list.** A list keeps you from forgetting things, and makes it easier to decide what *not* to take.

- ✔ **Figure out your limits.** Will you need to tote everything yourself to get on a train or boat, for example? If so, figure out who carries what and make sure each person can really carry his or her assigned items. If you rent a car at the airport, you don't have to carry everything at once, but it does have to fit in the car's trunk.

- ✔ **Start packing early.** You won't believe how much space all your stuff takes until you see it all together. If you start early enough, you'll have time for alternatives, such as buying smaller gear or arranging to rent gear at your destination.

- ✔ **Bring an extra collapsible bag.** One can be great for items you pick up on the way, for dirty clothes, or for segregating stuff you don't need so that you can stash it somewhere.

- ✔ **Mail back the extras.** You don't have to haul around souvenirs you buy or items you aren't using. Have shops mail them home for you. If you brought along something that's hanging around your neck like a mill stone (a friend told me a hilarious story of a trip weighed down by an old manual typewriter), stop in at a post office, buy a box, and mail it back. I list the location of a local post office in the "Fast Facts" section for each town in this book.

✔ **Don't bring what you can buy cheaply.** For example, water bottles are sold everywhere now with drinking water. Use a bottle for a few days, then throw it away and buy another one.

✔ **Arrange to rent as much as you can.** I list outdoor rental agencies in Anchorage and Juneau, Alaska's key gateways, in Chapters 13 and 20, respectively. Make sure to call ahead and reserve what you need. You can rent camping equipment as well as large items such as bikes, canoes, and sea kayaks.

✔ **Careful with that camp stove.** Airlines do not allow camp stoves on board with even the slightest odor of fuel. That means you can't bring a stove with a fuel tank on board. Don't try, as you will have to throw away your stove or miss the plane. Buy a propane tank or fuel tank in Alaska, or, if your stove has an attached tank that you can't take off, buy a whole new stove in Alaska.

Part III
Anchorage and Environs

The 5th Wave   By Rich Tennant

"Okay, I've got room for five in my plane. Who wants to go fishing this afternoon?"

In this part . . .

I've given Anchorage and the easy day trips around the city an entire three-chapter part in this book, and not just because it's my hometown. Anchorage is a fun city to visit and a perfect base of operations for a survey of the largest part of Alaska. You can do and see most of what you've come for within half a day's drive of Anchorage, and you can be in spectacular wild country less than an hour from the largest downtown hotel. With all the aircraft and other transportation options available, in addition to its big stores and offices, the city serves as Alaska's circulatory heart.

I cover the essentials of settling into Anchorage, including the hotels and restaurants to choose. You can discover what to do for fun in Anchorage, with the cultural attractions and the abundant outdoor offerings right in town. I also highlight easy day trips from Anchorage on the scenic Seward Highway, to the ski resort in Girdwood, and on Prince William Sound from Whittier, and the offerings of the Mat-Su Valley.

Chapter 13

Settling into Anchorage

● ●

In This Chapter

▶ Making your way to Anchorage

▶ Orienting yourself to Anchorage

▶ Making your way around Anchorage

▶ Finding accommodations

▶ Finding a good meal

● ●

Anchorage isn't a beautiful city, but it's in a beautiful place, and that's good enough. The main part of the city lies in the Anchorage Bowl, which is rimmed by the Chugach Mountains and the broad mud flats and swirling gray water of Cook Inlet. Either way — by air over the water to the west or on foot or bicycle into the mountains to the east — wilderness is only minutes away. Yet the town itself is quite civilized and firmly linked to the rest of the United States in its culture and in the look of the place. On a city street, if you keep your eyes off the mountains, you could be almost anywhere. But a few steps off the street, and you're into a greenbelt or a big natural park, ready to encounter moose, eagles, or beluga whales.

I wouldn't recommend that anyone spend an entire vacation in Anchorage (well, maybe a skiing vacation), but you can and should use the city as a base. As I discuss in earlier chapters, Anchorage is the cheapest gateway into the largest part of the state, with the state's most complete services and transportation network. The city is a world transportation hub; the airport here sees as much air cargo pass through as any in the United States and has the world's busiest float-plane base at Lake Hood. The Alaska Railroad is based here, and the three busiest highways meet close by. You need Anchorage, just as Alaskans do.

But the city is more than a jumping-off point; it has its own attractions, including several options for rainy-day activities. The state's biggest museum, an extraordinary Native cultural center, and Alaska's only zoo are here. And some of the state's best outdoor activities are found within the (quite large) city limits or on easy day trips to Prince William Sound or to the mountains and rivers north and south of town. You even find a performing arts scene, a choice of superb restaurants, and plenty of places to shop for art or schlock.

In this chapter, I cover the practical stuff — how to get to Anchorage and be comfortable there. In Chapters 14 and 15, I get more deeply into all the fun that makes you want to visit this great city.

Getting to Anchorage

Most folks who vacation in Alaska at least pass through Anchorage. It's a simple gateway, much like other mid-sized American cities, but some details can ease your way.

Flying in

You'll probably fly into Anchorage at the start of your trip, as it has the most flights linking Alaska to the rest of the world. The **Ted Stevens Anchorage International Airport** is a major hub. Seattle has the most frequent flights to Alaska, with numerous domestic carriers flying non-stop all day (see Chapter 6). Within Alaska, many flights route through Anchorage, even for communities much closer to each other than either is to Anchorage. **Alaska Airlines** (☎ 800-252-7522; Internet: www.alaskaair.com) is the dominant carrier for Alaska destinations and the only jet operator to most Alaska cities (see Chapter 7).

Various commuter carriers link Anchorage to rural destinations not served by jet. **Era Aviation** (☎ 800-866-8394 or 907-266-8394; Internet: www.eraaviation.com) is one of the largest for South Central Alaska destinations and can be booked directly or through Alaska Airlines.

The airport is perpetually under construction, but getting around it is still pretty straightforward. Here are some tips to get you oriented in the airport:

- ✔ **Domestic flights** (except for Delta Airlines) all use one terminal.

- ✔ The **international terminal,** which also houses Delta Airlines during the construction, is reached from the domestic terminal by a free shuttle bus.

- ✔ **Baggage claim** is downstairs next to the lower ramp, where taxis, airport courtesy vans, and airport shuttles make their pickups.

- ✔ **Rental-car counters** are in the tunnel below the lower ramp, which accesses the parking garage.

✔ An **ATM** is located behind the United Airlines desk in the north end of the main ticketing area.

✔ **Visitor information desks** at the airport are in the baggage-claim area in the domestic terminal and in the international terminal, in the lobby, and in the secured transit area.

Getting into town from the airport

Ted Stevens International Airport is right in the city, an easy trip from downtown. However, Anchorage is so big and spread out, getting around beyond downtown can be expensive without your own car.

Renting a car

The most practical way to tour this part of Alaska is to rent a car. Even if you're just staying in Anchorage, taxis are expensive to use because of the spread-out urban design. Most visitors travel to sites beyond downtown at least once a day for hiking, skiing, sightseeing, dining, or accommodations. Chapter 7 covers tips on renting a car or RV in Anchorage. Pick up your baggage and head down to the tunnel under the lower ramp, where the car-rental desks are located.

As you leave the airport, a divided highway leads east (toward the mountains); this is International Airport Road. At the first intersection, Spenard Road leads to the left, toward the main area of airport hotels. The next intersection is a large interchange. Follow the signs to head north on Minnesota Drive, which leads downtown.

Catching a cab or shuttle

Some hotels have free courtesy vans. That's the cheapest way to get to your hotel, and it allows you to postpone renting a car until you really need it. Find out the arrangement for getting the van when you reserve your room. If your hotel doesn't have a courtesy van, a taxi is the easiest way to get to your accommodations and costs little more than taking a shuttle even for a person traveling alone. The ride downtown from the airport costs about $14 (plus tip, about 15 percent is fine) and takes 15 to 30 minutes, depending on traffic. Try **Alaska Cab** (☎ **907-563-5353**).

You have a number of private airport shuttle options. One, the **Borealis Shuttle** (☎ **888-436-3600** or 907-276-3600; Internet: www.borealisshuttle.com), covers the whole city, charging by zones; from the airport to downtown, they charge $12 for the first person plus $2 for each additional person.

Arriving by car

Only one road connects Anchorage to the rest of the world: the Glenn Highway, which starts downtown as 5th and 6th avenues. From Anchorage, it leads through the Mat-Su Valley area and Glennallen to Tok, where it meets the Alaska Highway, 330 miles from Anchorage. To go to Denali National Park and Fairbanks, take the Parks Highway, which branches from the Glenn Highway 30 miles out of Anchorage. Alaska's highways are covered in Chapter 18. The Mat-Su area is in Chapter 15.

The only other road out of town, the Seward Highway, leads south to the Kenai Peninsula (see Chapters 15 and 16). If you arrive in the region by cruise ship or ferry, your ship will probably land in Seward, 124 miles from Anchorage. Cruise lines take care of the bus or rail transfer to Anchorage. The highway becomes Ingra and Gambell streets in downtown Anchorage, where it meets the origin of the Glenn Highway.

Arriving on the train

Some cruise-ship passengers arrive in Anchorage by rail from Seward. The depot is downtown on 2nd Avenue, a short cab ride to any downtown hotel.

Figuring Out Anchorage

Navigating Anchorage is easy if you just remember that the mountains are to the east. The "Anchorage" map, later in this chapter, gets you familiar with the major streets, but to find a particular address, you need to pick up a more detailed map at one of the visitor centers I mention in the "Street Smarts: Information After You Arrive" section, later in this chapter.

Downtown

Many visitors here for only a day never make it beyond the **downtown** area, the old-fashioned grid of streets at the northwest corner of town where the large hotels and the gift shops are located. Street numbers and letters work on a simple pattern. Numbered avenues run east and west. Lettered streets run north and south. East of A Street, north–south streets have the alphabetized names of Alaska places (Barrow, Cordova, Denali, Eagle, and so on). Check out the "Downtown Anchorage" map, later in this chapter, for a detailed look at this easy-to-navigate area.

Midtown and the rest of the Anchorage Bowl

Most of Anchorage beyond the compact downtown area is a newer creation, built in the western model of commercial strips along big roads. **Midtown,** just south of downtown, is the main added-on commercial center. South Anchorage is roughly everything south of Dimond Boulevard and includes **Hillside,** the district east of the Seward Highway in the foothills and mountainsides of the Chugach Range. It's not important for you to remember the names of most other neighborhoods.

Three major north–south thoroughfares run from downtown, through Midtown, to the shopping malls and residential districts of **South Anchorage.** These are **Minnesota Drive,** which becomes I and L streets downtown; **C Street** and **A Street;** and the **New Seward Highway,** which is Ingra and Gambell streets downtown and heads out of town to the south. Major east–west roads in the grid are Fifth and Sixth avenues, becoming the **Glenn Highway** and leading out of town to the north; **Northern Lights Boulevard** and **Benson Boulevard,** running across the city in Midtown; and **Dimond Boulevard,** in South Anchorage.

Beyond the Bowl

Some parts of Anchorage are outside the Bowl defined by the Chugach Mountains. The communities of **Eagle River** and **Eklutna** are northeast of Anchorage on the Glenn Highway; go a little farther that way and you reach the **Mat-Su Valley. Girdwood** and the **Portage Glacier** are on the Seward Highway, to the south. A tunnel near the glacier leads to **Whittier** and **Prince William Sound.**

Street Smarts: Information After You Arrive

Besides the information desks at the airport, you can get questions answered at the **Log Cabin Visitor Information Center,** downtown at Fourth Avenue and F Street (☎ **907-274-3531**). It's open daily June through August 7:30 a.m. to 7:00 p.m., in May and September 8 a.m. to 6 p.m., and October through April from 9 a.m. to 4 p.m. The **Anchorage Convention and Visitor Bureau** (☎ **907-276-4118**; Internet: www.anchorage.net) operates the information center.

Diagonally across the street is an indispensable stop for anyone planning an outdoors trip, the **Alaska Public Lands Information Center,** at 605 W. Fourth Ave. (☎ **907-271-2737;** TTY: 907-271-2738; Internet: www.nps.gov/aplic). It's open daily from 9 a.m. to 6 p.m. in summer and Monday through Saturday 9 a.m. to 4 p.m. in winter. Not just a place to get advice and information, it's also an outdoors museum. Located in a 1930s post office and federal courthouse, this information center boasts exhibits in a grand room with high ceilings. All the land agencies are represented, you can buy ferry tickets from the Alaska Marine Highway System, an excellent selection of trail and field guides is available, and rangers are on hand with advice based on personal experience.

Getting Around Anchorage

In 1970, the population of Anchorage was less than half of what it is today, and large sections of today's city were forest and swamp. It achieved its current form and size by 1985. That's just 15 years to build a city. Maybe there wasn't enough time to do it right. In any event, Anchorage ended up as one big sprawl.

If you plan to break out of the older, pedestrian-friendly downtown area, you're almost forced to rent a car. Taxis often cost as much or more, and taxis in Anchorage are of low quality. The bus transit system is inadequate and a poor use of valuable vacation time. Bus tours are available; they're good for orientation or to get to the Alaska Native Heritage Center, but otherwise not a good way to get around (find out more about guided tours in Chapter 14).

Driving around town

Driving in the city is simple, at least in the warm months. The roads are wide and straight, turning right at a red light is permitted, finding your way with a map is easy (just remember the mountains are east), and parking is not a problem (half the town is parking lots). If you have trouble finding a space downtown, just duck into one of the many pay-to-park public lots or garages. The fees don't break you at any of these places, but you pay cheaper fees farther east.

The allowable blood alcohol level in Anchorage is low: 0.08 percent. Penalties for driving while intoxicated are extremely stiff: Besides mandatory jail time, big fines, and fees, Anchorage police can take away your car and sell it.

Winter driving can be a challenge. The roads are slick and the lines between lanes become invisible under snow and ice. Winter driving is a skill, but the principles are simple: go slow, accelerate gradually, and plan ahead so that you are prepared to stop safely. When starting from a stop, apply as little gas as possible; avoid spinning your wheels. Renting a four-wheel-drive vehicle is probably worth the money. Avoid a car with rear drive wheels; front-wheel drive handles much better on ice.

For winter drives to outlying areas, such as the ski resort in Girdwood, check on road conditions with the Alaska Department of Transportation's hot line or Web site (☎ **800-478-7675;** Internet: `www.dot.state.ak.us`). Occasionally, the road to Girdwood, the Seward Highway, is closed by avalanche conditions or is undrivable because of wet ice. See earlier in this chapter and Chapter 7 for more information on driving in Alaska.

Grabbing a cab

If you can't drive, taking a taxi is your second best choice. Because of the size of the city, taxis are an expensive way to get around, but if you plan your trips carefully and don't go anywhere way out — such as the zoo, Chugach State Park, or Eklutna — you can make it work. The other problem with using cabs in Anchorage is that they tend to be poorly maintained and some of the drivers are pretty weird. Because of the way the cab system is set up here, money goes into the pockets of middlemen, not into maintaining the cars or paying the drivers. I've had the best luck with Alaska Cab (☎ **907-563-5353**), but don't take that as an enthusiastic endorsement.

Hailing a cab usually isn't possible, so you need to call. Normally, a cab comes within ten minutes of being called, but if you need one around the time the bars close (2 a.m.) or near the start of the workday, and you want to be on time, allow at least half an hour extra. If you leave something in a cab, call the cab company. To file a complaint, call the Transportation Inspection Division (☎ **907-786-8525**).

Waiting for the bus

It takes a long time to go far using the **People Mover** bus system (☎ **907-343-6543;** Internet: `www.peoplemover.org`), but if saving money is your primary concern, it is inexpensive and covers most of the city (but not the airport). Bus fares all over town are $1.25 for adults, 75¢ for ages 5 to 18. You need exact change, or you can buy tokens at the downtown transit center at Sixth Avenue and G Street. A free zone in the downtown core is called DASH. Most buses come every half-hour during peak hours, but are less frequent off-peak and on weekends. You spend a lot of time waiting for the bus and transferring, so most of the system's users are people who have no other way to get around.

Riding a bike

The network of bike trails is a great way to see the best side of Anchorage, but not a practical means of transportation for most people. The city is just too large. The **Tony Knowles Coastal Trail** comes right downtown, linking to trails that weave along greenbelts all over town. The trails and bike rental are covered in Chapter 14.

Using shoe leather

In the downtown area, the simplest way to get around is on foot. If you're spending only a day in Anchorage before heading off to activities elsewhere in the state, you don't need to go any farther than downtown for an interesting visit, and so you don't need transportation.

Where to Stay in Anchorage

Find a place in Anchorage you can use as a handy base for your trip. If you're using the airport frequently for getting around the state, staying in that part of the city makes sense. If you don't plan to rent a car, renting a room downtown gives you foot and bike access to the greatest number of attractions. If you're renting a car, you can stay anywhere in the city. If you reserve the same room for each time you pass through the city, you can stow extra baggage there and, when you come back for your subsequent stay, receive an extra level of hospitality.

Anchorage is a good place to consider staying in a bed-and-breakfast or small inn for two reasons. First, compared to a similar room in a hotel, you save at least $50 a day with the lower rate and the breakfast that is included. Second, it offers a chance to make a personal link with a local, your host, who can give you insider advice and regale you with stories of Alaskan adventure (the visitor bureau gives all residents an annual exam to make sure we have enough bear stories).

I've searched for some of the best small places, choosing those with character and reasonable prices. Anchorage has hundreds more, many of them just as good. One cool way to shop for a room is on the cooperative Web directory maintained by the **Anchorage Alaska Bed and Breakfast Association** at www.Anchorage-BnB.com. The many links go straight to the Web sites of individual B&Bs, and members police each other's quality. The association's hotline (☎ **888-584-5147** or 907-272-5909), answered by members in turn, offers referrals to places that meet callers' requirements. **Alaska Private Lodgings,** P.O. Box 200047, Anchorage, AK 99520-0047 (☎ **800-401-7444** or 907-258-1717; Fax: 907-258-6613; Internet: www.alaskabandb.com), represents B&Bs, cabins, and the like in Anchorage and over much of the state and can help with itinerary planning. Their directory of B&Bs is on the Web site, with pictures.

The top hotels and B&Bs

Aurora Winds Inn B&B Resort
$$$$ Hillside

This massive house far up the hillside in South Anchorage (near the zoo and Glen Alps trailhead) has rooms so grand and theatrically decorated you feel as if you're in a James Bond movie. Bed-and-breakfast is a misleading term here; whoever heard of a B&B with a dining room that looks like a ballroom, a lap swimming pool, a well-equipped gym, and a sound-proof theater with a huge projection TV? (They also offer a sauna, laundry machines, and fish freezing.) Each of the five bedrooms has a sitting area and decorative details that make it unique, elegant, or even campy, and amenities such as VCRs, dataports, coffeemakers, hair dryers, and irons. The bathrooms are also showplaces: Three have Jacuzzis, and one is larger than a lot of hotel rooms, with an "environmental habitat chamber." One lovely room has windows overlooking the deck and forest on three sides. The large outdoor hot tub is set in luxuriant gardens. You need a rental car to stay here.

7501 Upper O'Malley Rd., Anchorage, AK 99516. ☎ *907-346-2533. Fax: 907-346-3192. Internet:* www.aurorawinds.com. *Rack rates: High season $125–$195 double, low season $75–$155 double; extra person $15 in high season, $10 in low season. Rates include full breakfast. AE, DC, DISC, MC, V.*

Caribou Inn
$$ Downtown

Some of the rooms are large and the location is prime; right downtown. The carpet and fabrics were in good shape when I visited, but the Caribou is an old wooden building in need of some work, and much of the furniture is garage-sale style. All 14 rooms are nonsmoking, although a cigarette odor hangs in common rooms. Five rooms share bathrooms. Full kitchens are available, and many rooms have VCRs or refrigerators. The inn has a self-serve laundry. You'll do no better on price for respectable hotel lodgings downtown, especially when you count the money saved on the included breakfast, airport transfer, and parking pass. And you run into other budget-conscious summer visitors, not the flophouse clientele at downtown hotels charging comparable rates. If the hospitality isn't exactly warm, think of the money you're saving.

Anchorage

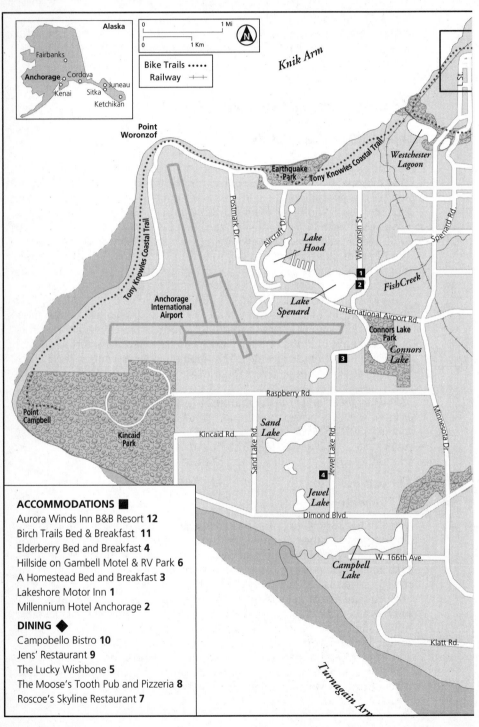

ACCOMMODATIONS ■
Aurora Winds Inn B&B Resort **12**
Birch Trails Bed & Breakfast **11**
Elderberry Bed and Breakfast **4**
Hillside on Gambell Motel & RV Park **6**
A Homestead Bed and Breakfast **3**
Lakeshore Motor Inn **1**
Millennium Hotel Anchorage **2**

DINING ◆
Campobello Bistro **10**
Jens' Restaurant **9**
The Lucky Wishbone **5**
The Moose's Tooth Pub and Pizzeria **8**
Roscoe's Skyline Restaurant **7**

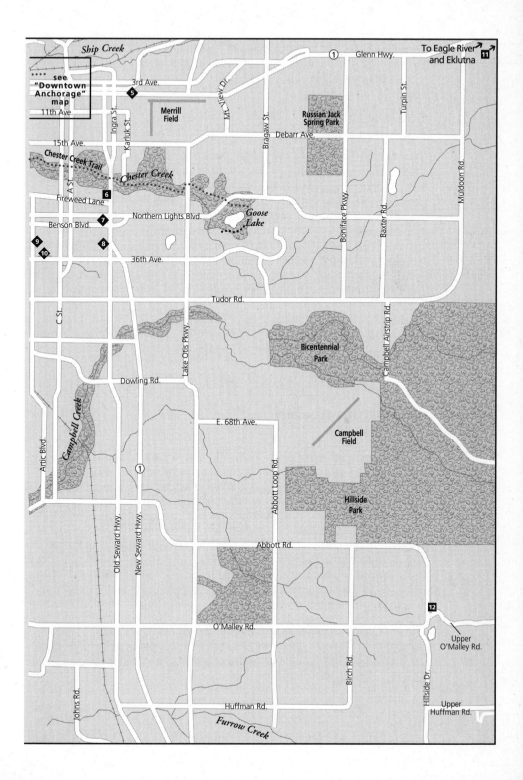

501 L St., Anchorage, AK 99501. ☎ ***800-272-5878*** *or 907-272-0444. Fax: 907-274-4828. Internet:* www.alaska.net/~caribou. *Rack rates: Summer $89 double with shared bathroom, $99 double with private bathroom; winter $49 double with shared bathroom, $59 double with private bathroom; $15 each additional person. Rates include full breakfast. AE, DC, DISC, MC, V.*

Copper Whale Inn

$$$$ **Downtown**

The Copper Whale consists of a pair of clapboard houses right downtown. They overlook the water and Elderberry Park on the Coastal Trail, with 18 charming rooms of every shape and size. (The inn rents bikes for the trail.) The place has a wonderfully casual feeling, with a host who serves a full breakfast and befriends guests. The rooms in the newer building, lower on the hill, have cherry-wood furniture and high ceilings on the upper level. Two rooms that share a bathroom in the old building have great views. A separated annex lacks the same charm. Rooms don't have TVs, but in some you can get one hooked up by request. All have dataports and irons. High-speed Internet is available in the lobby.

440 L St., Anchorage, AK 99501. ☎ ***866-258-7999*** *or 907-258-7999. Fax: 888-WHALE-IN or 907-258-6213. Internet:* www.copperwhale.com. *Rack rates: High season $120 double with shared bathroom, $155–$185 double with private bathroom; low season $69 double with shared bathroom, $95 double with private bathroom; extra person $10. Rates include full breakfast. AE, DISC, MC, V.*

Duke's 8th Avenue Hotel

$$$ **Downtown**

This cinderblock apartment house downtown was converted into surprisingly light and comfortable one- and two-bedroom suites with full kitchens. A family or business party on a long stay can save a lot of money here: The basic rate on two-bedroom units accommodates four adults, and children 12 and under stay free (the one-bedroom-unit rates are for two people, but could sleep a family of five for the base price). Moreover, the cooking and dining setup is adequate for real meals. On the downside, the four-story building has no elevator and is not accessible for the disabled, and the lowest level, with room numbers starting with 100, is a half basement. Each of 28 units has two telephones and an extra line for your computer. A cheap self-serve laundry is available, too.

630 W. Eighth Ave., Anchorage, AK 99501. ☎ ***800-478-4837*** *or 907-274-6213. Fax: 907-272-6308. Internet:* www.hotel.alaska.com. *Rack rates: High season $140–$165 suite, low season $80–$105 suite; children 12 and under stay free in parents' room. AE, DC, DISC, MC, V.*

Hillside on Gambell Motel and RV Park
$$ Midtown

On a busy highway near a car dealership and self-storage business, this funny little motel is a friendly oasis. The 26 rooms are clean and well maintained and have features — such as microwave ovens, refrigerators, coffeemakers, dataports, and hairdryers — that make them quite practical, if not luxurious or up to date. Six have kitchenettes, and you'll also find a cabin for four and a coin-op laundry. The wooded Lanie Fleischer Chester Creek Trail, for biking, walking, or Nordic skiing, is just beyond a gate in the RV park (full hookups are $24). You need your own wheels to stay here.

2150 Gambell St., Anchorage, AK 99503. ☎ *800-478-6008 or 907-258-6006. Fax: 907-279-8972. Internet:* www.hillside-alaska.com. *Rack rates: High season $89–$129 double, low season $60–$86 double, extra person $10. AE, DISC, MC, V.*

A Homestead Bed and Breakfast
$$ Airport

This is a real 1930s homestead house built of logs, once remote but now just a few minutes from the airport and Kincaid Park. Frank and Patricia Jasper have lived in the house for more than 30 years, and they've kept it an authentic slice of Alaska. One of the rooms is a charming log cabin with plank floors, the other is a many-room upstairs suite with four beds, an outside entrance, and many odd corners and pieces of furniture. Both rooms have cooking facilities. It's a great deal. (Beware, an entirely different place on Spenard Road has an almost identical name.)

6141 Jewel Lake Rd., Anchorage, AK 99502. ☎ *907-243-5678. Fax: 907-248-6184. E-mail:* jasper@chugach.net. *Rack rates: Summer $95 double, winter $65 double; extra person $20. Rates include full breakfast in summer, continental in winter. MC, V (5% surcharge for credit cards). No smoking.*

Hotel Captain Cook
$$$$$ Downtown

This is Alaska's great, grand hotel, where royalty and rock stars stay. (For a mere $1,500 a night, you can stay in the same suites they do.) Former governor Wally Hickel built the first of the three towers after the 1964 earthquake, and now the hotel fills a city block and anchors the downtown skyline. Inside, the brown decor has a fully realized (maybe a little excessive) nautical theme, with art memorializing Cook's voyages and enough teak to build a square-rigger. The regularly updated rooms are decorated in a rich, sumptuous style using exquisite fabrics, unique pieces of custom-built furniture, and lots of varnished trim. It works, but with dark colors that are not currently fashionable — you can't find a scrap of pale wood or generic beige in the whole place. Rooms are comfortable in size, but not as large as modern upscale chains, and all have a choice only of a king or two twin beds. Amenities include in-room Internet, voice mail, dual-line dataports, hair dryers, and irons. Lots of custom tile and mirrors make up for the relatively small size of the bathrooms. The hotel offers great views from all sides, and you don't pay more to be higher. The pool and health club with racquetball courts in the basement are among the best in town, and the business center is exceptional, like a real office.

Sophisticated continental food and elaborately formal service justify the high prices at **The Crows Nest,** the city's most traditional fine-dining restaurant, located on the hotel's top floor. Pheasant, quail, bison, and venison were on recent menus, as well as the usual seafood, beef, and lamb. All tables have stupendous views, and high-backed booths lend a sense of intimacy. The deliberate service requires that you set aside a full evening for a special meal — dinner unfolds gradually, with almost theatrical formality. Main courses range from $26 to $50. **Fletcher's,** off the lobby, is an English pub serving good Italian-style pizza and sandwiches. **The Pantry** is more than a typical hotel cafe, with excellent service and interesting entrees mixed in with more predictable choices. The **Whale's Tail** serves light meals with a long bar in a sort of men's club barroom.

Fourth Ave. and K St. (P.O. Box 102280), Anchorage, AK 99510-2280. ☎ 800-843-1950 or 907-276-6000. Fax: 907-343-2298. Internet: www.captaincook.com. *Rack rates: High season $240–$250 double, $260–$1,500 suite; low season $130–$140 double, $150–$1,500 suite; extra person $20. AE, DISC, MC, V.*

The Oscar Gill House Bed & Breakfast

$$ **Downtown**

On the Delaney Park strip, just a few blocks from downtown, this is truly the oldest house in Anchorage. Named after an early civic leader, the house itself has a complicated history. It was built in 1913, in Knik (before Anchorage was founded), and moved here on a barge a few years later. The house was to be torn down in 1982 but was moved to storage by a historic preservation group; Mark and Susan Lutz saved it in 1994, transferring it to its present location and, with their own labor, restoring it authentically as a cozy, friendly bed-and-breakfast. Now it's on the National Historic Register. The house is full of appropriate antiques, and manages to be both homey and immaculate. The Lutzes are good people and like to get to know their guests. The three rooms have TVs, dataports, hair dryers, and irons; one has its own bathroom. Free bikes are available. The breakfast is great. Book early, as they fill; you can check availability and even select a room on their Web site.

1344 W. 10th Ave., Anchorage, AK 99501. ☎ *and Fax:* **907-279-1344.** *Internet:* www. oscargill.com. *Rack rates: High season $95 double with shared bathroom, $110 double with private bathroom; low season $65 double with shared bathroom, $75 double with private bathroom; extra person $15. Rates include full breakfast. AE, MC, V.*

The Voyager Hotel
$$$$ **Downtown**

Thanks to its exacting proprietor, Stan Williams, the Voyager is just right, down to the quality of the linen. The size is small (38 rooms); the location central; the rooms large and light, all with well-designed kitchenettes; and the housekeeping exceptional. The desks have speaker phones, high-speed dataports, and extra electrical outlets; and the hospitality is warm yet highly professional. The hotel offers nothing ostentatious or outwardly remarkable, yet the most experienced travelers rave about it the loudest.

501 K St., Anchorage, AK 99501. ☎ **800-247-9070** *or 907-277-9501. Fax: 907-274-0333. Internet:* www.voyagerhotel.com. *Rack rates: high season $169 double; low season $89 double; extra person $10. AE, DC, DISC, MC, V. No smoking.*

Runner-up accommodations

Anchorage Marriott Downtown
$$$$$ **Downtown**   This is a newer high rise with a nice pool and fabulous views from rooms with wall-size picture windows. *820 W. Seventh Ave.* ☎ **800-228-9290** *or 907-279-8000. Internet:* www.marriotthotels.com.

Birch Trails Bed & Breakfast
$$ **Eagle River/Chugiak**   A half-hour out of town, this home-style B&B belongs to a dog-mushing family offering rides (see Chapter 14). The 24 dogs bed down in the yard just outside. They have a hot tub and serve a full breakfast — the inn, not the dogs. *22719 Robinson Rd., Chugiak, AK 99567.* ☎ **907-688-5713.** *E-mail:* birchtrails@excite.com.

Elderberry Bed and Breakfast
$ **Airport**   If you enjoy staying in a family home, this one has hosts who socialize with guests and tell about their Alaska experiences. *8340 Elderberry St., Anchorage, AK 99502.* ☎ **907-243-6968.** *Internet:* www.elder berrybb.com.

G Street House
$$ **Downtown**   An elegant home hosted by a wonderful family (he's on the city assembly, and she's an expert on local history). *1032 G St., Anchorage, AK 99501.* ☎ **888-235-2148** *or 907-276-3284.*

Lakeshore Motor Inn

$$$ **Airport** At $129 double in the peak season, this place has the lowest priced, consistently acceptable standard hotel rooms I have found near the airport. *3009 Lakeshore Dr., Anchorage, AK 99517.* ☎ *800-770-3000 or 907-248-3485. Internet:* www.lakeshoremotorinn.com.

Millennium Hotel Anchorage

$$$$$ **Airport** The lobby, with warm colors and fly rods and animal mounts on display, suggests a huge fishing and hunting lodge. Rooms are luxurious and well equipped. *4800 Spenard Rd., Anchorage, AK 99517-3236.* ☎ *800-544-0553 or 907-243-2300. Fax: 907-243-8815.*

Susitna Place

$$ **Downtown** An eight-room B&B with a handy downtown location and lovely views over Cook Inlet from atop a bluff on a quiet side street. *727 N St., Anchorage, AK 99501.* ☎ *907-274-3344. Internet:* www.susitnaplace.com.

Where to Dine in Anchorage

Anchorage offers some great dining experiences. The regional cuisine of fresh salmon, halibut, shellfish, and sometimes game dominates all fine dining establishments, and as long as they don't overcook the fish or keep it frozen for too long, you can't go wrong. The very best restaurants, however, use these ingredients creatively, combining various international styles in exciting and unexpected ways. (And you can always get a steak, too.)

But dining in style is expensive and takes a long time. Most people can't afford to do it every night. Moreover, some of our family and friends who have come to Alaska are already tired of salmon by the time they get to our house, and I'm ready to throw a sockeye fillet on the grill. So I include plenty of other, less expensive places, too. If I've listed them here, they're good, but read on to discover which places offer a unique Alaskan experience and which just serve satisfying meals.

The top restaurants

Campobello Bistro

$$ **Midtown** **Northern Italian/Bistro**

This quiet little strip mall restaurant is amazingly like stepping into northern Italy, except for the Alaska seafood. Even the service has the

Downtown Anchorage

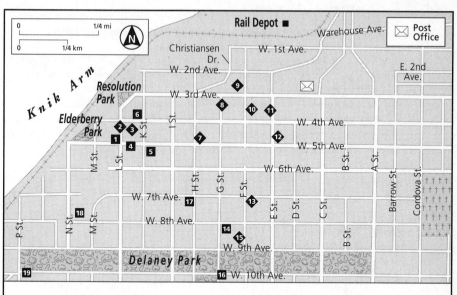

ACCOMMODATIONS ■
Anchorage Marriott Downtown **17**
Caribou Inn **4**
Copper Whale Inn **1**
Duke's 8th Avenue Hotel **14**
G Street House **16**
Hotel Captain Cook **6**
The Oscar Gill House Bed & Breakfast **19**
Susitna Place **18**
The Voyager Hotel **5**

DINING ◆
Cilantro's Mexican Restaurant **15**
Club Paris **12**
Dianne's Restaurant **13**
Downtown Deli and Cafe **11**
Glacier Brewhouse **7**
Kumagoro **10**
The Marx Brothers Cafe **9**
Orso **7**
Sacks Cafe **8**
Simon and Seafort's Saloon and Grill **2**
Snow City Cafe **3**

quality of jocular professionalism that I remember from Italy. Unlike most of Anchorage's best restaurants, they don't try to reinvent the cookbook here. Most of the menu consists of recognizable dishes, such as veal Marsala or Italian sausage and polenta. Meals are bold, highly flavored, and entirely satisfying. The seafood crepe is fantastic. Those seeking the bland tomatoes and cheese of a typical Italian family restaurant should go elsewhere. (Sorrento's and Romano's, both on Fireweed Lane, each do that tried-and-true formula well.) The wine list and food are reasonably priced.

661 W. 36th, Ste. 10. ☎ ***907-563-2040.*** *Lunch: $8–$13. Dinner main courses: $13–$23. DC, MC, V. Open: Mon–Fri 11:00 a.m.–2:30 p.m., Tues–Sat 5–9 p.m.*

Cilantros Mexican Restaurant

$ **Downtown Mexican**

Authentic, inexpensive Mexican food is served in this charming little house on the park strip. Each cheerful but sparsely decorated dining room is large enough for only a few tables, and the Spanish-speaking staff whizzes past over scuffed wood floors. Our meals were just right: from the warm, thick chips with salsa that hit the table when we did, to the ample and flavorful main courses that came not much later, to the bill, which, including everything for two, amounted to $14. They serve from the entire, very long menu all day, including breakfast; the huevos rancheros are great. They serve no alcohol.

611 W. Ninth Ave. ☎ *907-279-8226. Breakfast: $4.25–$6. Lunch and dinner: $5–$11. MC, V. Open: Mon–Fri 11 a.m.–10 p.m., Sat–Sun noon to 9:30 p.m.*

Club Paris

$$$$ **Downtown Steak/Seafood**

Coming in from a bright spring afternoon into midnight darkness, under a neon Eiffel Tower and past the bar, I sat down at a secretive booth for two, and felt as if I should lean across the table and plot a shady 1950s oil deal with my companion. And I would probably not have been the first. In contrast to Sullivan's Steakhouse across the street, which contrives a masculine, retro feel, Club Paris is the real thing, decorated with mounted swordfish and other cocktail-era decor. The club is the essence of old Anchorage boomtown years, when the streets were dusty and an oil man needed a class joint in which to do business. Steak, of course, is what to order, and rare really means rare. Ask for the blue cheese stuffing; the stuffed filet is worth the years it probably takes off your coronary arteries.

417 W. Fifth Ave. ☎ *907-277-6332. Internet:* clubparisrestaurant.com. *Reservations recommended. Lunch: $5.75–$15. Dinner main courses: $14–$44. AE, DC, DISC, MC, V. Open: Mon–Sat 11:30 a.m.–2:30 p.m. and 5–11 p.m., Sun 5–10 p.m.*

Dianne's Restaurant

$ **Downtown Soup/Sandwich**

This is my first choice for a quick, healthful, inexpensive lunch downtown. Located in the base of a tall, glass office building, Dianne's cafeteria line fills with well-dressed folk seeking the hearty, freshly baked bread, soups, sandwiches, and specials turned out for the lunch hour. The atmosphere is bright and casual, and you don't waste your day eating. No liquor license.

550 W. Seventh Ave., Ste. 110. ☎ *907-279-7243. All items: $4–$7.75. AE, DISC, MC, V. Open: Mon–Fri 7 a.m.–4 p.m.*

Glacier Brewhouse

$$$ Downtown   Grill/Seafood/Pizza

An eclectic and ever-changing menu is served in a large dining room with lodge decor, where the pleasant scent of the wood-fired grill hangs in the air. They brew eight or more hearty beers behind a glass wall. It's noisy and active, with lots of agreeable if trendy touches, such as the bread, made from spent brewery grain, that's set out on the tables with olive oil. An advantage for travelers is the wide price range — a feta cheese, spinach, and artichoke pizza is $10; crab legs are $34. The food is usually quite good. Choose it for a boisterous meal with quick, casual service that gets you out in time to do something else with the evening (although you may have to wait for your table, even with a reservation).

737 W. Fifth Ave. ☎ *907-274-BREW. Internet:* www.glacierbrewhouse.com. *Reservations recommended for dinner. Lunch: $8–$15. Dinner main courses: $9–$34. AE, DC, DISC, MC, V. Open: High season daily 11 a.m.–11 p.m., low season Mon 11:00 a.m.–9:30 p.m., Tues–Thurs 11 a.m.–10 p.m., Fri–Sat 11 a.m.–11 p.m., Sun 4:00–9:30 p.m.*

Jens' Restaurant

$$$$ Midtown   International

Chef Jens Hansen is truly gifted. His restaurant is for the kind of diner who loves exciting food, surprises, beautiful plates of new tastes and textures, and meals that are about the food, sharing bites, and saying "Wow" and "How did he do that?" I won't call it experimental, because I've never had a meal here that wasn't perfect, but the cuisine is highly eclectic and there's often only one item on the changing menu that isn't unusual or challenging: the superb pepper steak. Like everything, even that dish has a sauce, and it is complex and memorable. The wine list is exceptional and reasonably priced, and you can sip it while dining inexpensively on appetizers in a pleasant bar area; try the incredible spinach ravioli with Gorgonzola, for example. Desserts also are sublime, such as the chocolate pâté with chocolate sauce, laced with black raspberry sauce. The dining room is light and clean, decorated with modern art. Service is highly professional, with each formally attired waiter assigned to just a few tables. Lunch is a different experience; for the full treatment, go for dinner.

701 W. 36th Ave. ☎ *907-561-5367. Internet:* www.jensrestaurant.com. *Reservations recommended. Lunch: $9–$16.50. Dinner main courses: $18–$28. AE, DC, DISC, MC, V. Open: Mon–Fri 11:30 a.m.–2:00 p.m., Tues–Sat 6–10 p.m. Closed Jan.*

The Lucky Wishbone

$ Downtown   Diner

This Anchorage institution (in high school, we called it "The Bone") is where the locals go for a delicious, not-too-greasy fried chicken dinner and famous milk shakes (try the hot fudge) and other delights from the fountain. One section of the counter is reserved for discussion of aviation and golf, or you can pull up to the drive-in. When the beloved owners outlawed smoking years ago, it made the front page of the newspaper. You see few other tourists, as the location, among the car dealerships at the extreme east end of downtown, is too far to walk to from the hotels, but I ran into Alaska's powerful senior U.S. senator, Ted Stevens.

1033 E. Fifth Ave. ☎ 907-272-3454. All items: $3–$9.25. MC, V. Open: Summer, daily 10 a.m.–11 p.m.; winter, daily 10 a.m.–10 p.m.

The Marx Brothers Café
$$$$ Downtown   Eclectic/Regional

A restaurant started by three friends back when gourmet food was an exotic hobby in Anchorage is now a standard of excellence in the state. Treatments of Alaska seafood that started as cutting-edge creative cuisine here now turn up in many of the best restaurants. Chef Jack Amon still presides in the kitchen of the cottage downtown, one of the city's first houses. And maître d' Van Hale still presides out front, preparing his famous Caesar salad at tableside, a ritual that allows him to schmooze with anyone he chooses in the tiny dining rooms. His attitude mirrors the casual elegance of the entire evening. The cuisine is varied and creative, ranging from Asian to Italian. A meal is an experience that takes much of the evening. Waiting in the small entryway can be uncomfortable if your table isn't ready. The wine cellar is famous.

627 W. Third Ave. ☎ 907-278-2133. Internet: www.marxcafe.com. *Reservations required. Main courses: $19.50–$42.50. AE, DC, MC, V. Open: Summer, daily 5:30–10:00 p.m., winter, Mon–Thurs 6:00–9:30 p.m., Fri–Sat 5:30–10:00 p.m.*

The Moose's Tooth Pub and Pizzeria
$ Midtown   Pizza

The best pizza and beer in Anchorage undoubtedly comes from this fun and friendly place. The microbrewery came first, but the pizza really is the greater accomplishment. It has a soft, light crust like Italian pizza but the oomph of American pizza. They offer many ingenious toppings, but not just to dump on: The combinations really work. Dine inside (perhaps in the "hippie pad"), or at picnic tables outside in a tent that's open year-round — that's the best place in town to take kids for dinner. The same hip guys also own the Bear Tooth Café, at 1230 W. 27th Ave. (☎ 907-276-4200), where they serve pizzas, burritos, and wraps from 11 a.m. to 11 p.m. daily, next door to their cinema/pub (see Chapter 14).

3300 Old Seward Hwy. ☎ 907-258-2537. Internet: www.moosestooth.net. *Large pizza: $12.50–$25. DISC, MC, V. Open: Summer, Sun–Thurs 11 a.m. to midnight, Fri–Sat 11 a.m.–1 a.m., winter, Sun–Mon 11 a.m.–11 p.m., Tues–Thurs 11 a.m. to midnight, Fri–Sat 11 a.m.–1 a.m.*

Roscoe's Skyline Restaurant

$$ Midtown   Soul Food/Southern

Roscoe built up this large mall restaurant from a shack where he used to barbecue out back in a cut-off steel barrel. The place hasn't lost any of the authenticity or friendly, homey service in the transition, but now the dining room is comfortable and well appointed. Roscoe still table-hops to make friends by talking about food and his impressive collection of black entertainment memorabilia. The barbecue and fried chicken are justly famous.

600 E. Northern Lights Blvd. (in the Sears Mall). ☎ *907-276-5879. Lunch: $6–$8. Dinner main courses: $11–$16. AE, MC, V. Open: Mon–Thurs 11 a.m.–9 p.m., Fri–Sat 11 a.m.–10 p.m., Sun noon to 6 p.m.*

Sacks Café

$$$ Downtown   Creative/Eclectic

This is the most fashionable restaurant in town, and also one of the best. The storefront dining room, in warm Southwest colors and sharp angles, resembles a showcase for the food and diners, who can sit at tables or a tapas bar. It was remodeled by one of the city's most exciting architects, Mike Mense. The cuisine defies categorization, but is consistently interesting and creative, frequently with Thai influences. The menu changes, but one recent offering was chicken with scallops, shiitake mushrooms, snow peas, udon noodles, ginger cream sauce, and black bean salsa. Vegetarians do as well as meat eaters. For lunch, the sandwiches are unforgettable, with choices such as shrimp and avocado with herb cream cheese on sourdough. The beer and wine list is extensive and reasonably priced. They serve brunch Saturday and Sunday.

328 G St. ☎ *907-274-4022. Internet:* www.sackscafe.com. *Reservations recommended for dinner (reserve a day ahead for weekend nights). Lunch: $5.25–$12.95. Dinner main courses: $15–$28. AE, MC, V. Open: Daily 11 a.m.–3 p.m., Sun–Thurs 5:00–9:30 p.m., Fri–Sat 5:00–10:30 p.m.*

Simon and Seafort's Saloon and Grill

$$$$ Downtown   Steak/Seafood

Simon's, as it's known, is the most fun fine-dining place in town, a jolly beef and seafood grill where voices boom off the high ceilings. On sunny summer evenings, the rooms, fitted with brass turn-of-the-century saloon decor, fill with light off Cook Inlet, down below the bluff. The views are magnificent. The food is consistently very good. A long list of nightly specials includes items as exotic as a tasty crab- and macadamia-stuffed halibut, but most of the cuisine is simpler. The service, too, stands out; warm and professional, and quick enough to allow time for other evening activities. Children are treated well. To enjoy the place on a budget, order a sandwich and soup for lunch in the well-stocked bar.

420 L St. ☎ *907-274-3502. Reservations recommended (make dinner reservations a couple of days in advance in summer). Lunch: $7–$15. Dinner main courses: $16–$40. AE, MC, V. Open: Mon–Fri 11:15 a.m.–3:30 p.m. and 5–10 p.m., Sat–Sun 5–10 p.m.*

Runner-up restaurants

Downtown Deli and Café

$ **Downtown   Deli** A good sandwich restaurant founded by former Governor Tony Knowles before his success in politics. Best choices are the quiche of the day, breakfasts, and the salmon dinner. Kids are treated well. *525 W. Fourth Ave.* ☎ *907-276-7116. All items: $6.25–$12. AE, DC, DISC, MC, V. Open: Summer, daily 6 a.m.–10 p.m., winter, Sun 9 a.m.–4 p.m., Mon–Tues 7 a.m.–4 p.m., Weds–Sat 7 a.m.–9 p.m.*

Kumagoro

$$$ **Downtown   Japanese** A good, authentic Japanese restaurant right on the main tourist street downtown. Try the lunch box ($14.30), a large sampler of many dishes, including sushi and sashimi. The dining room is pleasantly low-key, with tables in narrow rows. Beer and wine license. *533 W. Fourth Ave.* ☎ *907-272-9905. Lunch: $6.50–$14.30. Dinner main courses: $13.20–$39. AE, DC, DISC, MC, V. Open: Summer, daily 11:00 a.m.– 10:45 p.m., winter, daily 11:00 a.m.–9:45 p.m.*

Orso

$$$ **Downtown   Italian** A large, theatrically decorated place serving a combination of northern and southern Italian cuisine with some local seafood inventions. The menu is set up in the multi-course Italian style, but the huge portions are designed to make a meal of just one course. *737 W. Fifth Ave.* ☎ *907-222-3232. Reservations recommended. Lunch: $8–$14. Dinner main courses or pasta: $12–$26. AE, DC, DISC, MC, V. Open: Summer, Mon–Fri 11:00 a.m.–2:30 p.m., 4:30–11:00 p.m., Sat–Sun 4:30–11:00 p.m., winter, Sun–Mon 4:30–9:30 p.m., Tues–Thurs 4:30–10:00 p.m., Fri–Sat 4:30–11:00 p.m.*

Snow City Café

$ **Downtown   Vegetarian/Home Style** This meeting place for a young, environmentally conscious crowd serves good food with interesting flavors and styles of preparation, including many vegetarian dishes. Breakfast is something of an event (the restaurant is full of people on weekends), with eggs Benedict, salmon cakes, homemade granola, and so on (served all day). *1034 W. Fourth Ave.* ☎ *907-272-CITY. Lunch: $5–$10. AE, DISC, MC, V. Open: Mon–Fri 7 a.m.–4 p.m., Sat–Sun 8 a.m.–4 p.m.*

Chapter 14

Exploring Anchorage

● ●

In This Chapter

▶ Discovering the top sights

▶ Getting outside and finding more to do

▶ Planning an Anchorage itinerary

▶ Shopping, Alaska style

▶ Painting the town at night

● ●

*Y*ou can find plenty to do for a few days in Anchorage, but not all of it is indoors. As good as a museum may be, it's got nothing on flying over Mount McKinley in a classic DC-3. (Compare perusing regional art with the most spectacular hours you ever spend.) The process of setting priorities isn't difficult. If the sun is out, stay outside. If it rains, check out the indoor attractions until it stops. That's how Alaskans do it, with one exception. They stay outside in the rain, too.

Now, a quick note on definitions. I define anything that involves the world out of doors as *outdoors,* not just bear wrasslin' or rock climbing with your fingernails. Driving to a fabulous mountain overlook or riding in a classic aircraft over a wildly rugged terrain counts as outdoors in this book, too. So you don't have to be active to see the good stuff. You *do,* however, need an interest in the outdoors, for participation or observation. But don't get me wrong: The indoor stuff isn't bad, either. This chapter helps you plan your Anchorage explorations, and it includes two maps, "Anchorage Attractions" and "Downtown Anchorage Attractions," to help you chart your course.

Hitting the Top Sights

Alaska Native Heritage Center
Muldoon (east of downtown)

Alaska Natives built this extraordinary center to bring their cultures to the visitors. It's Alaska's best Native cultural attraction. What makes it so is not the graceful building or the professional and informative

Anchorage Attractions

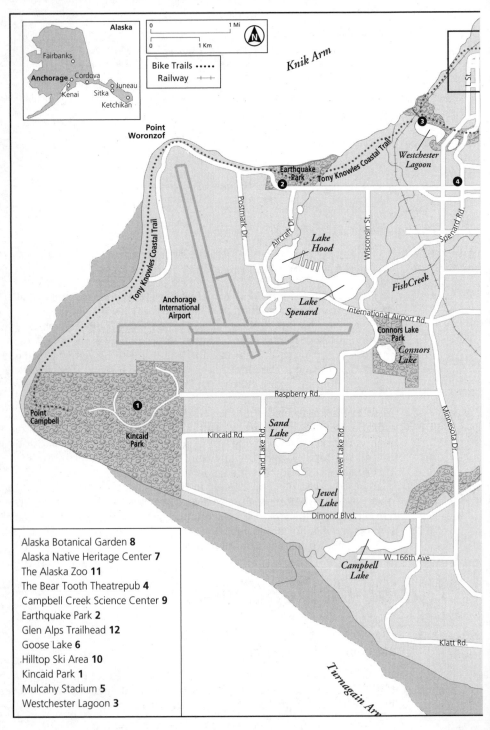

Alaska Botanical Garden **8**
Alaska Native Heritage Center **7**
The Alaska Zoo **11**
The Bear Tooth Theatrepub **4**
Campbell Creek Science Center **9**
Earthquake Park **2**
Glen Alps Trailhead **12**
Goose Lake **6**
Hilltop Ski Area **10**
Kincaid Park **1**
Mulcahy Stadium **5**
Westchester Lagoon **3**

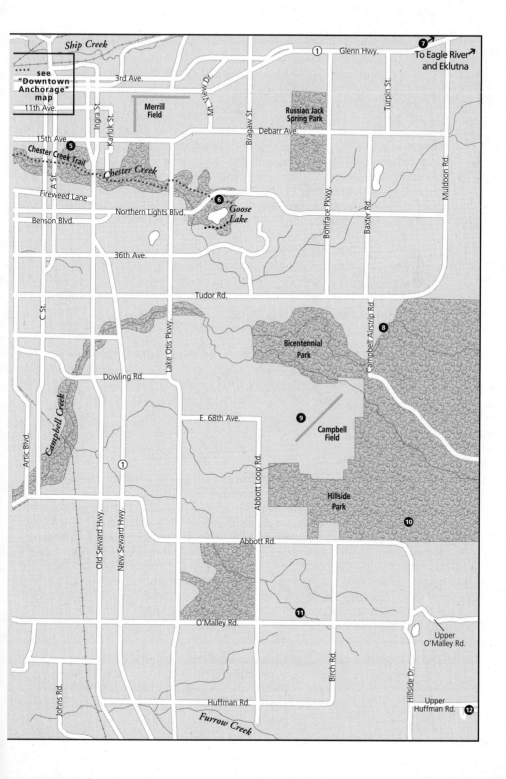

Ship Creek

see "Downtown Anchorage" map

3rd Ave.
11th Ave.

Merrill Field

Ingra St.
Kartuk St.
A St.

Mt. View Dr.

Bragaw St.

Glenn Hwy.

Turpin St.

To Eagle River and Eklutna

Russian Jack Spring Park

Debarr Ave.

15th Ave.

Chester Creek Trail

Chester Creek

Fireweed Lane

Northern Lights Blvd.

Goose Lake

Boniface Pkwy.

Baxter Rd.

Muldoon Rd.

Benson Blvd.

36th Ave.

Tudor Rd.

C St.

Lake Otis Pkwy.

Bicentennial Park

Campbell Airstrip Rd.

Dowling Rd.

Campbell Creek

E. 68th Ave.

Campbell Field

Artic Blvd.

Old Seward Hwy.

New Seward Hwy.

Abbott Loop Rd.

Hillside Park

Abbott Rd.

O'Malley Rd.

Birch Rd.

Upper O'Malley Rd.

Johns Rd.

Huffman Rd.

Furrow Creek

Hillside Dr.

Upper Huffman Rd.

displays, but the Native people themselves, real village people, who often make a personal connection with visitors and, at least on our visits, rarely come across as practiced or distant.

The three main parts of the center take much of a day to absorb; allow three hours, not for the exhibits, but to have time to interact with the people. First, storytellers and dancers perform in a hall with two 30-minute programs rotating through the day. The second part features a 10-minute film, a gallery of educational displays, and a series of workshops, where artisans practice and show off traditional crafts. Finally, don't miss the pond surrounded by five traditional Native dwellings representing five cultural groups, each with a Native host. Complete your day at the snack bar for soup and sandwiches. Then stop by the gift shop where inexpensive items are mixed in with real Native arts and crafts for sale by the center, or on consignment from Native artisans.

The center is about the same distance from downtown as the airport, but to the east. It's a 10- to 25-minute drive, depending on traffic. You can take a cab or choose one of two tours from downtown (see "Seeing Anchorage by Guided Tour," later in this chapter). Or rent a car, perhaps for the same amount you'd pay to take a taxi or a tour, depending on the size of your party. That way, you have the car for dinner out or other explorations.

From the Glenn Hwy. (Sixth Avenue downtown), take the North Muldoon exit. ☎ *800-315-6608. Internet:* www.alaskanative.net. *Open: Summer, daily 9 a.m.–6 p.m., winter, at least Sat–Sun noon to 5 p.m., call for additional hours and winter discounts. Admission: $19.95 adults, $14.95 children 5–12. AE, MC, V.*

The Alaska Zoo
Hillside

It's no big-city zoo, but the Alaska Zoo has a charm all its own. Anchorage residents have developed personal relationships with the animals, many of which are named. Watch Oreo and Ahpun, the brown and polar bear buddies, play and swim underwater (they have a Web cam, too). Gravel paths meander through the woods past large enclosures with natural flora for bears, seals and otters, musk oxen, Dall sheep, moose, caribou, waterfowl — all the animals you were supposed to see in Alaska but may have missed. (Your Alaskan trip itinerary definitely *didn't* include an elephant, Siberian tigers, or Bactrian camels, though all are residents of the Alaska Zoo. But try to keep them out of your snapshots — they blow your best wildlife stories.)

You can easily spend half a day wandering the zoo, but if it's raining, you may not want to, because the zoo offers little shelter. A snack bar serves basic meals, and a large gift shop is on site. Getting there is practical only if you have your own wheels, as the drive from downtown is 25 minutes without traffic. (Take the New Seward Hwy. to O'Malley Rd., then turn left and go 2 miles.)

*4731 O'Malley Rd. ☎ **907-346-3242**. Internet:* www.alaskazoo.org. *Open: Daily from 10 a.m., closing time varies by season, summer educational Tuesdays at 7 p.m. Admission: $8 adults, $7 seniors, $5 children 12–17, $4 children 3–11, free under 3. MC, V.*

Anchorage Museum of History and Art
Downtown

The state's largest museum doesn't have its largest collection, but unlike the Alaska State Museum in Juneau or the University of Alaska Museum in Fairbanks, the Anchorage museum has the room and staff both to teach and to serve as a center of contemporary culture of a regional caliber. Most visitors tour the large Alaska Gallery, an informative and enjoyable walk through the history and some of the anthropology of the state. In the art galleries, you can see what's happening in art in Alaska today; Alaska art isn't all scenery and walrus ivory, but the grandeur of the state does influence almost every work. The Anchorage museum also gets or mounts the best touring and temporary exhibits; recent shows on Yupik masks, Russian exploration, and Rockwell Kent were unforgettable. It's the only museum in Alaska that requires more than one visit, but you can get a good taste in two hours. The restaurant, operated by the excellent Marx Brothers Café (see Chapter 13), serves some of the best lunches downtown. Call for lectures, openings, and jazz happenings many summer evenings.

*121 W. Seventh Ave. ☎ **907-343-4326**. Internet:* www.anchoragemuseum.org. *Open: May 15–Sept 15, Fri–Wed 9 a.m.–6 p.m., Thurs 9 a.m.–9 p.m. Sept 16–May 14, Tues–Sat 10 a.m.–6 p.m., Sun 1–5 p.m. Admission: $6.50 adults, $6 seniors 65 and older, free for children 17 and under.*

The Imaginarium
Downtown

This science museum is one of my kids' favorite places. It's geared to children, with few words and lots of fun learning experiences. The idea is that while they're running around having a great time, the kids may accidentally learn something; at least, the displays will excite a sense of wonder that is the start of science. A strong Alaska theme imbues many of the displays. The saltwater touch tank is like an indoor tide pool. Allow an hour or two. Grownups will enjoy it along with children, but perhaps not without such accompaniment.

*737 W. Fifth Ave., Ste. G. ☎ **907-276-3179**. Internet:* www.imaginarium.org. *Open: Mon–Sat 10 a.m.–6 p.m., Sun noon to 5 p.m. Admission: $5 ages 13–64, $4.50 ages 2–12 and 65 and older.*

Getting Outdoors: Summer and Winter in the City

In most cities, you have to go somewhere else for a natural outdoor experience. In Anchorage, you may be able to do it right from your hotel. The city is a shallow scratch of civilization on a vast wilderness that otherwise remains intact. You find big parks with plenty of wildlife right in among the cars and strip malls. Just beyond the last houses, but still within the city limits, is Chugach State Park, one of the largest and most beautiful in the nation (indeed, many *national* parks don't come close). You can drive right to some of its most impressive views.

If you miss the outdoors, you're missing the whole point of Anchorage.

I cover some indispensable outdoor day trips in Chapter 15: Although you can't do them all, you should do at least one. Here I cover the top outdoor places and activities right in town, including activities that take place far afield but begin and end at the airport here (such as flightseeing and fly-in fishing).

In town, the city's bike trails connect through greenbelts that span the noisy, asphalt urban core with soothing creekside woods. Kincaid Park

Gearing up in Anchorage

You can rent almost anything you need for outdoor activities in Anchorage.

✔ **Backcountry gear and Nordic skis:** You can get advice and rent sea kayaks, cross country skis, snowshoes, bear-proof containers, and mountaineering equipment at **Alaska Mountaineering & Hiking,** at 2633 Spenard Rd. (☎ 907-272-1811; www.alaskan.com/amh). It's a small shop where the staff takes the time to help you plan a trip. A block away, at 1200 W. Northern Lights Blvd., **REI** has a large store (☎ 907-272-4565; www.rei.com) that rents a wide range of gear, including lightweight canoes with car-top carriers, camping gear, and packs.

✔ **Bikes:** The **Copper Whale Inn,** at the corner of Fifth and L (☎ 866-258-7999 or 907-258-7999), rents good street bikes. The Inn is near Elderberry Park downtown, at the start of the Tony Knowles Coastal Trail. They charge $15 for a half day, $30 for 24 hours. In midtown, **The Bicycle Shop,** at 1035 W. Northern Lights Blvd. (☎ 907-272-5219), rents and services a wide selection of street and mountain bikes, charging $20 the first day, $15 for additional days, or $85 a week.

✔ **Downhill skis:** Each of the downhill ski areas listed under "Wintertime outdoor activities," below, has a full rental operation.

✔ **Ice skates:** Skates rent for $5 a day at **Champions Choice,** in the University Center Mall at Old Seward Highway and 36th Avenue (☎ 907-563-3503).

Downtown Anchorage Attractions

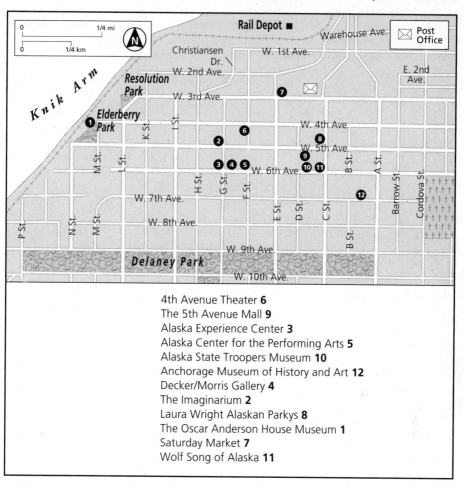

4th Avenue Theater **6**
The 5th Avenue Mall **9**
Alaska Experience Center **3**
Alaska Center for the Performing Arts **5**
Alaska State Troopers Museum **10**
Anchorage Museum of History and Art **12**
Decker/Morris Gallery **4**
The Imaginarium **2**
Laura Wright Alaskan Parkys **8**
The Oscar Anderson House Museum **1**
Saturday Market **7**
Wolf Song of Alaska **11**

and Far North Bicentennial Park are both on the trail system within the city, and encompass scores of miles of trails for Nordic skiing, mountain biking, and horseback riding. The Chugach Mountains, which form the backdrop to the town, offer tundra hiking, backpacking, mountain biking, and climbs that range from easy to technical. Or you can just drive up and take a look at the view.

Summertime outdoor activities

Don't be overwhelmed by the length of this section. I can only boil down warm-weather activities so far while still offering something for every ability level. Use this alphabetized listing here to jump to what you are interested in doing, and then choose the place to go to match your interests and energy level.

Biking and walking on pavement

Anchorage has an award-winning network of paved **bike trails** spanning the city along wooded greenbelts. You rarely see a building and almost always cross roads and rail lines through tunnels and over bridges, so you're never in traffic. Here are two of the best:

- ✔ **Tony Knowles Coastal Trail:** Leading 10 miles from the western end of Second Avenue along the shore to **Kincaid Park,** the coastal trail is a unique pathway to the natural environment from the heart of downtown and is among my favorite things about Anchorage. I've been stopped by moose on the trail near the Kincaid Park end; closer to downtown, I've ridden parallel to beluga whales swimming along the trail at high tide. The most popular entry is at **Elderberry Park,** at the western end of Fifth Avenue. **Westchester Lagoon,** a large dammed pond, is 10 blocks south of Elderberry Park, making for a lovely stroll. It's an equally enjoyable destination for a picnic or to feed the ducks and geese. A couple of miles farther, the trail comes to Earthquake Park and Point Woronzof, mentioned in the upcoming section, "Driving to beautiful places."

- ✔ **Lanie Fleischer Chester Creek Trail:** Starting at an intersection with the Coastal Trail at Westchester Lagoon, the trail runs about 4 miles east along the greenbelt to **Goose Lake,** where you can swim in a cool woodland pond at the end of a hot bike ride — still, improbably enough, in the middle of the city. South from the lake, a wooded trail leads partway through the University of Alaska Anchorage campus.

Driving to beautiful places

If you're not up to muscle-powered sports, and you don't want to spend the money it takes to go flightseeing, you can still get a taste of Anchorage's beauty behind the wheel of a rental car. Here are directions to some lovely places in town (don't miss the day trips mentioned in Chapter 15, either):

- ✔ **Glen Alps Overlook:** High in the mountains above Anchorage, the popular trailhead also has a short, easy trail to a spectacular overlook with interpretive signs. For directions, see "Hiking and mountain biking," below.

- ✔ **Point Woronzof:** A parking lot here sits atop a bluff over the edge of Cook Inlet with the best sunset views in town. A short scramble down the bluff leads to a broad pebble beach. Drive west on Northern Lights, past Earthquake Park (see the "Discovering More Cool Things to See and Do" section, later in this chapter); after the road makes a sharp left near the water, look for the sign on the right.

✔ **Potters Marsh:** A short boardwalk leads into an enormous wetland rich in waterfowl and other bird life. Take the New Seward Highway south, turning left just past the Rabbit Creek exit.

Fishing

Hatchery salmon run in many of Anchorage's streams, and stocked trout, salmon, or char in more than 25 lakes, so you need not leave town to catch a fish. The **Alaska Department of Fish and Game,** 333 Raspberry Rd., Anchorage, AK 99518-1599 (☎ **907-267-2218;** Internet: www.state.ak.us/adfg, click on the Sport Fish link), publishes informative booklets on the Web and on paper. Also, a recorded information line (☎ **907-267-2503**) has all the details on what's hot and lots of other advice.

✔ **Fly-in fishing (guided):** Use Anchorage as a base from which to fly to a remote lake or river with more fish and fewer people. Even folks who are less than enthusiastic about fishing may find such a flight an unforgettable experience, and it's a good opportunity to learn how to hook a salmon. The plane lifts off from Anchorage's Lake Hood floatplane base and within half an hour smoothly lands on a lake or river that often has no one else in sight. You climb out and watch as the plane lifts off and disappears, leaving behind the kind of silence unique to true wilderness. It's on such trips that avid anglers are made — or spoiled. I've heard people complain of how sore their arms got from pulling in too many salmon.

Several companies offer fly-in trips; two of the largest and best established are **Ketchum Air Service** (☎ **800-433-9114** or 907-243-5525; Internet: www.ketchumair.com) and **Rust's Flying Service** (☎ **800-544-2299** or 907-243-1595; Internet: www.flyrusts.com). They can take you out guided or on your own, just for the day or to stay for a while in a cabin or lodge. If you fly to a lake, they provide a boat. They can't make fish appear if none are running, but they try to take you to the hot spots. You can bring your own gear, or they can provide it. Prices for a guided day trip start about $400 per person, with a two-person minimum.

✔ **Roadside fishing (unguided):** Although the setting (under a highway bridge in an industrial area) may not be the wilderness experience you've dreamed about, the 40-pound king salmon you pull from **Ship Creek** may make up for it. From downtown, just walk down the hill to the railroad yard. A couple of shacks sell and rent gear in the summer. Fishing for kings is best in June and for silvers in August and September. Fish at or near high tide, especially at the end of the rising tide. You need rubber boots, preferably neoprene chest waders, for the muddy banks, but don't go too far out, as the mudflats are dangerous. **Bird Creek,** 25 miles south of Anchorage on the Seward Highway (see Chapter 15), carries a strong hatchery run of silver salmon, peaking in August. When silver fishing is hot, it gets crowded and parking is a problem. Pink salmon run from late June to early August. Other creeks along the Arm have similar but smaller runs.

Flightseeing

Small planes are the blood cells of Alaska's transportation system, and Anchorage is its heart. Anchorage hosts several busy airports, and Lake Hood is the world's busiest floatplane base. More than two dozen operators want to take you on a flightseeing tour. For a small plane, check the visitor center for a referral or use one of the operators listed under "Fishing" — but the most comfortable and memorable flights are aboard the restored DC-3s operated by **Era Aviation** (☎ **800-843-1947** or 907-266-8351; Internet: www.eraaviation.com). The planes re-create 1940s air travel in vintage aircraft, but it's their speed, range, and comfort that make them perfect for these trips. The windows are large, you can wander the aisles and even visit the cockpit (or the bathroom), and champagne flows freely. The views on any of the flights are extra-ordinary, but seeing Mount McKinley's spires and chasms on a clear day from this vantage is simply unbelievable. The daily summer flights leave from hangars on Carl Brady Drive, off Raspberry Road, with itineraries determined daily by the weather and viewing opportunities: McKinley, Prince William Sound, or Kenai Fjords National Park's Harding Ice Field. A 90-minute flight is $225 per person. Era also offers helicopter flightseeing.

Hiking and mountain biking

Choices of where to hike or mountain bike are arranged in order of convenience to downtown, but all are best reached by rental car.

- ✔ **Kincaid Park:** Covered in more detail later in this chapter, under "Skiing," Kincaid Park is an idyllic summer setting for mountain biking and day hikes. Moose sightings are a daily occurrence on the wide dirt trails that snake for about 30 miles through the birch and white spruce of the park's hilly 1,400 acres of boreal forest. You get many views of the sea and mountains beyond. Within the park, wooded Little Campbell Lake is a picturesque but little-used swimming hole and a fun spot for family canoeing and fishing for stocked trout, salmon, and char; keep in mind, though, that the lake has no lifeguard. To get there from downtown, take Minnesota Drive (I Street) south beyond the airport interchange to Raspberry Road, which leads right into the park.

- ✔ **Far North Bicentennial Park:** The 4,000-acre park, on the east side of town (also known as the Campbell Tract), is a unique patch of urban wilderness, a habitat for bears, moose, and spawning salmon. People use it for dog mushing and skiing in winter, and for exceptional mountain biking and day hiking in summer. The Alaska Botanical Garden and Hilltop Ski Area both are within the park's boundaries. A good place to start a hike or ride through the woods is the **Campbell Creek Science Center** (☎ 907-267-1257), an educational facility operated by the Bureau of Land Management, where staff are often on hand to answer questions and where you can consult books and maps and look at salmon in a big aquarium. To get there from downtown, take Gambell Street (which becomes New Seward Highway) south to Dowling Road, go east (toward the mountains), and turn right on Lake Otis Road and left on 68th Avenue, following it to the end.

✔ **Glen Alps Trailhead and Flattop Mountain:** You can find many ways to reach the alpine tundra, intoxicating fresh air, and cinematic views of the Chugach Mountains behind Anchorage, but the easiest and best developed are at Chugach State Park's **Glen Alps Trailhead.** Even if you're not up to hiking, a drive and a walk on a short, paved overlook loop with incredible views and good interpretive signs is well worth the effort. If you are ready for a hike, you can start at the trailhead for trips of up to several days, following the network of trails or taking off across dry, alpine tundra by yourself, but usually within cellphone range. Camping is permitted anywhere off the trails.

Flattop Mountain is the most popular hike from the Glen Alps Trailhead, and a great family climb, if a bit crowded on weekends. It's a steep afternoon hike, easy for fit adults and doable by school-age children. If you make it all the way to the top, you can't avoid a bit of a scramble near the summit: stick to the painted markers on the rocks. Also, don't forget to dress warmly and don't go in the rain. For a longer or less steep hike or a mountain-biking trip, follow the broad gravel trail that leads up the valley from the Glen Alps Trailhead to several other great routes. Trails lead all the way over the mountains to Indian or Bird Creek, on Turnagain Arm, up some of the mountains along the way, or to round alpine lakes in high, rocky valleys. You're always above the tree line, so you don't need to follow a trail if you have a good map. The area is wonderful backpacking country.

To get to the trailhead, take New Seward Highway to O'Malley Road, head east toward the mountains, then turn right on Hillside Drive and left onto Upper Huffman Road. Finally, turn right on the narrow, twisting Toilsome Hill Drive. Don't forget to bring cash for a self-service day-use fee of $5.

✔ **Eagle River Valley and Crow Pass:** The **Eagle River Nature Center,** at the end of Eagle River Road, 12 miles up Eagle River Valley from the Glenn Highway exit (☎ 907-694-2108; Internet: www.ernc.org), is like a public wilderness lodge, with hands-on naturalist displays about the area and guided nature walks or talks daily in the summer and weekends year-round (2 p.m. weekends, call for other times). Operated by a nonprofit concessionaire for Chugach State Park, it's open in summer Sunday through Thursday 10 a.m. to 5 p.m., Friday and Saturday 10 a.m. to 7 p.m.; spring and fall Tuesday through Sunday from 10 a.m. to 5 p.m.; winter Friday through

Sunday 10 a.m. to 5 p.m. Expect a $5 parking fee. The ¾-mile **Rodak Nature Trail,** with interpretive signs, leads to a viewing platform over a beaver pond. The **Albert Loop Trail** is a 3-mile route; a geology guide from the center matches with numbered posts on the way. Both have good bird- and wildlife-watching. The 25-mile **Crow Pass Trail,** a portion of the historic Iditarod Trail, continues as a backpacking route up the valley into the mountains along the river, eventually surmounting the Chugach in alpine terrain, and passing near Raven Glacier before descending into Girdwood (see Chapter 15).

✔ **Thunderbird Falls and Eklutna Lake:** The hike to Thunderbird Falls is an easy, 1-mile forest walk with a good reward at the end; you can see the falls without the steep final descent to their foot. Take Glenn Highway north to the Thunderbird Falls exit, 25 miles from Anchorage. Continuing 10 miles up the gravel Eklutna Lake Road, you come to the glacial lake, a place for canoeing, hiking, and exceptional mountain biking. The Lakeside Trail leads 13.5 miles to Eklutna Glacier. Rental bikes, kayaks, and other equipment, and guided kayak and boat tours, are offered by **Lifetime Adventures,** with a booth at the trailhead (☎ **800-9KATMAI** or 907-746-4644; Internet: www.lifetimeadventures.net). For $70, you can kayak 8 miles to the other end of the lake and pick up a bike there to ride back. This glacial melt is also where Anchorage gets most of its city water. People bottle it and sell it as "glacier water."

Rafting

Several white-water rivers are within a 90-minute drive of Anchorage. **Nova Raft and Adventure Tours** (☎ 800-746-5753 or 907-745-5753; Internet: www.novalaska.com) has more than 25 years of experience offering multi-day trips all over the state, and four different half-day floats in the Anchorage area. Rafting trips are available ranging from relatively easygoing Class II and III rapids on the Matanuska River to the Class IV and V white water of Six-Mile Creek, for which you may be required to prove your swimming ability before you can get in the boat. Self-paddling or hiking add-ons are options on some trips. White-water rafting always entails risk, but Nova's schedule allows you to calibrate how wild you want to get. The half-day trips range in price from $65 to $125. Children 5 to 11 can go on the calmer Matanuska River float for $35. Other trips are suitable only for older children and adults. You need your own transportation to the river and may need to bring your own lunch.

Chugach Outdoor Center (☎ 866-277-RAFT or 907-277-RAFT; Internet: www.chugachoutdoorcenter.com) also offers rides on Six-Mile Creek, with dry suits, and longer expeditions.

Sea kayaking

Except at Eklutna Lake (see "Hiking and mountain biking," above), kayaking day trips from Anchorage go through Whittier, on Prince William Sound (see Chapter 15).

Getting outdoors questions answered

The **Alaska Public Lands Information Center,** at Fifth Avenue and F Street down-town (☎ **907-271-2737;** Internet: www.nps.gov/aplic), offers guidance for all outdoor activities all over the state, especially around Anchorage. For information on the bike trails, cross-country skiing parks, and other city recreation, contact the **Municipal Division of Sports & Recreation** (☎ **907-343-4474;** Internet: www. muni.org/parks). For advice specific to **Chugach State Park** (including their *Ridgelines* newsprint guide), contact the public lands center, or the park directly (☎ **907-345-5014;** Internet: www.alaskastateparks.org, click on the Individual Parks link). The best trail guide to the entire region is Helen Nienhueser and John Wolfe, Jr.'s *55 Ways to the Wilderness,* published by The Mountaineers (Internet: www.mountaineersbooks.org). It costs $16.95 and is available in any bookstore in the area. The best trail map is the Chugach State Park topographic trail map published in 2000 by Imus Geographics and sold at either of the sporting-goods stores mentioned in the "Gearing up in Anchorage" sidebar, earlier in this chapter.

Wintertime outdoor activities

If you don't enjoy winter sports, Anchorage during the snowy months (that's normally at least November through March) probably isn't for you. Less active summer activities such as fishing, walking, or driving are difficult, impossible, or just plain chilly. But cold weather doesn't feel so cold when you're active. Mushers, skiers, and snowmobilers pray for snow. Around here, their prayers get answered pretty consistently.

Dog mushing

In the last 20 years, dog mushing has become a recreational sport as well as the utilitarian transportation it once was in the bush and the professional sport it has been for years. But keeping a dog team is more than a hobby — it is a lifestyle revolving around the feeding, care, and exercise of at least a dozen dogs (the pros sometimes have 200). Some mushers offset the great expense by offering rides.

In the Anchorage area, among the best are friendly and casual Angie and Tom Hamill, who keep two dozen dogs at their home in the Chugiak area, half an hour north of downtown on Glenn Highway, and run them on the wooded trails of the mushing park there. In winter only, they offer rides of various lengths starting at 2 miles, with guests riding in the sled basket while they drive, for $35. That's really too short, however; you just get the idea of how powerful and intelligent the dogs are, as they speed along responding to voice commands to make turns and deal with unexpected situations along the trail. For $195, the Hamills teach you to mush during a 2½-hour session; they make guests feel like friends — it isn't intimidating. They offer overnight expeditions, too, and own a bed-and-breakfast (see Chapter 13). The business is called **Birch Trails Adventures,** 22719 Robinson Rd., Chugiak, AK 99567 (☎ and Fax: **907-688-5713;** E-mail: birchtrails@ excite.com). For another mushing option, see the section on Girdwood in Chapter 15.

Ice skating

Westchester Lagoon, just 10 blocks from downtown (see "Biking and walking on pavement," earlier in this chapter), is a skating paradise in the winter. When the ice gets thick enough, usually by mid-December, the city clears a large rink and over a mile of wide paths that wind across the pond, mopping the ice regularly for a smooth surface. In recent years, a 1-kilometer speed-skating loop has linked with the paths. Skaters gather around burn barrels, well stocked with firewood, to socialize and warm their hands, and on weekends, vendors often sell hot chocolate and coffee.

Skiing

Kincaid Park is one of the best **cross-country skiing** areas in the country, with the first World Cup certified trails in the United States. More than 50 kilometers of trails are geared to every ability level, but mostly intermediate and expert. Besides the superb trails, Kincaid is a beautiful place to ski, through rolling hills of open birch and spruce, with views of the mountains and ocean. Trails are groomed for skating and classical techniques. Sixteen kilometers are lighted (an important feature on short winter days). The **Kincaid Park Outdoor Center** (☎ **907-343-6397**) is open Monday to Friday from 1:00 to 9:45 p.m. and Saturday and Sunday from 10:00 a.m. to 9:45 p.m. A gate closes at 10 p.m., so park outside it if you plan on skiing later. Skiing often lasts through March, when big races occur.

Far North Bicentennial Park also has some excellent trails — 32 kilometers total, 7 kilometers lighted — and a slightly longer season because of its hillside location. Start at Hilltop Ski Area. Many other parks and the bike trails have lengthy skiing routes, too, much of it lighted; ski right from downtown on the Tony Knowles Coastal Trail. See the "Gearing up in Anchorage" sidebar, earlier in this chapter, for ski rentals.

Anchorage has several **downhill ski areas.** The best, **Alyeska Resort,** is described in the Girdwood section of Chapter 15. **Hilltop Ski Area,** in Bicentennial Park in town, is a great place to start skiing, with one long beginner slope, at 7015 Abbott Rd. (☎ **907-346-1446;** Internet: www.hilltopskiarea.org).

Discovering More Cool Things to See and Do

You need wheels for these attractions, except the Oscar Anderson House Museum, which is downtown.

✔ **Walk a wooded garden trail.** The **Alaska Botanical Garden** (☎ 907-770-3692; Internet: www.alaskabg.org) is young, and the volunteer staff has filled only 4 acres of its wooded, 110-acre site, but already the garden is a restful place to discover native flora and see what else grows in Alaska while sitting in peaceful shade on benches and watching birds and squirrels. A fine 1.1-mile nature trail with explanatory signs leaves from the garden and proceeds down to Campbell Creek, where you may see salmon swimming. To get there from downtown (a 20-minute drive), take New Seward Highway (Gambell Street) to Tudor Road, exit to the east (left), turn right off Tudor onto Campbell Airstrip Road, and park at the Benny Benson School. A donation is requested; it's open in summer daily from 9 a.m. to 9 p.m.

✔ **Catch a large-format movie.** Two downtown theaters show large-format films aimed at visitors. **The Alaska Experience Center** (☎ 907-272-9076) is on the northwest corner of Sixth Avenue and G Street, partly in a dome tent. A 40-minute Omnivision wrap-around movie about Alaska costs $7 for adults, $4 for children, showing hourly. An Alaska Earthquake display that really shakes is $5 for adults and $4 for children ages 5 to 12. Combination tickets are discounted. The film shows in summer daily from 9 a.m. to 9 p.m.; in winter the last showing is at 6 p.m. In the summer, large-format films often play as well at the **Alaska Center for the Performing Arts,** 621 W. Sixth Ave. (☎ 800-GR8-SEAT; Internet: www.alaskapac.org). Recently, they've shown *Alaska: Spirit of the Wild* and a film about bears, starting hourly from 9 a.m. to 9 p.m. No need to buy in advance; just walk in and get your ticket for about $10 from a card table in the lobby.

✔ **See the remains of the continent's biggest earthquake.** On Good Friday, 1964, the biggest earthquake ever recorded in North America hit South Central Alaska, registering at 9.2 on the Richter Scale, killing 131 people, and flattening much of the region. **Earthquake Park** preserves some of the landscape that was thrown into a chaos of slides, cracks, and wave-like humps, and a sculpture and excellent interpretive signs have been added to commemorate and explain the event. Anyone can get to the interpretive area, but the land devastated by the earthquake is overgrown and requires climbing down the bluff through the woods (well worth the effort, but use care and go to the right, not over the guard rail). Earthquake Park is a good access point to the Coastal Trail. From downtown, take L Street (it becomes Minnesota Drive) to Northern Lights Boulevard and turn right. The park is on your right after you cross Lakeshore Drive.

✔ **See a mysterious Native cemetery.** The Athabascan village of Eklutna has a fascinating old cemetery, still in use, in which each grave is enclosed by a highly decorated spirit house, the size of a large dollhouse. These little shelters excite the imagination in a way no ordinary marker can. Two small Russian Orthodox churches are also on the tribal Eklutna Historic Site (☎ **907-688-6026** or 907-696-2828; Internet: www.eklutna.com), including one built of logs sometime before 1870, making it among the oldest buildings in the South Central region. Walk through by yourself or take an informative 30-minute tour for the same price ($6 adult, $3 ages 6 through 17). It's open in summer daily from 8 a.m. to 6 p.m. Wear mosquito repellent. To get there, drive the Glenn Highway 26 miles to the Eklutna exit, then go left over the overpass. If you come out this far, don't miss the Thunderbird Falls, described earlier in this chapter under "Hiking and mountain biking."

✔ **Tour an old house.** The **Oscar Anderson House Museum** (☎ **907-274-2336** or 907-274-3600; Internet: www.anchoragehistoric properties.org), moved to a beautiful site in downtown's Elderberry Park over the water, shows how an early Swedish butcher and entrepreneur lived. The house is quaint and dates from the city's founding in 1915. The 45-minute guided tour gives a good overview of Anchorage's short history. Admission is $3 adults, $1 children 5 through 12, and it is open summer only Monday to Friday from noon to 5 p.m. If you come at Christmas, don't miss the Swedish Christmas tours, the first two weekends in December.

✔ **Attend a summer-league baseball game.** Perhaps the best way to spend a fresh summer evening in Anchorage is at **Mulcahy Stadium,** watching the Anchorage Glacier Pilots (☎ **907-274-3627;** Internet: www.glacierpilots.com) or the Anchorage Bucs (☎ **907-561-2827;** Internet: www.anchoragebucs.com). You hear, smell, and feel the rhythm of the game when you sit so close in the tiny park. The teams are made up of college players spending their summer in the six-team Alaska League. Among famed alumni are Mark McGwire, Rick Aguilera, Tom Seaver, Dave Winfield, Barry Bonds, Wally Joyner, and Randy Johnson. Check the *Anchorage Daily News* or team Web sites for game times. Mulcahy is at 16th Avenue and A Street, a long walk or a short drive from downtown. Tickets are under $5. Dress warmly for evening games; a blanket is rarely out of order.

✔ **Visit a couple of quirky little museums.** Near the northwest corner of Sixth Avenue and C Street are two interesting little museums. **Wolf Song of Alaska** (☎ **907-274-9653;** Internet: www.wolf songalaska.org) is simply stuffed with information about wolves, including dioramas, exhibits, artwork, and videos. Admission is $4 adults, $2 ages 6 to 18. A couple of doors to the west is the **Alaska State Troopers Museum** (☎ **800-770-5050** or 907-279-5050; Internet: www.alaska.net/~foast), a trove of law enforcement insignia, police equipment, a 1952 Hudson Hornet, photographs, and other memorabilia. The place brims with pride.

Seeing Anchorage by Guided Tour

The best **guided walking tour** of the historic downtown area is given by **Anchorage Historic Properties,** 645 W. Third Ave. (☎ **907-274-3600;** Internet: www.AnchorageHistoricProperties.org), a city-endowed historic preservation group. They offer 2-hour, 2-mile walks June to August, Monday to Friday at 1 p.m. The volunteer guides are fun and knowledgeable. Meet at the lobby of Old City Hall, 524 W. Fourth Ave., next door to the Log Cabin Visitor Information Center. Tickets cost $5 for adults, $1 for children.

If you want to break the bonds of downtown Anchorage but don't want to rent a car, taking a **guided bus tour** is a reasonable option. You get an overview of what the city really looks like (beyond downtown, there really are businesses other than T-shirt shops), and you can get to some of the top sights as part of the package.

The **4th Avenue Theater** (☎ **907-263-2787;** Internet: www.fourth avenuetheater.com) is a historic Art Deco movie house between F and G streets downtown that was saved by a wealthy businessman and made into a gift shop and tourist dinner theater. Out front, a red bus made up to look like a trolley carries visitors on hour-long city tours. The $10 tour goes to the Lake Hood floatplane base, Point Woronzof, Earthquake Park, and West Chester Lagoon, sites on the west side of town; you don't get off the bus. A trolley shuttle to the Alaska Native Heritage Center is also available for $10.

For a more complete tour, **Gray Line of Alaska** offers a city tour that includes the Alaska Native Heritage Center for $40 adults, $20 children (☎ **800-544-2206;** Internet: www.graylineofalaska.com). The tour's okay for a quick overview, but when I went to the Heritage Center, I spent three hours there and could have stayed longer.

Spending 1, 2, and 3 Days in Anchorage

If I had a nickel for every time I've been asked, "What should I do in just one day in Anchorage?" I'd have a big bag of nickels. I long ago gave up asking people to read over all the choices I've written about and make choices based on their own interests. You want me to do all the work! So here are ideas for how to spend a day, two, or three in Anchorage, with my standard disclaimer: I think Alaska is about nature and the outdoors, even in the state's biggest city. So if you ask my advice, I'm going to send you out under the sky. Also, consider the day trips from the city that I cover in Chapter 15.

For simplicity's sake, I've set these itineraries up with the assumption that you're staying downtown, but they work from anywhere in town. Also, I have not set these days up in priority order: choose any of the three for a great one-day itinerary in Anchorage, or pair them up in any combination. You can find more information throughout this chapter about the attractions mentioned in the itineraries. For details on the lodging and dining recommendations, check out Chapter 13.

Day 1 in Anchorage

In the morning, head out to the **Alaska Native Heritage Center** to meet Alaska's indigenous people and discover their culture. Arrive there close to the 9 a.m. opening time so that you can get back downtown for lunch. Eat casually but well at the **Glacier Brewhouse,** then check out the shops in the area, including the string of galleries and offbeat businesses along G Street. When you're done shopping, walk 5 blocks west on Fifth Avenue to **Elderberry Park, the Tony Knowles Coastal Trail, and the sea.** Walk the coastal trail to see the ocean, mudflats, and wildlife, or if you have the energy, **rent bikes at the Copper Whale Inn** (at Fifth Avenue and L Street) and ride the trail. The ducks of **West Chester Lagoon** make a good, close destination; in less than an hour, you can bike to **Earthquake Park** and **Point Woronzof.** If you're a hardcore bicyclist, you can ride 10 miles all the way through the woods to **Kincaid Park.** At the end of your coastal trail sojourn, back at Elderberry Park, you'll be a block from one of the best restaurants in town, **Simon and Seafort's** (but you must reserve a table a day or two ahead). After dinner, if you still have energy, this may be the night to catch the **Whale Fat Follies** at Mr. Whitekeys' Fly By Night Club.

Day 2 in Anchorage

This morning, prepare with sweaters, jackets, and a picnic and drive up to the **Glen Alps Trailhead** for a hike (or mountain bike) above the tree line with the wonderful views and clear, crisp air. You can spend the whole day there, but if that's too much, spend part of the afternoon at **Alaska Zoo,** on the drive back down the mountain. In the early evening, catch the classic **DC-3 flightseeing excursion** with Era Aviation (the light is best on the 6 p.m. flight); if you're lucky with the weather, you may fly through the canyons of Mount McKinley and get as intoxicated on the scenery as on the champagne served on board. Afterward, go for a long, special dinner at **Jens',** which takes up the rest of the evening.

Day 3 in Anchorage

Start the day at the **Anchorage Museum of History and Art.** See the Alaska Gallery for a survey of Alaska's history and culture and then continue into the art galleries to see the best attempts at capturing

Alaska on canvas. Lunch at the **Marx Brother's Café** at the Museum. Now drive out the Glenn Highway to the **Eagle River Valley** and the nature center and trails there, perhaps joining a naturalist program. If time remains, you may also want to drive a bit farther to see **Thunderbird Falls** and the **Eklutna Historical Park.** Back in town, catch a **summer league baseball game** at Mulcahy Stadium and dine on hot dogs and beer under the midnight sun.

Saving Time for Alaska Shopping

You can buy any of Alaska's unique creations in Anchorage — Alaska Native arts and crafts, furs, and fine art interpreting Alaska. The city has some of the state's best galleries and all its largest fur shops, and it's big enough to have a few quirky and offbeat places, too.

Finding the best shopping areas

Most of the shopping choices that interest visitors are found downtown. This section takes you to a couple of clusters of good shops.

A walk down G Street

G Street from Sixth to Third avenues has the city's greatest concentration of interesting and unusual shops; here are some highlights, starting on Sixth Avenue and working north:

- ✔ **Decker/Morris Gallery** (621 W. Sixth Ave.; ☎ **907-272-1489;** Internet: www.deckermorrisgallery.com) is one of Alaska's best and most uncompromising art venues. The owners are real leaders in serious contemporary art.

- ✔ **Aurora Fine Arts** (737 W. Fifth Ave.; ☎ **907-274-0234**) is another gallery, with more gifts and crafts. It's a block north of Decker/Morris, at Fifth and G.

- ✔ Continuing north, **Uncle Joe's Pizzeria** (428 G St.; ☎ **907-279-3799**), offers good pie by the slice.

- ✔ **Darwin's Theory** (426 G St.; ☎ **907-277-5322**) is a friendly, old-fashioned bar with character that shows up in an Indigo Girls song ("Cut It Out").

- ✔ **Suzis' Woollies** (420 G. St.; ☎ **907-277-9660;** Internet: www.suzis woollies.com), a Celtic shop carrying imported sweaters, jewelry, and CDs, entertains with live Irish music Saturday afternoons.

- ✔ **Denali Wear** (416 G St.; ☎ **907-278-9327**) is Tracy Anna Bader's studio and shop of bright, graphic wearable art.

- ✔ In addition to your favorite coffee drink, at **Side Street Espresso** (412 G St.; ☎ **907-258-9055**) you can get into a lively discussion on art or politics and make contact with thinking people.

✔ Next, **Charlie's Alaska Trains** (410 G St.; ☎ 907-278-7426;
Internet: www.ptialaska.net/~aktrains) is a retired couple's
labor of love, which sells little other than Alaska Railroad models
and memorabilia.

✔ Across the street, at Fourth and G, is **Cabin Fever** (☎ 907-278-
3522), one of the classier gift shops in town.

✔ And finally, the next block north contains **Artique** (314 G St.;
☎ 800-848-1312 or 907-277-1663; Internet: www.artiqueltd.com),
a high-end gallery of popular work that also has a large print
collection.

Near Fourth and D streets

The biggest shopping place in Anchorage is the **5th Avenue Mall,**
covering two full blocks between Fifth and Sixth avenues and C and
E streets. It has a Nordstrom and many other popular stores, but
they're mostly national chains that you can find at home. Down at
street level are a few more unique places.

✔ **Laura Wright Alaskan Parkys** is on Fifth between C and D streets
(343 W. Fifth Ave.; ☎ 907-274-4215; Internet: www.alaskan.com/
parkys). Seamstresses inside sew custom Eskimo coats.

✔ Just west of D on Fifth, **Cook Inlet Books** (415 W. Fifth Ave.; ☎ 800-
240-4148 or 907-258-4544; Internet: www.cookinlet.com) carries
an exhaustive selection on Alaska, probably unmatched anywhere
in the world.

✔ North on D, the **Rondy Shop** (402 D St.; ☎ 907-274-1196) sup-
ports the Anchorage Fur Rendezvous, the annual winter festival
and sled dog race.

✔ At Fourth and D is **Cyrano's Off-Center Playhouse** (413 D St.;
☎ 907-274-2599; Internet: www.cyranos.org), with its Eccentric
Theater Company, Bistro Bergerac, and bookstore. Stop in for a
snack or to find out what's playing. The company is really good;
the tiny theater can cause quite a stir in town.

✔ Along Fourth near here are the best of Anchorage's fur shops, a
good Native crafts store called **The Rusty Harpoon** (see "Alaska
Native arts and crafts," later in this chapter, for more details),
and the **Army Navy Store** (320 W. Fourth Ave.; ☎ 907-279-2401;
Internet: www.army-navy-store.com), where people go to stock
up on ultra-warm winter wear before heading to the Arctic.

Saturday Market

If you can be in town on a Saturday during the summer, be sure to visit
the **Saturday Market,** in the parking lot at Third Avenue and E Street,
a big street fair with food, music, and hundreds of miscellaneous crafts
booths.

What to look for and where to find it

This section tells you where to pick up some of the uniquely Alaskan gift items (and a couple of not-so-unique things).

Alaska Native arts and crafts

Many stores in Anchorage carry Native Alaskan arts and crafts. Before making major purchases, know what you're buying. Please read up on this subject in Chapter 11. If you're going to the bush, you can find lower prices there but less selection.

Nowhere else can you find a business like the **Oomingmak Musk Ox Producers' Co-operative** (☎ **888-360-9665** outside Alaska or 907-272-9225; Internet: www.qiviut.com), located in the house with the musk ox on the side at Sixth Avenue and H Street. Owned by 250 Alaska Native women in villages across the state, the co-op sells only scarves and other items they knit of *qiviut* (*ki*-vee-ute), the light, warm, silky underhair of the musk ox, which is collected from shedding animals. Each village has its own knitting pattern. They're expensive — adult caps start at $140 — but the quality is extraordinary. The Web site contains the women's fascinating correspondence.

The shop at the Anchorage Museum of History and Art has superb Native art. The Alaska Native Heritage Center shows some original work, too. **The Rusty Harpoon** (411 W. Fourth Ave.; ☎ **907-278-9011;** Internet: www.rustyharpoongifts.com) also has authentic Native items, less expensive crafts, and reliable, longtime proprietors. Both of these locations buy only direct from Native artists they know. Farther afield, the **Alaska Fur Exchange,** at 4417 Old Seward Hwy., near Tudor Road (☎ **907-563-3877;** Internet: www.alaskafurexchange.com), is a cross between an old-time wilderness trading post and a modern factory outlet. Rural residents bring in furs and crafts to sell and trade, which are displayed in great profusion and clutter. If you're in the market for pelts, go no farther.

Probably the best place for Native crafts in Anchorage is the **Hospital Auxiliary Craft Shop** in the Alaska Native Medical Center, off Tudor east of Bragaw (☎ **907-729-1122**), where everything is made by folks eligible to use the hospital. The work you find here is all authentic and entirely traditional. The shop is open Monday to Friday 10 a.m. to 2 p.m. and the first and third Saturday 11 a.m. to 2 p.m. You can see exceptional Native art on the walls of the hospital, too.

Furs, kuspuks, and parkas

If you're in the market for a fur, Anchorage has a wide selection and no sales tax. **David Green Master Furrier,** at 130 W. Fourth Ave. (☎ **907-277-9595;** Internet: www.davidgreenfurs.com), is an Anchorage institution. Others are nearby.

Laura Wright Alaskan Parkys (see "Near Fourth and D streets" earlier in this chapter) makes and sells *kuspuks,* the brightly trimmed summer parkas really worn by Eskimos that are cool enough for wear in temperate climes. Their winter-wear *parkys* usually have fur trim, but that isn't a requirement for beauty and authenticity. Most of the coats are made to order by the friendly women in the shop.

Gifts

You'll find lots of places to buy both mass-produced and inexpensive handmade crafts that aren't from the bush. The **Saturday Market** street fair, in the parking lot at Third Avenue and E Street, has hundreds of booths. You won't have any trouble finding gift shops on Fourth, including the ones I mention earlier in this chapter. The **Kobuk Coffee Company,** at Fifth Avenue and E Street, next to the town square (☎ 907-272-3626), occupies one of Anchorage's earliest commercial buildings; it's a cozy little candy, coffee, and collectibles shop. In midtown, on International Airport Road between the Old and New Seward highways, **Alaska Wild Berry Products** (☎ 800-280-2927 or 907-562-8858; Internet: www.alaskawildberryproducts.com) is a fun store to visit, with a chocolate waterfall and a big window where you can watch the candy factory at work. The chocolate-covered berry jellies are simultaneously addictive and rich enough to make you dizzy if you eat more than a few.

Fine art

Downtown has several galleries, the best of which I mention above under "A walk down G Street." Openings at all the galleries happen on the first Friday of each month, allowing for an evening of party hopping to meet artists and non-tourists of like interests.

Getting Out in the Evening

Anchorage isn't exactly a nightlife capital, but you can find something to do in the evening.

Attending the performing arts

To find out what's happening, pick up a copy of Friday's edition of the *Anchorage Daily News* for the "8" section, which includes event listings and information on the club and arts scene. The paper's Web site, www.adn.com/weekend, allows you to check the calendar and listings from afar, or on days other than Friday. **Tickets.com** (☎ 800-478-7328), of Concord, California, is the main ticket agency. For a list of current events, go to its site and search under "Anchorage." Tickets.com has box offices at the Anchorage Center for Performing Arts and at Carrs/Safeway grocery stores. The arts season begins in the fall and ends in the spring, but in the summer, you can catch traveling performers and music festivals.

The **Anchorage Concert Association** (☎ 907-272-1471; Internet: www.anchorageconcerts.org) offers a fall through spring schedule of classical music, theater, dance, and other performing arts. **Whistling Swan Productions** (Internet: www.whistlingswan.net) promotes folk and acoustic alternative performers in intimate venues. The **Anchorage Symphony** (☎ 907-274-8668; Internet: www.anchoragesymphony.org) performs during the winter season.

Anchorage also has lots of community theater, opera, and limited professional theater, including the experimental **Out North Contemporary Art House** (☎ 907-279-8200; Internet: www.outnorth.org), which produces local shows and imports avant-garde performers. Downtown, **Cyrano's Off Center Playhouse** (☎ 907-274-2599; Internet: www.cyranos.org), at Fourth Avenue and D Street, is a tiny theater with its own semiprofessional repertory company.

Hitting the city's nightclubs and bars

For a fun, funny night out, nothing in town compares to **Mr. Whitekeys' Fly By Night Club,** on Spenard Road south of Northern Lights Boulevard (☎ 907-279-SPAM; Internet: www.flybynightclub.com). The goateed proprietor, a consummate vulgarian, ridicules Anchorage in his crude, political, local-humor musical comedy shows, in which he co-stars with a fallen former Miss Anchorage. If you can laugh at dog poop, you'll love it. The summer show is at 8 p.m. Tuesday to Saturday, with no smoking allowed Tuesday to Thursday; live music follows Fridays and Saturdays. Tickets are $12 to $19, and reservations are necessary well in advance. They serve good food, too. (Believe me, I was praising Mr. Whitekeys' long before they started using a piece of my writing in one of their shows.)

Blues Central/Chef's Inn, 825 W. Northern Lights Blvd. (☎ 907-272-1341), is dedicated to showcasing the best blues performers available, virtually every night. Major names come through on a regular basis. Shows start at 9:30 p.m. They also serve excellent beef. The huge **Chilkoot Charlie's,** at Spenard Road and Fireweed Lane (☎ 907-272-1010; Internet: www.koots.com), has two stages for rock and one for swing. The place is huge, but can be claustrophobic when crowded, with low ceilings and a dark, roadhouse atmosphere.

For your personal safety, downtown has lots of bars and nightclubs to avoid, mostly along Fourth Avenue. You can find safe drinking places in the hotels, or try **Humpy's,** at 610 W. Sixth Ave. (☎ 907-276-2337), a popular tavern with a young crowd and live music (but little room for dancing); **Darwin's Theory,** 426 G St. (☎ 907-277-5322), a good elbows-on-the-table hangout; or the bar at **Simon & Seafort's,** 420 L St. (☎ 907-274-3502), an upscale after-work place for the professional set.

Spending a night at the movies

The most fun place to see a movie is the **Bear Tooth Theatrepub,** at 1230 W. 27th Ave. (☎ **907-276-4200;** Internet: www.beartooththeatre. net), where you can watch art films and second-run movies while sipping craft brews and eating gourmet tacos, pizzas, and the like. Arrive early, as films often sell out and parking is terrible. Check out the Web site for monthly concerts.

Anchorage has several multiplexes playing all the current Hollywood output; check the *Anchorage Daily News* for listings. The closest larger theaters, the **Century 16** (301 E. 36th Ave.; ☎ **907-929-FILM;** Internet: www.centurytheatres.com) and the **Fireweed 7 Theater** (661 E. Fireweed Ln.; ☎ **907-566-3328;** Internet: www.regalcinemas.com), are a short cab ride away in midtown.

Fast Facts: Anchorage

ATMs

A bank is rarely far away, and grocery stores also have ATMs. Downtown, **Wells Fargo** (☎ 907-263-2501) has a branch in the 5th Avenue Mall (Fifth Avenue and D Street) that offers full foreign currency exchange and wire transfer services. It's open Monday through Saturday 10 a.m. to 6 p.m.

Emergencies

Dial ☎ **911** for all emergency services.

Hospitals

Alaska Regional Hospital is at 2801 DeBarr Rd. (☎ 907-276-1131), and **Providence Alaska Medical Center** is at 3200 Providence Dr. (☎ 907-562-2211).

Information

Contact the **Anchorage Convention and Visitor Bureau,** (☎ 907-276-4118; www. anchorage.net), or drop by their **Log Cabin Visitor Information Center,** downtown at Fourth Avenue and F Street (☎ 907-274-3531). It's open daily June through August, 7:30 a.m. to 7:00 p.m., May and September, 8 a.m. to 6 p.m., October through April 9 a.m. to 4 p.m.

Internet Access

Downtown, **Mail Boxes Etc.,** at 645 G Street, next to City Hall (☎ 907-276-7888), has three public computers with DSL connections and makes a point of serving visitors. The **Z. J. Loussac Library,** midtown at 3600 Denali St. (☎ 907-343-2975), offers free access.

Mail

The downtown post office is in the lower level of the brown building at Fourth Avenue and D Street.

Maps

Ordinary street maps are available at the visitor center or any grocery store. Outdoors maps and guidebooks are for sale at the **Alaska Public Lands Information Center** at Fourth Avenue and F Street (☎ 907-271-2737; www.nps.gov/aplic). **The Maps Place,** 601 W. 36th Ave. (☎ 907-562-7277), carries every conceivable map of Alaska, including all USGS topographic maps.

Newspapers/Magazines

Cook Inlet Books, at 415 W. Fifth Ave. (☎ 907-258-4544), is the handiest downtown source of out-of-town newspapers and has an extensive selection of magazines. **Barnes & Noble** is in midtown, at the corner of Northern Lights Blvd. and A Street (☎ 907-279-7323).

Pharmacies

Anchorage has no pharmacy downtown. The closest is in the **Carrs/Safeway** store at 1340 Gambell St. (☎ 907-297-0260), but that's not a great neighborhood. You may feel more comfortable a mile south on the same road at the pharmacy in the **Fred Meyer** grocery store at 1000 E. Northern Lights Blvd. (☎ 907-264-9633).

Police

For emergencies, dial ☎ **911**. The **Anchorage Police Department** has main offices at 4501 S. Bragaw Rd., south of Tudor Road; for a nonemergency, call ☎ 907-786-8500. For nonemergency police business outside the city, call the **Alaska State Troopers**, 5700 E. Tudor Rd. (☎ 907-269-5511).

Restrooms

The public restrooms in hotel lobbies and public buildings are your best bet. Any business serving food also is required to have them, which includes grocery stores.

Safety

Muggings are rare in Anchorage, but sexual assault is not. Women need to be especially careful, especially around the rough downtown bars or in lonely places at night. The area of downtown east of Cordova Street (beyond the big Sheraton Hotel) is run-down and frequented by suspicious-looking characters, although I make no effort to avoid it.

Smoking

Anchorage outlaws smoking in virtually all indoor public places except for bars. Many accommodations don't allow smoking in any rooms, and some small places don't even allow smoking outside. Check when you reserve.

Taxes

Anchorage has no sales tax. The bed tax and rental car tax is 8%.

Taxis

See Chapter 13 for a discussion of using taxis in Anchorage. One operator is **Alaska Cab** (☎ 907-563-5353).

Transit

The bus system is called the **People Mover** (☎ 907-343-6543; www.peoplemover.org). See Chapter 13 for advice on using it.

Weather Updates

The National Weather Service maintains an **Alaska Weather Line** at ☎ 907-266-5145 from Anchorage or from outside Alaska, or ☎ 800-472-0391 toll free anywhere within Alaska. Or check the forecast at www.arh.noaa.gov.

Chapter 15

Side Trips from Anchorage

In This Chapter

▶ Enjoying the vertical landscape of Seward Highway

▶ Taking in some winter (and summer) activities in Girdwood

▶ Cruising Prince William Sound

▶ Breaking away in the Mat-Su Valley

A base in Anchorage puts you close enough to some of Alaska's most appealing destinations for you to experience them as day trips. Few days that you spend in town can compare with what you'll see on some of the outings discussed in this chapter.

Driving between Mountain and Sea on the Seward Highway

One of the world's great drives starts in Anchorage and leads roughly 50 miles south on the Seward Highway to Portage Glacier. The trip, and not the destination, is what makes the drive worthwhile. The two-lane highway is chipped from the foot of the rocky Chugach Mountains along the waters of Turnagain Arm, providing a platform to see a magnificent, ever-changing, mostly untouched landscape full of wildlife.

I list the sights in the style of a highway log because you'll find interesting stops all along the road. This route also leads to several other great places: Girdwood's ski slopes, Whittier and Prince William Sound (covered later in this chapter), and the Kenai Peninsula (in Chapter 16).

Getting there

Getting lost on the Seward Highway is hard to do. It leaves downtown Anchorage under the name Gambell Street, becomes a limited-access freeway through the rest of the city, and then narrows to two lanes at Potter Marsh as it leaves the developed part of Anchorage (even though you remain within the city limits almost all the way on this drive). From the marsh, the highway traces the edge of Turnagain Arm.

Taking a tour

If you don't want to drive, a number of bus tours follow this route and visit Portage Glacier. **Gray Line of Alaska** (☎ 800-544-2206 or 907-277-5581; Internet: www.graylineofalaska.com) offers a seven-hour trip that includes a stop in Girdwood and a boat ride on Portage Lake for $59 adults, $30 ages 2 through 11, twice daily in summer. You can take the boat ride separately, too. (See the information on Portage Glacier in the section, "Seeing the sights.")

A sightseeing drive takes at least half a day round-trip, and you can find plenty to do if you want to make it an all-day excursion. Use your headlights for safety even during daylight and be patient whenever you get stuck behind a summertime line of cars — even when you pass, you're likely to just come up behind yet another line ahead of you again.

If you're taking the train to Seward or driving elsewhere on the Kenai Peninsula later in your trip, don't take this day trip, because you'll be covering the same ground.

Seeing the sights

The sights described in the following listing are in order of the highway mileage markers that you'll encounter on the way from Anchorage:

- ✔ **Potter Marsh (mile 117):** Heading south from Anchorage, the Seward Highway descends a bluff to cross a broad marsh formed by water impounded behind the tracks of the Alaska Railroad. Beside the marsh is a boardwalk from which you can watch a huge variety of birds. Salad-green grasses grow from sparkling, pond-green water.

- ✔ **Potter Section House (mile 115):** Located at the south end of Potter Marsh, the section house was an early maintenance station for the Alaska Railroad. Today it contains offices of Chugach State Park, open during normal business hours, and outside features a few old train cars and interpretive displays. Across the road is the trailhead for the **Turnagain Arm Trail,** a mostly level path running down the arm well above the highway with great views breaking now and then through the trees. You can follow the trail for 9 miles to Windy Corner, or break off where it meets the McHugh Creek picnic area and trailhead, about 4 miles out.

- ✔ **McHugh Creek (mile 111):** Four miles south of Potter is an excellent state park picnic area and a challenging day hike with a 3,000-foot elevation gain to **Rabbit Lake,** which sits in a tundra mountain bowl, or a 4,301-foot ascent to the top of **McHugh Peak.** You don't have to climb all the way; spectacular views are to be had within an hour of the road.

✔ **Beluga Point (mile 110):** The state highway department probably didn't need to put up scenic overlook signs on this pull-out, 1½ miles south of McHugh Creek, because you'd probably figure it out on your own. The terrain is simply awesome, as the highway traces the edge of Turnagain Arm below the towering cliffs of the Chugach Mountains. If the tide and salmon runs are right, you may see beluga whales, which chase the fish toward fresh water. Sometimes they overextend their pursuit, stranding themselves farther along the run by the dozens in the receding tide, but they usually aren't harmed.

✔ **Windy Point (mile 106):** Be on the lookout for Dall sheep picking their way along the cliffs on the mountain side of the road. It's a unique spot, because the sheep get much closer to people here than is usual in the wild; presumably, they know they're safe. Windy Point is a prime spot, but you also have a good chance of seeing sheep virtually anywhere along this stretch of road. Whenever cars are stopped, sheep-viewing is probably the reason why; so, get well off the road and pay attention to traffic, which still will be passing at high speeds.

✔ **Bird Ridge Trail (mile 102):** This trail is a lung-busting climb of 3,000 feet in a little more than a mile. It starts as an easy, accessible trail but then rises steeply to views that start at impressive and become even more amazing as you climb.

✔ **Bird Creek (mile 100):** With the southern exposure, the creek is dry early in the year. Across the creek, you'll find a short trail, interpretive signs, an overlook, and a platform that makes fishing easier for people with disabilities. Pink salmon run late June to mid-August; silver salmon, mid-July to August.

✔ **The Flats (miles 96 to 90):** At **Bird Point,** with a large wayside, the highway descends from mountainside to mudflats. A fragment of a bike trail parallels the highway for this 6-mile stretch. At high tide, water comes right up to the road. At low tide, the entire Arm narrows to a thin, winding channel through the mud. Since the 1964 Good Friday earthquake, the Arm hasn't been navigable; before the earthquake, no one ever had much reason to navigate it. The first to try was Captain James Cook in 1778, when he was searching for the Northwest Passage on his final, fatal voyage of discovery (he was killed by Hawaiians later that year). He named this branch of Cook Inlet "Turnagain Arm," because the strength of the currents and shoals forced his boat to keep turning around.

✔ **Turnoff to Girdwood (mile 90):** The attractions of Girdwood, which I cover later in this chapter, are worth a visit, but the shopping center here at the intersection is not chief among them. Stop for a simple meal, a restroom break, or to fill your gas tank for the last time for many a mile.

✔ **Old Portage (mile 80):** All along the flats at the head of Turnagain Arm are large marshes full of what looks like standing driftwood. These are actually the remnants of trees killed by salt water that flowed in when the 1964 quake lowered the land by as much as 10 feet. On the right, 9 miles beyond the turnoff for Girdwood and across from the former rail depot, a few ruins of the abandoned town of Portage still are visible almost 40 years after the great earthquake. (See Chapter 14 for details about Earthquake Park in Anchorage, which offers additional information about this devastating earthquake.)

The turnouts offer good bird-watching spots, but venturing out on Turnagain Arm's tidal mud carries the real risk of getting stuck in quicksand-like mud and drowning in the tide.

✔ **Big Game Alaska Wildlife Center (mile 79):** A 140-acre fenced compound on this glacial valley provides shelter for injured or orphaned deer, moose, eagles, owls, elk, bison, musk ox, bear, and caribou (☎ **907-783-2025;** Internet: www.biggamealaska.com). One moose is a movie star, but the animals, for the most part, spend their lives on display for visitors, who pick up a cassette tape and map and drive a short course looking at them in 3- to 5-acre enclosures. The center offers easy ways for children to see wildlife that they may not have patience to wait for in the wild. A large log gift shop is at the end of the tour. Admission is $5 for adults, $3 for military, seniors, and children ages 4 to 12, with a maximum of $20 per vehicle. In summer, it's open daily from 8 a.m. to 8 p.m.; in winter, daily 10 a.m. to 6 p.m.

✔ **Portage Glacier (take the 5.5-mile spur road at mile 78):** The named attraction has largely melted, receding out of sight of the visitor center. (The glacier that you can see is Burns Glacier.) When the center was built in 1985, Portage Glacier was predicted to keep floating on its 800-foot-deep lake until the year 2020. Instead, it withdrew to the far edge of the lake in 1995. Today, the exhibits in the lakeside **Begich, Boggs Visitor Center** (☎ **907-783-2326**) focus on the Chugach National Forest as a whole, rather than just the glacier; the exhibits are well worth an hour or two to become oriented to the area's nature, history, and lifestyles.

Several short trails start near the center. Rangers lead nature walks on the ¼-mile, paved Moraine Trail up to six times a day. Another trail leads less than a mile to Byron Glacier, in case you're interested in getting up close to some ice. Always dress warmly, because cold winds are the rule in this funnel-like valley.

A **day boat** operated by **Gray Line of Alaska** (☎ **800-544-2206** Seattle, 907-277-5581 Anchorage, or 907-783-2983 at the lake; Internet: www.graylineofalaska.com) traverses the lake to get right up to Portage Glacier on hour-long tours, ice conditions permitting. It costs $25 adults, $12.50 ages 2 to 12, and operates five times daily in summer, every 90 minutes starting at 10:30 a.m. If this is your only chance to see a glacier in Alaska, it's probably a

good example, but if your itinerary includes any of the great glaciers in Prince William Sound, Kenai Fjords National Park, or the
like, you won't be as impressed by Portage. You also can get a free
view of the glacier by taking a left just before the visitor center
and stopping at a pullout on the way to the Whittier Tunnel.

Enjoying the Slopes of Girdwood

Girdwood, 37 miles south of Anchorage, is proof that a charming little
town can coexist with a major ski resort, as long as the resort goes
undiscovered by the world's skiers. Girdwood still has a sleepy, offbeat
character. Retired hippies, ski bums, a U.S. senator, and a few old-timers
live in the houses and cabins among the big spruce trees in the valley
below the Mount Alyeska lifts. They all expected a development explo-
sion to follow the construction of an international resort here a few
years ago, but it hasn't happened. Although that may not be good news
for the investors in the resort, it's great for skiers and other visitors
who discover this paradise. They find varied, uncrowded skiing through
long winters, superb accommodations, and an authentically funky
community.

The primary summer attractions are the hiking trails, the tram to the
top of **Mount Alyeska,** and the **Crow Creek Mine,** described later in
this chapter. In winter, it's skiing. Mount Alyeska doesn't have the size
of some of the famous resorts in the Rockies, but it's large and steep
enough. Better still, it isn't crowded, half the mountain is above the
tree line, and the snow lasts a long time. Olympian Tommy Moe trained
here. Skiers used to tamer, busier slopes rave about the skiing here,
with long, challenging downhills, no lift lines, and stunning views of the
Chugach Mountains above and glistening Turnagain Arm below.

Getting there

A **rental car** is the most practical mode of transportation to Girdwood.
The preceding section gives directions for driving from Anchorage to
Girdwood. In summer, you can come down for the sights and hikes; in
winter, you can make it a day trip for winter sports. If you plan to stay
at the resort for skiing, however, you may not need a car. Call the
resort to find out whether shuttle service is available.

Seeing the sights

Crow Creek Mine
Girdwood

This mine opened in 1898 and operated until 1940. The Toohey family
has turned the paths and 14 small buildings into a charming tourist

attraction where you can witness the frontier lifestyle and watch rabbits and ducks wandering around. A bag of dirt that's guaranteed to have some gold in it is provided for you to experience what panning for gold was like, and you can dig and pan to get more, if you have the patience for it — which few people do. Note that Crow Creek Road, off the Alyeska Highway, is quite rough and muddy during the spring.

Crow Creek Road (off the Alyeska Highway), Girdwood, AK 99587. ☎ 907-278-8060. Open: May 15–Sept 15 daily 9 a.m.–6 p.m. Admission: $3 adults, free for children 11 and younger. Gold panning $5 adults, $4 children.

Mount Alyeska Tram
Girdwood

The tram isn't cheap, but it's worth the price if you otherwise may not make it to high alpine tundra during an Alaska trip. (In winter, ride on your lift ticket; in summer, ride free while taking in a meal at the Seven Glaciers Restaurant at the top — covered later in this chapter.) The tram takes seven minutes in summer to rise to the 2,300-foot level, where it stops at a station with an attractive but overpriced cafeteria. The tram presents an opportunity for everyone, no matter how young, old, or infirm, to experience the pure light, limitless views, and crystalline quiet of an Alaskan mountaintop. Take the opportunity to walk around and enjoy it. Dress very warmly.

At the Alyeska Prince Hotel (see below). $16 adults ($12 Alaska residents), $15 ages 55 and older, $10 ages 8–17, $7 ages 7 and younger.

Getting outdoors in Girdwood

For additional information about activities in this area, contact the **Alyeska Resort** (see "Where to stay," below).

Skiing

Mount Alyeska, at 3,939 feet, has 1,000 acres of skiing, operated by Alyeska Resort (☎ 907-754-2285; Internet: www.alyeskaresort.com), beginning from a base elevation of only 250 feet and rising 2,500 feet. The normal season is early November to April, though skiing often lasts through Memorial Day weekend. Winters without plenty of snow are rare. The average snowfall is 721 inches, or 61 feet. Because it's near the water, the weather is rarely very cold. Light is more of an issue, with the short days in midwinter.

You can ski after dark (after 3 p.m. in mid-winter) on 27 lighted trails covering 2,000 vertical feet on Friday and Saturday evenings mid-December to mid-March, but the best Alaska skiing is when the days get longer and warmer during the spring. The resort has nine lifts, including the tram. Two chairs serve beginners, with a vertical drop of around 300 feet. The other 89% of the mountain is geared for intermediate to expert skiers. The mountain is steep, and the expert slopes are pretty extreme, but more than half are rated intermediate. Helicopter skiing starts out right from the hotel as well.

An all-day lift ticket costs $45 for adults, $27 for ages 14 to 17, $20 for those 8 to 13 or 60 to 69, and $7 for ages 7 and younger or older than 70. Private and group instruction is available, and a basic rental package costs $22 a day for adults, $12 for ages 13 and younger or older than 60.

The resort also has groomed **cross-country trails** and gear for rent, but the best Nordic skiing is in Anchorage (see Chapter 14).

A utilitarian **day lodge** with snack and rental counters is located at the front of the mountain, as is the **Sitzmark Bar,** a more comfortable place for a meal (burgers are about $8). The hotel is on the other side of the mountain, connected to the front by the tram to the top and beginner-level chair 7 (you can ski right from the door). The hotel is a quieter and more genteel starting point for day-trippers and guests, because it has its own rental counter and day lockers. The hotel has several dining choices, two at the top of the tram (see "Where to dine," below).

A center operated by **Challenge Alaska** (☎ **907-783-2925** or 907-344-7399) enables skiers with disabilities to use the mountain, skiing down to the lift to start and back to the center at day's end.

Snowmobiling and dog mushing

Alaska Outdoor Adventures (☎ **888-414-7669** or 907-783-7669; Internet: www.snowmobile-alaska.com), in a cabin at the base of the mountain, offers snowmobile tours in Turnagain Pass for raw beginners, with everything provided, but it isn't the hand-holding experience you expect from a commercial tour: Guests are soon flying off through the snow in exciting style, using their own judgment. The guides are professional and the machines powerful. Three-hour trips are $110 (an additional rider is about half off). A five-hour tour to the Placer Glacier, for $175, is a better choice for sightseeing and exploring rather than just playing. Hour-long dog-sled rides also are offered ($70 adults, $50 children). You ride in the sled, and then get to drive the dogs yourself.

Hiking

A couple of great hiking trails begin in Girdwood. The **Winner Creek Trail** runs 5 miles through forest from behind the Alyeska Prince Hotel to a roaring gorge where Winner Creek and Glacier Creek meet; it's muddy and snowy in the spring. The winter ski trail takes a separate route, through a series of meadows, to the same destination. The **Crow Pass Trail** rises into the mountains and passes all the way over to Eagle River, after a 26-mile hike that you can do in a couple of days. But you can make a long day hike of it to the pass and see the glaciers, wildflower meadows, and old mining equipment. The trailhead is up Crow Creek Road, off the Alyeska Highway.

Where to stay

Besides the resort hotel, plenty of condos and B&Bs are in town. **Alyeska Accommodations,** on Olympic Circle (☎ **888-783-2001** or 907-783-2000; Internet: www.alyeskaaccommodations.com), offers condos, chalets, and houses. The **Girdwood Bed and Breakfast Association** (☎ **907-222-4858;** Internet: www.gbba.org) networks B&Bs in the area that are inspected for quality.

Alyeska Prince Hotel
$$$$$ Girdwood

The Alyeska Resort's hotel is Alaska's best. The beauty of the building alone separates it from the competition. Standing in an unspoiled mountain valley among huge spruce trees, studded with dormers and turrets, it impresses on first sight. Inside, sumptuous cherrywood and rich colors unite the welcoming common rooms and elegant guest rooms. Although not large, the rooms have every convenience, and the maintenance and housekeeping are exceptional. The swimming pool is magnificent, with a cathedral ceiling and windows by the spa overlooking the mountain. They offer children's programs, and a tour-desk personnel in the lobby can take care of booking your activities.

Four restaurants vie for attention, including the cafe and mountaintop cafeteria. The **Seven Glaciers,** 2,300 feet above the lobby by tram on Mount Alyeska, serves trendy and beautifully presented dinners in a sumptuous dining room floating above the clouds (wear a coat on the unheated tram). The hotel's Japanese cuisine also has developed a reputation, and off the lobby is a teppanyaki dining room, where chefs create your meal at your table.

One warning: On winter weekends, especially around holidays, families from Anchorage, like mine, descend on the hotel with noisy children. Couples would do well to come midweek.

1000 Arlberg Ave. (P.O. Box 249), Girdwood, AK 99587. ☎ 800-880-3880 or 907-754-2111. Fax: 907-754-2200. Internet: www.alyeskaresort.com. *Rack rates: Summer and Christmas $195–$435 double, $800–$1,600 suite; winter $145–$280 double, $600–$1,100 suite; extra adult $25; children stay free in parents' room. AE, DC, MC, V.*

Where to dine

Chair 5
$$ Girdwood   Seafood/Burgers/Pizza

This is where Girdwood locals meet their friends and take their families for dinner, and it's one of our favorites after skiing. One afternoon, Bob

Dylan music accompanied a friendly game of pool while men with pony-tails and beards sipped microbrews. Another evening, a guy in the entry-way entertained the children with magic tricks, and a waitress asked them to draw pictures to enter into a contest. The menu offers choices pleasing to all, including pizza, burgers, fresh fish, and steaks.

5 Linblad St., town square. ☎ *907-783-2500. Internet:* www.chairfive.com. *All meals: $8–$20; large pizza: $15.75–$19.75. AE, MC, V. Open: daily 11 a.m. to midnight.*

Double Musky Inn

$$$$ Girdwood   Cajun

The ski-bum-casual atmosphere and rambling, cluttered dining room among the trees match the wonderful Cajun and New Orleans food in a way that couldn't have been contrived — it's at once too improbable and too authentic. Service is relaxed to a fault, and food takes a long time to arrive, but when it does it's flawless. However, the place isn't to every-one's liking. Your senses can feel raw after the extreme noise, highly spiced food, and crowds, and parking can be difficult. Loud groups will enjoy it more than couples, and families don't really fit. They have a full bar.

Mile 3, Crow Creek Rd., Girdwood. ☎ *907-783-2822. Internet:* www.double muskyinn.com. *Main courses: $18–$32. AE, DC, DISC, MC, V. Open: Tues–Thurs 5–10 p.m., Fri–Sun 4:30–10:00 p.m. Closed Nov.*

Embarking on Prince William Sound from Whittier

Almost all of Prince William Sound is in Chugach National Forest, the nation's second largest. The Sound is a world to itself, one largely free of people, with 3,500 miles of shoreline coursing its folded islands and deeply penetrating fjords and passages. And Whittier is Anchorage's portal to this vast wildness.

Although Anchorage itself is on Upper Cook Inlet, that muddy, fast-moving waterway is little used for recreational boating. Whittier, on the other hand, stands on the edge of a long fjord in the northwest corner of the sound, where clear waters are full of salmon, orcas, and otters, and bounded by rocky shores, rain forests, and glaciers. The water also is calmer here than on excursions to Kenai Fjords National Park (cov-ered in Chapter 16), so seasickness is rare, and the glaciers are more numerous.

I consider Whittier a day trip in the purest sense of the term, and because I can think of no reason to spend the night there, I don't list any accommodations in this section. Other than a trip on the Sound, you have little reason to go to Whittier — unless you're on a quest to find the oddest towns in America. Most of the 182 townspeople live in a single 14-story concrete building with dark, narrow hallways. The grocery store is on the first floor and the medical clinic on the third. **The Begich Towers,** as the dominant structure is called, was built during the 1940s, when Whittier's strategic location on the Alaska Railroad and at the head of a deep Prince William Sound fjord made it a key port in the defense of Alaska. Today, with its barren gravel ground and ramshackle warehouses and boat sheds, the town has a stark military-industrial character. An **ATM** is located at the liquor store near the boat harbor, but Whittier lacks a bank and other services, so bring what you need.

Getting there

If you plan to take a day trip on the Sound from a base in Anchorage — the way most people use Whittier — leave the car behind and take a train or bus all the way. Tour boat operators (listed below) will book the transportation from Anchorage for you, greatly simplifying the process and assuring that you'll be on time for the boat. If you have a party of more than two, however, you'll save money by driving. Likewise, drive whenever you plan to continue through the Sound by ferry. In that case, carefully read "By car," later in this chapter, to find out about the unusual process of getting through the tunnel to Whittier.

By bus

Boat tour operators put visitors on buses and vans from Anchorage that can save more than the price of riding the train; expect to pay round-trip fares of $40 or $45. Reserve and get details when you buy your boat cruise ticket.

By train

The **Alaska Railroad** (☎ **800-544-0552** or 907-265-2494; Internet: www.alaskarailroad.com) runs a daily train with self-propelled cars, similar to those used on commuter lines, timed to match the schedules of Prince William Sound tour boats. Unless you have planned an activity or tour on the water, however, you'll find the six-hour stay in Whittier is too long just to hang around. The round-trip fare is $55, one-way $45, half price for ages 2 to 11. The large tour operators will book it for you when you buy your boat ticket. However, if you're traveling with at least one more person, a rental car saves you money.

By car

Take the Seward Highway, as described in "Driving between Mountain and Sea on the Seward Highway," earlier in this chapter, to the Portage Glacier Road, at mile 78 (48 miles from Anchorage). Allow at least an hour from Anchorage without stops. The road through the 2.8-mile-long World War II–era rail tunnel to Whittier is only one lane that also is used to accommodate trains, so you may have to wait your turn. Check the schedule at the tunnel's Web site (link to it from www.dot.state.ak.us), on its phone recording (☎ 877-611-2586 or 907-566-2244), or on the radio (1610 AM in Portage or 530 AM in Whittier). You may be able to time your passage so that you keep the length of your trip to an hour.

Checking the schedule helps you avoid a wait of an hour or more caused by missing the opening for your particular direction of travel. Nevertheless, you may still have to wait if you arrive during peak periods and too many other vehicles are in line ahead of you also waiting to get through during a single open period. You'll wait for your open period in a staging area with standing lanes similar to what you'd find when driving your car onto a ferry. For the best chance to get through the tunnel, choose the shortest line, as each line gets an equal amount of time for driving through.

Summer tunnel hours are daily 6 a.m. to 11 p.m.; winter hours are shorter and are subject to change, so check ahead. The tunnel closes altogether at night. The tolls are $12 for cars and $20 for RVs, cars with trailers, or large vans. The fee is levied only on vehicles headed toward Whittier. Special permits are required for really huge vehicles (higher than 14 feet or wider than 10 feet). Parking in Whittier is $5 a day. As I mention in the introduction of this section, Whittier really isn't worth the trouble unless you're going out on the water.

By ferry

The **Alaska Marine Highway System** ferry *Bartlett* (☎ 800-642-0066 or 800-764-3779 TTY; Internet: www.alaska.gov/ferry) makes a seven-hour run to Valdez several times a week, where you can drive north on the beautiful Richardson Highway, making a complete circle back to Anchorage in two days or more. That's covered in Chapter 18.

Getting out on the Sound

Whittier is the entrance to western Prince William Sound, at the end of one of many long, deep fjords where marine mammals and eagles are common. You can ride one of the tour boats that cruise these waters from Whittier, viewing glaciers at the heads of many of the fjords.

Large tour boats

Several companies with offices in Anchorage compete for your business, offering day-trip tours to the Sound's western glaciers. Besides having incredible scenery, the water is calm, making seasickness unlikely — for the queasy, this is a much better choice than Kenai Fjords National Park. Each operator times departures to coordinate with the daily Alaska Railroad train from Anchorage, described in the "Getting there" section, earlier in this chapter. That means they have up to six hours for the trip. Some tour companies try to show you as much as possible, while others take it slower so that you can savor the scenery and wildlife sightings. Between train and boat fares, expect to spend $145 to $185 per person for this day's outing, leaving Anchorage at 10:00 a.m. and returning at 9:30 p.m. You can save $10 to $15 a person and up to three hours by taking a bus that the tour boat company arranges instead of the train. When you have three or more people, you can save by renting a car and driving. You'll also have to buy some meals, although lunch is included with the price of the tour on some boats.

Major Marine Tours

This company operates a smaller, 149-passenger vessel at a slower pace than Phillips — they visit a mere ten glaciers, but spend more time waiting for ice to calve, that is, fall from glaciers. The route goes up Blackstone Bay. The boat is comfortable, with reserved table seating. They also put more emphasis on their food, which costs extra; the salmon and prime rib buffet is $12 for adults, $6 for children. Time on the water is five hours.

411 W. Fourth Ave., Anchorage, AK 99501. ☎ *800-764-7300 or 907-274-7300. Internet:* www.majormarine.com. *Price: $99 adults, $49 children ages 11 and under.*

Phillips' Cruises and Tours

The 26-glacier cruise travels the Sound on a fast three-deck catamaran, counting the glaciers as it goes. The boat ride is 4½ hours, so if you use their bus, your total time from Anchorage is less than 8½ hours.

519 W. Fourth Ave., Anchorage, AK 99501. ☎ *800-544-0529 or 907-276-8023. Internet:* www.26glaciers.com. *Price: $129 adults, $69 children younger than 12.*

Small tour boats

Instead of getting on a giant tour boat with a mob of people, you can go on a small boat with a local who you'll get to know as he shows off favorite places and lands on beaches to picnic and walk. If you see a whale or other point of interest, you stay as long or as short a time as you like. What you give up are the creature comforts of a larger, tour-bus-like vessel, and most small boats have a four-person minimum.

Honey Charters

This family-run operation offers small boats licensed for six to ten passengers, specializing in personal tours, water transportation, and kayaker drop-offs. Honey Charters operates with a minimum of four passengers; by paying the four-person minimum, you can have the boat to yourself. For larger groups, a new boat can carry 18 kayakers or 30 on a sightseeing cruise.

On the Whittier waterfront (P.O. Box 708), Whittier, AK 99693. ☎ *888-477-2493 or 907-472-2493. Internet:* www.honeycharters.com. *Price: 3-hr. cruise: $99 per person; 6 hrs.: $149 per person; 11 hrs.: $199 person.*

Sound Eco Adventures

Gerry Sanger, a retired wildlife biologist who spent years researching the waterfowl and ecology of Prince William Sound, now carries up to six passengers at a time on wildlife and glacier tours and drops off kayakers from his 29-foot aluminum boat, which has a landing-craft-like ramp that's perfect for landing on gravel beaches and is suitable for wheelchairs. He claims better than a 90-percent success rate on whale-watching trips, quite high for the Sound.

P.O. Box 707, Whittier, AK 99693. ☎ *888-471-2312 or 907-472-2312. Internet:* www.SoundEcoAdventure.com. *Price: 10-hr. wildlife cruise: $195 per person; 5½ hrs: $165; or charter the entire boat for $145/hr.*

Fishing

More than a dozen charter fishing boats operate out of Whittier, the closest saltwater fishing to Anchorage, mostly targeting halibut but also hooking salmon at certain times. The Whittier Harbormaster can give you a list of operators (☎ **907-472-2330**). **Bread N Butter Charters** (☎ **888-472-2396** or 907-472-2396) has been around for a while. They charge $195 per person for a day of halibut fishing and have an office on the waterfront. Honey Charters, listed earlier in this chapter under "Small tour boats," has a similar service.

Sea kayaking

Whittier is a popular starting point for kayak trips to beautiful and protected western Prince William Sound. Day trips for beginners paddle along the shore near Whittier, often visiting a bird rookery, or you can take a boat 5 miles from the harbor to Shotgun Cove and paddle back. Longer multiday trips go by boat to even more interesting waters where you can visit glaciated fjords and paddle narrow passages. The following lists a couple of kayaking businesses compete in Whittier:

✔ **Alaska Sea-Kayakers** (☎ **877-472-2534** or 907-472-2534; Internet: www.alaskaseakayakers.com) offers three- and five-hour day trips for $70 and $140, respectively. Their paddles at Blackstone Glacier, which begin with a charter boat ride, cost $250. They offer extended trips, too. Self-guided kayakers can rent equipment at the Whittier office.

✔ The **Prince William Sound Kayak Center** (☎ **877-472-2452** or 907-472-2452; Internet: www.pwskayakcenter.com) offers guided three-hour trips starting at $55. They also take guests on day trips to Blackstone Bay, usually seen only on overnighters, and have escorted trips of two to four days. The two-day trip is $140 per person, with a two-person minimum.

Where to dine

You can get a meal in the triangle at the east end of the harbor, including a good Chinese food place, the **China Sea** (☎ **907-472-2222**). Away from the harbor, the **Anchor Inn** (☎ **907-472-2354**), near the town's main building, is a burger joint and bar of many years' standing.

Taking a Side Trip to the Mat-Su Valley

Here are some highlights of the **Matanuska** and **Susitna valleys,** the suburbs to the north of Anchorage commonly referred to as Mat-Su. You may want to spend a night there, but, more than likely, you'll merely pass through on a drive north, taking advantage of some of the area's attractions. The choice is yours. Reached by the Glenn Highway about 40 miles from Anchorage, the Mat-Su area is both a bedroom community for the city and a former frontier-farming region with its own quirky identity.

In this summary, I discuss a few highlights in the central area of the valley (the whole thing is the size of West Virginia). Other area highlights include Talkeetna, which is presented with Denali National Park in Chapter 19; rafting the Matanuska River (included in Chapter 14); and the Glenn Highway, which is covered in Chapter 18.

Seeing the valley's highlights

The only way to travel to the Mat-Su Valley is by car. Here are some stops to make if you're merely passing through or spending a little more time exploring the area.

Hatcher Pass

If you're headed north to Denali National Park or Fairbanks, the rough, winding gravel road through Hatcher Pass to Willow makes a glorious alpine detour around what otherwise would be the least attractive part of your drive. Past the mine and skiing area, the road is open only in summer and is not suitable for large RVs. Just after the Parks Highway branches from the Glenn Highway, exit to the right on the Trunk Road and keep going north on Fishhook Road. From the Glenn Highway near Palmer, take Fishhook just north of town. Check with the Alaska Department of Transportation for road conditions before you leave (☎ **800-478-7675;** Internet: www.dot.state.ak.us).

Even when you're not headed farther north, a trip to Hatcher Pass combines one of the area's most beautiful drives, access to great hiking or Nordic skiing, and interesting old buildings to look at. The **Independence Mine State Historical Park** (☎ **907-745-2827** or 907-745-3975; Internet: www.alaskastateparks.org, click on the Individual Parks link) takes in the remains of a hard-rock gold-mine operation that closed down in 1943. Some buildings have been restored, including an assay office (now a museum) and the manager's house (now a welcoming visitor center), while other structures sag and lean as picturesque ruins. The park is undergoing a renovation, so many details about it are changing. At present, $3 guided tours ($2 seniors, free for ages younger than 10) leave at 1:30 and 3:30 p.m. weekdays, plus 4:30 p.m. weekends, or you can wander with the help of an excellent walking-tour map. The visitor center is open 11 a.m. to 7 p.m. daily in the summer, but closes the week after Labor Day.

The high Talkeetna Mountains valley that the site occupies is ideal for a summer ramble in the heather or for downhill and backcountry skiing in winter. Four hiking trails and two mountain-biking routes are situated in the area — ask for directions at the visitor center. One great hike is the 8-mile **Gold Mint Trail,** which starts across the road from the Motherlode Lodge on Fishhook Road and ends at the Mint Glacier, where you have to turn around to hike back.

Along the Parks Highway

Driving north on the Parks Highway from Anchorage to Denali National Park or Fairbanks takes you through the populated central part of the valley. The area is not attractive — it looks like an unplanned highway development anywhere — but among some of the good stops to make, if you're of a mind, is **The Museum of Alaska Transportation and Industry,** off the Parks Highway at mile 47, west of Wasilla (☎ **907-376-1211;** Internet: www.alaska.net/~rmorris/matil.htm). Volunteers have gathered every conceivable machine and conveyance — 13 fire trucks, 7 locomotives, and 2 steam cranes, for example — and fixed up as many as they could to running condition. An indoor museum displays the finished masterpieces, while the 20 acres outside are crammed with future projects — trains, aircraft, tractors, fishing boats, and mining equipment — all grist for memories and imagination. The museum is open May through September, 10 a.m. to 6 p.m. daily; October through April, 9 a.m. to 5 p.m. Saturday only, or by appointment. Admission is $8 for adults, $5 for students and seniors, $14 for families, free for ages younger than 8.

Along the Glenn Highway

The Glenn Highway, north from the Parks Highway intersection and onward north of Palmer, is one of Alaska's prettiest drives. The road traces the edge of a rugged canyon over the Matanuska River and glacier. (More about that in Chapter 18.) Nearer Anchorage, the main attraction is the Alaska State Fair in Palmer, which takes place the week before Labor Day. See Chapter 2 for details.

Where to stay and dine

Best Western Lake Lucille Inn

$$$ Wasilla

For a spot along the Parks Highway, this well-run, attractive lakeside hotel right in Wasilla has the best standard hotel rooms in the valley. They're large and well appointed, and those facing the lake have balconies and a grand, peaceful view. Various kinds of boats can be rented for play on Lake Lucille, and flightseeing trips take off right from the dock below the lawn. The restaurant is one of the best in the area, with a light, quiet dining room looking out on the water. It's open for dinner only, with the beef and seafood dinner menu ranging from $15 to $38.

1300 W. Lucille Dr., Wasilla, AK 99654. ☎ *800-528-1234 for reservations, or 907-373-1776. Fax 907-376-6199. Internet:* www.bestwestern.com/lake lucilleinn. *Rack rate: High season $149 double, $209 suite; low season $92 double, $139–$159 suite; extra person $10. AE, DC, DISC, MC, V.*

Colony Inn

$ Palmer

This place is about an hour's drive from Anchorage, and ideal if you're traveling the Glenn Highway. This perfect country inn occupies a lovingly restored teacher's dormitory from the New Deal Colony Project, right in the middle of Palmer. The rooms are wonderfully old-fashioned, with rockers and comforters but also Jacuzzi bathtubs and big TVs with VCRs. A large sitting room and a dining room downstairs are decorated with historic photographs that help tell the building's story. Excellent lunches and inexpensive dinners are served here during the summer at the **Inn Cafe** (☎ **907-746-6118**).

325 E. Elmwood, Palmer, AK 99645. ☎ *907-745-3330. Fax: 907-746-3330. Rack rate: $85 double, $170 suite; extra person $5. AE, DISC, MC, V.*

Hatcher Pass Lodge

$$ Hatcher Pass

Nine good A-frame cabins with chemical toilets sit in the treeless bowl of the 3,000-foot alpine pass, deeply buried in snow in winter and surrounded by heather in summer. Running water and showers are available in the fun, funky little restaurant. It's a great family place where, in the winter, you can ski out the front door on up to 20 kilometers of Nordic trails. Cabins lack phones and have no TVs; it's a little like camping, which is why I think kids will enjoy it.

P.O. Box 763, Palmer, AK 99645. ☎ *907-745-5897. Internet:* www.hatcherpass lodge.com. *Rack rates: $95–$115 cabin for 2, extra person $15. AE, DC, DISC, MC, V.*

Part IV
Road Trips from Anchorage

The 5th Wave   By Rich Tennant

"The guests are getting hungry. You'd better push over another garbage dumpster."

In this part . . .

The easiest way to many of Alaska's best destinations is along the two-lane highways that wind through the mountains from the South Central coast into the Interior and beyond, all the way to the Arctic Ocean. With a car that you rent in Anchorage, you can get to the forests and ocean shores of the Kenai Peninsula, including Seward, Kenai Fjords National Park, Kenai, and Homer. You can drive to Fairbanks and explore the long Interior highways. And you can see the wildlife and scenery of Denali National Park.

Chapter 16

The Kenai Peninsula: Seward, Kenai Fjords National Park, Kenai, and Homer

. . . .

In This Chapter

▶ Anticipating the highlights in the Kenai Peninsula

▶ Discovering Seward

▶ Cruising Kenai Fjords National Park

▶ Fishing in Kenai and Soldotna

▶ Experiencing Homer

. . . .

The Kenai (*keen*-eye) Peninsula is a microcosm of what's most appealing about Alaska, and you can get to it without the expense and exhausting effort that can make traveling much of the state difficult. South of Anchorage, between Cook Inlet and Prince William Sound, the peninsula is a landmass large enough to show up on any globe. But it's not unimaginably vast and intimidating, the way so much of Alaska is. And it's accessible, with roads, rails, and frequent air service. Traveling here is a bit more like traveling anywhere else in America (if you leave aside the amazing beauty and huge undeveloped areas). You have no need for guides or tour buses; on the Kenai Peninsula, you can discover Alaska on your own.

Most of what you're looking for lies along a few hundred miles of blacktop, within reach of a rental car and perhaps a tour boat ticket: glaciers, whales, legendary sportfishing, spectacular hiking trails, interesting little fishing towns and art colonies, bears, moose, and high mountains. People from Anchorage go to the peninsula for the weekend to fish, hike, dig clams, and paddle kayaks. Certain places can become crowded. But it's easy to break past the humanity into places where you'll see few, if any, other people. There you can easily and inexpensively get beyond the road network altogether.

Discovering the Kenai Peninsula and Its Major Attractions

Set aside enough time to visit Kenai Fjords National Park from Seward, at least one overnight from Anchorage. For Homer or Kenai, allow two or more nights, because driving around that area takes time when you consider how tempting it is to stop along the way to view all the open and beautiful public land. The following sections contain a few of the highlights you need to look for while you're here. And check out "The Kenai Peninsula & Prince William Sound" map in this chapter.

Seward

Seward, which is situated at the head of a large fjord opening on the Pacific Ocean called Resurrection Bay, was the traditional gateway into most of Alaska beginning with the earliest explorers and continuing through the age of rail, until modern jet travel started bringing people straight into Anchorage. An attractive little town, its main claim to fame is as a gateway. Visitors come to Seward to get out on the water and to visit Kenai Fjords National Park. The town lies 124 miles by road or rail from Anchorage on the southeastern side of the peninsula. While in Seward, be sure to

- ✔ **Visit the Alaska SeaLife Center,** a research aquarium where you can see marine mammals and birds up close.
- ✔ **Fish salmon in the ocean** from charter boats; they fish halibut here, too.
- ✔ **Sea kayak** among sea otters and along rocky shores and streams where salmon spawn.

Kenai Fjords National Park

This **marine park** is a place where mile-high mountains jut straight up out of the sea. Glaciers burst over the mountains' shoulders and dump big chunks of blue ice into the water. Craggy islands poke out of the sea, serving as hosts to thousands of nesting sea birds, and whales and other marine mammals cruise through regularly. Visitors arrive at the park on day-tour boats from Seward. The park also has a back door, **Exit Glacier,** accessible by land from Seward. Walk up for a close, personal look.

The Kenai Peninsula & Prince William Sound

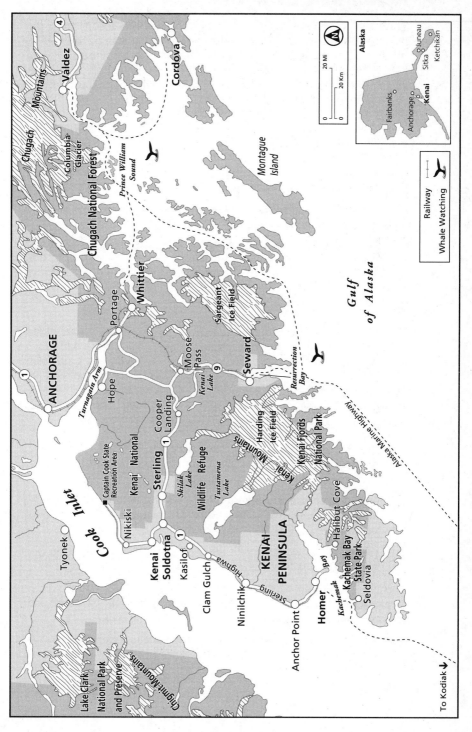

Kenai and Soldotna

The towns of Kenai and Soldotna sit on the banks of a supremely productive salmon stream, the **Kenai River,** which produces the world's biggest king salmon and many other species of fish. Visitors come to fish, but nonfishing members of the family can easily find some sightseeing to interest them, too. Alaska's most easily accessible canoe route is close at hand in the **Kenai National Wildlife Refuge** (which is *not* part of Kenai Fjords National Park). Kenai is about three hours' drive from Anchorage on the peninsula's west side. While you're there, check out what it's like to go

✔ **Salmon fishing in the Kenai River,** which is one of Alaska's top attractions. It's a chance to catch enormous, hard-fighting fish.

✔ **Walking through Russian heritage and contemporary art** during an interesting afternoon in the town of Kenai.

✔ **Exploring the lovely Kenai National Wildlife Refuge on an overnight canoe trip.**

Homer

This hip, artsy, and vigorous little town is on the shore of **Kachemak Bay,** which stretches out across the community's front yard like an outdoor smorgasbord. After seeing the galleries in town, you'll also want to take this opportunity to get across the water, beyond the road network, to experience Alaska directly. Take at least a couple of days to sample a taste of it and to justify the 4½-hour drive down from Anchorage to the end of the road. While in Homer, you can

✔ **Visit the galleries and the Pratt Museum.** View the output of Alaska's most active art colony and find out about the area's natural history.

✔ **Go tide-pooling and take a nature walk.** The nonprofit Center for Alaska Coastal Studies leads visitors on educational outdoor ventures.

✔ **Hook into a monstrous halibut.** The state's biggest charter boat fleet goes after fish that can top 300 pounds.

✔ **Sea kayak among tiny islands.** The waters of Kachemak Bay are also home to some fascinating wildlife, including sea otters and puffins.

✔ **Mountain bike and hike beyond the reach of cars.** A water taxi can take you for a day to wonderful paths and byways off the road network.

✔ **Dine at a watery art colony.** Boats are the only vehicles in the village of Halibut Cove, near Homer.

Exploring Seward Is No Folly

This agreeable little town started life as a place to fish and to get off
the boat for Alaska, and then it continued as a place for Alaskans and
visitors to get *on* boats to see the bay and Kenai Fjords National Park
(described in the "Enjoying the Wilds of Kenai Fjords National Park"
section, later in this chapter). With the growth of the cruise industry,
Seward again is a place to get *off* the boat. Most cruises that cross the
Gulf of Alaska start or end here, with their passengers taking a bus or
train to or from the airport in Anchorage. That flow of people has
brought considerable tourist development to town, mostly of a quality
that hasn't damaged the town's character.

Located by the broad fjord of Resurrection Bay, Seward is a mountainside grid of streets lined with old wood-frame houses and newer fishermen's residences (see the "Seward" map later in this chapter). It's long
been the sort of place where pedestrians casually wander across the
road, hardly glancing for cars, for there likely won't be any. Or, if there
are, they're ready to stop. The growing tourism industry brings more
traffic, but most of what's new has been good for the town. The largest
addition, the Alaska SeaLife Center, is a research aquarium that's open
to the public. Combined with Seward's excellent ocean fishing, the
national park, the wonderful hiking trails, and the unique and attractive
town itself, the new center makes Seward well worth a two-day visit.

Getting there

The easiest route to Seward is by car from Anchorage. But several
other options offer some unique (well, not so unique for Alaska) traveling opportunities.

By car

The 124-mile drive down from Anchorage on the Seward Highway is
easy and especially scenic. It takes about 2½ hours without stops, so
you need to allow at least an additional hour to get out and look at the
scenery, which is one of the highlights of a trip to Seward. The first 48
miles of this drive are described in detail in Chapter 15. For tips on
renting a car, see Chapters 7 and 13.

By train

The **Alaska Railroad** (☎ **800-544-0552** or 907-265-2494; Internet: www.
alaskarailroad.com) offers passenger service from Anchorage to
Seward and back daily during summer. The route is even prettier than
the highway, passing close to glaciers and following a ledge halfway up
the narrow, vertical Placer River gorge, where it ducks into tunnels and
pops out at bends in the river. The landscape looks the way it did when
the first person beheld it. The railroad's young guides are well trained.
The fare is $55 one-way, $90 round-trip; children ages 2 to 11 ride for
half price.

The railroad also offers money-saving lodging and sightseeing packages through its Web site (but don't try to do Seward as a day trip). A rental car is cheaper for all but single travelers, and more convenient when you get to Seward, but the train ride is unforgettable and getting around Seward is manageable without a car. Seward is the end of the line, however, so you'll just have to ride the same rails back to Anchorage.

By air

F.S. Air (☎ **907-248-9595** in Anchorage or 907-224-5920 in Seward) serves Seward with small-prop planes from Anchorage twice a day for $69 one-way, $99 round-trip.

By ferry

The ferry *Tustumena,* of the Alaska Marine Highway System (☎ **800-642-0066,** Seward terminal at 907-224-5485; Internet: www.alaska.gov/ferry), calls on Seward a few times a month bound for Valdez to the east or Kodiak to the west. Once a month in summer, the *Kennicott* travels from Juneau across the Gulf of Alaska to Valdez and then Seward. The $169 fare is a bargain, but it takes 50 hours. The terminal is at the cruise-ship dock, on the outside of the small-boat harbor.

Getting around

If you didn't bring a car, you can easily cover downtown Seward on foot, although a little help getting back and forth from the boat harbor is handy. **Glacier Independent Taxi** (☎ **907-224-5678**) is one of the cab companies, but you'll need your own wheels to travel to Exit Glacier (see the "Enjoying the Wilds of Kenai Fjords National Park" section, later in this chapter). To rent those wheels in Seward, try **Hertz,** 600 Port Ave. (☎ **907-224-4378**).

In addition to walking, however, Seward offers a couple of other interesting transport alternatives:

- ✔ If it isn't raining, a bike may be the best alternative. **Seward Mountain Bike Shop** (☎ **907-224-2448**), in a railcar near the depot at the harbor, rents high-performance mountain bikes and models good for just getting around town, in addition to accessory equipment. A cruiser is $12 half day, $19 full day.

- ✔ The **Chamber of Commerce Trolley** runs every half-hour from 10 a.m. to 7 p.m. daily in summer; it goes south along Third Avenue and north on Ballaine Street, stopping at the railroad depot, the cruise-ship dock, the Alaska SeaLife Center, and the harbor visitor center. The fare is $2 per trip, or $4 to ride all day. It's a convenient, money-saving system.

Seward

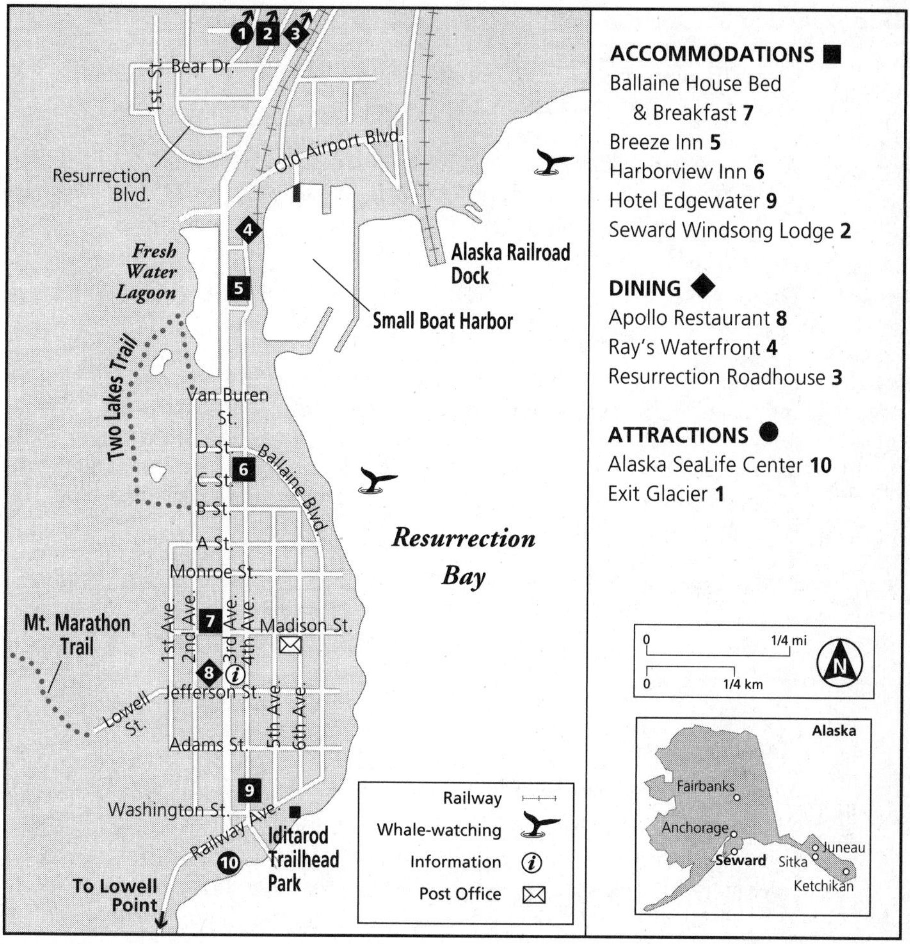
ACCOMMODATIONS ■
Ballaine House Bed & Breakfast 7
Breeze Inn 5
Harborview Inn 6
Hotel Edgewater 9
Seward Windsong Lodge 2
DINING ◆
Apollo Restaurant 8
Ray's Waterfront 4
Resurrection Roadhouse 3
ATTRACTIONS ●
Alaska SeaLife Center 10
Exit Glacier 1
Bear Dr.
1st. St.
Resurrection Blvd.
Old Airport Blvd.
Fresh Water Lagoon
Alaska Railroad Dock
Small Boat Harbor
Two Lakes Trail
Van Buren St.
D St.
C St.
B St.
A St.
Ballaine Blvd.
Monroe St.
Resurrection Bay
Mt. Marathon Trail
1st Ave.
2nd Ave.
3rd Ave.
4th Ave.
Madison St.
Jefferson St.
Lowell St.
Adams St.
5th Ave.
6th Ave.
Washington St.
Railway Ave.
Iditarod Trailhead Park
To Lowell Point
Railway
Whale-watching
Information
Post Office
0 1/4 mi
0 1/4 km
N
Alaska
Fairbanks
Anchorage
Seward
Sitka
Juneau
Ketchikan

Where to stay

Alaska's Point of View Reservation Service (☎ **907-224-2323;** Internet: `www.alaskasview.com`) is a Seward lodging and tour-booking agency. The Web site has an impressive search function for B&B lodgings. You also can get a list of B&Bs from the Chamber of Commerce visitor center (see "Fast Facts: Seward," later in this chapter).

Ballaine House Bed & Breakfast

$ Downtown Seward

This 1905 house near downtown is a classic B&B, with wooden floors, a large living room, and tall, double-hung windows. It's on the National Register of Historic Places and the town walking tour. The hostess,

Marilee Koszewski, is accommodating and fun. She decorates the B&B with antiques and handmade quilts, and provides raincoats, binoculars, and other gear for outings. She cooks breakfast to order and even does laundry. She also gives back the commission on boat bookings, which normally amounts to a discount of up to 20%. The four rooms are not large, and all bathrooms are shared.

437 Third Ave. (P.O. Box 2051), Seward, AK 99664-2051. ☎ 907-224-2362. Rack rate: $82 double; extra person $10. Rates include full breakfast cooked to order. No credit cards. No smoking. No children under 10.

The Breeze Inn
$$–$$$ Boat harbor

Located right at the busy boat harbor, this large, three-story, motel-style building offers good standard accommodations with the most conven-ient location in town for a fishing trip or a Kenai Fjords boat trip. Rooms are frequently renovated and have refrigerators and coffee makers. An annex building has excellent upscale rooms, some overlooking the harbor.

1306 Seward Hwy. (P.O. Box 2147), Seward, AK 99664-2147. ☎ 888-224-5237 in Alaska only, or 907-224-5238. Fax: 907-224-7024. Internet: www.breezeinn.com. *Rack rates: Summer $119–$160 double, winter $49 double; extra person $10. AE, DC, DISC, MC, V.*

Harborview Inn
$$$ Near the boat harbor

The energetic and hospitable Jerry and Jolene King take great pride in their inn, which grew from their bed-and-breakfast operation, for good reason — because theirs are among the most attractive rooms in town, with plenty of light, Mission-style furniture, and Tlingit art based on Jolene's tribal crest. The rates are good by Seward standards, and the location, midway between the Small Boat Harbor and downtown, puts both within long walking distance. A couple of two-bedroom apartments on the beach along Ballaine Avenue, perfect for families, rent for $149 a night. A nice one-bedroom apartment is in the main section, too.

804 Third Ave. (P.O. Box 1305), Seward, AK 99664. ☎ 888-324-3217 or 907-224-3217. Fax: 907-224-3218. Internet: www.SewardHotel.com. *Rack rates: High season $129 double, off-season $59 double; extra person $10. AE, MC, V.*

Hotel Edgewater
$$$$ Downtown Seward

Standing right across the street from the ocean and the SeaLife Center, this hotel has excellent views from two sides and a three-story atrium inside. The rooms have fine furniture and the hotel has upscale amenities, but it has cut more corners than you'd expect at a top-end place (lower-quality carpeting and wall coverings and a utilitarian elevator, for example), so it misses that opulent feel. A few rather claustrophobic rooms that face the atrium instead of the bay rent for $99 double occupancy. The room rate includes a continental breakfast.

200 Fifth Ave. (Box 1570), Seward, AK 99664. ☎ _888-793-6800 or 907-224-2700. Fax: 907-224-2701. Internet:_ www.hoteledgewater.com. _Rack rates: High season $99–$245 double, low season $65–$105 double; extra person $10. AE, DISC, MC, V._

Seward Windsong Lodge
$$$$ North of Seward

This big hotel is the only one at Kenai Fjords National Park with a national park atmosphere: The 12-unit buildings with mock log siding and the large restaurant and lobby buildings sit among spruce trees on the broad valley of the Resurrection River. The rooms are crisp and trim; all have two queen beds and rustic-style furniture. The price is high, however. The hotel restaurant, the **Resurrection Roadhouse,** is covered later in this chapter in the "Where to dine" section.

Mile 0.5, Herman Leirer Rd., also known as Exit Glacier Road. (Mailing address: 2525 C St., Ste. 405, Anchorage, AK 99503.) ☎ _888-959-9590 or 907-265-4501 in Anchorage, or 907-224-7116 in Seward. Internet:_ www.sewardwindsong.com. _Rack rates: High season $189 double, $239 suite; low season $129 double, $179 suite; extra person older than age 11 $10. AE, DISC, MC, V. Closed Oct–Apr._

Where to dine

You can find various places at the harbor to grab a sandwich or a quick meal on the way out to sea; they change too frequently for me to include here. Downtown, the **Ranting Raven,** at 228 Fourth Ave. (☎ **907-224-2228**), is a great little gift and coffee shop serving pastries, sandwiches, and soup; it's open April through Christmas.

Apollo Restaurant
$$ Downtown Seward   Mediterranean/Seafood

This is a surprisingly good small-town restaurant. Seward families come back for a menu that includes anything they may want: Greek and southern Italian cuisines, seafood, pizza, and more. But the overall cuisine is far more sophisticated and expertly turned out than you'd expect in such a place, especially the seafood dishes, and the service is fast and professional. The dining room, with many booths, takes the Greek theme as far as it will go — I especially enjoyed the miniature Doric columns. The same folks own Apollo II, selling pizza, sandwiches, and the like at the north end of the boat harbor.

229 Fourth Ave. ☎ *907-224-3092. Open: Daily 11 a.m.–11 p.m. Main courses: $10–$18. AE, MC, V.*

Ray's Waterfront
$$$ Boat harbor   Steak/Seafood

The lively, noisy dining room looks out from big windows across the Small Boat Harbor, with tables on terraces so everyone can see. The atmosphere is fun and the consistently good food is just right after a day on the water. Although not perfect, the fare is more nuanced than typical harborside places; the seafood chowder is great. More important, Ray's doesn't overcook the fresh local fish — and that's really all you can ask. Full liquor license.

At the Small Boat Harbor. ☎ *907-224-5606. Open: Daily 11 a.m.–11 p.m. Closed Oct to mid-Mar. Main courses: $16–$25; lunch: $6–$15. AE, DC, DISC, MC, V. 15% gratuity added for parties of 6 or more.*

Resurrection Roadhouse
$$$ North of town   Steak/Seafood/Pizza

This place (at the Seward Windsong Lodge, see the listing earlier in this chapter) has sometimes been subject to an annual shift in quality that's typical of seasonal restaurants, but I've had wonderful food here. The menu includes fish, venison, and ribs smoked in-house. Hand-thrown gourmet pizzas also are served. The dining room lacks life, but the mountain view is great, and you have plenty of space. The bar's collection of Alaskan craft brews on tap is exhaustive.

Mile 0.5, Herman Leirer Rd. (also known as Exit Glacier Road). ☎ *907-224-7116. Open: Daily 7:00 a.m.–2:30 p.m., 5–10 p.m.; closed mid-Oct to mid-Apr. Main courses: $9–$24; lunch $9–$13. AE, DISC, MC, V.*

Seward's top attractions

Well, Seward really has only one *top* attraction. I cover other in-town pastimes later in this chapter under "Other cool things to do in Seward."

Alaska SeaLife Center
Downtown Seward

The Alaska SeaLife Center is a serious research institution and a superb aquarium of creatures from the nearby Alaska waters. You may have seen puffins diving into the water from a tour boat; here you can see what they look like flying *under* the water. Seabirds, harbor seals, and sea lions reside in three large exhibits that you can see from above or below. Some smaller tanks house fish, crab, and other creatures, and a touch tank enables you to handle starfish and other tide-pool animals. Federal grants and *Exxon Valdez* oil-spill settlement winnings from Exxon built the center, and an exhibit updates the status of spill-damaged populations of birds and marine mammals. Not as large as a big-city aquarium, you're not likely to spend more than an hour or two visiting the center. Programs for kids and adults take place throughout the day: To make the most of the admission price, call ahead to catch a program that interests you.

301 Railway Ave. (P.O. Box 1329), Seward, AK 99664. ☎ 800-224-2525 or 907-224-6300. Internet: www.alaskasealife.org. *Open: Daily May–Aug 8 a.m.–8 p.m., Oct–Mar 10 a.m.–5 p.m., Sept and Apr 9 a.m.–6 p.m. Admission: $12.50 adults, $10 children 7–12, free for children 6 and younger.*

Getting outdoors in Seward

In this section, I describe things to do outdoors in Seward, other than visiting the national park, which includes the fjords and Exit Glacier, which is described in the "Enjoying the Wilds of Kenai Fjords National Park" section, later in this chapter.

Boating and sea kayaking

Miller's Landing, at Lowell Point 3 miles south of town (☎ **866-541-5739** or 907-224-5739; Internet: www.millerslandingak.com), is a good place to know about whenever you intend to spend any time outdoors around Seward. They offer sea-kayak lessons and tours and fishing charters with experienced skippers (and a campground and a boat launch with skiffs and sea kayaks for rent). Guided kayaking day trips are $50 to $180. The water-taxi operation charges flat rates for transportation to remote beaches and public cabins around the bay or the national park, for sea kayakers or those who just want to go off on their own.

Miller's Landing's kayak lessons are a good value: $50 for four hours of instruction, and then for only $25 more, a three-hour guided paddle to salmon-choked (in season) Tonsina Creek. Fishermen hang around the shop trading tall tales and advice (5 cents, with a money-back guarantee). The staff teaches you how to fish for salmon and sends you out on your own or on a guided charter.

Sunny Cove Sea Kayaking (☎ **800-770-9119** for reservations, or 907-224-8810; Internet: www.sunnycove.com) offers day trips suitable for beginners as part of the Kenai Fjords Tours trips to its Fox Island, and day trips and multiday trips into the fjords themselves. See the "Enjoying the Wilds of Kenai Fjords National Park" section, later in this chapter. Sunny Cove has earned a good reputation. On a budget, you can take one of their tours right from Seward. They launch from Lowell Point, following the shore toward Caines Head State Recreation Area, where you can see sea otters, seabirds, intertidal creatures, and the salmon in

Tonsina Creek. Three-hour paddles are $59; eight-hour trips are $125. A trip to Fox Island is more expensive but comes with a fjords boat tour, so it's roughly the same value.

Fishing

Seward is renowned for its saltwater silver salmon fishing. The silvers start showing up in the bay in mid-July and last through September. You can catch the fish from shore, from Lowell Point south of town, or even near the boat harbor, but your chances for success are far greater from a boat. I prefer small, six-passenger boats, because you can get to know the skipper better and use that contact to learn more about fishing. When your party has the entire boat, you can control where it goes, perhaps adding whale-watching or sightseeing to the day. The going rate for a guided charter, with everything provided, is about $170 per person, or $225 to fish for salmon and halibut on the same day. You can choose from among many charter services; most are booked through central charter agencies, which makes life simpler for visitors. But a couple of good ones are

- ✔ Andrew Mezirow, a marine biologist and diver for the SeaLife Center, tells you about the bay while you find fish on his large, comfortable boat; his business is **Crackerjack Sportfishing Charters** (☎ **907-224-2606;** Internet: www.crackerjackcharters.com).

- ✔ **The Fish House,** located at the Small Boat Harbor, books charters, sells and rents ocean-fishing and spin-casting gear, and carries some fly-fishing supplies. For charters, reserve ahead at P.O. Box 1209, Seward, AK 99664 (☎ **800-257-7760** or 907-224-3674; Internet: www.thefishhouse.net).

Hiking

You'll find some excellent hiking trails near Seward. You can obtain a complete list and directions at the Kenai Fjords National Park Visitor Center (see the upcoming section about the park).

- ✔ The **Mount Marathon Trail** is a tough hike to the top of a 3,000-foot mountain, with a couple of trails of varying skill level. The route of the famous Mount Marathon footrace is the more strenuous choice, basically going straight up from the end of Jefferson Street; the hikers' route starts at the corner of First Avenue and Monroe Street. Either trail rises steeply to the top of the rocky pinnacle and the incredible views you'll find there. Allow an entire day, unless you're a racer; in that case, expect to make it to the top in less than 45 minutes.

- ✔ The **Caines Head State Recreation Area** (Internet: www.alaskastateparks.org; click on the link to individual parks) has a 7-mile coastal trail south of town. Parts of the trail are accessible only at low tide, so it's best done either as an overnight or with someone picking you up or dropping you off in a boat at the far end. (The Miller's Landing water taxi, mentioned under "Boating and sea kayaking," earlier in this chapter, offers this service for $30 adults one-way, kids half price.) The trail has some gorgeous views, rocky shores, and a fascinating destination at the end: a towering cliff with the concrete remains of Fort McGilvray, a World War II defensive emplacement. Take flashlights and you can poke around in the spooky, pitch-dark underground corridors and rooms and imagine what each was used for (going in without lights would be foolhardy). I've rarely enjoyed a hike more. The trailhead is south of town on Lowell Point Road; pull off in the lot right after the sewage plant, then cross the road through the gate and follow the dirt road a bit until it becomes the actual trail. Stop at the Kenai Fjords National Park Visitor Center at the boat harbor for tide conditions and advice.

Sled dog mushing

The dog-driving Seavey Family, including the four boys (one is a Junior Iditarod champ), shows off their kennel on Old Exit Glacier Road off Herman Leirer Road, offering summer rides in Seward and winter rides in Sterling (near Soldotna). The summer ride uses a wheeled sled and a full, 12-dog team — not the real thing (no snow), but you nevertheless gain a feel for the dogs' power and intelligence. The 90-minute tour costs $39 for adults, $19 for children 11 and younger. Husky puppies are available for cuddling, too. They call their company **IdidaRide** (☎ **800-478-3139** or 907-224-8607; Internet: www.ididaride.com).

Other cool things to do in Seward

Most of Seward's attractions are of the modest, small-town variety and involve exploring downtown and the waterfront on foot:

- ✔ **Walk along the beach** on Ballaine Avenue. The broken concrete and twisted metal you see are the last ruins of the Seward waterfront that was destroyed by a tsunami wave that resulted from the 1964 earthquake. Sometimes you can see sea otters swimming just offshore.

- ✔ **Visit the Seward Museum** at Third and Jefferson (☎ **907-224-3902**). It's a charming grandma's attic of a place, with clippings, memorabilia, and curiosities recalling town history, painter Rockwell Kent, and the ways of the past. Admission is $3 for adults, 50¢ for ages younger than 18. It's open during the summer daily from 9 a.m. to 5 p.m.; in winter, it's usually open weekends (call ahead).

- ✔ **See the steep-roofed St. Peter's Episcopal Church,** a delightful little chapel under the mountains at First Avenue and Adams Street; a mural in the front of the church shows what the Resurrection would have looked like if it had happened in front of Seward locals in the 1930s.

> ✔ **Stop for coffee at the Resurrect Art Coffee House Gallery,** at 320 Third Ave. (☎ 907-224-7161), which occupies an old church. It's a gathering place showing local fine art.

Fast Facts: Seward

ATMs

First National Bank of Anchorage, 303 Fourth Ave., has an **ATM.** You can also find ATMs at the Eagle Quality Center grocery store at Seward Highway mile 2, and other places.

Emergencies

Dial ☎ **911.**

Hospital

Providence Seward Medical Center is at 417 First Ave. (☎ 907-224-5205).

Information

Contact the **Seward Chamber of Commerce,** P.O. Box 749, Seward, AK 99664 (☎ 907-224-8051; www.sewardak.org).

Internet Access

Free at the **Seward Public Library,** Fifth and Adams (☎ 907-224-3646).

Police

For nonemergency situations, call the **Seward Police Department** (☎ 907-224-3338) or, outside the city limits, the **Alaska State Troopers** (☎ 907-224-3346).

Post Office

At Fifth Avenue and Madison Street.

Taxes

Sales tax is 5%. The **room tax** totals 9%.

Enjoying the Wilds of Kenai Fjords National Park

Kenai Fjords National Park is all about remote rocks, mountains, and ice that meet the ocean, and the animals that live there. The park comprises 670,000 acres of the south coast and interior landmass of the Kenai Peninsula. The shore here is exposed to the Gulf of Alaska, where wild, recurrent storms beat against the mountainous shore unbuffered by any landmasses from the vast expanses of the Pacific to the south. Wildlife thrives, but humans have never made a mark.

The majority of the area, in the impossibly rugged interior of the Kenai Peninsula, was likely first seen by human eyes only in 1968, when mountain climbers initially crossed the **Harding Ice Field,** which covers most of the national park (Native Americans avoided that area). **Exit Glacier** and all the glaciers of Kenai Fjords flow from this Ice Age leftover, which may be a mile thick. The ice field lies in a high bowl of mountains that jut straight out of the ocean to heights of 3,000 to 5,000 feet.

Visitors travel the park's marine periphery, seeing the glaciers that dip into the sea, the shore's razor-sharp mountains, and the abundant wildlife that lives in the water, on the rocks, and in the air. A large vessel, such as a tour boat operating out of Seward, is the only practical way for most people to do this, and that, by no means, is cheap or quick, and better destinations are available for people subject to seasickness (for example, Prince William Sound, discussed in Chapter 15). But if you go, you'll experience a ride into primeval wilderness that's pretty much unequaled.

Getting there

Seward is the threshold to the park. Exit Glacier is 13 miles from the town by road; the Kenai Fjords National Park Visitor Center is at Seward Small Boat Harbor; tour boats that visit the park also leave from the harbor.

Don't try to see the park in a day, coming from Anchorage by train or road, touring the park by boat, and then returning that evening. For a better glimpse of the park, you need to take an all-day boat trip — most half-day trips barely leave Resurrection Bay and see hardly any of the park proper. Besides, the trip down from Anchorage and back in one day, especially by train, is too tiring. That kind of a day amounts to 16 hours of near-constant boat and train rides. Spending a night in Seward and taking in the full Kenai Fjords boat trip and Exit Glacier visit is a better plan.

Getting park information

At the **Kenai Fjords National Park Visitor Center,** Seward Small Boat Harbor (P.O. Box 1727), Seward, AK 99664 (☎ **907-224-3175;** Internet: www.nps.gov/kefj/), rangers answer questions about the park, provide information on the all-important tour boats, and operate a good bookstore. The center is open June to August, daily from 8 a.m. to 7 p.m. and September to May, Monday to Friday from 8 a.m. to 5 p.m.

The rangers do a great deal, but they can't help you find a hotel room in the park: there are none. Indeed, virtually no facilities of any kind are situated on park land. Seward is the place to stay, eat, and do any non-wilderness activities.

Enjoying the park

Kenai Fjords is essentially a marine park. On a boat tour, you'll see its mountains, glaciers, and wildlife. On any of the tours, you're sure to see sea otters and sea lions, and you have a good chance of seeing humpback whales, orcas, mountain goats, and black bears. I saw all that wildlife on one trip to Aialik Bay. Gray whales come in the early spring and huge fin whales show up sometimes, too (but are hard to see). Bird-watchers can see bald eagles, puffins (both tufted and horned), marbled and Kittletz's murrelets, cormorants (red faced, pelagic, and double-breasted), murres (common and thick billed), rhinoceros and parakeet auklets, and various other sea ducks, alcids, and gulls.

The farther you go into the park, the more you'll see. If you really want to see Kenai Fjords National Park and glaciers that drop ice into the water, the boat has to go at least into **Aialik Bay** to **Holgate Glacier. Northwestern Glacier** is even deeper in the park. Half-day **Resurrection Bay** cruises offer plenty of impressive scenery but pass only one glacier, and that at a distance, leaving you with fewer opportunities for seeing whales and puffins and other birds. The longest trips into the heart of the park proper encounter the greatest variety and number of birds and animals. If you're lucky with the weather, you can make it to the exposed **Chiswell Islands,** which are home to some of the greatest bird rookeries in Alaska, supporting more than 50,000 seabirds of 18 species. I've seen clouds of puffins swarm here. The daylong trips also provide more time to linger and really witness the behavior of the wildlife. Whatever your choice, binoculars are a necessity; you may be able to rent them on board.

Deciding on a tour

One important factor to consider when choosing your boat tour is your susceptibility to seasickness. Vessels must venture into the unprotected waters of the North Pacific to reach the heart of the park. Large rolling waves are inevitable on the passage from Resurrection Bay to the fjords themselves, although once you're in the fjords, the water is calm. On a rough day, most boats turn back for the comfort of the passengers and change the full-day trip into a Resurrection Bay cruise, refunding the difference in fare. Of course, they'd rather not do that, and the decision may not be made until the vessel is pretty far out, often after many of the passengers are already vomiting over the side. If you get seasick easily, my advice: Stick to the Resurrection Bay cruise, or take a boat tour in protected Prince William Sound out of Whittier, where the water is smooth. In any event, ask about the tour company's policy on turning back and refunds, and take some motion-sickness remedy *before* leaving the dock, because doing so once you're underway is probably too late to do any good.

Prices are about $150 to go to Northwestern Glacier in Northwestern Fjord off Harris Bay, a ten-hour trip; $110 to go to Holgate Glacier in Holgate Arm off Aialik Bay, which takes six to eight hours; and $60 to $70 for a three- to four-hour Resurrection Bay tour, which doesn't go to the national park at all. I have seen misleading publicity material from the tour operators, so ask exactly where the boat goes (or get a map of the route). Children's prices are usually about half off.

Although you can sometimes obtain early season or Web specials, fares with each operator differ little. Instead, shop for the destination, length of trip, food service, interpretation, and size or intimacy of the boat. Ask how much deck space is outside so that you can really see. What seating arrangements are enforced inside? How many passengers will be on board and how many crewmembers can answer questions? Is lunch provided, and what does it consist of? Another important point of comparison is whether you have a ranger providing the commentary, or only the captain — some captains don't know when to shut up and can give inaccurate information.

Try to schedule loosely so that if the weather is bad on the day you choose for your boat trip, you can wait and go the next day. If the weather's bad, you'll be uncomfortable, and the animals and birds won't be as evident, or the boat may not go out at all. If you pay up front to hold a reservation on a boat — probably a good idea in the busiest months — find out the company's policies regarding refunds and rescheduling.

Choosing a tour operator

Most operators offer packages with the Alaska Railroad and the SeaLife Center, which may save you money, but make sure that you have enough time to do everything you want to do in Seward. All have offices at the Small Boat Harbor in Seward. In addition to the large operators listed in full below, **Renown Charters and Tours** (☎ **800-655-3806** or 907-272-1961; Internet: www.renowncharters.com) has smaller (but still substantial) vessels, offering shorter, lower-priced cruises, and year-round operations. They can get you out for four hours of whale-watching on the bay for $59, including lunch.

See the preceding "Deciding on a tour" section for general information on tour-boat fares and what to look for in a tour-boat operator.

Kenai Fjords Tours

Kenai Fjords Tours is the dominant tour operator, having the most daily sailings and choices of destination. The main part of the operation uses 90- to 150-passenger vessels, some of which have forward-facing seats, like the ones on an airplane. They're professionally staffed, but when ships are crowded, the experience can be impersonal. The captain provides the commentary instead of a ranger. However, the same company also owns **Mariah Tours,** which operates 16-passenger vessels and whose trips are more spontaneous and go farther. The downside: The smaller boats are less stable in the waves.

Most of the large Kenai Fjords vessels call on a lodge that the company owns on **Fox Island** in Resurrection Bay. It sits on the long cobble beach of **Sunny Cove,** where painter Rockwell Kent lived in seclusion with his son in 1918 and 1919 and produced both the art that made him famous and his classic book *Wilderness: A Journal of Quiet Adventure in Alaska* (Wesleyan University Press). It is an inspiring spot. The lodge itself stands on a narrow strip of land between the beach and a pond that visitors can view from the large wooden decks. Boats stop for lunch of grilled salmon or a family-style dinner, and some passengers spend the night. Half-day sea-kayaking paddles from the island are offered for $149 to $169, including a Resurrection Bay tour-boat ride for day-trippers. Sunny Cove Sea Kayaking, the company mentioned later in this chapter, provides guide service at Fox Island, but Kenai Fjords Tours books the trips and collects the money. See "Spending the night on an island," for an overnight option.

At the Seward Small Boat Harbor. ☎ *800-478-8068, 907-224-8068 in Seward, or 907-276-6249 in Anchorage. Internet:* www.kenaifjords.com.

Major Marine Tours

This company pioneered first-class onboard dining and, at this writing, is the only cruise that brings along a park ranger to assure high-quality commentary, a decisive advantage in my judgment. After all, you're here for the park. Their boats are slower than some of the competitor's, so they don't make the long trip to Northwest Glacier; they head either into Aialik Bay to see Holgate Glacier or just tour Resurrection Bay around Seward. Instead of bringing sandwiches or stopping for a meal, they serve a buffet of salmon and prime rib on board for $12 per person, $6 for children. The food is surprisingly good. Although I prefer their table-seating arrangement to forward-facing seats, it can be an uncomfortable crush when the boat is crowded. Your seat is assigned, so you don't need to rush aboard or try to stake out your spot.

411 West Fourth Ave., Anchorage. ☎ *800-764-7300 or 907-274-7300, or 907-224-8030 in Seward. Internet:* www.majormarine.com.

Sunny Cove Sea Kayaking

Seeing the fjords from a sea kayak is quieter and more intimate than a big boat with too many people. Even beginners can do it on a guided day trip. Sunny Cove Kayaking takes guests for a wildlife tour to Aialik Bay on a small charter boat, then launches kayaks for a paddle in front of the glacier. The price of $289 for the one-day outing isn't much more than you'd pay for a separate boat tour and guided kayaking back in Resurrection Bay. If you're sure you like kayaking, spend a couple of days; a two-night trip costs $849.

Point Lowell in Seward. ☎ *800-770-9119 for reservations, or 907-224-8810. Internet:* www.sunnycove.com.

TIP

Spending the night on an island

Fox Island stands with high, rocky pinnacles like a castle over Resurrection Bay, a seductive destination for anyone exploring those waters. For a price, you can spend a night or two there, on the same beach where artist Rockwell Kent found inspiration. Sea kayaking outings among the sea otters, puffins, and sheer rocks are an essential add-on, priced at $79 to $89 per person for lodge guests. An overnight package on the island costs $220 per person, meals included. See the Kenai Fjords Tours listing in the "Choosing a tour operator" section, earlier in this chapter, for contact information to make a reservation.

Checking out Exit Glacier

The only land-accessible part of the park is the engaging Exit Glacier, one of the few glaciers in Alaska that you can stroll up to. Approaching the glacier, you can see the pattern of vegetation reclaiming the land that the melting ice has uncovered, a process well explained by inter- pretive signs and a nature trail. At its face, cold, dense spires of ice loom over you, breathing chilled air like an open freezer door.

The National Park Service's low-key presentation of the site makes it a casual, pleasant visit for an hour or two (longer if you want to take a hike). The easiest way to get to the glacier is to drive. Take the Seward Highway 3.7 miles north of town to the clearly marked 9-mile route to the glacier, recently renamed Herman Leirer Road. In winter, the road is closed to vehicles. If you don't have a car, van service usually is avail- able; check with the Kenai Fjords National Park Visitor Center (see the "Getting park information" section, earlier in this chapter) to see who currently offers this service.

Following the road along the broad bed of the wandering Resurrection River, you can observe, in reverse order, the succession of vegetation, from mature Sitka spruce and cottonwood trees down to smaller alders and shrubs. It takes time for nature to replace the soil on sterile ground left behind by a receding glacier. As you get closer, watch for signs with dates starting a couple of centuries in the past; they mark the retreat of the glacier through time. At the glacier itself, nothing grows at all.

At the end of the road, an entrance booth charges a **user fee of $5 per vehicle.** A simple **ranger station** and pit toilets are located near the parking lot. **Ranger-led nature walks** start here on a sporadic schedule; check at the visitor center. The short **trail** to the glacier leads to the glacier's face. Take a good look, but don't go beyond the warning signs, because huge pieces of ice sometimes fall. The pile of gravel in front of the glacier is called a *glacial moraine* that still is under construction.

The slowly moving glacier chips rock off the mountain, leaving the chips as the moraine. Long, narrow hills all over northern North America are glacial moraines left over from the last Ice Age; Cape Cod is a moraine.

An all-day hike, 7 miles round-trip, climbs along the right side of the glacier to the **Harding Ice Field** — Exit Glacier gets its name for being an exit from that massive sheet. The walk is a challenging 3,000-foot elevation gain, but it's the easiest access I'm aware of to visit an ice field on foot. Because of snow, the trail doesn't open until late June or early July. The ice field itself is cold and dangerous. If you want to risk it, the Park Service sometimes offers guided hikes up the trail.

It's (Nearly) All about Fishing in Kenai and Soldotna

The largest sport-caught king salmon in the world, almost 100 pounds, came from the Kenai River. That's why people come here. The Kenai's kings run so large that the river has a different trophy class. Everywhere else in the state, the Alaska Department of Fish and Game certifies a 50-pounder as a trophy, but on the Kenai, your catch has to be at least 75 pounds. That's because kings in the 60-pound class — with enough wild muscle to fight ferociously for hours — are just too common here. Anglers prepared to pay for a charter will be in their element on the river when the fish are running hot. Catching a big king isn't easy or quick, however, and success rates vary greatly year to year and week to week.

Visitors who aren't interested in fishing find less than a day's sightseeing in these towns. Instead, they can use the towns as bases for the outdoors. Kenai has a strangely beautiful ocean beach and the Kenai River mouth, in addition to exceptional bird-watching. Outside of town, you find terrific canoeing waters in the lake-dotted **Kenai National Wildlife Refuge,** which has headquarters in Soldotna.

Getting there and getting around

The drive on the Seward and Sterling highways to the Kenai/Soldotna area from Anchorage is 147 miles and takes a good three hours without stops. In summer, traffic slows you down, and in winter, speeds are limited by ice and the fear of hitting moose. (The first 48 miles of this leg are covered in Chapter 15.) Bear right onto the Sterling Highway about 90 miles from Anchorage. Car rental in Anchorage is covered in Chapters 7 and 13.

By air, Kenai receives frequent flights from Anchorage via **Era Aviation** (☎ 800-866-8394; Internet: www.eraaviation.com). Among the rental companies at the Kenai airport are **Hertz** (☎ **800-478-7980** or 907-283-7979; Internet: www.hertzcars.com) and **Payless** (☎ **800-729-5377** or 907-283-6428; Internet: www.paylesscarrental.com).

The area is too spread out to walk, and you won't find public transportation. You can get by without a car only when you do nothing but fish and you eat at your lodgings; then you can get the rides you need from your guide, host, or a taxicab. Of the several cab companies in the area, try **Alaska Cab** (☎ **907-283-6000** in Kenai or 907-262-1555 in Soldotna).

Where to stay

Rates at all the hotels in the area are on seasonal schedules with three, four, or even more levels linked to the salmon runs. When I list high- and low-season rates in this section, I'm talking about the highest and lowest rates of the year.

Great Alaska Adventure Lodge

$$$$$ **Sterling**

For anglers, location is what counts, and a third of a mile of river frontage where the Moose and Kenai rivers converge has been a hot fishing spot since time immemorial, as an ancient Native legend about the site attests. In the evening, the lodge keeps a guide on the beach and a campfire burning so that you can keep casting in the midnight sun. For guests interested in seeing wildlife and the glorious backcountry of the Kenai National Wildlife Refuge, cushy tent camps enable you to use some muscle and yet sleep and eat in comfort. A bear camp across Cook Inlet features day trips and overnights to watch three-dozen resident brown bear up close, engaging in their natural behavior. The lodge cabins, in Sterling, recently were remodeled.

Moose River, 33881 Sterling Hwy., Sterling, AK 99672 (in winter, P.O. Box 2670, Poulsbo, WA 98370). ☎ *800-544-2261 or 907-262-4515. Fax: 907-262-8797 in summer, 360-697-7850 in winter. Internet:* www.greatalaska.com. *Rack rates: Ranging from $175–$249 for a day trip without lodging to $3,495 for a 7-day package. Rates include all meals, guide service, and travel from Anchorage. AE, MC, V. Closed mid-Oct to mid-May.*

Harborside Cottages Bed and Breakfast

$$$ **Kenai**

On a grassy compound at the top of the bluff above the mouth of the Kenai River in Old Town, the little white cottages of Harborside Cottages Bed and Breakfast make the most of a perfect site. The view and quiet can keep you occupied all day in a peaceful reverie. Inside, the cottages are as immaculate as if they were brand-new, each with its own light country decoration. The hostess stocks a self-serve breakfast the night before in kitchen areas equipped with a microwave, fridge, and coffee-maker. The bathrooms have no tubs, only shower stalls. Outside is a deck with a picnic table and gas barbecue.

813 Riverview Dr. (P.O. Box 942), Kenai, AK 99611. ☎ ***888-283-6162*** *or 907-283-6162. Internet:* www.harborsidecottages.com. *Rack rates: High season $150 double, low season $125 double. Rates include continental breakfast. AE, DISC, MC, V. Closed Nov through April.*

Kenai River Lodge
$$$ Soldotna

Overlooking the river, next to the bridge in Soldotna, the roadside Kenai River Lodge has the advantage of predictable standard rooms with refrigerators and coffeemakers in a great location for anglers. The grassy front yard descends right to the water, with a barbecue where you can cook up your catch. The lodge operates fishing charters right from the motel.

393 Riverside Dr., Soldotna, AK 99669. ☎ ***888-966-4292*** *or 907-262-4292. Fax: 907-262-7332. Internet:* www.kenairiverlodge.com. *Rack rates: High season $140 double, low season $60 double; year-round $240 suite; extra person $10. Fishing packages available. DISC, MC, V.*

Log Cabin Inn
$$ Kenai

Ted and Carol Titus built this big log house specifically to be a B&B, but with its huge common room — with fireplace and towering cathedral ceiling — it feels more like a luxurious wilderness lodge. Located off Kalifornsky Beach Road a little south of the bridge in Kenai, the house stands over an active beaver pond, with a deck and plenty of windows from which to watch the beavers. The upstairs rooms, which cost $10 more, are well worth it — they're large and airy. A room on the main floor has French doors to a deck over the pond. All the rooms are attractively decorated in a country style, with quilts, rag rugs, and pictures of the Titus' ten grandchildren. Carol cooks a large breakfast at the time of your choosing. They have a wheelchair lift.

9840 Eider Rd. (P.O. Box 2886), Kenai, AK 99611. ☎ *and Fax:* ***907-283-3653***. *Internet:* www.acsalaska.net/~ted.titus. *Rack rates: High season $90–$100 double, low season $70–$90; extra adult $25, extra child $10. Rates include full breakfast. AE, MC, V.*

Where to dine

Franchise fast-food and burger-steak-seafood places dominate in Kenai and Soldotna. Here are two of the few places that aren't familiar brands.

Charlotte's Bakery, Café, Espresso
$ **Kenai   Sandwiches**

Rich-textured bread from the bakery anchors the sandwiches, and lettuce from a nearby garden completes the large, filling salads, but the motherly owner doesn't make a point of that — hers is not a trendy or gimmicky place. Locals fill the big wooden chairs in the bright dining room because the food is wonderfully flavored, the service sweetly attentive, and the prices reasonable.

115 S. Willow, Kenai. ☎ *907-283-2777. Open: Mon–Fri 7 a.m.–4 p.m. All items: $5–$9. MC, V.*

Sal's Klondike Diner
$ **Soldotna   Diner**

It certainly looks corny and touristy from the outside, but Sal's turns out to be a classic Western highway diner, with huge portions, fast service, and nothing fancy that doesn't have to be. Sandwiches, burgers, and halibut fish-and-chips top the menu for a quick lunch, and your coffee cup stays full. The children's menu is good and inexpensive.

44619 Sterling Hwy., Soldotna. ☎ *907-262-2220. Open: Daily 24 hours. Lunch: $4.50–$9; dinner main courses: $7–$10. AE, MC, V.*

Fishing in Kenai/Soldotna

Fishing the Kenai River is the point of coming to the area for most visitors. Check at the visitor centers (see "Fast Facts: Kenai and Soldotna," later in this chapter) for information and regulation booklets. Or contact the **Alaska Department of Fish and Game (ADFG),** 43961 Kalifornsky Beach Rd. Suite B, Soldotna, AK 99669 (☎ **907-262-9368** or 907-262-2737, for a recorded fishing report; Internet: www.alaska.gov/adfg). Serious anglers shouldn't miss that Web site; you can find treatises on Kenai River biology and fishing techniques, check current fish counts and escapement goals, and purchase licenses on the site. (You can also buy fishing licenses in virtually any sporting-goods store in Alaska.)

The Kenai River has more than two-dozen public-access points along its 80-mile length. A **guide brochure** with a map is available from the state **Division of Parks,** P.O. Box 1247, Soldotna, AK 99669-1247 (☎ **907-262-5581;** Internet: www.alaskastateparks.org); you also can pick up a copy at one of the town visitor centers.

Anglers who are interested in less competition and more of a wilderness experience find that Kenai is a gateway for vast wild lands accessible by air on the west side of Cook Inlet where you can fish a stream packed with salmon without competition. Among others, **High Adventure Air** (☎ **907-262-5237;** Internet: www.highadventureair. com) has day trips and packages with fly-in cabins. For a day trip, you'll pay $250 to $325 per person.

The following sections discuss the top sportfish in the Kenai River and how to catch them.

Fishing for king salmon

King salmon, the monsters of the river, come in two runs. The early run, which sometimes has been limited to catch-and-release, occurs late May to the end of June, peaking in mid-June. These usually are smaller fish and less plentiful, in the 20- to 40-pound range. The second run occurs during July and includes massive fish that range up to 90 pounds. Regulations usually allow only the use of artificial lures with a single hook. Most people fish kings from a boat, floating with the current as the lure bounces along the bottom. Some also keep the boat stationary or back slowly down the river. Your chances from the bank are low; on average, with or without a boat, it takes 29 hours of fishing to land a king (you're likely to get at least a dozen strikes for every fish that makes it into the boat). With a guide, the average time to land a fish is cut in half, but that still means that if you fish for only one day, chances are good that you'll get skunked. Three anglers in a boat on a half-day guided charter have roughly a 50% chance of landing a king between them. You can increase your chances by fishing for several days, or when king and silver salmon are both in the river and both biting the same lures — a narrow window in late July.

A guided charter averages $125 to $150 for a six-hour, half-day trip, $225 to $250 full day. Contact the visitor center in Kenai or Soldotna to get in touch with one of the dozens of guides (see "Fast Facts: Kenai and Soldotna," later in this chapter). Remember that many hotels and lodges have their own guides. The **Sports Den,** at 44176 Sterling Hwy. in Soldotna (☎ **907-262-7491;** Internet: www.alaskasportsden.com), is one charter operator that offers river and ocean trips, fly-in fishing, and hunting. I've found them friendly and helpful.

Fishing for red salmon

The area really goes crazy when the red, or sockeye, salmon join the kings in the river from mid-July to early August. You can fish reds from the bank or from a boat. Reds are plankton eaters and won't strike a lure. In the most popular fishing areas, near the confluence of the Russian River or Moose River with the Kenai River, regulations allow only the use of flies. Most people around here cast the flies with spinning gear, weighting the line 18 inches from the fly so that it bounces along the bottom. Cast upstream from shore and allow the fly to drift down, keeping near the bank. The fish probably don't actually attack the flies, but, instead, get caught when they instinctively move their mouths in an eating motion, which they do in quick-moving water.

Fishing for silver salmon

Silvers come in two runs. The first, heavier run is late July to August, and the lighter run arrives in September. They're easiest to catch anchored in a boat, but you can also do well from shore. Lures work well, and so does bait of salmon eggs; however, eggs aren't always allowed.

Fishing for other species

Trophy-size rainbow trout and Dolly Varden char also come out of the river. Anglers using light tackle may also get some enjoyment out of catching pink salmon, but most Alaskans turn up their nose at this 4-pound fish, which is plentiful in the Kenai during even-numbered years.

Canoeing in Kenai/Soldotna

Floating through the Kenai National Wildlife Refuge in a canoe narrows the world into a circle of green water, spruce, and birch. You can paddle and hike for days without encountering more than a few other people. Your only expenses are the costs of your canoe and the vehicle that carried you to the trailhead. Most of the western half of the Kenai Peninsula lies within the 2 million acres of the refuge — it's almost as large as Yellowstone National Park — much of which is impossibly remote and truly dedicated to the wildlife. Canoeists use the lowlands on the west side, west of the Sterling Highway and north of Kenai and Soldotna. The region is a maze of lakes connected by trails. You can reach more than 70 lakes on canoe routes that stretch more than 150 miles. It's the easiest way to real Alaska wilderness that I know.

Stop in at the **Kenai National Wildlife Refuge Visitor Center,** Ski Hill Road (P.O. Box 2139), Soldotna, AK 99669 (☎ **907-262-7021;** kenai. fws.gov), for guidance before plunging into the wilderness. The staff offers advice and sells books and maps that you'll definitely need for a successful backcountry trip. To find the center, turn left just south of the Kenai River bridge, taking the dirt road uphill from the building-supply store. It's open in summer, Monday to Friday from 8 a.m. to 5 p.m., and Saturday and Sunday from 9 a.m. to 6 p.m.; in winter, Monday to Friday from 8:00 a.m. to 4:30 p.m., and Saturday and Sunday from 10 a.m. to 5 p.m. The Web site also contains detailed trip-planning information for the canoe routes.

I haven't provided detailed driving instructions because you'll need detailed maps to go at all. You can order a good one printed on plastic from **Trails Illustrated** (☎ **800-962-1643;** Internet: www.trails illustrated.com). A serviceable free map is distributed by the refuge visitor center. *Note:* It's best to rent your equipment in Anchorage (see Chapter 14).

Guided canoe trips are available from Blue Moose Lakeside Lodge (☎ 877-256-6673 or 907-262-0669; Internet: www.blue-moose.com). But you don't need a guide when you already know how to canoe and camp. Instead, get the invaluable book, *The Kenai Canoe Trails,* by Daniel L. Quick, published by Northlite Publishing Company (33335 Skyline Dr., Soldotna, AK 99669-9752).

The refuge has two main canoe routes, both reached from Swanson River and Swan Lake roads, north of the Sterling Highway from the town of Sterling.

✔ The **Swan Lake Canoe Route** is a 60-mile network of 30 lakes connected by channels or *portages,* paths on which you carry a canoe or kayak from one point of water to another. It meets Swan Lake Road twice, allowing a loop of several days, and in-between adventurers can penetrate deep into the wilderness, visiting many remote lakes that they'll have all to themselves. Canoeing through to the Moose River and riding its current 17 miles over a long day back to the Sterling Highway also is possible. However, getting anywhere requires frequent portages of a quarter mile or so, and more ambitious routes have mile-long portages.

✔ You can skip the portaging, however, by floating two days down the **Swanson River** to its mouth, at the Captain Cook State Recreation Area north of Kenai. Join the river at a landing at mile 17.5 of Swanson River Road. The water is slow and easy all the way. All routes have many dozens of remote campsites — just lakeside areas of cleared ground with fire rings — and most of the portages are well marked and maintained with wooden planking over wet areas.

Other things to do in Kenai and Soldotna

The following list offers some of the (generally) nonfishing-related activities you can do in Kenai and Soldotna:

✔ **Viewing art, history, and natural history displays** at the **Kenai Visitors and Cultural Center** at 11471 Kenai Spur Hwy., Kenai, AK 99611 (☎ **907-283-1991**; Internet: www.visitkenai.com). A highlight is the "King of Snags" — an immense conglomeration of lost fishing lures and sticks from the bottom of the river. In the summer, superb temporary art exhibitions are mounted, too. Summer admission to the museum portion is $3, free for students through high school; off-season, admission is free. It is open summer, Monday to Friday from 9 a.m. to 8 p.m., and Saturday and Sunday from 10 a.m. to 7 p.m.; and off-season, Monday to Friday from 9 a.m. to 5 p.m., and Saturday from 10 a.m. to 4 p.m.

✔ **Walking Kenai's historic area.** Start at the visitor and cultural center mentioned above and get a copy of the _Old Town Kenai Walking Map;_ follow the numbered markers. Not many of the simple, weathered buildings remain from Kenai's life before it became an oil boom town, but those that do are interesting and lie only a few blocks down Main Street from the center, along the Cook Inlet bluff, including the 1895 **Holy Assumption Russian Orthodox Church.** It's a quaint, onion-domed church, brightly kept but with old icons. A donation is requested.

✔ **Watching fishing boats and whales in the river mouth.** The best vantage point is from Erik Hansen Scout Park, at Cook and Mission avenues, near the church mentioned above. When the salmon are running, you can occasionally see white beluga whales chasing them upstream from here, sometimes in great numbers, competing with the transiting fishing boats and personal-use dipnet fishermen.

✔ **Walking the sandy beach.** From the Kenai Spur Highway, turn left on South Spruce Street where you'll find a simple beach park and a place to begin a walk. On a calm day, the beach sand, the mudflats, and the Inlet's gray, glacial water seem to meld together into one vast shimmering plain. Walking south, the beach wraps around and becomes the shore of the Kenai River. The water is far too cold for swimming.

✔ **Bird-watching.** One of the best places for serious bird-watching is the tidal marsh along Bridge Access Road, which branches from the Spur Highway. The state of Alaska has developed a viewing area near the bridge.

✔ **Swimming in a great public pool.** The magnificent **North Peninsula Recreation Area Nikiski Pool** (☎ **907-776-8472**), 10 miles north of Kenai on the Kenai Spur Road, occupies a large gold dome and has a 136-foot water slide, mushroom fountains of water, and a raised hot tub from which parents can watch their children play in the pool below. The water slide is open Tuesday to Sunday from 1 to 5 p.m. and 6 to 9 p.m. in the summer (swimming without the slide opens those days at 7 a.m.); the winter hours are complicated, with the slide open only Friday through Sunday, so call for details. Pool admission is $3, or $6 to use the slide and pool. Weekends can be crowded.

Fast Facts: Kenai and Soldotna

ATMs

Banks are on the Kenai Spur Highway in the middle of town; in Soldotna, on the Sterling Highway commercial strip. In addition, ATMs are in grocery stores all across the area.

Emergencies

Dial ☎ **911.**

Hospital

Central Peninsula General is in Soldotna at 250 Hospital Pl. (☎ 907-262-4404); from the Sterling Highway, take Binkley Street to Marydale Avenue.

Information

The **Kenai Visitor and Cultural Center** is at 11471 Kenai Spur Hwy., Kenai, AK 99611 (☎ 907-283-1991; www.visitkenai. com). It's described earlier in the "Other things to do in Kenai and Soldotna" section. The **Soldotna Visitor Information Center**, 44790 Sterling Hwy., Soldotna, AK 99669 (☎ 907-262-9814 or 907-262-1337; www. SoldotnaChamber.com), is located on the south side of town; drive through the commercial strip and turn right after the Kenai River Bridge. It's open daily in summer

from 9 a.m. to 7 p.m.; in winter, Monday to Friday 9 a.m. to 5 p.m.

Internet access

Connect to the Web for free at the **Kenai Public Library**, 163 Main St. Loop (☎ 907-283-4378), or at the **Soldotna Public Library**, 235 Binkley St. (☎ 907-262-4227).

Police

For nonemergencies in Kenai, call the **Kenai Police Department** (☎ 907-283-7879); in Soldotna, call the **Soldotna Police Department** (☎ 907-262-4455); outside city limits, call the **Alaska State Troopers** (☎ 907-262-4453).

Taxes

5% **sales tax** in Kenai and Soldotna, and 2% outside city limits.

Coming to the End of the Line in Homer

Homer is at the end of the road. The nation's paved highway system comes to an abrupt conclusion at the tip of the Homer Spit, a narrow strip of land almost 5 miles out in the middle of Kachemak Bay. That geography has brought together a wonderfully odd collection of artists and retired people, fundamentalist preachers and New Age healers, wealthy North Slope oil workers and land-poor settlers with no visible means of support to the area. They're all people who live here simply because they choose to. The choice is understandable. Homer lies on the north side of Kachemak Bay, a branch of lower Cook Inlet of extraordinary biological productivity. The halibut fishing is especially exceptional. The town has a breathtaking setting on the spit and on a wildflower-covered bench high above the bay. Outdoor opportunities here are among Alaska's best, and the arts community has developed into an attraction of its own.

You'll be disappointed, however, if you expect a charming little fishing town. Poor community planning has created a town that doesn't live up to its setting. Homer Spit in summer is a traffic-choked jumble of cheap tourist development and RVs. Ignore that. It's where the spit goes that counts. At its tip, out in the middle of the bay, you feel like you're at sea. The town depends on that unique finger stretching out into the ocean — an exceptional launching point to one of the world's great marine recreation areas.

Homer

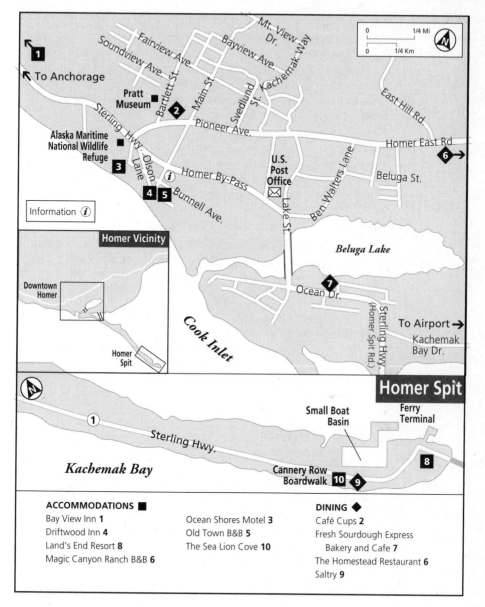

Homer Vicinity

Homer Spit

Small Boat Basin

Ferry Terminal

Cannery Row Boardwalk

ACCOMMODATIONS ■		DINING ◆
Bay View Inn **1**	Ocean Shores Motel **3**	Café Cups **2**
Driftwood Inn **4**	Old Town B&B **5**	Fresh Sourdough Express
Land's End Resort **8**	The Sea Lion Cove **10**	Bakery and Cafe **7**
Magic Canyon Ranch B&B **6**		The Homestead Restaurant **6**
		Saltry **9**

Getting there

Homer is at the end of the road, not the end of the rails. The rails end way before you get to Homer. You can, however, get to Homer using one of these reliable options.

By car

The scenic 235-mile drive from Anchorage to Homer takes roughly 4½ hours by car, that is if you don't stop at any of the many interesting or beautiful places along the way. Follow the Seward Highway south from Anchorage (the first hour of the drive is detailed in Chapter 15), then join the Sterling Highway at the Tern Lake junction (about 90 miles from Anchorage). You'll pass Soldotna and Kenai on your way to Homer. Save time for the view from Baycrest Hill as you enter town. Car rental in Anchorage is covered in Chapters 7 and 13.

By air

Era Aviation (☎ 800-866-8394; Internet: www.eraaviation.com) serves Homer from Anchorage several times a day. Small air-taxi operators use Homer as a hub for outlying villages and the outdoors.

By ferry

The **Alaska Marine Highway System** (☎ 800-642-0066; Internet: www.alaska.gov/ferry) connects Homer to Seldovia, Kodiak, and points west along the Alaska Peninsula and Aleutian Archipelago, and to Seward and Valdez to the east, with the ferry *Tustumena*. The **Homer ferry terminal,** run by a contractor, has its own toll-free number and Web site (☎ 800-382-9229 or 907-235-8449; Internet: www.akmhs.com) and is potentially an easier avenue than through the state number mentioned before to get in touch with someone who can answer questions and book trips anywhere in the system. The Homer terminal is open (and employees answer phones) Monday through Saturday from 7 a.m. to 5 p.m.

Getting around

Homer is spread out and has no public transportation, so the best way to get around is by car. (See the nearby "Homer" map.) If you fly or arrive by ferry, you can rent a car at the airport from **Hertz** (☎ 800-654-3131 or 907-235-0734; Internet: www.hertz.com) or three local firms.

Homer has two taxi companies in town: **CHUX Cab** (☎ 907-235-CHUX) and **Kache Cab** (☎ 907-235-1950).

Where to stay

Homer has many good B&Bs. The Web site of the Homer Chamber of Commerce (www.homeralaska.org) has links to a bunch of them.

Driftwood Inn

$ **Downtown Homer**

This historic building, a block from Bishop's Beach and across from the Bunnell Gallery, resembles a lodge or B&B with its large fireplace of

TIP

Crossing the bay in a different kind of taxi

To enjoy the best of the Homer area, get on and across Kachemak Bay. Using a system of water taxis that run from the small boat harbor on Homer Spit to beaches and docks that are half an hour and a world away is easy. Go for hiking, mountain biking, or self-guided sea kayaking. Rates vary little, about $50 to get to Kachemak Bay State Park, for example.

✔ **Jakolof Ferry Service** (☎ 907-235-2376 or 907-235-6384 summer only; Internet: www.jakolofferryservice.com) operates handsome wooden boats that carry up to 18 passengers, mostly seated outside, landing right on the beach.

✔ **Mako's Water Taxi** (☎ 907-235-9055; Internet: www.makoswatertaxi.com) carries passengers and rents sea kayaks and drops them both off at a starting point; with Mako's advice, experienced kayakers can plan their own one-way paddle, with the water taxi providing a lift at each end.

✔ **Bay Excursions** water taxi and tour (☎ 907-235-7525; Internet: www.bayexcursions.com) offers those services and specializes in hosting serious birders.

rounded beach rock, the hot coffeepot and inexpensive self-serve break-fast in the lobby, and a friendly attitude. Sloping floors and worn carpets and fixtures somehow enhance the cozy feel. Most of the rooms are like Pullman compartments in size and configuration, but they're cute and clean and have some real style. And they're inexpensive. Nine bedrooms share two bathrooms. Larger rooms have more amenities, but not as much charm. The walls are thin, so a no-noise policy is enforced during evening hours. A coin-operated laundry is on site.

135 W. Bunnell Ave., Homer, AK 99603. ☎ *800-478-8019 or 907-235-8019. Internet:* www.thedriftwoodinn.com. *Rack rates: High season $65–$120 double, low season $45–$68 double; extra person $10. DISC, MC, V. No smoking.*

Land's End Resort
$$–$$$$ Homer Spit

Traditionally, *the* place to stay in Homer, Land's End would be popular no matter what it was like inside because of its location at the tip of Homer Spit — the best spot in Homer and possibly the best spot for a hotel in all of Alaska. It's composed of a line of weathered buildings that straggle along the beach crest like driftwood logs. Inside, the local owners keep high standards in rooms, and public areas are decorated with town history and old photographs, nautical memorabilia, and bold colors. The place has plenty of intentional charm. About a dozen differ-ent classes of rooms (and a complex rate schedule to match) range from cute ship-like compartments with fold-down Murphy beds to two-story affairs. The resort also owns a series of townhouses next door that you can reserve through the hotel. The hotel is near the boat harbor, and you can fish right from the beach in front. The hotel has several resort-like facilities, too, such as a small lap pool, work-out facility, sauna, and outdoor hot tub.

The **Chart Room restaurant** makes good use of its wonderful location, looking out over the beach and bay from big windows, with a casual, relaxing atmosphere in its long, wood-trimmed dining room. The deck outside has glass windshields, making it a warm, satisfying place to sit with a cup of coffee on a sunny day. You can watch otters, eagles, and fishing boats while you eat. Excellent chefs have passed through from year to year, so it's hard to predict the quality of the cuisine — locals discuss the current food at Land's End the way some towns talk about their baseball players. I've had simply prepared fresh seafood there that couldn't have been better. The extensive appetizer and bar menu offer an inexpensive way to enjoy the atmosphere. Main courses are about $20.

4786 Homer Spit Rd., Homer, AK 99603. ☎ *800-478-0400 or 907-235-0400. Fax: 907-235-0420. Internet:* www.lands-end-resort.com. *Rack rates: High season $119–$193 double; low season $86–$137 double; extra person $10. AE, DC, DISC, MC, V.*

Magic Canyon Ranch Bed and Breakfast
$–$$ East of downtown

At the top of a canyon road off East End Road, the Webb family shares their charming home, 74 unspoiled acres, a treehouse, and sweeping views with guests, a cat, and a herd of retired llamas. The air is mountain clear and quiet between the high canyon walls — you start to relax as soon as you get out of the car. The Webbs serve sherry in the evening and a full breakfast in the morning. The four rooms, some nestled cozily under the eaves, are decorated in country and Victorian styles, with some family antiques.

40015 Waterman Rd., Homer, AK 99603. ☎ *and Fax: 907-235-6077. Internet:* www.magiccanyonranch.com. *Rack rates: High season $85–$100 double, low season $55–$70 double; extra adult $25, extra child $20. Rates include full breakfast. MC, V.*

Ocean Shores Motel
$$ Downtown Homer

Buildings on a grassy compound overlook Kachemak Bay, with a path leading down to Bishop's Beach, yet the location is right off the Sterling Highway as you enter town, within walking distance of downtown Homer. Rooms are fresh and bright, most with private balconies, refrigerators, and microwaves; four have full kitchens (one rents for only $99). The less expensive rooms lack the views and are older, but recently were upgraded and have cute touches. Smoking is allowed in only one room. The place is decorated with photographs and art collected during the owners' five generations in Alaska.

451 Sterling Hwy. no. 1, Homer, AK 99603. ☎ *800-770-7775 or 907-235-7775. Fax: 907-235-8639. Internet:* www.oceanshoresalaska.com. *Rack rates: High season $99–$149 double, low season $59–$75 double; extra person $5. AE, DISC, MC, V.*

Old Town Bed and Breakfast
$ **Downtown Homer**

These rooms combine the artiness of the excellent Bunnell Street Gallery downstairs and the funky, historic feel of the old trading post/hardware store that the building used to house. The wood floors undulate with age and settling, and the tall, double-hung windows, looking out at Bishop's Beach, are slightly cockeyed. Antiques and handmade quilts complete the charming ambience. A full breakfast is served on weekends, and during the week you get a continental breakfast at the wonderful Two Sisters Bakery, downstairs. Not a good choice for people who have trouble with stairs.

106 W. Bunnell, Homer, AK 99603. ☎ *907-235-7558. Fax: 907-235-9427. Internet:* www.xyz.net/~oldtown. *Rack rates: High season $70 double shared bath, $85 double private bath; low season 25% discount; extra person $15. Rates include breakfast. MC, V.*

Runner-up accommodations

Bay View Inn
$–$$$ **West of Homer** You'll find good budget lodgings here at the top of Baycrest Hill before you come into town on the Sterling Highway, with amazing views and attractive little rooms. *2851 Sterling Hwy., Homer, AK 99603.* ☎ *877-235-8485 or 907-235-8485. Internet:* www.bayviewalaska.com.

The Sea Lion Cove
$$ **On the spit** Above the Sea Lion Gallery on Homer Spit are two comfortable rooms with kitchens and a deck right over the beach. *4241 Homer Spit Rd. (P.O. Box 2095), Homer, AK 99603.* ☎ *907-235-3400 in summer or 907-235-8767 in winter. Internet:* www.AlaskaOne.com/sealion.

Where to dine

Besides these free-standing restaurants, try the **Chart Room,** at Land's End Resort, described earlier under "Where to stay."

Café Cups
$$$ **Downtown Homer** **Seafood/Sandwiches**

The facade of the yellow house on Pioneer Avenue is unmistakable with its elaborate bas-relief sculpture. The small dining room is a work of art, too, a masterpiece of wood, light, and space. Jennifer Olsen seats guests, and her husband, David, is the chef. As the owners, they combine a love for good food with practicality in a small town: The menu contains many mainstream and inexpensive dishes in addition to more ambitious specials and thoughtfully seasoned seafood. Gone is the amazing creativity of earlier years; most of the flavors I experienced were familiar, and the portions a bit too large. Beer and wine are served.

162 W. Pioneer Ave. ☎ 907-235-8330. Reservations recommended. Open: High season Mon–Sat 11 a.m.–10 p.m.; low season Mon–Sat 11 a.m.–9 p.m. Lunch: $6–$10; dinner main courses: $16–$23. MC, V.

Fresh Sourdough Express Bakery and Café
$$ Near Homer Spit   Bakery/Café

Ebullient Donna and Kevin Maltz's organic eatery is quintessential Homer, starting with its motto: "Food for people and the planet." But you won't find New Age dogma here. Fresh Sourdough Express is fun and tasty, even as it grinds its own grain and recycles everything in sight. An inexpensive lunch menu includes many vegetarian choices in addition to hearty sandwiches. The evening menu takes in seafood and inexpensive choices. From a new drive-up window, you can get food in a bag for a day on the water. Don't miss dessert from the scratch bakery.

1316 Ocean Dr. ☎ 907-235-7571. Internet: www.freshsourdoughexpress. com. Open: High season daily 7 a.m.–9 p.m.; low season daily 8 a.m.–3 p.m.; closed Oct to mid-Apr. Breakfast: $4–$8; lunch: $5.50–$7.50; dinner main courses: $7.50–$18. DISC, MC, V.

The Homestead
$$$ East of Homer   Steak/Seafood

The ambience is that of an old-fashioned Alaska roadhouse, in a large log building decorated with local art and plenty of summer light. The food is wonderfully satisfying. After a day outdoors, it's a warm, exuberant place for dinner. Many menu items are charbroiled, but the cuisine is more thoughtful than you'd find in your typical steak-and-seafood place, including adventurous and creative concoctions together with the simple, perfectly broiled fish and meat. Service is cordial but sometimes slow. The restaurant has a full bar.

Mile 8.2, East End Road. ☎ 907-235-8723. Reservations recommended. Open: Summer daily 5–10 p.m.; low season Wed–Sat 5–9 p.m.; closed Jan–Feb. Main courses: $17–$25. AE, MC, V.

Saltry
$$$ Halibut Cove   Seafood

This restaurant is about 5 miles across the water from the boat harbor on Homer Spit; going there is a wonderful day's outing to a remote art colony. A classic wooden boat, the **Danny J,** leaves Homer daily in the summer at noon for lunch and takes over dinner guests at 5 p.m. (Seating on the *Danny J* is mostly outdoors, so don't go in the rain.) Each trip allows time to wander the charming boardwalks and galleries of Halibut Cove, a tiny seaside village without roads where boats take the place of cars. The restaurant itself sits on pilings above the edge of the smooth, deep green of the cove's main watery avenue. You can sit back in the deck gazebo and sip microbrews and eat fresh baked bread, mussels, sushi, and locally grown salads, followed by fresh fish grilled over charcoal. For a basic lunch, however, you'll have few choices other than fish chowder and bread. And those who don't eat seafood also have few choices. In addition to the price of the meal, budget for the boat ride: the noon trip is $44 for adults and the dinner trip is $22; kids 12 and younger are $22 for either trip; seniors $36 at noon and $12 for dinner. Make meal and boat reservations a day or two ahead at the same telephone number.

On the main channel, Halibut Cove. ☎ *907-235-7847. Reservations required. Open: Lunch and dinner seatings coordinate with daily **Danny J** schedule (see above); closed Labor Day to Memorial Day. Lunch: $10–$18; dinner main courses: $18–$20. MC, V.*

Finding Homer's top attractions

Homer is not the place to go for indoor activities: I think only one place makes the grade as a top attraction. But the town is one of the best places in Alaska to shop for art. I provide guidance on spending a rainy day in the galleries later in the "Other things to do in Homer" section.

Pratt Museum
Downtown Homer

The Homer Society of Natural History's museum is as good as any you'll find in a town of this size, and it has achieved a well-deserved national reputation. The Pratt displays art and explains local history, too, but it is strongest in natural history. Volunteers pioneered new technology that enables visitors to watch birds inside nesting burrows on Gull Island and bears feeding at the McNeil River State Game Sanctuary (the Gullcam and Bearcam), and you can zoom and pan the cameras live from controls in the museum. If that doesn't impress the kids, the saltwater aquarium of local marine life will. If you're curious about all the fishing boats down in the harbor, you can find out about the different types of gear and the fish they catch. In the garden outside, you can discover how to identify all the local wildflowers, and a forest trail enlightens you about the ecology along its course.

3779 Bartlett St. (at Pioneer Avenue). ☎ *907-235-8635. Internet:* www.pratt museum.org. *Admission: $6 adults, $5.50 seniors, $3 children ages 6–18; $20 family rate. Open: High season daily 10 a.m.–6 p.m.; low season Tues–Sun noon to 5 p.m.; closed Jan.*

Getting outdoors in Homer

For summer outdoor activity, Homer offers quite a variety of options, from road trips (in the car or on a bike) to water trips (via sea kayak). This section discusses some of the leading activities.

Driving or mountain biking

Several gravel roads around Homer make for exquisite drives or bike rides. Mountain bikers can use any of the hiking trails, too (see "Hiking," later in this section). Drive out **East End Road,** through lovely seaside pastures, a forest, and the village of Fritz Creek, and then follow the bluff line through meadows toward the head of the bay. When the road gets too rough, explore onward on a mountain bike. **Skyline Drive** has extraordinary views of high canyons and Kachemak Bay; drive up East Hill Road just east of Homer.

If you take a boat across the bay, you find an incredible wealth of mountain-biking routes that you can have all to yourself on the far side of Kachemak Bay. Rent a bike in town and take it on a water taxi to the **Jakolof Bay Dock.** Supreme mountain biking roads lead along the shore and right across the peninsula through forests and meadows for berry picking. A maintained 10-mile road west leads along the shore to the charming village of Seldovia. For more about water taxis, check the sidebar, "Crossing the bay in a different kind of taxi," in this chapter.

Homer Saw and Cycle, 1532 Ocean Dr. (☎ **907-235-8406;** E-mail: homersaw@xyz.net), rents mountain bikes and trailers, starting at $15 for a half day; keeps track of trail conditions; and offers gear and repairs. They're open Monday to Friday from 9:00 a.m. to 5:30 p.m., and Saturday from 11 a.m. to 5 p.m. Reserving bikes a day or two ahead of time is wise, especially when an outing depends on getting one.

Outdoors advice: Whom to ask

The **Alaska Maritime National Wildlife Refuge Visitor Center,** on the right as you come into Homer (509 Sterling Hwy.; ☎ **907-235-6961**), is the place to stop for outdoor information wherever you go in the area. It's open in summer daily from 9 a.m. to 6 p.m., winter by appointment. Rangers offer bird and beach walks frequently in the summer, and show natural history films and give programs at the center. Call for times.

The **Kachemak Bay State Park District Office,** 4 miles out on the way into town (mile 168.5, Sterling Hwy.; ☎ **907-235-7024**), helps answer questions about planning a trip to the trails and beaches across Kachemak Bay. Depending on staffing, the office should be open Monday through Friday from 9 a.m. to 5 p.m.

Fishing

Homer is known for **halibut,** those huge, flat bottom fish, and the harbor is full of charter boats that can take you out fishing for the day for about $180 per person in the high season. Every day, a few people catch fish that are larger than they are, and halibut weighing more than 50 pounds are common. You can participate in a summer-long Jackpot Halibut Derby with a prize that tops $30,000 for the biggest fish, generally more than 300 pounds; tickets are $10 per day (☎ **907-235-7740;** Internet: www.homerhalibutderby.com).

Getting out to where the fish are plentiful requires an early start and a long ride to unprotected waters. People prone to seasickness shouldn't go, because the boat wallows on the waves while you're fishing. (Take your favorite motion-sickness remedy *before* you set out; if you wait, it probably won't do any good.) One good, large operator is **Silver Fox Charters** (☎ **800-478-8792** or 907-235-8792; Internet: www.silverfoxcharters.com). Their Web site has a handy primer on fishing Kachemak Bay. Or contact **Central Charters** (see the "Booking your outing" sidebar, in this chapter).

Flightseeing and bear-viewing

Several good air taxis in Homer provide access to the very remote areas of the southern Kenai Peninsula and lower Cook Inlet that you can't easily reach by boat, but **Kachemak Bay Flying Service** (☎ **907-235-8924;** Internet: www.alaskaseaplanes.com) is really special. It offers spectacular scenic flights over the bay and glaciers starting at $120 per person. The personable Bill de Creeft, flying out of Homer since 1967, is experienced enough to qualify as a pioneer aviator, but the real old-timer is his favorite plane, a restored **1929 Travel Air S-6000-B,** one of only six remaining examples of the executive aircraft, with mahogany trim and wicker seats. He'll also fly you to backcountry lakes.

For bear-viewing, contact **Emerald Air Service** (☎ **907-235-6993;** Internet: www.emeraldairservice.com), operated by de Creeft alumni. They even helped the National Wildlife Federation film an IMAX movie, starring in it along with the bears.

Hiking

The 6-mile **Homestead Trail** is an old wagon road used by Homer's early settlers. The largely informal trail is lovely and peaceful, tunneling through alders, crossing fields of wildflowers, and passing old homestead cabins with great views. A trailhead is at the reservoir on Skyline Drive — drive up West Hill Road from the Sterling Highway, turn right, and follow Skyline Drive, turning left before the pond.

If you are a bit more adventurous, one of Alaska's great outdoor opportunities awaits you in Homer: **a hike in Kachemak Bay State Park.** The park comprises much of the land across the water that makes all those views from Homer so spectacular. For less than $50, you can get a water-taxi ride (and the skipper can give you all the advice you need). Have the boat drop you off in the park after breakfast, walk the beach, hike in the woods, climb the mountains, then meet your boat in time to be back in Homer for dinner and to see the first other people you've seen all day. (See the sidebar, "Crossing the bay in a different kind of taxi," in this chapter.) The park has about 80 miles of trails, mostly linking at a ranger station at a dock in Halibut Cove Lagoon. A free trail guide is available there, but you're well advised to get a good map before leaving Homer. The trails generally start at tidewater among a lush, mossy forest and rise into the craggy mountains — up sharp peaks to a glacier, or, if you don't want to climb, over the hills to the next secluded beach. Bring mosquito repellent and review bear avoidance skills (see Chapter 9). Sources for park information are listed in this chapter in the "Outdoor advice: Whom to ask" sidebar.

Natural history tours

The nonprofit **Center for Alaska Coastal Studies** (☎ 907-235-6667; Internet: www.akcoastalstudies.org) is dedicated to educating the public about the natural environment around Homer. Near town, their **Wynn Nature Center** offers you a chance to discover the ecology of the area on an easy guided walk across 130 acres of spruce forest and wildflower meadow off Skyline Drive, with an 800-foot boardwalk accessible to people with disabilities. It is open daily from 10 a.m. to 6 p.m. mid-June through Labor Day, with guided walks every two hours. Fees for adults are $5, seniors $4, younger than age 18 $3. Call about the weekly programs.

For a more ambitious and truly memorable outing, take the center's daily trip across Kachemak Bay to its facility in the Peterson Bay area. If the tides are right, guests are led on a fascinating guided tide-pool walk; if not, you can take a woodland nature walk and visit an archaeological site. The center has saltwater tanks containing creatures from the intertidal zone, and microscopes to inspect your finds. It's a relaxed and truly Alaskan outing. The center also offers sea kayaking and overnights. Reserve through Jakolof Ferry Service (see the sidebar, "Crossing the bay in different kind of taxi"). The price is $75 adults, $60 ages 3 to 11. Pack your own lunch or buy a light lunch there; bring footwear suitable for hiking and beach walks and warm clothing for the boat ride.

Sea kayaking

The protected waters, tiny islands, and remote settlements across Kachemak Bay are fascinating places to paddle. You're likely to see sea otters and puffins and other sea birds. Floating above the shore gives a great view of the life in the intertidal zone — tide-pool creatures above or below the waterline. You have to take a boat ride first to go sea kayaking in Homer, so it costs more than in some other places, but it's worth it to get away from town. **True North Kayak Adventures** (☎ 907-235-0708; Internet: www.truenorthkayak.com) offers an eight-hour beginner day trip for $125, including lunch and passage across the bay.

Booking your outing

Setting up a day on or across the water in Homer is easy because almost everything can be set up through central agencies that represent many businesses.

✔ **Central Charters** (☎ **800-478-7847** or 907-235-7847; Internet: www.central charter.com), a long-established booking agent, represents the largest and most popular activities, including halibut fishing, boat tours, and the like. It has a ticket office on the right side of the spit as you drive out.

✔ **The Bookie** (☎ **888-335-1581** or 907-235-1581; Internet: www.alaskabookie. com) represents more than 100 small, owner-operated businesses, including B&Bs and other businesses on land, as well as fishing, kayak tours, and water taxis.

It feels more like a mini expedition than a tame day trip. True North also offers more challenging overnight and multiday trips to remote waters in the area and a $199 package that includes the day tour, a night in the attractive Hesketh Island Cabins, and a second day of hiking. Various other companies offer Kachemak Bay kayak trips, too; make a choice through one of the agencies listed in the "Booking your outing" sidebar.

Other things to do in Homer

Homer is known for its artists and galleries. Take an afternoon to check out some of these choices.

✔ **Bunnell Street Gallery,** 106 W. Bunnell Ave. (☎ **907-235-2662;** Internet: www.xyz.net/~bunnell), is a nonprofit gallery, located in a perfect space in an old hardware store near Bishop's Beach at the lower end of Main Street. My favorite gallery in Alaska, Bunnell was made by and for artists, and the experience is noncommercial and often challenging. It's open in summer, daily from 10 a.m. to 6 p.m.; in winter, Monday to Saturday from 10 a.m. to 6 p.m.; closed January.

✔ **Norman Lowell Studio & Gallery** is on Sterling Highway at milepost 160.9, near Anchor Point, about 12 miles from Homer (☎ **907-235-7344**). Lowell built his own huge gallery on his homestead to show his life's work. The immense oils of Alaska landscapes, which are not for sale, hang in a building that counts as one of Alaska's larger art museums. Lowell or his wife, Libby, often serve as host to guests walking through and sell smaller paintings and prints from their shop. Their original homestead cabin also is a museum. Hours are Monday to Saturday from 9 a.m. to 7 p.m., and Sunday from 1 to 5 p.m.; closed October through April. Admission is free. No credit cards for purchases.

✔ For some more **gallery hopping downtown,** a widely distributed brochure lists most of the galleries in town, with a map. Most are close together on Pioneer Avenue. Among my favorites are **Ptarmigan Arts,** at 471 E. Pioneer Ave. (☎ **907-235-5345;** Internet: www.ptarmiganarts.com), a cluttered artists' co-op showing a cross-section of what the area offers; the **Fireweed Gallery** (☎ **907-235-3411**), right next door in an elegant, airy new space; and the large, friendly **Art Shop Gallery** (☎ **907-235-7076**), in the octagonal wood building at 202 W. Pioneer Ave.

Nightlife

The **Pier One Theatre** (☎ **907-235-7333;** Internet: www.pierone theatre.org) is a strong community theater group, housed in a small, corrugated-metal building on the spit, just short of the small-boat harbor on the left, that presents serious drama, musicals, and comedy — not just schlock. The group also produces dance, classical music, and youth theater events during the summer. Check the *Homer News* for current listings. Tickets are available at the door or can be reserved by phone.

The landmark **Salty Dawg Saloon** is a small log cabin on the spit with a lighthouse on top (you can't miss it). This is the place to swap fish stories after a day on the water.

Fast Facts: Homer

ATMs

Wells Fargo, with an ATM, is on the Sterling Highway near Heath Street.

Emergencies

Dial ☎ **911.**

Hospital

South Peninsula Hospital is at the top of Bartlett Street, off Pioneer Avenue (☎ 907-235-8101).

Information

The Homer Chamber of Commerce Visitor Information Center, 201 Sterling Hwy. (P.O. Box 541), Homer, AK 99603 (☎ 907-235-7740; www.homeralaska.org), is on the right as you enter town. Summer hours are daily from 9 a.m. to 8 p.m.; winter Monday through Friday 8 a.m. to 5 p.m.

Internet Access

Eagle Eye Photo and Communications, 601 E. Pioneer Ave. (☎ 907-235-8525), offers $5-an-hour Internet access and photo processing and business services.

Police

For nonemergencies within the city limits, call the **Homer Police Department** (☎ 907-235-3150); outside the city, phone the **Alaska State Troopers** (☎ 907-235-8239). Both have offices located across Pioneer Avenue from the intersection with Heath Street.

Post Office

At Sterling Highway at Heath Street.

Taxes

Sales tax in Homer is 5.5%. Outside the city, you pay 2%.

Chapter 17

Fairbanks

• •

• •

As Alaska's second largest city and the site of the University of Alaska's main campus, you may expect Fairbanks to be somewhat cosmopolitan. Not only would you be wrong, your expectation could hurt people's feelings. Fairbanks doesn't pride itself on being at the center of things; it likes being out on the edge. The city is the last out-post before the great, unpeopled expanse of Alaska, a town with a self-image of being tougher and more extreme than anyplace else. It's got a full range of eccentrics, from granola-crunching university types who climb glaciers to bear-eating gold prospectors who would like to see Alaska become its own nation. And not many people in the middle — most live here for a reason, not because it's just where they happened to end up. Winter days can drop to 40 degrees below zero. They claim to like it. Nothing stops them.

Individualism and toughness are Alaskans' favorite qualities about themselves (whether in truth or in myth), and Fairbanks is the essential Alaska town. But truth be told, individualism and toughness can have their downside. Fairbanks is not a pretty town: The downtown area has been sucked dry by its outskirts, and the outskirts look like any suburban commercial area in the United States, with lots of malls and parking lots. Sightseeing in town is limited to the **university,** with its museum, a big community park, and several commercial tourist attractions. Indeed, some visitors tell me Fairbanks was a disappointment.

But I love going to Fairbanks, especially if I've got my children along. The Chena River runs through town; you can float right up to a restau-rant for dinner. With its many accessible river floats, Fairbanks is Alaska's canoeing capital. **Pioneer Park** (formerly called Alaskaland) charms and amuses my entire family for hours. And the outlying residential areas and the roads out of town are lovely, with big rounded hills clothed in birch and spruce trees. A little farther afield, **Chena Hot Springs Road** leads to wonderful day hikes and swimming at the springs.

If you can get into the lusty spirit of the place, Fairbanks can be a lot of fun.

Getting There

Fairbanks is a transportation hub, whether by plane, train, or automobile. This section details your options for getting to town. And check out the "Fairbanks" map in this chapter for more information.

By car

Many roads lead to (and from) Fairbanks. The Richardson Highway heads east 98 miles to Delta Junction, the end point of the Alaska Highway, then south to Glennallen and Valdez. The Parks Highway heads due south from Fairbanks to Denali National Park, 120 miles away, and then on to Anchorage, 358 miles south. These are all paved two-lane highways, and you can usually do 65 miles an hour.

I think it makes most sense to rent a car or RV in Anchorage and make Fairbanks the far point in a driving loop that includes the Richardson Highway and Denali National Park. The next chapter explains the highway layout and suggests some loop itineraries. But you can also fly into Fairbanks and rent a car here. Details are in Chapter 7 and later under "Getting around by car."

By train

The **Alaska Railroad** (☎ 800-544-0552; Internet: www.alaskarailroad.com) links Fairbanks with Denali National Park and Anchorage. Tour commentary is provided on the nicely appointed full-service trains. The high season, one-way fare is $50 from Denali and $175 from Anchorage (more than twice the cost of flying between the cities). The train is slow, taking 12 hours to get to Anchorage — and that's without delays (which are not infrequent). Driving takes under seven hours, and flying takes about one hour, not counting security and so forth.

By air

Alaska Airlines (☎ 800-252-7522; Internet: www.alaskaair.com) connects Fairbanks to Anchorage. Advance purchase round-trip fares are about $200, and sales go as low as $100. The airport is a hub for various small carriers to Alaska's Interior and Arctic communities. A cab downtown from the airport is $16 to $18 with **Yellow Cab** (☎ **907-455-5555**).

Orienting Yourself in Fairbanks

The **downtown** area and **College,** which once was a separate town and is the site of the University of Alaska campus, are the two original sections of Fairbanks. The downtown area sits in a bend in the Chena River, which bisects Fairbanks. You won't find an awful lot there, but you can spend a couple of hours walking around (see the "Other cool things to see and do" section and the "Downtown Fairbanks" map, later in this chapter). College is to the west. The airport and the Parks Highway (the way to Anchorage) are both near College. The two areas are linked by Airport Way, which is a major commercial strip and a kind of spine through the city, and by the Johansen Expressway (part of an outsized road network that makes getting around very speedy). From the east side of downtown, the Steese Highway leads north to several important places, including Chena Hot Springs Road and the suburban town of Fox.

Getting around by car

Fairbanks is designed for the car, and that's the practical way to get around. Without one, you'll stay downtown the whole time and leave with a low opinion of the place. The city is too spread out to use taxis much. If you fly or take the train to Fairbanks, you can find many car-rental agencies. At the airport, you can rent from Avis, Dollar, Hertz, National, Payless, and Thrifty (contact information is in the appendix of this book). Downtown, **National Car Rental,** at 1246 Noble St. (☎ **800-227-7368** or 907-451-7368), rents SUVs and allows some of its vehicles to go on gravel roads such as the Dalton Highway, an important consideration in this region. Several local firms rent RVs in Fairbanks, including **Diamond Willow RV Rentals,** 350 Old Steese Hwy. N. (☎ **888-724-7373** or 907-457-2814).

Getting around by bus

If saving money is your only consideration, you can use the Fairbanks North Star Borough's **MACS bus system** (☎ **907-459-1011**; Internet: www.co.fairbanks.ak.us/transportation). Buses link the university, downtown, the nearby North Pole community, shopping areas, and some hotels. Service is every 30 minutes, at best, worse Saturday, and nonexistent Sunday, so getting around this way takes a lot of time. Pick up timetables at the visitor center. All buses connect at the transit park downtown, at Fifth Avenue and Cushman Street. The fare is $1.50.

Getting information

The **Fairbanks Log Cabin Visitor Information Center** is in a large log building at 550 First Ave., on the Chena River downtown at Cushman Street, Fairbanks, AK 99701 (☎ **800-327-5774** or 907-456-5774; Fax: 907-452-4190; Internet: www.explorefairbanks.com). The staff provides a road map and detailed walking and driving tour maps, and will help you find a room with their daily vacancy listing. The center is open summer daily 8 a.m. to 7 p.m., winter Monday through Friday, 10 a.m. to 5 p.m. They also have desks at the airport and train depot.

For advice on activities outdoors, don't miss the **Alaska Public Lands Information Center,** 250 Cushman St. (at Third Avenue), Suite 1A, Fairbanks, AK 99701 (☎ **907-456-0527;** Internet: www.nps.gov/aplic). The staff is remarkably knowledgeable and can tell you about trips and activities based on first-hand experience. Besides providing maps and other details, the center houses a small museum about the state's regions and the gear needed to explore them. Daily free films and naturalist programs show in a small auditorium. Open daily 9 a.m. to 6 p.m. in summer, and Tuesday through Saturday 10 a.m. to 6 p.m. in winter.

Where to Stay in Fairbanks

Going the bed-and-breakfast route is a smart choice in Fairbanks, where good budget motel rooms are few. Besides those I list, you can find more through the **Fairbanks Association of Bed and Breakfasts,** P.O. Box 73334, Fairbanks, AK 99707-3334, which lists many on its Web site at www.ptialaska.net/~fabb. Or contact the **Bed and Breakfast Reservation Service,** 763 Seventh Ave., Fairbanks, AK 99701 (☎ **888-451-6649** or 907-479-8165; Fax: 907-474-8448; E-mail: inn@alaska.net).

All Seasons Inn
$$–$$$ **Downtown**

This charming and comfortable country inn stands on a pleasant residential street a couple of blocks from the downtown core. Each cozy room has its own inspired decorative details in bold colors, and the housekeeping has always been perfect on my many visits. Rooms have showers, not baths, and the TVs are small. For socializing with the personable hostess or other guests, a series of large, elegant common rooms connect downstairs, where you'll find a bar with hot drinks and a sun porch with books and games. Complimentary newspapers come with the full breakfast. Shoes must be removed at the front door.

763 Seventh Ave., Fairbanks, AK 99701. ☎ 888-451-6649 or 907-451-6649. Fax: 907-474-8448. Internet: www.allseasonsinn.com. Rack rates: High season $120–135 double, low season $75 double; extra person $25. Rates include full breakfast. AE, DC, MC, V. No smoking.

Fairbanks

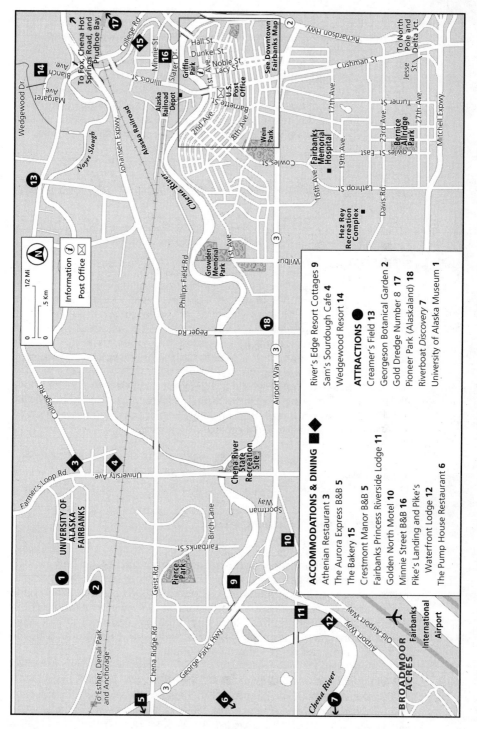

ACCOMMODATIONS & DINING ◼

Athenian Restaurant **3**
The Aurora Express B&B **5**
The Bakery **15**
Crestmont Manor B&B **5**
Fairbanks Princess Riverside Lodge **11**
Golden North Motel **10**
Minnie Street B&B **16**
Pike's Landing and Pike's
Waterfront Lodge **12**
The Pump House Restaurant **6**
River's Edge Resort Cottages **9**
Sam's Sourdough Cafe **4**
Wedgewood Resort **14**

ATTRACTIONS ●

Creamer's Field **13**
Georgeson Botanical Garden **2**
Gold Dredge Number 8 **17**
Pioneer Park (Alaskaland) **18**
Riverboat *Discovery* **7**
University of Alaska Museum **1**

Crestmont Manor Bed and Breakfast

$-$$ **College**

Phil and Connie Horton built this masterpiece of pale custom woodwork to be their home and inn (Phil is a builder), and filled it with handmade quilts (Connie is a quilter), splashes of bright colors, warm decorative themes, and huge impressionistic oil paintings (their son is an artist). The house sits on the side of Chena Ridge, overlooking the west side of town, near the university and the best restaurants. One small room with two twin beds and a separated bathroom rents for $75 in summer; the rest are typically sized with attached bathrooms with shower stalls.

510 Crestmont Dr., Fairbanks, AK 99709. ☎ **888-283-3831** *or 907-456-3831. Fax: 907-456-3841. Internet:* www.mosquitonet.com/~crestmnt. *Rack rates: High season $75–$115 per room, low season $65 per room. AE, DISC, MC, V. Rates include full breakfast.*

Fairbanks Hotel

$-$$ **Downtown**

Four women transformed a notorious flophouse into this trim Art Deco–style historic hotel, in the core of downtown. The proprietors aim for the feel of a small European hotel. Although quite small, the rooms are light and attractively decorated, including brass beds and other period touches. A few rooms just big enough for one person rent for only $55 a night. The neighborhood remains gritty, however, and the building has quirks, so it's wise to choose your room when checking in. Five rooms share a bathroom if you don't get your own. Only the bottom floor of three is nonsmoking. The hotel offers a courtesy van and bike rentals. In the winter, you can rent arctic parkas, boots, hats, and mittens for $5 a day (also available for $20 a day for nonguests).

517 Third Ave., Fairbanks, AK 99701. ☎ **888-329-4685** *or 907-456-6411. Fax: 907-456-1792. Internet:* www.fbxhotl.com. *Rack rates: High season $85–$109 double, low season $40–$59 double. AE, DC, DISC, MC, V.*

Minnie Street Bed & Breakfast Inn

$$-$$$$ **Downtown**

Just across the river from the downtown center, near the rail depot, two buildings around a garden courtyard contain clean, large, brightly decorated rooms with many amenities, custom-designed carpeting, handmade quilts, and stylish furniture. A full breakfast is served in a dining room with a high vaulted ceiling. Huge one- and two-bedroom suites have kitchens, one guest room has a Jacuzzi, and a guest computer is in the common area. Four rooms share bathrooms.

345 Minnie St., Fairbanks, AK 99701. ☎ **888-456-1849** *or 907-456-1802. Fax: 907-451-1751. Internet:* www.minniestreetbandb.com. *Rack rates: High season $100–$130 double, $145–$195 suite; low season $50–$65 double, $95 suite; extra person $25. Rates include full breakfast. AE, DISC, MC, V.*

River's Edge Resort Cottages

$$$$ College

An afternoon on a sunny riverbank exemplifies the best of Interior Alaska; and this place is built around that knowledge. Trim little cottages stand in a grassy compound along the gentle Chena River, where guests can fish for grayling. Inside, each light, airy cottage is an excellent standard hotel room, with high ceilings and two queen beds. Outside, the cottages seem like a little village, where guests can sit on the patio, watch the river go by, and socialize. The owners got the idea for the place from their RV park next door when they noticed how their guests enjoyed visiting together in the open with their own private units to retreat to. It's perfect for families, as the outdoor areas are safe for playing and noise inside won't bother the neighbors. A large, summer-only restaurant sits at the river's edge, with dining on a deck or inside at round, oak tables. Dinner entree prices range up to $30 — on the menu is steak, seafood, and down-home cooking. A burger is $8.

4200 Boat St., Fairbanks, AK 99709. Take Sportsman Way off Airport Way to Boat Street. ☎ *800-770-3343 or 907-474-0286. Fax: 907-474-3665. Internet:* www.rivers edge.net. *Rack rates: High season $173 double, low season $89 double; extra person age 12 and older $10. AE, DISC, MC, V.*

Wedgewood Resort

$$$–$$$$ North of downtown

Located off College Road near the Creamer's Field Refuge, this well-kept hotel sprawls across a grassy, 23-acre complex in eight large buildings. Seven of them are converted three-story apartment buildings, regularly refitted, without elevators but with large living rooms, separate dining areas, fully equipped kitchens, air conditioners, two TVs, balconies, and phones with voice mail in both the living room and bedroom. The main difference from your home is that someone else cleans up after you — a perfect setup for families or business people who want to cook their own food. At $150, these accommodations are a real bargain. The remaining 157 standard hotel units are large and thoughtfully designed but mostly house package tour groups in summer and are closed in winter. I would choose an apartment, but if you don't have your own car, you'll be hiking back and forth to the buildings and up the stairs a lot, so travelers with mobility issues may prefer the more centrally located though smaller regular rooms. A scheduled courtesy van runs to the airport, train depot, and various tourist sites in the summer. The same company owns **Sophie Station Hotel,** which is nearer the airport. It's similar to the Wedgewood but has smaller (although still large) suites. The Sophie boasts elevators and is all in one building.

212 Wedgewood Dr., Fairbanks, AK 99701. ☎ *800-528-4916 or 907-452-1442. Fax: 907-451-8184. Internet:* www.fountainheadhotels.com. *Rack rates: High season $185 double, $150 apt for 2; low season $70 apt, regular double rooms not offered; extra person in apt $10. AE, DC, DISC, MC, V.*

Runner-Up Accommodations

You'll have no trouble finding chain hotels in Fairbanks. Here are some places with more character, or where you can find a bargain.

Aurora Express Bed and Breakfast

$$–$$$ **South of Fairbanks** If you like trains, don't miss this B&B, where a family has installed one at their house on a mountain 6½ miles south of town, with a pair of 1956 Pullman sleepers, a dining car, a locomotive, a caboose, and a World War II hospital car. Some cars are close to their original form, others are elaborately remodeled into small rooms on themes related to Fairbanks history. A full breakfast is served in the dining car. *1540 Chena Ridge Rd. (P.O. Box 80128), Fairbanks, AK 99708.* ☎ ***800-221-0073*** *or 907-474-0949. Fax: 907-474-8173. Internet:* www.aurora-express.com.

Fairbanks Princess Riverside Lodge

$$$$$ **Airport** This enormous cruise-line-operated hotel with many amenities has an opulent style, which consists of lavish colors and prints, a pleasing mish-mash of faux-rustic Alaskan touches, and gold rush excess. Rooms are not large but are well turned out and many have river views. *4477 Pikes Landing Rd., Fairbanks, AK 99709.* ☎ ***800-426-0500*** *or 907-455-4477. Fax: 907-455-5094. Internet:* www.princessalaskalodges.com/fairbanks.htm.

Golden North Motel

$–$$ **Airport** The Baer family, owners since 1971, keep this two-story motel in good shape. The small, dated rooms are a good bargain favored by Alaskans who've come to town from the bush to shop or visit. *4888 Old Airport Way, Fairbanks, AK 99709.* ☎ ***800-447-1910*** *or 907-479-6201. Fax: 907-479-5766. Internet:* www.goldennorthmotel.com.

Marriott SpringHill Suites of Fairbanks

$$$$ **Downtown** This is the best downtown hotel property, a grand new building outside with well-equipped little suites inside. However, the service was poor when I visited. *575 First Ave., Fairbanks, AK 99701.* ☎ ***888-236-2427*** *or 907-451-6552. Fax: 907-451-6553. Internet:* www.springhillsuites.com.

Pike's Waterfront Lodge

$$$$ **Airport** The owners packed this riverside hotel with every amenity they could think of; the overall feeling is pampered hospitality, although the building and exterior are rather ordinary. *1850 Hoselton Rd., Fairbanks, AK 99709.* ☎ ***877-774-2400*** *or 907-456-4500. Fax: 907-456-4515. Internet:* www.pikeslodge.com.

A Taste of Alaska Lodge

$$$–$$$$ **Chena Hot Springs Road** Situated atop a grassy slope on 280 acres, facing Mount McKinley, the hand-crafted, log main building feels like a wilderness lodge but is less than half an hour from Fairbanks. Breakfast is served at 8 a.m. on the dot, and guests must remove their shoes at the door. *551 Eberhardt Rd. (turn right 5.3 miles out Chena Hot Springs Rd.), Fairbanks, AK 99712.* ☎ *907-488-7855. Fax: 907-488-3772. Internet:* www. atasteofalaska.com.

Westmark Fairbanks Hotel

$$$$ **Downtown** This is the city's grand hotel, taking up a full block downtown. A recent remodeling helps it hold that image, but the Westmark Fairbanks remains an old-fashioned property, with dark, heavy colors and rooms that show signs of age. *813 Noble St., Fairbanks, AK 99701-4977.* ☎ *800-544-0970 (reservations), or 907-456-7722. Fax: 907-451-7478. Internet:* www.westmarkhotels.com.

Where to Dine in Fairbanks

The Bakery

$–$$ **Near downtown** **Diner**

You can find an infinite number of old-fashioned coffee shops in and around Fairbanks — the kind of places where a truck driver or gold miner can find a hearty, down-home meal, a motherly waitress, and a bottomless cup of coffee. The Bakery is the best of the lot, which is really saying something. The sourdough pancakes are memorable, the menu is long and inexpensive, portions are huge (sometimes they require two plates), the service is fast and friendly, and the quality of the baked goods is proven. You can get breakfast all day (of course). They have no liquor license.

69 College Rd. ☎ *907-456-8600. Lunch items: $5.50–$9; dinner main courses: $8–$16. Open: Mon–Sat 6 a.m.–9 p.m., Sun 7 a.m.–4 p.m. MC, V.*

Gambardella's Italian Café

$$ **Downtown** **Italian**

This is a warm, charming restaurant right in the center of things. It's my first choice for dinner in Fairbanks. The chicken rustico on polenta, the halibut on pasta, and the lasagna all are tasty, well done, and reasonably priced. Dining rooms are narrow and segmented, so you always seem to be sitting with just a few other people. Elaborate decoration adds to a pleasingly busy feeling. Unlike the synthetic ambiance of some of Fairbanks' other fine dining places, Gambardella's feels homey; a place where the owners have worn down the wood floor over many years. On a sunny day, eat on the patio among the hanging flowers. They serve beer and wine.

706 Second Ave. ☎ *907-456-3417. Internet:* www.gambardellas.com. *Main courses: $9.50–$20, lunch $6–$10, 15% gratuity added for parties of 5 or more, or for split checks. Open: Mon–Sat 11 a.m.–10 p.m., Sun 4–10 p.m., closes an hour earlier off-season. AE, MC, V.*

Pike's Landing

$$$$ Airport Seafood

The fine dining here is Fairbanks' most formal (not such a high standard), and comes across as a little pretentious, but the food is good and the service professional. It overlooks the Chena River near the airport. The menu includes a nice spread of simple to more ambitious selections. The highlight I found was the appetizer of spicy crab-stuffed mushrooms with a thick, chowder-like sauce. Main courses come with a choice of three salads, including a flavorful Caesar. My halibut, however, was dry and the vegetables overcooked. Portions are quite large. Sunday brunch is big and delicious. For an inexpensive meal, the bar serves basic food on the deck over the river from 2:30 p.m. to closing time. The deck is a pleasant choice on a sunny day, less so in cool or rainy weather, when it remains in operation behind plastic.

4438 Airport Way. ☎ *907-479-6500. Main courses: $22–$33; lunch items $7.50–$10.75. Open: Daily summer 5–10 p.m., winter 5–9 p.m. AE, DC, DISC, MC, V.*

The Pump House Restaurant and Saloon

$$$–$$$$ College Regional/Steak/Seafood

The historic, rambling, corrugated tin building on the Chena River is elaborately decorated and landscaped with authentic gold rush relics. Sitting on the deck, you can watch the riverboat paddle by or a group in canoes stop for appetizers and drinks from the full bar. For dinner, the cuisine is a cut above the area's typical steak and seafood. Dishes such as the smoked salmon salad and the fish chowder — hearty, creamy, and flavorful — make the most of the regional ingredients without trying to get too fancy. Portions are ample — save room for one of the exceptional deserts. They serve a big Sunday brunch, too.

1.3 Mile, Chena Pump Road. ☎ *907-479-8452. Internet:* www.pumphouse.com. *Main courses: $17–$29. Open: Summer Mon–Sat 11:30 a.m.–2:00 p.m. and 5–10 p.m., Sun 10 a.m.–2 p.m. and 5–10 p.m.; winter Mon–Sat 5–9 p.m., Sun 10 a.m.–2 p.m. and 5–9 p.m. AE, DISC, MC, V.*

Thai House

$–$$ Downtown Thai

In a small, brightly lit storefront in the downtown area, this is a simple, family-run restaurant with authentic Thai cuisine. Every time we've dined here, the food came quickly and was deftly seasoned and cooked to a turn. And the first time I ate there, I re-checked the bill because it seemed too small. You can rely on the servers, beautifully attired in national

Downtown Fairbanks

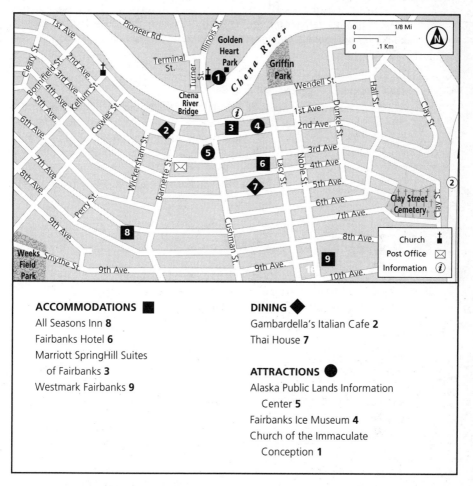

ACCOMMODATIONS ■

All Seasons Inn **8**

Fairbanks Hotel **6**

Marriott SpringHill Suites
of Fairbanks **3**

Westmark Fairbanks **9**

DINING ◆

Gambardella's Italian Cafe **2**

Thai House **7**

ATTRACTIONS ●

Alaska Public Lands Information
Center **5**

Fairbanks Ice Museum **4**

Church of the Immaculate
Conception **1**

costumes, to help you order; just remember that when they say hot, they really mean it. Such gems may be common in cities with large ethnic communities, but in Fairbanks, this place stands out.

526 Fifth Ave. ☎ *907-452-6123. Main courses: Lunch $6.75–$8, dinner $9–$12. Open: Mon–Sat 11 a.m.–4 p.m. and 5–10 p.m. MC, V.*

Runner-Up Restaurants

Athenian Restaurant

$$ College   Greek   A great little place in a minimall with an extensive, reasonably-priced menu for lunch or dinner, good quick service, and deliciously seasoned food. *At University and College roads.* ☎ *907-458-2171.*

Sam's Sourdough Café

$ College Burgers/Diner This is a masterpiece in the art of the greasy spoon, with quick and friendly service, good burgers, great milk shakes, and breakfast all day. *3702 Cameron St., off University Road.* ☎ *907-479-0523.*

Two Rivers Lodge/Tuscan Gardens

$$–$$$$ Chena Hot Springs Road Northern Italian If you're out this direction, perhaps staying at Chena Hot Springs Resort and looking for a little variety, you may enjoy an intimate meal here. It's an old fashioned roadhouse turned into a white-tablecloth restaurant inside that also features a deck over a duck pond outside where meals are served from a brick Tuscan oven in fine weather. *4968 Chena Hot Springs Rd.* ☎ *907-488-6815.*

Exploring Fairbanks

Let go of your expectations and give in to Fairbanks — a little hokey, a little rough, but with a heart of gold. All it takes to have fun here is the sure knowledge that your explorations are not at the center of the universe, but somewhere out around the ragged edges.

The top attractions

Gold Dredge Number 8

Fox

This historic gold-mining site is the best in the area. Built on a real site, the centerpiece is a 1928 gold dredge standing five decks tall. The dredge stands on a barge floating in a pond it created. When it operated, huge scoops would dig from one end, the mechanism inside would digest the gold from the gravel, and then it would dump the spoils out the back — in this way, the pond and the dredge it supports crept 3½ miles across the frozen ground north of Fairbanks. Many sterile areas you see in this area were created by these earth-eaters, for nothing grows on their tailings for decades. The tour company that bought the historic site added museums housed in relocated gold camp buildings, showing the drab life the miners lived. A 90-minute tour starts with a film, then a half-hour on the dredge, and finally a chance to pan for gold yourself, with success assured. A good tour, but I consider the admission price to be high.

1755 Old Steese Hwy., Fairbanks, AK 99712. To get there, go north on the Steese Expressway from town, turn left on Goldstream Rd., and again on the Old Steese Hwy. ☎ *907-457-6058. Internet:* www.golddredgeno8.com. *Admission: $17 adults, $13 children ages 4–12; add $4 for gold panning; add another $8.50 for a cafeteria lunch. Open: Mid-May to mid-Sept tours hourly 9:30 a.m.–3:30 p.m.*

Pioneer Park
West of downtown

This city park contains the boiled down essence of Fairbanks. Created as Alaskaland in 1967 for the centennial of the Alaska purchase, it was renamed in 2002 because they thought the old name promised too much. It's true; this is no theme park. But it is worth your time. The park is relaxing and low-key; entrancing for young children, and interesting for adults if you can give in to the charm of the place. Plan on looking around for at least a couple of hours. The centerpiece is the SS *Nenana* (☎ 907-456-8848), a large sternwheeler that plied the Yukon and Tanana rivers until 1952, with five decks of sumptuous mahogany, brass, and white-painted promenades. Additionally, many of Fairbanks's small historic buildings have been moved to the park. And near the park entrance sits President Warren Harding's railcar, from which he stepped to drive the golden spike on the Alaska Railroad.

The Pioneer Air Museum (☎ 907-451-0037) is housed in a geodesic dome toward the back of the park. Other attractions include a gold rush museum, an illustrated gold rush show, a dance hall, and an art gallery. The park also offers canoe, kayak, and bike rentals. And if you have children, you certainly won't escape without a ride on the Crooked Creek and Whiskey Island Railroad that circles the park twice, with a tour guide pointing out the sights. Kids also enjoy the large playground, with equipment for toddlers and older children, the 36-hole miniature golf course, and an old-fashioned merry-go-round, the park's only ride. And adults will appreciate the revue and salmon bake (see "Nightlife," later in this chapter).

At Airport Way and Peger Road. ☎ *907-459-1087. Internet:* co.fairbanks. ak.us/Parks&Rec/pioneerpark. *Admission: Free to the park; fees for individual attractions are less than $5 each. Attractions open: Memorial Day to Labor Day, daily from 11 a.m. to 9 p.m.*

The Riverboat Discovery
Airport

The *Discovery* belongs to the pioneering Binkley family, who has been in the riverboat business since the Klondike gold rush and has run this attraction for 50 years. The *Discovery* is a real stern-wheeler, a 156-foot steel vessel carrying 700 passengers on as many as three trips a day. The 3½-hour ride is hardly intimate or spontaneous (it mostly carries package-tour passengers off fleets of buses), but the Binkleys still provide a fun, educational experience that doesn't feel cheap or phony. After loading at a landing with shops off Dale Road, near the airport, the boat cruises down the Chena and up the Tanana past demonstrations on shore. Demonstrations include a bush plane taking off and landing, fish cutting at a Native fish camp, and a musher's dog yard. (In recent years, it was four-time Iditarod champion Susan Butcher's yard, and she'd often show off the dogs herself.) Finally, the vessel pulls up at the bank for an hour-long tour of a mock Athabascan village.

1975 Discovery Dr., Fairbanks, AK 99709. ☎ *866-479-6673 or 907-479-6673. Internet:* www.riverboatdiscovery.com. *Admission: $44.95 adults, $29.95 ages 3–12. Sailings: mid-May to mid-Sept daily at 8:45 a.m. and 2:00 p.m.*

University of Alaska Museum
College

This rich, interdisciplinary museum explains the nature and culture of each of the state's regions. It's Alaska's best natural history museum and its most scholarly, with information presented at advanced as well as elementary levels. Some of the objects have a real wow factor, such as Blue Babe, the mummified Steppe Bison; a 5,400-pound copper nugget; and the state's largest collection of gold. Use an audio tour guide or join free 20-minute talks offered through the day on the university's specialties, including wildlife, the aurora, Alaska art and culture, and so on. Despite the museum's small size, a curious person can spend half a day here. The only major weakness is that it tries to do too much in such a small space and seems cluttered, but that will be addressed by a $31-million expansion under construction in 2003, which will double the museum's size, adding an art gallery, café, and auditorium. While the work is going on, the museum's acclaimed theater presentations on the Northern Lights and Alaska Native culture will be moved to the Salisbury Auditorium on the lower campus for one daily showing only; call for details. Other attractions on campus are under "Other cool things to see and do," later in this chapter.

907 Yukon Dr. (P.O. Box 756960), Fairbanks, AK 99775-6960. ☎ *907-474-7505. Internet:* www.uaf.alaska.edu/museum. *Admission: $5 adults, $4.50 ages 60 and older, $3 ages 7–17, ages 6 and younger free. Open: Summer daily 9 a.m.– 7 p.m.; winter Mon–Fri 9 a.m.–5 p.m., Sat–Sun noon to 5 p.m.*

Getting outdoors in Fairbanks

You'll find plenty to do outdoors in and around Fairbanks — I expect that's why most people live here — but don't expect spectacular, sweeping vistas. And you'll find most of what you do here is self-guided. Be sure to take a look at "A Side Trip on Chena Hot Springs Road," later in this chapter. The Chena Hot Springs Resort offers many guided activities.

Canoeing

The Chena River is slow and meandering as it flows through Fairbanks, and you have your pick of restaurants on the bank. Farther up river, canoes pass wilder shores. For a wonderfully relaxing afternoon, rent a canoe at Pioneer Park and paddle down to the Chena Pump House Restaurant for dinner. **Alaska Outdoor Rentals & Guides,** located on the riverbank at the park (☎ **907-457-BIKE;** Internet: www.akbike.com), rents canoes and offers pickup or drop-off along the river for flat rates.

For example, to float from the park to the Pump House is $29 for the canoe and $15 for the pickup. They also offer lessons and drop-offs for longer paddles.

Hiking and bird-watching

Creamer's Field, at 1300 College Rd. (☎ **907-459-7307**), right in Fairbanks, is a 1,800-acre former dairy farm made into a migratory waterfowl refuge by a community fund drive in 1966. The pastures are a prime stopover point for Canada geese, pintails, and golden plovers in the spring and fall. Sandhill cranes, shovelers, and mallards show up all summer. The **Friends of Creamer's Field** (Internet: www.creamers field.org) operates a small visitor center with displays on birds, wildlife, and history, open June through August daily 10 a.m. to 5 p.m. You can also take guided nature walks in summer on Saturday and Wednesday at 9 a.m. and Tuesday and Thursday at 7 p.m. You don't need a guide, however; I especially enjoyed the boreal forest nature walk, interpreted by an excellent booklet you can pick up at the visitor center or from a kiosk at the trailhead when the visitor center is closed.

See "Getting outside on Chena Hot Springs Road," later in this chapter, for a discussion of longer hikes along Chena Hot Springs Road.

Mountain biking

Hiking trails around Fairbanks are open to bikes, and the cross-country ski trails described in the following section are fine mountain bike routes in summer, too. You can get many other good ideas from a couple of good bike rental agencies in town. **Beaver Sports** is at 3480 College Rd. (☎ **907-479-2494;** Internet: www.beaversports.com), and **Alaska Outdoor Rentals & Guides** is at Pioneer Park and at the Fairbanks Hotel, downtown at 517 Third Ave. (☎ **907-457-BIKE;** Internet: www.akbike.com). People around here bike summer and winter: In the cold months, they just use studded tires.

Winter recreation

Fairbanks has real Jack London winters. The visitor bureau guarantees it. Fairbanks is the place for the growing number of visitors who want to experience deep cold, see the Aurora Borealis, and ride a dog sled. Chena Hot Springs Resort, covered near the end of this chapter, is the best destination for winter immersion, but you can also have a good time in town, especially in March, when the days lighten up, temperatures moderate, and the town gets busy with dog mushing and the ice-carving contest (see Chapter 2).

  ✔ **Aurora-viewing:** Fairbanks is famous for the Northern Lights. Some of the world's top scientists studying the phenomenon are at the University of Alaska's Geophysical Institute (check out their predictions at www.gi.alaska.edu). The cold, dark months are the best times to see the Aurora, and the best places are away from city lights. Chena Hot Springs Resort specializes in Aurora-viewing, but all you really need is warm clothing and someone to wake you up. Many accommodations in town offer Aurora wake-up calls.

✔ **Dog mushing:** The long winters and vast wild lands make the Fairbanks area a center of dog sledding, both for racers and recreationists, and plenty of people are willing to take you for a lift, an experience not to be missed. I've heard good things about **Sun Dog Express Dog Sled Tours** (☎ 907-479-6983; Internet: www.mosquitonet.com/~sleddog), which charges $25 for a quick spin, or up to $250 to learn to drive a team in a half-day. They also have summer cart tours. Two local accommodations described elsewhere in this chapter include mushing in their offerings, A Taste of Alaska Lodge and Chena Hot Springs Resort.

✔ **Nordic skiing:** The **Birch Hill Recreation Area,** off the Steese Expressway just north of town (look on the right for the signs and follow them carefully), has about 25 kilometers of good cross-country ski trails, most groomed for classical or skate skiing, and a warm-up building to change clothes. Several loops of a few kilometers each offer advanced skiing on the steep southern side of the hill; loops of up to 10 kilometers provide more level terrain to the north. The area has a lighted loop, too. For information, contact the local Parks & Recreation Department at ☎ 907-459-1070. At the **University of Alaska Fairbanks,** trails start from the west end of Koyukuk Drive, near the satellite dishes. Although not as extensive or as well groomed as Birch Hill, they're well worth a try. Diagonal striders can go quite a distance, but skaters have a shorter network to use.

Other cool things to see and do

If you have extra time in Fairbanks, you'll find enough to do to fill several days. I've gathered some additional highlights here:

✔ **Walk the historic downtown area.** You can pick up a walking-tour map at the visitor center at First and Cushman. The town's most interesting building is right across the river, the Roman Catholic **Church of the Immaculate Conception.** The white clapboard structure, built in 1904, has gold rush decoration inside, rare for its authenticity, including a pressed-tin ceiling and stained-glass windows.

✔ **Encounter ice (even in summer).** The **Fairbanks Ice Museum,** downtown at 502 Second Ave. (☎ 907-451-8222), shows what winter is like year-round, with a freezer you can enter to feel the cold and view 60,000 pounds of ice sculptures. A striking high-tech slide show plays hourly, explaining the annual World Ice Art Championships. Admission is $9 for adults, $8 seniors, $4 ages 6 to 12. It's open 10 a.m. to 6 p.m. daily June to mid-September.

✔ **See the University campus.** A free two-hour walking tour, led by students, meets at the University of Alaska Museum Monday through Friday at 10 a.m., June to August except July 4. Call ahead (☎ 907-474-7581) to confirm the time and any weather cancellations. (See `www.uaf.edu/univrel/Tour/index.html` for information on all university tours and maps.)

✔ **Walk in a research garden.** The University of Alaska's **Georgeson Botanical Garden** is a pleasant mix of science and contemplation. Plots are laid out to compare seeds and cultivation techniques, usually well posted with explanatory information on the experiment; but at the same time, the flowers and vegetables are spectacular, and you'll find peaceful memorials and places to picnic. It's not large, so allow no more than an hour. The garden is on West Tanana Drive at the bottom of the campus (☎ 907-474-6921; Internet: `www.uaf.edu/salrm/gbg`). Admission is $1.

✔ **See a working gold mine.** The **Fort Knox Gold Mine** (☎ 907-488-GOLD), an open pit mine, is Alaska's largest and operates the largest mill in the United States, recovering 1,200 ounces of gold a day. It's a heavy industry site where you can see immense equipment and machinery. The mine is 25 miles north of town on the Steese Highway. Admission is $21 adults, $17 children. Call a day or two ahead for reservations. The tour is not a good choice for people with mobility problems.

✔ **Pan gold at an educational mining tour.** At the **El Dorado Gold Mine,** a train carries visitors through an impressively staged tour, including a tunnel through the permafrost. Visitors gather around a sluice to hear the amusing and authentic Dexter and Lynette (a.k.a. Yukon Yonda) Clark and watch a swoosh of water and gold-bearing gravel rush by. You pan the resulting pay dirt, and everyone goes home with enough gold dust to fill a plastic locket — typically $5 to $35 worth. Drive out to the mine after making reservations, or take a free shuttle. It's nine miles north of town, off the Elliot Highway (☎ 866-479-6673 or 907-479-6673; Internet: `www.eldoradogoldmine.com`). Admission is $27.95 adults, $19.95 ages 3–12 (a bit high, in my opinion).

Spending 1, 2, or 3 days in Fairbanks

Here are some ideas of how to organize your time during a stay in Fairbanks. I'm not sure I'd spend three days in Fairbanks if I had only limited time in Alaska (better to add more time somewhere like Denali National Park), but you can certainly have fun if you do. Each element of the following itinerary is reviewed in more detail elsewhere in this chapter.

Day 1 in Fairbanks

Head to the **University of Alaska Museum** in the morning. It's the most interesting place to visit in town, and it provides a good introduction to the region and the whole state. After a couple of hours there, take a walk on campus, perhaps strolling through the **Georgeson Botanical Garden.** Lunch at the **Athenian Restaurant,** just off campus. In the afternoon, take a cruise on the **Riverboat *Discovery.*** For dinner, dine downtown at **Gambardella's Italian Café.**

Day 2 in Fairbanks

Go to **Pioneer Park** in the morning, and be sure to see the stern-wheeler *Nenana* as well as whatever other attractions catch your fancy — it's a good place to wander. Eat lunch at one of the small restaurants or food booths and then walk to the riverbank and **rent a canoe.** Take your time floating downstream, getting out to look around wherever you choose. Finish the paddle at the **Chena Pump House Restaurant,** where you can dine and have the canoe rental agency pick you and the canoe up for the ride back to your car.

Day 3 in Fairbanks

Take a morning walk at **Creamer's Field** to see the birds and enjoy the peaceful forest trails. If you have time left in the morning, take a look at **New Horizons Gallery** downtown, then lunch at **Thai House.** In the afternoon, drive up the Steese Highway to Fox to see **Gold Dredge Number 8** (you'll also see the Trans-Alaska Pipeline along the road here). After the dredge tour, head back to town to dine at the **salmon bake at Pioneer Park** and see the **Golden Heart Revue** there.

Shopping

Fairbanks isn't a shopping destination by any means, but downtown does have a few good shops.

- ✔ The **Arctic Travelers Gift Shop,** at 201 Cushman St. (☎ **907-456-7080**), specializes in Native crafts, carrying both valuable art and affordable but authentically Alaskan gifts.

- ✔ **Big Ray's Store,** 507 Second Ave. (☎ **907-452-3458**), makes an interesting stop, even if you aren't interested in buying anything: It's known for heavy-duty winter wear, camping gear, and work clothes favored by Alaskans who make their living outdoors all over the state.

- ✔ **New Horizons Gallery,** at 519 First Ave. (☎ **907-456-2063**), occupies a large space with a combination of gifts, inexpensive prints, and large oils by Alaska's best serious artists, and is open every day.

- ✔ Near the airport, at 4630 Old Airport Rd., the **Great Alaskan Bowl Company** (☎ **907-474-9663;** Internet: www.woodbowl.com) makes and sells bowls of native birch — salad bowls, of course, but also for many other purposes. They can carve up to eight nested bowls from one piece of wood and even laser-engrave a photo inside one. Through a glass wall looking into the shop, you can see workers cutting the bowls from raw logs.

Nightlife

Fairbanks has a lot of tourist-oriented evening activities, as well as entertainment also attended by locals. Call the 24-hour event recording of what's playing currently (☎ **907-456-INFO**) or get a copy of the *Fairbanks Daily News-Miner.*

One pleasant way to spend a warm evening is the salmon bake and revue at Pioneer Park. Dinner is served in the evening mid-May to mid-September at the **Alaska Salmon Bake,** in the park's mining valley area (☎ **907-452-7274**), with indoor or outdoor seating areas. Prices for halibut, cod, brown-sugar salmon, or prime rib are under $24. Beer and wine are available. The **Golden Heart Revue** is at the park's Palace Theatre (☎ **907-456-5960;** Internet: www.akvisit.com) nightly at 8:15 p.m. during the same months. It covers the story of the founding of Fairbanks with comedy and song in a nightclub setting; admission is $14 for adults.

The Ester Gold Camp (☎ **800-676-6925** or 907-479-2500; Internet: www. akvisit.com) is an 11-building historic site, an old mining town that's been turned into an evening tourist attraction. The main event is a gold rush theme show at the Malamute Saloon, with singing and Robert Service poetry, nightly at 9 p.m.; admission is $14. A "photosymphony" slide show about the Aurora takes place a couple of times a night in the summer and costs $8. A restaurant serves a buffet and has mess-hall seating; it costs $16, or $26 if you have crab. The gift shop is open in the evening, and the old gold mine bunkhouse offers simple, inexpensive rooms, or you can check out the campground.

Fast Facts: Fairbanks

ATMs
Fairbanks has numerous banks with **ATMs** in the downtown area and along the commercial strips. **Key Bank** is at 100 Cushman.

Emergencies
Dial ☎ **911.**

Hospital
Fairbanks Memorial is at 1650 Cowles St. (☎ 907-452-8181).

Internet Access
Café Latte is at 519 Sixth Ave. (☎ 907-455-4898).

Police
For nonemergency police business, call the **Alaska State Troopers** (☎ 907-451-5100) or, within city limits, the **Fairbanks Police Department** (☎ 907-459-6500).

Post Office
At 315 Barnette St.

Taxes
Fairbanks has no sales tax. Bed tax is 8%.

A Side Trip on Chena Hot Springs Road

The 57-mile paved Chena Hot Springs Road traces the Chena River through the wooded hills east from Fairbanks. It's an avenue to an enjoyable day trip or a destination for outdoor activities and hot-spring swimming. The road crosses the Chena River State Recreation Area, a place for spectacular hikes and float trips, and leads to the Chena Hot Springs, a year-round resort perfect for soaking in hot mineral springs and a useful base for summer or winter outdoor day trips. The resort is as popular in the summer, when you can hike or ride horseback, as in the winter, when you can watch the Aurora, ski, and ride snowmobiles and dog sleds. (The slow seasons are spring and fall.) Swimming in the hot water, indoors or outdoors, goes on all year, regardless of the weather. The paved road itself is a pleasant drive at any time, about 1¼ hours each way from Fairbanks, but not particularly scenic.

Getting there

Chena Hot Springs Road meets the Steese Expressway about 10 miles north of downtown Fairbanks. (Details on renting a car in Fairbanks can be found earlier in this chapter.) The resort offers rides from any-where in Fairbanks for $80 round-trip for one or two people, $40 for each additional person.

Where to stay and dine

Besides the **Chena Hot Springs Resort,** two other places along the road are described earlier in the chapter with other Fairbanks estab-lishments: **Two Rivers Lodge,** a fine-dining establishment and bar, and **A Taste of Alaska Lodge,** a bed-and-breakfast.

Chena Hot Springs Resort
$$$–$$$$ Chena Hot Springs

This unsophisticated family resort, set on 440 acres of land in a bowl of mountains, invites a slow pace, with plenty of time spent soaking or in the woods. Winter is the high season, when the Aurora-viewing is excep-tional, away from city lights. You can enjoy Nordic ski trails groomed for classical or skating techniques, snowmobile tours, ice skating, sled dog rides, winter biking, and more. An Aurora-viewing station, with a warm-up lodge, is established on a hilltop, where guests can flop back in the snow under a dizzying dome of stars and colors. In the summer, you can go horseback riding, rafting, canoeing, hiking, gold panning, flightseeing, or mountain biking. All activities are guided and carry extra fees, start-ing at a large activity building that also has indoor diversions, such as virtual golf. There are no rentals, except for cold weather clothing.

The rooms range from the crude, original cabins built by the prospectors who discovered the area to large hotel rooms with televisions, phones, and coffeemakers. The newest rooms, in the Moose building, are large and nicely done up, but noise can be a problem at night; light sleepers may prefer the smaller but still comfortable older buildings. The larger cabins — not the prospectors' originals — are crude but adequate for a family or group looking for inexpensive lodgings and not particular about indoor plumbing. The main lodge building contains the restaurant and bar, with a brief but sufficiently varied menu with prices only slightly above those in town. Over all, this is a good place to have fun in the real Alaska, but be ready for some rough spots — it's a sprawling, old-fashioned resort owned and operated by locals. Service has been quite inconsistent.

Mile 56.5, Chena Hot Springs Rd. (P.O. Box 58740), Fairbanks, AK 99707. ☎ *800-478-4681 or 907-451-8104. Fax: 907-451-8151. Internet:* www.chenahotsprings.com. *Rack rates: $125–$170 double, $190–$200 suite; extra person $20. AE, DC, DISC, MC, V.*

Getting outside on Chena Hot Springs Road

The best trail hikes in the Fairbanks area are in the Chena River State Recreation Area, and excellent guided activities are available at the resort at the end of the road. Here are the highlights:

- **Hike the Angel Rocks Trail.** A sometimes steep 3½-mile loop to an immense granite outcropping, this impressive destination has good views of the valley below. The trailhead is at mile 48.9 of the road.

- **Backpack or hike the Granite Tors Trail.** A 15-mile loop starting at mile 39 of the road, it leads to towering granite tors that stand at random spots on the broad Plain of Monuments. The tors look like a surrealist experiment in perspective, at first confounding the eye's attempts to gauge their distance and size. Water is scarce, so bring along plenty. This is an excellent overnight hike, with the driest ground for camping right around the tors. You'll find a public shelter halfway along.

- **Float part of the Chena River.** Where you choose to start depends on your expertise. Easier water is downstream from Rosehip Campground (mile 27), with the slowest of all nearer Fairbanks, but the upper portion is more popular if you are up for something a bit more challenging. **Canoe Alaska** (☎ **907-883-2628;** Internet: www.canoealaska.net) specializes in whitewater canoe instruction for beginners and intermediate paddlers, and leads guided canoe and raft outings and expeditions; an introductory clinic is $165. See "Getting outdoors in Fairbanks," earlier in this chapter, for information on canoe rental.

✔ **Swim and soak in the hot springs.** You don't have to stay at the resort to enjoy the pools and outdoor hot pond, all fed naturally by geothermal springs. Swim passes come with your room if you're staying at the resort; for day-trippers, a day pass is $10 adults, $7 ages 6 to 13, free for children 5 and younger. To get there, just drive to the end of the road.

✔ **Explore the woods on horseback or a bike, on skis or a snowmobile.** The resort offers a full range of outdoor activities, all guided by the staff at the on-site recreation center. The description of the lodge above has a complete list.

✔ **View the Aurora from a mountaintop.** The resort maintains an Aurora-viewing facility on one of the rounded mountains that surround it. Visitors lie on their backs to watch the displays, periodically stepping inside to warm up.

The **Alaska Division of Parks** (☎ **907-451-2695;** Internet: www.alaska stateparks.org, click on the Individual Parks link) manages Chena River State Recreation Area and produces trail, river, and road guides, which are available at trailhead kiosks, on the Web site, or in their brochure, *The Chena Trailmarker,* which you can also order from the Web. Or, get all that and answers to your questions in Fairbanks at the **Alaska Public Lands Information Center,** 250 Cushman St. (at Third Avenue), Suite 1A (☎ **907-456-0527;** Internet: www.nps.gov/aplic).

Chapter 18

Driving Alaska's Highways

- -

In This Chapter

▶ Getting a handle on Alaska's highways

▶ Looping the loop, part one (Anchorage to Whittier to Valdez to Glennallen)

▶ Looping the loop, part two (Anchorage to Glennallen to Fairbanks to Denali)

▶ Braving the Arctic and other extremes

- -

*W*hen you're used to a drive being a chore and a highway being an interstate that looks about the same no matter where you are, prepare for something completely different when driving in Alaska. The great majority of the state's highway miles are lonely two-lane roadways stringing together tiny settlements that are hundreds of miles apart, with nothing in-between but spectacular wild country.

A long drive in Alaska is a form of wilderness travel. The radio goes dead. You cross great rivers and mountain ranges, see moose and other wildlife, but encounter few other cars and virtually no buildings. The landscape evolves and storms cross the skies. A winding road slowly unfolds the world, unfolds land that belongs to you. Alaska is almost all public land; you can get out anywhere to walk through the heather, smell the cottonwood trees by a roaring river, or feel the cool air of a bright midnight on your cheek.

Road trips take a long time around here: You must cover a lot of ground. If you're really ambitious, you'll need a car that you can take over gravel roads; that's a problem whenever you're renting a car here, because I know of only one good agency that lets you drive off-pavement with its rental vehicles (the National Car Rental office in Fairbanks — see "Driving to the Arctic and Other Extremes," later in this chapter). On the other hand, you have little need to fear the unknown on an Alaskan road trip during the warm months — you won't be eaten by wild animals. It is a long way between services, but people are friendly and helpful, and you'll muddle through whenever you have a problem.

Winter driving on Alaska highways is beautiful (at least during the brief hours of daylight), but safely taking a long winter's drive requires some preparation and knowledge. Consider flying and traveling by train instead during the winter. For winter or summer trips, check out the safety tips in Chapter 7.

I structure this chapter differently than the others. First, I summarize the qualities of the few main highways. Reviewing this summary with a map in your hand orientates you with the routes and what they are like. Next, I describe some of the best driving itineraries, starting with the loops that most people want to drive, followed by the more extreme and lengthy remote drives.

Understanding Alaska's Road Map

Losing your way on Alaska's highways is pretty difficult, because there just aren't enough of them. One leads in and out of the state, another connects Anchorage and Fairbanks, another heads to the Arctic, another to Prince William Sound, and another ends at the Kenai Peninsula. Despite the state's enormous size, a usable highway map can essentially fit on a cocktail coaster, because you need only a few simple lines to show the entire network of roads.

For planning your trip, you nevertheless need some critical information that's far more difficult to come by (that I'm about to give you): the drives that really are worth doing. Alaska has plenty of miles — plenty of 100-mile stretches, in fact — that are as boring as driving through a tunnel of brush can be. So get out your map (or use the "Alaska Highways" map provided in this chapter) and follow me through this menu, derived from many long road trips across Alaska. I provide cross-references for places to check out in other chapters; otherwise, look for more detailed information later in this chapter. I mention only the paved roads here. Remote, gravel highways are covered in the section about "Driving to the Arctic and Other Extremes," later in the chapter:

> ✔ **Alaska Highway** (Route 2 from the border to Delta Junction): Running nearly 1,400 miles from Dawson Creek, British Columbia, to Delta Junction, Alaska, a couple of hours east of Fairbanks on the Richardson Highway, this World War II road is paved, but that doesn't mean it's always smooth. Like other northern highways, it's subject to bone-jarring frost heaves and spring potholes. And the 200 miles in Alaska are pretty dull; the prettiest part is on the Canadian side, in the Kluane Lake area.

Alaska Highways

Glenn Highway (Route 1 from Anchorage to Tok): From the Alaska Highway, this road is how you get to South Central Alaska, including Anchorage, 330 miles southwest of Tok. The northern section, from Tok to Glennallen (sometimes called the Tok Cutoff), borders Wrangell–St. Elias National Park, with broad tundra and boreal forest (also known as *taiga*) broken by high, craggy peaks — a pretty drive, but not top-five material by Alaska standards. The section from Glennallen to Anchorage, however, is truly spectacular. The road passes through high alpine terrain frequented by caribou. It then claws its way along the walls of a deep canyon close by the Matanuska Glacier and the river that flows from it.

✔ **Parks Highway** (Route 3): The George Parks Highway is a straight line from Anchorage to Fairbanks, 358 miles to the north, providing access to Denali National Park (see Chapter 19). Although this highway features some vistas of Mount McKinley from south of the park and nice views on the wide tundra of Broad Pass, it is mostly a transportation route, less scenic than the Richardson or Glenn highways.

✔ **Richardson Highway** (Route 4 from Valdez to Delta Junction, Route 2 from Delta Junction to Fairbanks): Leading 364 miles from tidewater in Valdez to Fairbanks, this route is the most beautiful paved drive in the Interior. I've been hypnotized into awed reverie on this drive; you just can't absorb so much beauty hour after hour. From the south, the road begins with a magnificent climb through Keystone Canyon and steep Thompson Pass, just outside of Valdez, then passes the huge, distant peaks of southern Wrangell– St. Elias National Park. North of Glennallen, the road climbs into the Alaska Range, snaking along the shores of long alpine lakes and crossing the dizzyingly huge spaces of the tundra slopes, which are good areas for spotting wildlife. The road descends again to the forested area around Delta Junction and meets the Alaska Highway before arriving in Fairbanks (see Chapter 17). The state's first highway, it lost much of its traffic to the Parks Highway, which trims more than 90 miles from the drive between Anchorage and Fairbanks, and to the Glenn Highway, which shaves about 120 miles off the trek from Glennallen to Tok. The other highways' gains are also your gains, because you rarely see another car.

✔ **Seward Highway** (Route 1 from Anchorage to Tern Lake, Route 9 from Tern Lake to Seward): The highway leaves Anchorage on the 124-mile drive to Seward following the rocky edge of mountain peaks above a surging ocean fjord. Abundant wildlife and unfolding views often slow cars (see Chapter 15 for more information about this stretch of highway). Later, the road climbs through high mountain passes above the tree line, tracing sparkling alpine lakes before descending through forest to Seward (see Chapter 16).

✔ **Sterling Highway** (Route 1 from Tern Lake to Homer): Leading 142 miles from the Seward Highway to the tip of the Kenai Peninsula, the highway has some scenic spots but is mostly a way to get to Kenai, Soldotna, and Homer, places that are discussed in Chapter 16.

Driving Loop 1: Anchorage to Whittier to Valdez to Glennallen

Here's a great way to see Prince William Sound, the coastal mountains, and the spectacular Glenn Highway sections from Glennallen to Anchorage, including a trip on the Alaska state ferry from Whittier to Valdez.

Day 1: Anchorage to Valdez

The loop starts with a drive south from Anchorage to Whittier of about an hour's duration if you don't stop. But making stops on this stretch of road is part of the fun. You can spend a full day in the scenic **Girdwood** and **Portage Glacier** areas, all of which I discuss in Chapter 15. Near Portage Glacier, you drive through the unique 2-mile tunnel to Whittier. I also include plenty of important tips about that strange passage in Chapter 15.

In Whittier, put your car on the **Alaska Marine Highway ferry** *Bartlett* (☎ **800-642-0066** or 907-465-3941; Internet: www.alaska.gov/ferry). The ship shuttles back and forth between Whittier and Valdez several times a week. The ride takes seven hours, and every minute of it is scenic and relaxing. If the weather is fine, sit on the top solarium deck and keep an eye out for whales. A Chugach National Forest ranger interprets the scenery in the observation lounge, and a serviceable little restaurant is onboard. The fare is $78 for a car up to 15 feet long, plus $65 for an adult passenger (including the driver), with ages 2 to 11 roughly half price. You do need to reserve ahead, but a few weeks usually is sufficient.

In Valdez, check in to the **Aspen Hotel** at 100 Meals Ave. (☎ **888-478-4445** or 907-835-4445; Internet: www.aspenhotelsak.com), which has nice upscale rooms for $129 to $149 double in the high season. Dine at **Mike's Palace Ristorante** on the harbor (☎ **907-835-2365**). Besides being a good family restaurant that serves Italian and Greek food, it's historic: Captain Joe Hazelwood was waiting for a take-out pizza here when he slipped next door for his last cocktail before boarding the fateful voyage of the *Exxon Valdez.*

Day 2: A day in Valdez

Following are a list of entertainment options for spending the day in Valdez:

- ✔ **The Valdez Museum and Historical Archive,** at 217 Egan Dr. (☎ **907-835-2764**; Internet: www.alaska.net/~vldzmuse), showcases regional history.

- ✔ The **Solomon Gulch Salmon Hatchery,** on Dayville Rd. (☎ **907-835-1329**), is a place to see millions of swarming fish on a free, self-guided tour.

- ✔ Take an outdoor sea kayaking outing to Shoup Glacier with **Pangaea Adventures** (☎ **800-660-9637** or 907-835-8442; Internet: www.alaskasummer.com), or go whitewater rafting with **Keystone Raft and Kayak Adventures** (☎ **800-328-8460** or 907-835-2606; Internet: www.alaskawhitewater.com).

✔ Hike and fish while armed with info you obtained from the **Visitor Information Center,** operated by the Valdez Convention and Visitors Bureau, at 200 Chenega Ave., a block off Egan Drive (P.O. Box 1603), Valdez, AK 99686 (☎ **800-770-5954,** 907-835-4636, or 907-835-2984 in winter; Internet: www.valdezalaska.org).

Day 3: Valdez to Glennallen

If the weather is clear, the drive north from Valdez on the Richardson Highway will be a highlight of your trip. The road traces the rocky slot of **Keystone Canyon** and then climbs straight up the side of the sheer coastal mountains to high alpine country in **Thompson Pass.** This spot has the distinction of being on the receiving end of the biggest snowfall ever to occur in Alaska during a 24-hour period (5 feet) and the most during a season (81 feet). A glacier that you can walk right up to is located here. A little farther along, you see the silvery Trans-Alaska Pipeline snaking along to the left.

About 100 miles from Valdez, you come to **Copper Center,** a tiny community known as Athabaskan. It's growing up these days, thanks to the proximity of Wrangell–St. Elias National Park and a new 85-room luxury hotel, the **Copper River Princess Wilderness Lodge** (☎ **800-426-0500** or 907-822-4000; Internet: www.princessalaskalodges.com/copper.htm). High season rates are $189 double. Stop here for lunch in the top-rated restaurant. Staying here a couple of days so that you can see the park, especially the mining ghost town of **Kennecott,** is well worth the expense. You can make park arrangements through the lodge. However, unless you can allocate at least that much time, don't bother staying: Getting into the park is a major undertaking. In any event, check out the National Park Service visitor center in Copper Center to find out about Wrangell–St. Elias, which by far is the largest and most rugged of all national parks.

Another 15 miles north of Copper Center, you reach the little town of **Glennallen,** which lies at the junction of the Richardson and Glenn Highways. If you want to continue on Loop 2, the northern loop that includes Fairbanks and Denali National Park, continue north (or straight), bearing left at the second major Y, and skip to "Day 2" in the "Driving Loop 2: Anchorage to Glennallen to Fairbanks to Denali" section, later in this chapter. Otherwise, to continue with Loop 1, turn left onto the Glenn Highway.

Heading west from Glennallen, the Glenn Highway crosses tundra, swamp, and taiga that are typical of Interior Alaska and a good place to spot caribou and moose over wide and distant vistas. The road then rises into the craggy peaks of two converging mountain ranges, the Talkeetna and Chugach mountains. Stop about 70 miles beyond Glennallen at **Sheep Mountain Lodge** (☎ **877-645-5121** or 907-745-5121;

Internet: www.sheepmountain.net), a friendly and authentic mountainside roadhouse. Eat simply in their dining room, take a sauna or a walk on the high tundra trails, and bed down in one of the cute cabins, which rent for $125 double.

Day 4: The road back to Anchorage

Anchorage is only another 115 miles away, but you have plenty to do on the way. First comes the enormous **Matanuska Glacier.** See it from the Matanuska Glacier State Recreation Site, an overlook with a 1-mile nature trail with explanatory signs at mile 101 of the highway. More country-style development crops up along the road as you approach urban Alaska. Chickaloon is the base for **Nova Raft and Adventure Tours,** the river-riding company listed in Chapter 14; if you already plan to pass through here, you may want to stop and arrange a float. Sutton is a little town left behind by a coal mine that once operated in these mountains. The charming little historic park there is worthy of a stop to stretch your legs. Next comes Palmer (see the section that covers a side trip to the Mat-Su Valley in Chapter 15). Anchorage is an hour farther, but you can still consider stops on the way at Eklutna Historical Park, Eklutna Lake, or Thunderbird Falls (all described in Chapter 14).

Driving Loop 2: Anchorage to Glennallen to Fairbanks to Denali

Most people who come to Alaska want to see Denali National Park, for reasons that become obvious in Chapter 19. The best way to get there is in the rented car you pick up in Anchorage (see Chapter 13). But there's much more country to see than just Denali. This part of the trip takes you over one of the world's most beautiful loop drives before arriving at the park.

If you have the time, consider traveling both loops that I describe in this chapter. They overlap at Anchorage and Glennallen. You can start with Loop 1, driving south to Whittier, crossing Prince William Sound, and driving north on the Richardson Highway; then join Loop 2 by continuing north at Glennallen all the way to Fairbanks, then south to Denali, and back to Anchorage.

Day 1: Anchorage to Glennallen

Leave Anchorage northbound on the Glenn Highway (Sixth Avenue as you depart downtown). This day reverses the Day 4 itinerary of Loop 1, taking you past Palmer, Sutton, and the Matanuska Glacier to the Sheep

Mountain Lodge. If you're not ready to stop there (perhaps you're driving through and skipping the sights), go another 70 miles to Glennallen, eat comfort food at the **Caribou Restaurant** and stay at the **New Caribou Hotel** (☎ **800-478-3302** or 907-822-3302; Internet: www.alaskan.com/caribouhotel), where good standard rooms rent for $137 in summer. Be sure to call ahead, however, because they book up fast.

Day 2: Glennallen to Fairbanks

Drive north on the Richardson Highway, turning left at the T at the end of the Glenn Highway and continuing to bear left. The next 150-mile stretch passes north through the Alaska Range to Delta Junction and its extraordinary scenery. The road rises from the forest, past a series of lakes, to an enormous area of alpine tundra, traced topographically by more long alpine lakes. Scan those wide vistas for wildlife. Although sightings of the Trans-Alaska Pipeline are frequent, few other structures interrupt your view along the way, and you can stop and take a walk virtually anywhere you like.

You may want to pack a picnic for this drive, because the area has few worthy places to dine. Or you can eat when you arrive in the little farming town of Delta Junction; turn left at the junction with the Alaska Highway and stop at the **Buffalo Center Diner** (☎ **907-895-5089**), on the right, a good, clean local hangout. If you need a room at this point, the funky but charming **Kelly's Country Inn** (☎ **907-895-4667;** Internet: www.kellysalaskacountryinn.com) is right at the junction, charging $89 to $109 double.

Or you can continue 100 miles west to Fairbanks, with one good stop 10 miles along the way at **Rika's Roadhouse and Landing** (☎ **907-895-4201;** Internet: www.rikas.com), a historic way station from the days when this part of the highway was a dog-sled journey of many days. Rika's is a good indoor and outdoor museum of pioneer life, with a simple restaurant. Nearby, the Alaska pipeline suspension bridge over the Tanana River is well worth a look. Spend the night in Fairbanks. I often choose the **All Seasons Inn;** it and other accommodations and restaurants are listed in Chapter 17. Dine at **Gambardella's Italian Café.**

Day 3: A day in Fairbanks

Spend a day (or more) in Fairbanks. The area offers a wide variety of things to do, from gold-mining sites to hot springs and other outdoor destinations to even an ice museum. You can find a good list of ideas of what to do in Chapter 17.

Day 4: Fairbanks to Denali

Driving south from Fairbanks on the Parks Highway, the first worth-while stop you come to is Nenana, about 60 miles along the way. It's a town straight out of a Mark Twain novel: a sleepy, dusty riverside barge stop. Riverboats, in fact, still load with cargo for villages up and down the nearby Tanana River. Visit the nostalgia-jogging **Depot Museum** and the cultural center on the waterfront, with its own little museum and Native craft shop. Stop in at the visitor center on the Parks Highway to find out about the **Nenana Ice Classic** (www.nenanaakiceclassic. com), a contest to guess the exact minute the ice on the Tanana breaks up and starts to go out. It had a jackpot of $300,000 for the 2002 time (May 7th, at 9:27 p.m.).

You should still be able to make Denali National Park for lunch, 120 miles south of Fairbanks. Stop just short of the park in Healy to eat at the **Black Diamond Grill** (☎ **907-683-4653**) and check in at the **Motel Nord Haven** (☎ **800-683-4501** or 907-683-4500; Internet: www.motel nordhaven.com). In the afternoon, visit the **Denali National Park Visitor Center** to become oriented to the park. Take a hike in the front country or go on a river-rafting ride in the Nenana Canyon. In the evening, catch a dinner theater show. All the Denali options are discussed in Chapter 19.

Day 5: A day in Denali

Get up as early as possible to board a shuttle bus (that you've reserved at least a few weeks in advance) into the park. Your chances of seeing brown bear, moose, and caribou are excellent, and you may even see wolves, Dall sheep, and other hard-to-find animals. Get off the bus for a walk on the tundra; go ahead and walk out of sight of the road so that you can find out how it feels to be all alone in the outdoors, and then return to the road to catch another bus back (make sure you can find your way back to the road). Stay out all day and dine at the **Summit Restaurant** in the **Denali Princess Lodge** (☎ **907-683-2282**).

Day 6: Denali back to Anchorage

Drive about three hours south of the park to Talkeetna and have lunch at **Talkeetna Alaska Lodge** (☎ **907-733-9500**; Internet: www.talkeetna lodge.com) before boarding a bush plane at the Talkeetna Airport for a flight over Mount McKinley and, in season, a landing on one of its glaciers. Details about the flight are found in Chapter 19. After the flight, drive two hours south to Anchorage to complete the loop.

Driving to the Arctic and Other Extremes

I spend few words reflecting on the remote, unpaved highways of the Arctic and Interior, because driving them is simply impractical for most visitors. Unless you bring your own car, you must rent an expensive SUV from one of the few agencies that allow any of their vehicles on these rough roads. One that does is **National Car Rental,** at 1246 Noble St. in Fairbanks (☎ **800-227-7368** or 907-451-7368). After you have something to drive, you need to prepare: You'll need extra gas, at least one full-sized spare, and other emergency equipment (see the lists in Chapter 7). On the longer routes, you also need food and bedding. When you're on the road, you'll find conditions are tough and services are crude and infrequent. Besides, these roads, although often quite scenic, don't always go anywhere that most visitors want to be. Once you're there, you may not find anything you like there after all.

Now, I must add that I personally love driving these remote highways in my own four-wheel-drive vehicle. Doing so is a real adventure and amazing things sometimes happen. When I recently was sleeping in the back of my 4-by-4 on the side of the Dalton Highway, I woke to see a moose mother and calf looking in at me. If you're prepared and motivated, go for it. The rest of this section provides you with a preview of what you can expect to see and do on these forgotten highways.

Dalton Highway (Route 11)

Built to haul equipment to the Prudhoe Bay oil fields about 500 miles north of Fairbanks, the Dalton punctures the heart of the wilderness, crossing the Brooks Range and the North Slope to the Arctic Ocean. The scenery is unbearably spectacular, the wildlife is abundant, and the destination is unique. But it takes a full tank of gas between stops, and prudence demands that you take extra gasoline in cans just in case. Services are gritty and rough, and any mishap leaves you far beyond any ordinary kind of assistance. Although the road is excellent in places, it can wash out or become rough and muddy for long stretches.

The Dalton ends at an oil field security checkpoint. From here, you must take a $37 guided tour offered by the **Arctic Caribou Inn** (☎ **877-659-2368** or 907-659-2368; Internet: www.arcticcaribouinn.com) just to get through to the water. You need to reserve at least 24 hours in advance to clear security, and be prepared to provide your name and an identification number that British Petroleum can use to run a background check before allowing you on the oil field: a driver's license, passport, or Social Security number works.

Denali Highway (Route 8)

I simply couldn't believe my eyes when I first drove this 133-mile gravel road connecting the midpoints of the Parks and Richardson highways. Stunning alpine vistas high in the Alaska Range rival those within Denali National Park, but they're open to all drivers, with a rich network of trails and mountain lakes offering you a good chance to see caribou, bear, moose, and waterfowl. The trouble is the road is falling apart. At this writing, it is best described as almost undriveable, with top speeds of 10 miles an hour. At best, it's a long, bumpy road with few services. In winter, the road is not maintained and is off limits.

Edgerton Highway and McCarthy Road (Route 10)

Running east from the Richardson Highway, south of Glennallen, the Edgerton leads to the tiny town of Chitina, where the McCarthy Road, a muddy one-lane track, penetrates Wrangell–St. Elias National Park to historic sites at McCarthy and Kennecott. The road actually is the railbed of the Copper River and Northwestern Railroad, which was abandoned in 1938, and it passes over high, one-lane trestles. The journey of 93 miles takes half a day, with no services and few views. But the wondrous ghost town of Kennecott is a great destination, with good places to stay and eat. The best choice to stay (where meals are included) is at the **Kennicott Glacier Lodge** (☎ **800-582-5128** or 907-258-2350; Internet: www.KennicottLodge.com). If you're not up for the perilous drive, the lodge can help you find an easier way to get there, too. See the "Driving Loop 1" section, earlier in this chapter, for another lodging and dining option for Kennecott.

The Klondike Loop

On the **Klondike Highway** (Yukon Highway 2), the **Top of the World Highway** (Yukon Route 9), and the **Taylor Highway** (Alaska Route 5), you make a big detour from the Alaska Highway to see the North's best historic gold rush treasures in Dawson City and Eagle. You can do it when you're driving your own car to Alaska, or when you're in Haines or Skagway and have a car you can drive over gravel roads (generally, not allowed with a rental car). From Whitehorse, Yukon, to Tok, Alaska, is 502 miles via a loop that is mostly unpaved and 127 miles longer than the direct and paved Alaska Highway between the two towns. Completing a circular loop by driving from Skagway to Dawson City to Haines and then taking the Alaska Marine Highway ferry back to Skagway adds more than 530 miles. So, if that's what you want to do, you'll spend a significant amount of your vacation driving.

Checking road conditions

Sometimes gravel highways are washed out or too rough to use, so it's a good idea to check with the Alaska Department of Transportation before you drive one of these remote routes, even in summer. Call ☎ 800-478-7675 or check the Web site at www.dot.state.ak.us. For conditions on the Alaska Highway in Canada, call the Yukon Department of Infrastructure at ☎ 867-456-7623 or check out www.gov.yk.ca/roadreport. In winter, check before you drive any highway, and it can't hurt to check on paved highways in summer to find out about possible construction delays.

What you see are historic Dawson City, Yukon, and the fabulous mountain scenery of the Top of the World Highway. Dawson was the destination of the 1898 gold rush; the bed of the Klondike River near there contained thick slabs of gold. The town maintains the look of those bygone days, when it was the second largest city on the west coast, after San Francisco. Many buildings are restored — part of the Klondike National Historic Sites — and are well interpreted by guides and museums; a working casino, vaudeville show, and other attractions of the era are operated primarily by **Parks Canada.** Get information from their **Dawson City Visitor Reception Centre,** King and Front streets (P.O. Box 390), Dawson City, YT, Canada Y0B 1G0 (☎ 867-993-7200; Internet: http://parkscan.harbour.com/khs). The **Klondike Visitors Association,** housed in the same building (P.O. Box 389P, Dawson City, YT, Canada Y0B 1G0; ☎ 867-993-5575; Fax: 867-993-6415; Internet: www.DawsonCity.org), offers information on local businesses, accommodations, and community events.

After passing into the United States on the Top of the World Highway (*note:* this border crossing is open only during the day, and only during the summer), a further detour leads north on the Taylor Highway to the forgotten town of Eagle (going south on the Taylor leads you back to the Alaska Highway). The trip to Eagle adds 66 miles each way on a winding, narrow dirt road; allow two hours one-way. But, if you have the time, the destination more than rewards the effort. Eagle is lost in time, a treasure of a gold rush river town with many original buildings full of original artifacts from a century ago. It's entirely authentic and noncommercial: You'll find few businesses other than a café, motel, and an office of the **Yukon–Charley Rivers National Preserve,** P.O. Box 167, Eagle, AK 99738 (☎ 907-547-2233; Internet: www.nps.gov/yuch). The **Eagle Historical Society and Museums** (☎ 907-547-2325) shows off the buildings and several museums of materials left behind in this eddy in the stream of history. Their three-hour walking tours start at 9 a.m. daily, Memorial Day to Labor Day, and cost $5.

Steese Highway (Route 6)

The Steese Highway is a gravel road that climbs the rounded tundra mountains 162 miles east of Fairbanks to the Native village of Circle, on the Yukon River. It's a bumpy route to Bush Alaska, quite scenic, with good hiking trails and river floats along the way. Get details from the Fairbanks **Alaska Public Lands Information Center,** 250 Cushman St. (☎ **907-456-0527;** Internet: www.nps.gov/aplic).

Chapter 19

Denali National Park

· ·

In This Chapter

▶ Discovering what's so special about visiting Denali National Park

▶ Planning's a necessity on this trip

▶ Making your way to the park

▶ Getting oriented after you arrive

▶ Riding the bus is a good thing

▶ Finding a soft bed and warm meal

· ·

Denali National Park is managed the way a park should be: for the animals, not the cars. That means it's different than other parks you may have visited, and it demands a different kind of visit with different plans and expectations. You get into the main part of the park on a bus (with or without narration from a guide). If you don't want to ride the bus, you shouldn't go to the park (though I do discuss some other options later in this chapter). But if you do ride the bus, you stand a good chance of experiencing a remarkable wildlife safari unlike anything else in the national parks system.

The bears here live entirely naturally, but they're used to these buses. I've seen them walk within a yard or two — not like the garbage-eating bears that used to climb on cars in some parks in the Lower 48, but rather just out of curiosity, like any bear living naturally. Elsewhere in Alaska, seeing a bear this way costs as much as $400 per person, because it requires flying out to a remote spot without other people. At Denali, it costs $20, because visitors are managed in a way that keeps them from scaring off the bears. You also have excellent chances for seeing moose, caribou, and Dall sheep, and to a lesser extent, wolves and beavers.

The shuttle bus also has another purpose that is just as important as the scenery and wildlife it enables people to see. It's a mass transportation system to pure wilderness. It allows people without special skills or experience to walk on untracked tundra under an immense sky and to feel what the real world beyond the reach of humanity is like. This is a big step beyond any trail hike. In most places, you need plenty of money or muscle to travel to such places. Here, anyone can do it. And when you reach your limit, you merely walk back to the road and catch another bus.

That's the secret of Denali National Park, and unfortunately, it remains a real secret. Plenty of visitors leave the park disappointed because they don't know about it. They can't separate from their cars, or they don't want to take a long bus ride, or they take a bus but don't understand why. Many gauge their successes purely on whether they see Mount McKinley, a recipe for disappointment, because most days you can't see it from within the park. Some tour companies add to the problem, rushing as many visitors through the park as they can in less than 24 hours, too little time to really enjoy what the park offers.

You need to spend at least two nights at Denali National Park. You need to spend one whole, long day on a shuttle-bus outing. You need to reserve that bus ticket far in advance. You need to remember that everything else at the park is simply garnish to this main course. Following this advice provides you a good opportunity for a truly remarkable experience, one you can't have anywhere else on the planet.

If the bus doesn't sound like your thing, you'll find a few good options at Denali beyond a traditional visit through the park entrance. South of the park, at Talkeetna, you can do most of the same activities as at the park entrance. The setting is more natural than the ticky-tacky highway strip near the park, and you have a better chance of seeing Mount McKinley, and maybe even saving money. Taking a flight around (or even onto) Mount McKinley with a Talkeetna glacier pilot is an experience not to be missed. Opportunities to view wildlife from the ground and to hike the vast tundra are what you give up by opting to go south of the park.

Going to and actually seeing Denali National Park means taking a long bus ride once inside the park. Because the park road is narrow and made of gravel, only lightweight vehicles similar to school buses are permitted to drive on it. They bounce and rumble along for a dusty eight hours or more on these trips. Moreover, the buses act like mountain goats on the heights of Polychrome Pass and near Eielson Visitor Center. The road climbs without guardrails, so if you're afraid of heights, that may not be to your liking. If you're in doubt, I say go: Life is short, and you can put up with a little discomfort to see such a beautiful place. But if you're pretty sure that you wouldn't enjoy it, consider going to Talkeetna instead and seeing the park by air.

Planning Ahead

More than at any other national park, making advance reservations is critical to the success of your trip to Denali. That's because the core of the park experience — riding the shuttle bus to see wildlife and access hiking areas — is rationed by the number of seats available, though you can't reserve individual seats. For the best bus seats, those early in the morning, for example, you must reserve well in advance of the high season. During some years, you have to make reservations by

March for a July visit; of late, however, with tourism down, a few weeks of advanced planning has been sufficient. Reserving your shuttle tickets and campsites as soon as you know the dates of your visit is safest. The availability of lodgings tightens in July but isn't as critical. Reserve as far ahead as you can, but don't worry about getting stuck in a dive if you don't get your first choice of rooms or cabins, because you'll find few really bad places near the park.

Reserving shuttle seats and campsites in advance

Sixty-five percent of shuttle-bus seats and all campground sites (except Morino, Sanctuary, and Igloo) can be booked by telephone, fax, or mail; the balance are held back for walk-ins (see the "Reserving when you arrive" section, later in this chapter). Reserve with the park concessionaire, **ARAMARK/Denali Park Resorts,** 241 W. Ship Creek Ave., Anchorage, AK 99501 (☎ **800-622-7275** or 907-272-7275; Fax: 907-264-4684; at Denali, summer only, ☎ 907-683-8200; Internet: www.denali parkresorts.com). Reservations by mail or fax open December 1 for the entire upcoming summer. Reservations by phone open in mid-February. After that date, lines are answered daily 7 a.m. to 5 p.m. Alaska time (that's four hours earlier than eastern standard time). By faxing, you can make reservations before the phone lines open. Reservation forms to fax or mail are available on ARAMARK's Denali Park Resorts Web site. You need to include the dates, times, and campgrounds that you want (plus alternate dates); the names and ages of the people in your party; and entrance and reservation fees (see the "Paying entrance fees" section, later in this chapter) along with a Visa, MasterCard, American Express, or Discover Card number, expiration date, and signature. You don't have to figure out the total. Expect to receive a **confirmation,** which should be sent out by mail or fax within two days of receipt. Take the confirmation to the will-call desk at the visitor center to exchange it for a camping permit and bus ticket when you arrive. If you're arriving after the center closes at 8 p.m., you must call ☎ **907-683-1266** in advance to avoid losing your site or shuttle seat.

Reserving when you arrive

Although phone, mail, and fax orders no longer are accepted the day before a visit begins, the park begins accepting walk-in reservations two days prior to the start of a visit, offering the remaining 35% of shuttle-bus seats and any leftover car-camping sites. During busier times of year, desirable shuttle reservations are snapped up early in the day, which means that instead of getting a good reservation the day of your arrival or even the day after, you may only get one the next day after that. That's why making reservations in advance is so critical.

On the other hand, don't despair when you arrive without reservations, because the flow of visitors rises and falls unpredictably. It's possible that you'll walk into the visitor center and get a shuttle seat on the same day.

Paying entrance fees

The **park entrance fee** of $10 per family or $5 per person is good for seven days. (An increase to $10 per person is under consideration at this writing.) With no entrance station to collect the fee, it automatically is added to your bill when you make shuttle or campground reservations. If you have a National Parks Pass or a Golden Age or Golden Access pass (see Chapter 5), mention it when you call, so you can receive your discount.

Reserving rooms

You won't find any hotels within the park — though the Kantishna area of the park has a few wilderness lodges. The park concessionaire operates hotels outside the park, mostly for passengers of escorted tours, but many other choices are available. I describe them later in this chapter in the "Where to Stay" section.

Packing for the park

The packing advice in Chapter 12 is especially important for a Denali National Park trip. Although it can be warm or even hot, you should be prepared for chilly, wet weather at any time of year by taking along waterproof rain gear, fleece jackets, sweaters, and wool socks; a wool hat and gloves come in handy, too. If you're camping, bring synthetic long underwear and warm sleeping bags. Everyone should bring hiking boots or sturdy walking shoes, binoculars, and insect repellent.

Getting There

Some methods of traveling to Denali National Park (particularly by train) can require some early planning. However, you have a number of options when it comes to getting there.

Driving to the park

A car gives you the greatest flexibility in getting to the park and back and forth to your accommodations, and is the lowest-cost alternative. However, you can only drive 14 miles into the park with a car — not far enough to see much (see "Riding the Shuttle Bus," later in this chapter). The park entrance is 4½ hours (240 miles) from Anchorage, 2½ from Fairbanks (120 miles), on a good two-lane road, the George Parks Highway. Talkeetna lies on a 13-mile spur road that branches from the

Parks Highway 100 miles north of Anchorage and 140 miles south of the park entrance.

Taking the train

The **Alaska Railroad** (☎ **800-544-0552** or 907-265-2494; Internet: www.alaskarailroad.com) serves Denali from both Anchorage and Fairbanks beginning at 8:15 a.m. daily, and arriving at 3:45 p.m. from Anchorage and at noon from Fairbanks. The two trains alternate between cities, timing their arrival at the opposite cities from the park at 8:15 p.m. *Note:* The trains travel much slower than cars. The one-way adult fares are $125 from Anchorage to Denali, $75 from Anchorage to Talkeetna, $50 from Fairbanks to Denali, and half price for children. The full, daily trains run only from mid-May to mid-September, with somewhat lower fares in the first and last few weeks of the season. You can save money by purchasing a hotel package from the railroad. The ride is comfortable, with assigned seating, two dining options, and well-trained guides in each car.

The same locomotives pull super-luxury cars owned by three of the cruise lines. Two of them also are available for use by independent travelers: **Princess Cruises and Tours** (☎ **800-PRINCESS**; Internet: www.princesslodges.com/rail.htm) and **Holland America Tours** (☎ **800-544-2206** or 907-277-5581; Internet: www.hollandamerica.com). Each passenger has a seat beneath a full dome with a white-table-cloth dining assignment. Fares are excessive, however, unless you buy a tour or lodging package.

Whenever you take the train, book your accommodations as a package at the same time. The tour operators usually take care of moving you and your luggage around at the park, so you won't need to rent a car or figure out the schedules of the buses that transport visitors between most of the hotels and the park entrance. Be sure, however, that you have plenty of time (see the introduction to this chapter). When you don't spend at least two nights, which gives you time to take an all-day shuttle ride deep into the park, experiencing a meaningful visit to Denali is difficult.

Taking the bus

Bus and van services bring passengers to Denali and Talkeetna in comfortable vehicles aimed at the tourist market. They are listed in Chapter 7.

Flying to Denali

Denali National Park has no regularly scheduled air service; flying to the park for your visit isn't an option. However, you can take a flight-seeing trip from Talkeetna (see below) or Anchorage (see Chapter 14)

Getting a look at the mountain

The 20,320-foot monolith of Mount McKinley, the tallest mountain in North America, is an indisputably awesome sight. The mountain rises straight up from an elevation of only 3,000 feet, giving it the *greatest relief* of any mountain in the world — it's the biggest single thing you'll ever see on the planet. The mountain's Great Gorge is deeper than the Grand Canyon, even though its floor is covered with an ice sheet that's 4,000 feet thick. A single sheer cliff is more than two miles high. No wonder visitors feel driven to see it and are disappointed when they fail.

Being able to see Mount McKinley, however, is far from assured. Although it often is clearly visible from Anchorage and Fairbanks in winter, each more than 100 miles away, during summer, clouds pile up daily on the mountain's flank, making it hard to see from anywhere near its base. You can never see it from the entrance to Denali National Park. If you take the shuttle bus to get closer, your chances are still less than 50%, because of the clouds. The general rule is: The earlier in the day you go, and the longer your bus ride, the better your chances. The closest you can get using the park bus service is 27 miles away, and that's at the far end of a wearying 12-hour round-trip bus ride. (Staying at a hotel south of the park, in Talkeetna, enhances your chances, because a clear view of the mountain right from the hotel means you'll be in place to look when the clouds clear.)

If seeing the mountain is your goal, your chances are far better, and the view much more impressive, from an aircraft. You can fly from the park's private airstrip, from Talkeetna, or from Anchorage. The Talkeetna option features pilots who routinely carry climbers to the mountain and offers you the opportunity to land on a glacier way up on the mountain, an unparalleled experience — indeed, a mountain-top experience. From Anchorage, you can sip champagne while riding on a classic DC-3 (see Chapter 14). You'll still have to wait for the weather, so if this is a key to your trip, plan two or three days of flexibility around your flight. Details are in the "Flightseeing" section of this chapter.

to see Mount McKinley. Your chances of viewing the mountain are by far better than going over land to its base. See the sidebar, "Getting a look at the mountain."

Learning the Lay of the Land

Denali National Park and Preserve is a huge slice of the Alaska Range that stands like a pivot in the center of Alaska. It encompasses 6 million acres, a roughly triangular polygon about 20% larger than Massachusetts. (For a glimpse of the park's layout, see the "Denali National Park" map in this chapter.) The Parks Highway provides access to the entrance, which lies at the northeast corner of the park. (Mount McKinley is to the southwest of the park.) A mile north of the park entrance on the Parks Highway, along a cliff-sided canyon of the Nenana River, hotels and restaurants have developed a seasonal town known locally as

Denali National Park

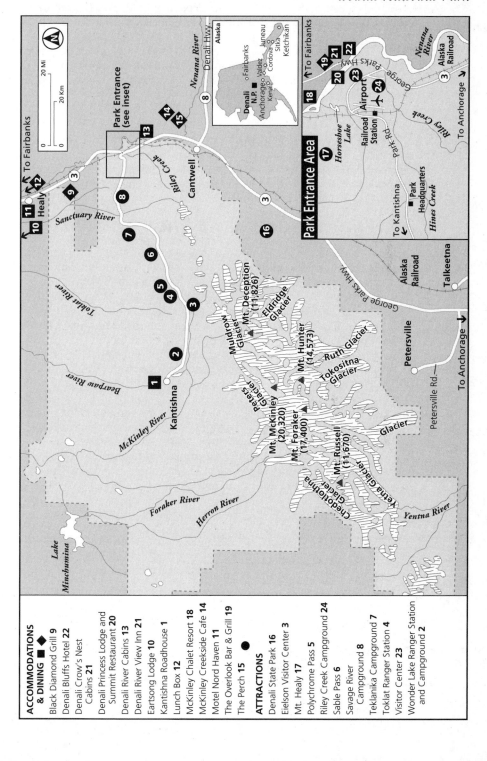

Park Entrance Area

ACCOMMODATIONS & DINING ◆ ■
Black Diamond Grill **9**
Denali Bluffs Hotel **22**
Denali Crow's Nest Cabins **21**
Denali Princess Lodge and Summit Restaurant **20**
Denali River Cabins **13**
Denali River View Inn **21**
Eartsong Lodge **10**
Kantishna Roadhouse **1**
Lunch Box **12**
McKinley Chalet Resort **18**
McKinley Creekside Cafe **14**
Motel Nord Haven **11**
The Overlook Bar & Grill **19**
The Perch **15**

ATTRACTIONS ●
Denali State Park **16**
Eielson Visitor Center **3**
Mt. Healy **17**
Polychrome Pass **5**
Riley Creek Campground **24**
Sable Pass **6**
Savage River Campground **8**
Teklanika Campground **7**
Toklat Ranger Station **4**
Visitor Center **23**
Wonder Lake Ranger Station and Campground **2**

Glitter Gulch, or for the benefit of tourists, the *Nenana Canyon Area.*
Other services are available at **Carlo Creek,** 14 miles south on the
Parks Highway, and in the year-round town of **Healy,** 10 miles north of
the park entrance. From the park entrance, a road accessible only by
shuttle bus leads west 89 miles through the park, past a series of campgrounds and a visitor center, and ends at the **Kantishna District,** a
patch of park-surrounded private land holdings with wilderness lodges.
Talkeetna lies well south of the park on the Parks Highway.

Arriving in the Park

Getting help upon your arrival at Denali depends on whether you go to
the park entrance or take the Talkeetna option. I cover each separately.

Arriving at the park's main entrance

On any self-guided trip (as opposed to an escorted tour), your first
stop should be the **Denali National Park Visitor Center,** also known as
the Visitor Access Center, on Denali Park Road, a half-mile from the
park entrance (P.O. Box 9), Denali National Park, AK 99755 (☎ 907-
683-2294; Fax: 907-683-9612; Internet: www.nps.gov/dena). Pick up
your previously reserved shuttle tickets and campsite permits, or
make new reservations at ticketing desks operated by the concessionaire, ARAMARK/Denali Park Resorts. The same rooms provide rangers
to answer questions and offer a backcountry desk for setting up backpacking trips.

Because the park has no entrance station, the center also is the place
for picking up the park map, a copy of the *Alpenglow* park newspaper,
and other handouts. A small bookstore offers a limited selection of
material about the area, and films and programs take place in an auditorium. The center is open June to mid-September, daily from 7 a.m.
to 8 p.m.; May and late September, daily 10 a.m. to 4 p.m. It's closed
October to April.

Caution: Construction ahead

Massive changes to the main Denali National Park visitor area are under construction through the 2004 season. The disruptions and noise of heavy equipment
and truck operations are inevitable; it may make sense to plan your trip so that you
don't spend much time in the area around the park entrance where most of the
work is taking place. The biggest project is a new Denali Science and Learning
Center and Visitor Center Campus. When completed, it will feature programs,
exhibits, a theater, a food court, dorms, a bookstore, parking, and so on. It's a
needed improvement, but it won't be such fun for people who visit before construction is complete.

The only means of travel into the heart of the park is covered in the section, "Riding the Shuttle Bus," later in this chapter. Getting around the entrance area is easy using your own car or various free shuttle buses that connect park facilities with nearby hotels. If you choose a hotel that's farther afield, it may have a courtesy van; some are handy, others are less frequent. If you visit without a car, get the scoop on whether your respective hotel's transportation service fits in with your schedule. Taxi service also is available from the summer-only **Caribou Cab** (☎ **907-683-5000**), which charges on a per-person basis ($4 from Glitter Gulch to the visitor center, for example), with a $7 minimum. You can also rent a car in Healy from **Teresa's Alaska Car Rentals** (☎ **907-683-1377**; Internet: www.denalicarrental.com). You can take the train to Denali, rent a car there, and drop it off in Fairbanks or Anchorage.

Arriving in Talkeetna

The **Denali National Park Talkeetna Ranger Station,** downtown Talkeetna (P.O. Box 588), Talkeetna, AK 99676 (☎ **907-733-2231;** Internet: www.nps.gov/dena), was built to serve climbers — Mount McKinley climbs start with flights from Talkeetna — and it makes a fascinating stop for anyone curious about mountaineering. Rangers are on hand to answer questions, too. It's open May through August, daily 8 a.m. to 6 p.m.; winter, Monday to Friday 8:00 a.m. to 4:30 p.m. For information about commercial services, stop at the **Talkeetna/Denali Visitor Center,** located in a tiny cabin at Parks Highway and Talkeetna Spur Road (P.O. Box 688), Talkeetna, AK 99676 (☎ **800-660-2688** or 907-733-2688; Internet: www.alaskan.com/talkeetnadenali). It's open daily 8 a.m. to 8 p.m. in summer, and responds to inquiries year-round with free trip-planning help. Keep in mind, though, that it is a business that profits from booking commissions.

Whenever you stay in Talkeetna, far south of the park, and you're not on an escorted tour, you need your own car to get around. On the other hand, if you arrange all your activities through a resort lodge, you can get to Talkeetna by bus or train and let the lodge schedule your transportation (see "Getting There," earlier in this chapter).

Riding the Shuttle Bus

As I explain in the introduction to this chapter, the centerpiece of a trip into Denali National Park is the shuttle bus ride. It's an inexpensive wildlife safari and an easy way to get to open country for off-trail wilderness hiking — with transportation always close at hand. This section provides tips to help you make the most of your ride.

Choosing your bus and destination

You have a couple of options for bussing through the park: the nonguided shuttle bus and the guided-tour buses. The shuttle bus rides aren't supposed to be narrated tours, because shuttle-bus drivers aren't trained to provide information, although some actually do a very good job of it. The guided-tour buses have trained narrators, and food is even served on the longer tours, but one disadvantage is that you can't get off and back on them to take a hike.

Shuttle bus options

You can buy shuttle tickets to the Toklat (*toe*-klat) River, 53 miles into the park; the Eielson (*aisle*-son) Visitor Center at 66 miles; Wonder Lake at 85 miles; or Kantishna, which is farthest from the park entrance at 89 miles. Going to Eielson balances the desire to see scenery and wildlife with the need for preserving your rear end from too much sitting, and in the process, saves you time for getting out and hiking. The Eielson round trip takes eight hours, and the fare is about $23 for adults, half price for ages 15 to 17, and free for ages 14 and younger. No extra fee is charged for getting off the bus at almost any spot of your choosing for a hike or picnic and then flagging down the next bus to travel onward. You have to bring your own food.

Narrated bus tours

All narrated tours use the same lightweight buses as the shuttles, which are similar to school buses but more appropriately sized for adult riders. The first two on the list are reserved through the concessionaire, like the shuttle; the Kantishna bus is independent.

- ✔ The **Natural History Tour** ($40 adults, $19 ages 12 and younger) travels only 17 miles down the park road, hardly farther than you can drive yourself, and misses 90% of what you come to Denali to see.

- ✔ The **Tundra Wildlife Tour** ($74 adults, $36 ages 12 and younger) travels to Toklat when Mount McKinley is hidden by clouds, and 8 miles farther, to Highway Pass, when it is visible. This route hits most of the highlights but skips the beautiful grizzly and caribou habitat toward the Eielson Visitor Center. Food is provided.

- ✔ **Kantishna Wilderness Trails** (☎ **800-942-7420** or 907-683-1475; Internet: www.denaliwildlifetour.com) covers the entire park road with a 190-mile, 13-hour marathon that includes lunch and dog-sled and gold-panning programs at the halfway mark at the Kantishna Roadhouse (see "Where to Stay"). The cost is $115.

Getting ready

Reserve your shuttle ticket for as early as you can stand to get up in the morning. This strategy gives you more time for day hikes and

Maintaining your wits in the park with kids

Denali can be a challenge for families. Young children tend to go nuts when subjected to an eight-hour bus ride, and they aren't often able to pick out the wildlife because the park isn't like a zoo; most animals blend in with their surroundings. Likewise, even older children have a hard time keeping their patience on these trips, as do many adults. The only solution: Get off the bus along the route and turn your trip into a romp in the heather. After you've had a chance to revive, catch the next bus. Besides, just because you buy a ticket to Eielson doesn't mean that you have to go that far. Keep in mind, too, that if your child normally needs a car seat, you must bring it along on the bus, or borrow one from the National Park Service.

enhances your chances of seeing the mountain and wildlife. During peak season, the first bus leaves the visitor center at 5:15 a.m. and then roughly every 15 to 30 minutes in the morning. A few buses leave in the afternoon, mostly to pick up stragglers on the way back, returning late under the midnight sun.

Here's a checklist for preparing the night before you catch your morning shuttle bus:

- ✔ Lunch (several restaurants pack them) and plenty of water

- ✔ Sturdy walking shoes and layers of warm and lighter clothing with rain gear packed

- ✔ Binoculars or a spotting scope

- ✔ Insect repellent

- ✔ Optional: Camera and plenty of film

- ✔ Optional: A copy of Kim Heacox's mile-by-mile *Denali Road Guide,* available for $6 at the visitor center bookstore

- ✔ For extensive hiking: A detailed topographic map ($9.95 at the visitor center) and a compass (not necessary if you're just walking a mile or two off the road)

Spotting wildlife on your way

The shuttle bus has no reserved seats, but if you arrive early, you can find a place on the left side, which has the best views on the way out. On most bus trips you can see grizzly bears, caribou, Dall sheep, moose, and occasionally wolves. Yelling whenever you spot any wildlife is common courtesy on the shuttle bus so that others can see it, too. Doing so cues the driver to stop, so that everyone can rush to your side of the bus. After you've had a look, give someone else a chance to look out your window or to take a picture. Try to be quiet and don't stick anything outside of the bus, because that can scare away the animals.

Hiking and Backpacking from the Shuttle Bus

Walking away from the road takes a little courage, but doing so may be the best chance you ever have for experiencing a place like this on your own. The major risks of hiking are avoidable. It can get cold and wet in midsummer, so you need to be prepared with layers of warm, waterproof clothing to avoid the spiraling chill of hypothermia. The rivers are dangerous because of their fast flowing icy cold water. Experienced backcountry trekkers plan their routes to avoid crossing sizable rivers. See Chapter 9 for other health and safety tips.

Day hikes by bus

For a first foray beyond the trails, consider joining one of the Park Service–guided hikes. Two daily **Discovery Hikes** take place somewhere near the Eielson Visitor Center and another nearer the entrance end of the park. A ranger leads only 15 hikers into wilderness, telling them about the nature of the places they visit. Plan for a 5- to 11-hour day, including the shuttle ride. Actual hiking time is about four hours. The hikes generally aren't too strenuous for families with school-age children, but inquiring about how steep they will be always is wise if you have any doubts. Hikes cost no more than the price of your shuttle ticket. You need to wear hiking shoes or boots and bring food, water, and rain gear. Reserve a place in advance, because hikes fill up in July, and you'll need to know when and where to catch special buses.

I list some good hiking areas along the park road shuttle-bus ride by milepost. You don't need a permit for any of these day hikes.

- ✔ **Mile 34:** Manageable climbs on Igloo, Cathedral, and Sable mountains take off along the road from Igloo Creek to Sable Pass.
- ✔ **Mile 53:** The bed of the Toklat River is a flat plain of gravel with easy walking. The glaciers that feed the river are 10 miles upstream.
- ✔ **Mile 58:** Highway Pass is the highest point on the road. In good weather, dramatic views of Mount McKinley start here. The alpine tundra from here to the Eielson Visitor Center is inviting for walking.
- ✔ **Mile 66:** The **Eielson Visitor Center,** the end of most bus trips, has flush toilets, a covered picnic area, and a small area of displays

where rangers answer questions. Starting in mid-June, a ranger-guided tundra walk occurs daily at 1 p.m. It lasts no more than an hour. You need to take a 9 a.m. or earlier bus to be there on time. If you leave the bus here for a hike, you can get a ride back later by signing up on the standby list kept by a ranger.

Backpacking

Imagine backpacking over your own area of wilderness, without trails, limits, or the chance of seeing other people. Retracing your route to get back to the bus isn't necessary: Anywhere you meet the 89-mile Denali Park Road, you can catch a bus back to the world of people. Any experienced backpacker should consider a backcountry trek at Denali.

This section distinguishes the more rigorous backpacking opportunities available in Denali from the more casual day hikes discussed in the preceding section. If you're not an experienced backpacker — and don't intend to do any camping on your hikes — stick with the easy, casual jaunts just off the bus.

You must be flexible about where you're going and prepared for any kind of terrain, because you can't choose the backcountry unit that you'll explore until arriving at the backcountry desk at the visitor center and finding out what's available. This information, and a map of the units, is posted on a board behind the desk. You can reserve permits for overnight backpacking only a day in advance, and although you're unlikely to get one for the day you arrive, you can reserve permits for continuation of your trip for up to 14 days at the same time. The first night of a trip is the hard one to get — for one thing, you can reserve only units that are contiguous to the park road for the first night — but after that, each night gets progressively easier. And if you decide to change your route, you have to return to the visitor center for a new permit. A couple of rangers are there to help you through the process.

Buy the *Denali National Park and Preserve* **topographical map,** published by Trails Illustrated, available for $9.95 from the Alaska Natural History Association (☎ **907-683-1272** summer, 907-683-1258 off-season; Internet: www.alaskanha.org). You'll also want a copy of *Backcountry Companion,* by Jon Nierenberg, which describes conditions and routes in each area and is published and sold by ANHA for $8.95. You'll find both for sale at the visitor center.

Great Activities off the Bus

You'll have time before and after your bus ride for other activities, or you can see the park from the air and skip the bus ride. Here are the options.

Day hiking near the park entrance

Without taking the backcountry shuttle, you can hike beyond trails at Savage River Day Use Area, at mile 15, which has a mile-long loop trail and longer informal routes for great alpine tundra hiking. You can drive there or take a $2 shuttle. Ranger-led hikes also start there.

Right at the park entrance, six short trails weave through the forest around small lakes, and so does one steep and spectacular hike to the **Mount Healy overlook,** a 5-mile round trip. The *Alpenglow* park newspaper contains a brief guide for these trails, and you can get a $5 natural history trail guide, *The Nature of Denali,* by Sheri Forbes, at the visitor center.

Flightseeing

Getting a good, close look at Mount McKinley is best accomplished by air. Frequently, you can see McKinley from above the clouds when you can't see it from the ground. You can make the flight from the park entrance, from Talkeetna, or from Anchorage (see Chapter 14).

From the park entrance

Small planes and helicopters fly from the park airstrip, private heliports and airstrips along the Parks Highway, and the Healy airstrip. **Denali Air** (☎ **907-683-2261;** Internet: www.denaliair.com) has an office in Glitter Gulch, and flight operations at mile 229.5 of the Parks Highway. An hour-long flight going within a mile of the mountain costs $205 for adults, $105 for children ages 2 to 12. **Era Helicopters** (☎ **800-843-1947** or 907-683-2574; Internet: www.eraaviation.com) has 50-minute flights for $229, including van pickup from the hotels. Their heli-hikes land for a four-hour walk on a mountain ridgeline, with the degree of difficulty tailored to customers' abilities. They also offer a 75-minute glacier-landing flight. Either costs $315.

From Talkeetna

McKinley climbs typically begin with flights from Talkeetna to the 7,200-foot level of the **Kahiltna Glacier.** You can go, too, and no more dramatic or memorable experience is available to the typical tourist in Alaska. Several operators with plenty of experience offer flights. The least expensive excursions cost about $120 (if the plane is full) and approach McKinley's south face. Rates often depend on how many flightseers are going, so if you can put together a group of four or five, or the operator can add you to a group, you can save as much as half.

Whenever possible — and if the weather is good — buying an extended tour that circles the mountain and flies over its glaciers, for $180 to $205 with a full plane, is better. Best of all, in early summer and in the fall, you can arrange a landing on the mountain itself, the way climbers do (the snow is too soft starting in mid-July). These landings are usually treated as tour add-ons, for an additional price of about $55 per person.

Try any of these three renowned glacier-flight operations, all operating out of the Talkeetna airport: **Talkeetna Air Taxi** (☎ **800-533-2219** or 907-733-2218; Internet: www.talkeetnaair.com); **K2 Aviation** (☎ **800-764-2291** or 907-733-2291; Internet: www.flyk2.com); and **Doug Geeting Aviation** (☎ **800-770-2366** or 907-733-2366; Internet: www.alaskaair tours.com).

Rafting

Rafting on the Nenana River, which borders the park along Parks Highway, is fun and popular. Several commercial guides float two stretches of the river: an upper portion, where the water is smoother and the guides explain passing scenery; and the lower portion, where the river roars through the rock-walled Nenana Canyon, and rafts take on huge splashes of silty, glacial water through Class III and IV rapids. Each session takes 2 to 2½ hours, including safety briefings, suiting up, and riding to and from the put-in and take-out points. Prices vary from $60 to $87 for adults, with discounted rates for children (from $10 and less to half off). **Denali Outdoor Center** (☎ **888-303-1925** or 907-683-1925; Internet: www.denalioutdoorcenter.com) is a professional operation, offering rafting trips and instruction in river techniques.

If you go to Talkeetna, **Talkeetna River Guides,** on Main Street (☎ **800-353-2677** or 907-733-2677; Internet: www.talkeetnariverguides.com), offers a two-hour wildlife river-rafting tour, without white water, over 9 miles of the Talkeetna River three times a day for $55 adults, $22 children younger than 12. They also offer longer trips and guided fishing expeditions.

Ranger programs

In high season, ranger programs and slide shows take place in the park auditoriums (at the visitor center — and at the soon-to-be finished educational campus), and at the Riley Creek, Savage River, and Teklanika campgrounds. A daily demonstration of the park's sled dog teams is a highlight at the kennels. I mention ranger-led hikes earlier in this chapter, in the "Day hikes by bus" section. All programs and times are listed in the *Alpenglow* park newspaper.

Where to Stay

At Denali, how much you pay depends on how far from the park entrance you stay. Ordinary hotel rooms rent for $140 to $200 in the tacky Glitter Gulch area next to the park entrance. Save 25% or more by staying 14 miles south of the park in Carlo Creek or 10 miles north in Healy.

I also include lodgings in Talkeetna, more than two hours south of the park. However, stay there only if you plan to spend all your time in that area and fly into the park.

The top hotels and lodges

Denali Bluffs Hotel
$$$$ **Glitter Gulch**

This hotel is a series of 12 buildings on a steep mountainside looking down on the Nenana Canyon area from above the highway. The light, tastefully decorated rooms have two double beds and good amenities, including satellite TV, and those on the upper floor have vaulted ceilings and balconies with great views. A courtesy van takes you anywhere in the area. The Mountain Café serves simple, American meals for breakfast and lunch.

Mile 238.4, Parks Hwy. (P.O. Box 72460, Fairbanks, AK 99707). ☎ *907-683-7000. Fax: 907-683-7500. Internet:* www.denalibluffs.com. *Rack rates: High season $185 double, low season $132 double; extra person $15. Rate includes continental breakfast. AE, DISC, MC, V.*

Kantishna Roadhouse
$$$$$ **Kantishna**

This well-kept property of many buildings along Moose Creek in the old Kantishna Mining District (a full day's bus ride into the park) trades on both mining history and outdoor opportunities in the area. Some accommodations are large and luxurious; others are in smaller single cabins with lofts. Guided hikes, wagon rides, biking, and gold panning are included in the rate. A sled dog demonstration (Internet: www.denali wildlifetour.com) coincides with the arrival of a day trip that the lodge offers called the Kantishna Wilderness Trails (the same bus brings lodge guests).

Kantishna District, Denali National Park (mailing address: P.O. Box 81670, Fairbanks, AK 99708). ☎ *800-942-7420 or 907-683-1475. Fax: 907-683-1449. (Winter:* ☎ *907-459-2120; fax 907-459-2160.) Internet:* www.kantishnaroadhouse.com. *$310 per person per night, double occupancy; $230 ages 3–11. Rates include all meals and activities. 2-night minimum. AE, DISC, MC, V.*

Motel Nord Haven
$$–$$$ **Healy**

This fresh little gray hotel with a red roof has large, immaculate rooms, each with one or two queen-size beds. They're equal to the best standard rooms in the Denali Park area and are much less expensive. Bill and Patsy

Nordmark offer free continental breakfast in the summer, along with newspapers, coffee, tea, hot chocolate, extra phone lines for the Internet, and a sitting room with a collection of Alaska books. The rooms, decorated with Alaska art and oak trim, all have interior entrances and have been smoke-free since their construction. Up to four people can stay in the rooms with two beds for the price of a double. Three units have kitchenettes. The motel packs sack lunches for $8 each.

Mile 249.5, Parks Hwy. (P.O. Box 458), Healy, AK 99743. ☎ *800-683-4501 or 907-683-4500. Fax: 907-683-4503. Internet:* www.motelnordhaven.com. *Rack rates: Summer $117–$140; spring/fall $84–$94; winter $75. AE, MC, V.*

The Perch

$–$$ Carlo Creek

In the trees along rushing Carlo Creek, 14 miles south of the park entrance, cabins range from large, modern units with private bathrooms to adorable, if spartan, A-frame cottages with lofts that share a bathhouse. Staying here, you have a sense of privacy and of being out in the woods along the wooden and gravel walkways. It's an exceptional value, open year-round. You need a car to stay here. The Perch has a good restaurant, too.

Mile 224, Parks Hwy. (P.O. Box 53), Denali National Park, AK 99755. ☎ *888-322-2523 or phone/fax: 907-683-2523. Internet:* www.denaliperchresort.com. *Rack rates: $65–$95 cabin for 2; extra person $10. AE, DISC, MC, V.*

Talkeetna Alaskan Lodge

$$$$ Talkeetna

The Cook Inlet Region Native corporation spared no expense building this magnificent hotel of big timbers and river rock, but it's no gaudy showplace. Instead, authenticity is present, right down to the hospitable locals working behind the desk. The view certainly can't be faked. Every common room and many guest rooms are oriented to a broad-canvas masterpiece of the Alaska Range, with Mount McKinley towering in the center. The hotel gains these views from its location atop a high river bluff. Rooms in the main building are preferable. They're somewhat larger and have either king or two queen-size beds, and the hallways connect to several sumptuous lobbies with reading areas. Dining is first class, with good service and surprisingly sophisticated cuisine produced by a year-round chef.

Mile 12.5, Talkeetna Spur Rd. (P.O. Box 93330, Anchorage, AK 99509-3330). ☎ *888-959-9590 or 907-265-4501 reservations; 907-733-9500 at lodge. Fax: 907-263-5559. Internet:* www.talkeetnalodge.com. *Rack rates: Summer $199 double; winter $149 double; extra person $12. AE, DISC, MC, V.*

Runner-up accommodations

Denali Crow's Nest Cabins

$$$$ **Glitter Gulch** Cabins perched in five tiers on the side of a mountain above the Nenana Canyon area create more of a true Alaskan feeling than the area's modern, standard rooms. *Mile 238.5, Parks Hwy. (P.O. Box 70), Denali National Park, AK 99755.* ☎ *888-917-8130 or 907-683-2723. Fax: 907-683-2323. Internet:* www.crowsnestalaska.com.

Denali River View Inn

$$$ **Glitter Gulch** Good standard rooms in a small motel as close as you can get to the park entrance. *Mile 238.4, Parks Hwy. (P.O. Box 49) Denali National Park, AK 99755.* ☎ *866-683-2663 or 907-683-2663; Fax: 907-683-7433. Internet:* www.denaliriverviewinn.com.

Earthsong Lodge

$$–$$$ **Healy** Cozy log cabins hosted by interesting year-round residents sit on open tundra with sweeping views of the Alaska Range and Mount McKinley — a 21-mile drive from the park entrance. *Stampede Trail, off the Parks Highway at mile 251 (P.O. Box 89), Healy, AK 99743.* ☎ *907-683-2863. Fax: 907-683-2868. Internet:* www.earthsonglodge.com.

Swiss-Alaska Inn

$$ **Talkeetna** Simple rooms in a family business where guests are made to feel like old friends. *F Street, near the boat launch (P.O. Box 565), Talkeetna, AK 99676.* ☎ *907-733-2424. Fax: 907-733-2425. Internet:* www.swiss alaska.com.

Campgrounds

The park has seven campgrounds, four of which have flush toilets and sites you can reserve in advance: Riley Creek, Savage River, Teklanika, and Wonder Lake. Of these four, you can drive to only two: Riley Creek and Savage River. Teklanika and Wonder Lake are in the backcountry, accessible along the park road by the shuttle-bus system. One exception: You can drive to Teklanika if you stay three days and don't move your car during that time. Use the reservation system described earlier in the "Reserving shuttle seats and campsites in advance" section. The three campgrounds that don't take reservations are Morino, Igloo Creek, and Sanctuary River. These are tiny, primitive campgrounds intended primarily for backpackers getting ready for a trek.

Other than Riley Creek and Savage River, these campgrounds aren't the car camping you may be used to. You'll be away from any services and away from even easy communication, so you must bring everything that you need.

✔ **Riley Creek:** A large campground near the park entrance, visitor center, store, showers, and so on. $16 per site. 100 sites.

✔ **Savage River:** A beautiful campground with great tundra views and hiking routes, and the only one you can readily drive to that's away from the entrance. 13 miles from park entrance. $12 per site. 33 sites.

✔ **Teklanika River:** Wake up here close to the heart of the park, cutting the time you must spend on the bus on daily explorations. 29 miles from entrance; accessible by bus. $12 per site. 53 sites.

✔ **Wonder Lake:** After six hours on the bus, you reach this coveted campground by a placid lake near the foot of Mount McKinley. The mosquitoes can be horrendous. 85 miles from entrance. $12 per site. 28 sites. Tents only. No campfires.

Where to Dine

I list a range of restaurants matching locations with your lodgings (in Talkeetna, try the hotels' own restaurants). If you don't have a car, don't try dining in areas other than the one where you're staying. Every restaurant listed here is closed during the off-season.

Black Diamond Grill

$$–$$$ Healy   Steak/Seafood/Italian

A menu mostly influenced by Northern Italian cookery includes lunch of sandwiches, such as a pesto chicken hoagie for $7.50, and dinner, such as halibut in parchment with fresh rosemary and garlic for $20. The dining room is light, with pine furniture and flowers on the table, but is somewhat cramped.

Mile 247 Parks Hwy. (take the highway north 10 miles, then turn left at Otto Lake Road). ☎ *907-683-4653. Internet:* www.blackdiamondgolf.com. *Lunch: $7.50–$9; dinner main courses: $14–$24. AE, DISC, MC, V. Open: Daily 9 a.m.–10 p.m.*

The Lunch Box

$ Healy   Take-out

This trailer produces good, inexpensive food in Asian, Italian, Mexican, and deli styles. Take it on a picnic or eat it back at the room. A hearty box lunch is $8, and the restaurant will bring it to your hotel the night before so that you can catch an early park bus.

Healy Spur Rd. (just off the Parks Highway across the street from the Mountain View Store). ☎ *907-683-6833. Lunch: $3.50–$8. No credit cards. Open: Mon–Fri 11:00 a.m.–6:30 p.m., Sat 11 a.m.–3 p.m. Closed Sunday.*

McKinley Creekside Café
$–$$$ Carlo Creek   Steak/Seafood/Sandwiches

This is a cozy and friendly spot in the Carlo Creek area, south of the park, where you can dine on steak or baked salmon with brown sugar, apples, and toasted almonds for about $20, or you can order a main-course salad or burger for about $8. The restaurant also packs substantial sack lunches for the shuttle bus ride.

Mile 224, Parks Hwy. ☎ *907-683-2277. Internet:* www.mckinleycabins.com. *Lunch: $6–$10; dinner main courses: $8–$21. DISC, MC, V. Open: Daily 6 a.m.– 10 p.m.*

The Overlook Bar and Grill
$$$–$$$$ Glitter Gulch   Burgers/Steak/Seafood

This fun, noisy place has the feel of a classic bar and grill, with a vaulted ceiling of rough-cut lumber and a spectacular view of the Nenana Canyon. A huge variety of craft beers is available, with several on tap. At times, I've gotten superb fare here, but at other times it has been merely acceptable.

Mile 238.5, Parks Hwy., up the hill above the Denali Canyon area. ☎ *907-683-2641. Lunch: $9–$15; dinner main courses: $16–$30. MC, V. Open: 11 a.m.–11 p.m. daily.*

The Summit Restaurant
$$$–$$$$ Glitter Gulch   Steak/Seafood

This is a terrific place for a special night dining out right near the park, in the huge Denali Princess Lodge. The dining room is perched on the edge of the Nenana Canyon and the food — steak and salmon, the usual choices for Alaska tourists — is done well.

In the Denali Princess Lodge, mile 238.5, Parks Hwy. ☎ *907-683-2282. Reservations recommended. Dinner main courses: $15–$30. AE, DC, DISC, MC, V. Open: Daily 6:30–10:30 a.m., 5:30–10:30 p.m.*

Denali dinner theater

Cabin Nite Dinner Theater, at the **McKinley Chalet Resorts** (☎ 800-276-7234 or 907-683-8200), is a professionally produced musical revue about a gold rush–era woman who ran a roadhouse in Kantishna. You can buy the $46 tickets (half price for ages 2–12) virtually anywhere in the area. The actors, singing throughout the evening, stay in character to serve big platters of food to diners sitting at long tables, doing a good job of building a rowdy, happy atmosphere for adults and kids.

Part V
Southeast Alaska

The 5th Wave   By Rich Tennant

WHALE-WATCHING IN JUNEAU

WHALE WATCH CAFE

"Would you like to watch the whale a little longer, sir, or should I ask him to leave?"

In this part . . .

Southeast Alaska is a world apart, a realm of water and mountains where charming old towns are tucked in wherever they fit among the peaks, bears, and big rain-forest trees. Getting around is made more complicated and yet more interesting by the region's lack of highways — getting from town to town requires you to board a boat or plane. Juneau, the state capital and Alaska's third largest city, is the hub for this area's transportation network. It's also a delightful place to visit with excellent access to outdoor activities. Skagway, north of Juneau, is a center of gold rush history. Sitka is full of charm and the history of Russian America, and has a spectacular setting for the outdoors.

Chapter 20

Juneau

● ●

In This Chapter

▶ Taking the good with the . . . wet

▶ Flying or sailing into Juneau (there's no other way)

▶ Finding the best places to sleep and eat

▶ Checking out what Juneau has to offer — indoors and out

▶ Planning a Juneau itinerary

● ●

*J*uneau stands out as a terrific town to visit. You get an inkling of that as your plane glides toward the airport on Gastineau Channel, viewing tall mountains above you on two sides, grassy wetlands and towering conifers below, and a great big nearby glacier that comes right up to a suburban neighborhood. The taxi ride downtown is a scenic side trip in most places, traveling at the base of mountains and along a coastal refuge full of eagles. Checking in at your hotel when you arrive downtown even takes effort, considering what you can do right outside the lobby — exploring steep, narrow streets, their sidewalks sheltered by awnings from charmingly weathered little buildings. Juneau is a thriving old-time downtown straight out of a movie, but in this case, it's real.

Few other towns in Alaska can justify a weeklong visit all by themselves, but in Juneau, lengthier stays make all kinds of sense. You encounter plenty to see in town and on the short road network, and the variety of outdoor activities you can do from here is unmatched anywhere in the state. Then, using Juneau as a base, you can explore fascinating and splendid places, such as Skagway; see the whales and glaciers of Glacier Bay National Park or Tracy Arm; or take a floatplane to a viewing area where you can watch brown bear fish for salmon from close up. Or, go dog mushing at the peak of summer on a glacier high above the city. By the end of your week, you'll have a good feeling for the town, and I'll even bet it becomes one of your favorite places, even though you haven't exhausted all of its possibilities.

That's my prediction, but, unfortunately, Juneau has a way of confounding predictions. The climate that produces those lush forests also produces torrential rains, rotten visibility, and canceled flights. When you're unlucky with the weather, a week in Juneau can make you feel like moss is growing between your toes. Even during the summer, it can rain for days, staying as cool and damp as winter in other places. In the fall, the rains here are biblical in proportions. Although rainy days do have a special charm here, especially when the soft light glows on rain-streaked facades and mist drifts among moss-shrouded branches, a little of that goes a long way.

Getting There

Juneau is a transportation hub without any road connection. Air and water are the only ways of getting there.

Arriving by air

Jet service is available only from **Alaska Airlines** (☎ **800-252-7522;** Internet: www.alaskaair.com), with several daily nonstop flights from Seattle and Anchorage, and from the smaller Southeast Alaska towns. Many of the region's commuter and air-taxi operators also maintain desks at the airport and have flights out of Juneau, including **L.A.B. Flying Service** (☎ **907-789-9160;** Internet: www.labflying.com) and **Wings of Alaska** (☎ **907-789-0790;** Internet: www.wingsofalaska.com).

Arriving by ferry

All the ferries of Southeast's main-line **Alaska Marine Highway System** (☎ **800-642-0066;** Internet: www.alaska.gov/ferry) stop at the terminal in Auke Bay (☎ **907-789-7453** or 907-465-3940 recording), 14 miles from downtown. The *Malaspina* runs daily up the Lynn Canal to Haines and Skagway and back in the summer. The passenger fare is $26 to Haines, $35 to Skagway. The *Malaspina's* cabins have been made into inexpensive private day rooms with outside windows — a relaxing, private way to travel.

Getting Downtown

The ride downtown from the airport is a long one, and from the ferry dock even farther, but at this writing, Juneau has no airport shuttle, and no public transportation at all to the dock. Maybe an airport shuttle will start operation again; ask at the visitor information desk in the baggage claim area. In any event, keep in mind that if your lodging has a courtesy van, it can save you more than $50 round-trip.

To overhead — meaning, you're screwed

Juneau's mist-shrouded airport, wedged between ocean and mountain, is tough to get into and can be a hair-raising place to land. That means that when you fly to Juneau, you can end up somewhere else, instead, maybe Anchorage or Seattle, or maybe even some little town that you never heard of. You never know. Landing in places other than Juneau is such a common experience, that the locals have a special word for it: *to overhead*. Here's an example of how you may hear it used:

"Why did you miss the fishing trip?"

"I overheaded three times and ended up sleeping in Ketchikan."

When your flight overheads, the airline puts you on the next plane back to Juneau. Even so, you may overhead again. Although people sometimes bounce back and forth like Ping-Pong balls, the airlines won't pay for hotel rooms or give you any refunds. Your only protection is a relaxed attitude, a loose itinerary that provides you with a chance for making up for lost time, and trip cancellation insurance (see Chapter 12).

When you're already in Juneau and the planes overhead, you're stuck there until the weather improves. You can call ahead, but the airline often wants you at the airport just in case the plane makes it in. That's why Juneau residents have the Channel Channel. It's a cable TV channel that silently broadcasts a view of the Gastineau Channel near the airport (hence the name). Locals can tell from that image whether going to the airport is worth the effort. An example of everyday usage:

"Did you see the Channel Channel? They'll overhead. Let's have another beer."

Navigating by taxi

A taxi is the handiest way for most people to get downtown from the airport, and the only way from the ferry terminal. **Capital Cab** (☎ 907-586-2772 or 907-789-2772) is one company. A cab ride in from the airport will cost you $20, from the ferry dock, $28.

Navigating by bus

An express **Capital Transit** city bus (☎ 907-789-6901) comes to the airport at 11 minutes past the hour on weekdays from 7:11 a.m. to 5:11 p.m. and costs $1.25; however, your luggage must fit under your seat or at your feet.

Navigating by rental car

You can get about in Juneau without a car, because the downtown area is compact, and to compound matters, parking can be a headache.

Operators of most outdoor activities come and get you at your hotel. On the other hand, you need wheels to visit some attractions, and having a car opens up more choices for dining and lodging in addition to some beautiful drives. Hertz, Avis, Budget, and National are based at the airport (national reservation contacts are listed in the appendix). When contemplating your costs, remember that you can save at least $40 for taxicabs from the airport. The airport and ferry dock are relatively close together, so when you come by ferry and want to rent a car, do it as soon as you arrive so that you save the cab fare downtown and back.

Orientating Yourself in Juneau

Juneau has three main parts: downtown, the Mendenhall Valley, and Douglas. (Check out the "Greater Juneau" map in this chapter.) **Downtown Juneau** is a numbered grid of streets (see the nearby "Downtown Juneau" map) overlying the uneven topography in the lap of the mountains. As you look at the city from the water, Mount Juneau is on the left and Mount Roberts on the right; Mount Roberts is a few hundred feet taller, at 3,819 feet. When the city outgrew its original site downtown, housing spread to the suburban **Mendenhall Valley,** about a dozen miles north out the Egan Expressway or the parallel, two-lane Glacier Highway. The glacial valley also contains the airport and **Auke Bay** area, where the ferry terminal is located. The road traverses a total of 40 miles to a place known as *The End of the Road.* Across a bridge over the Gastineau Channel from downtown Juneau is Douglas Island. Turn left for the town of **Douglas,** mostly a bedroom community for Juneau, and turn right for the North Douglas Highway.

Juneau is truly a pedestrian city, but if your feet get tired, taking a cab around downtown is cheap. Try **Capital Cab** (☎ **907-586-2772** or 907-789-2772). You can also hire a cab as a personal tour guide for $55 an hour. To go beyond downtown, you need a car.

Getting around by car

Rent a car whenever you want to stay, dine, or enjoy self-guided activities beyond the downtown area. Don't bother if you're happy downtown (by far the most interesting area) or if you want to take part in only guided outings — the operators usually take care of transfers. Hertz, Avis, Budget, and National are based at the airport (national reservation contacts are listed in this book's appendix).

If you rent a car, be sure to check with your lodgings about parking arrangements. Finding a place to park in downtown Juneau can be hard amid its narrow, crowded streets, many of which are very steep. Besides parking, Juneau can also be a challenging place just to drive.

Greater Juneau

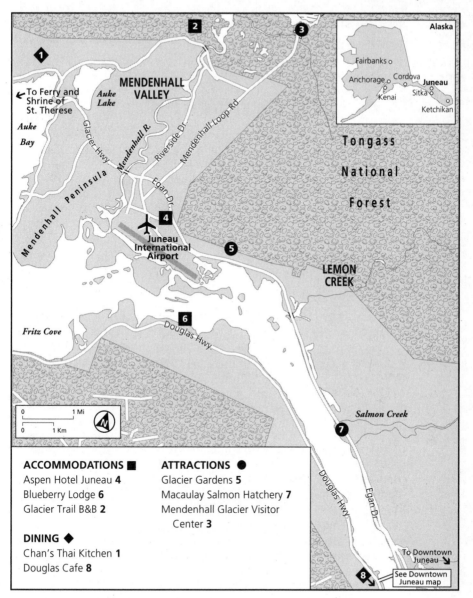

ACCOMMODATIONS ■
Aspen Hotel Juneau **4**
Blueberry Lodge **6**
Glacier Trail B&B **2**

DINING ◆
Chan's Thai Kitchen **1**
Douglas Cafe **8**

ATTRACTIONS ●
Glacier Gardens **5**
Macaulay Salmon Hatchery **7**
Mendenhall Glacier Visitor
    Center **3**

Getting around by bicycle

Strong bike riders can cover the town with a bike, but you must be able to handle the hills. Separate paths parallel many of the main roads, and downtown traffic is slow. The 24-mile round trip from downtown to Mendenhall Glacier keeps you on a bike path almost all the way. Bikes are for rent at the **Driftwood Inn,** 435 Willoughby Ave. (☎ **800-544-2239** or 907-586-2280; Internet: www.driftwoodalaska.com), for $25 a day, $15 half-day; they also have children's bikes, children's trailers that you can attach to your adult bike, and helmets and other safety equipment.

Where to Stay in Juneau

Hotel rooms are tight in the summer, so book ahead. Bed-and-breakfasts are a good way to go in Juneau. The Juneau Convention and Visitors Bureau's *Juneau Travel Planner* and Web site contain listings of the hotels and B&Bs, with their features and price ranges (☎ **888-581-2201;** www.traveljuneau.com). **Bed & Breakfast Association of Alaska, INNside Passage Chapter,** communicates through its Web site (www.accommodations-alaska.com), where you can find more than a dozen Juneau B&Bs listed with links to their own pages.

Baranof Hotel
$$$ Downtown

The Baranof is the only lodging in Alaska with the pedigree and style to pull off the role of the old-fashioned grand hotel. Built of concrete in 1939, it has served for decades as an informal branch of the state capitol, with legislators and lobbyists conferring in the dark, opulent lobby and restaurants. The structure itself constrains modernization — the bathrooms and many rooms tend to be small — but features such as glass door-knobs and pressed-tin ceilings remain, showing that it comes by its faults honestly. Recent remodeling has lightened many rooms while keeping the style. The upper-floor rooms have great views on the water side, while lower rooms were redone more recently. Many appealing suites are available. Although mainly configured for business travelers, they're comfortable for families, too.

The Art Deco **Gold Room** restaurant is Juneau's most traditional fine-dining establishment. The dining room combines intimacy and grandeur, a real showplace of shining brass, frosted glass, and rich wood. The food varies greatly in quality year to year. Most entrees are $20 to $25.

127 N. Franklin St., Juneau, AK 99801. ☎ *800-544-0970 or 907-586-2660. Fax: 907-586-8315. Internet:* www.westmarkhotels.com. *Rack rates: High season: $149–169 double, $229 suite; low season $129–$139 double, $199 suite; $15 each additional person older than 12. AE, DC, DISC, MC, V.*

Blueberry Lodge
$$ North Douglas Island

Staying here is like visiting a first-class wilderness lodge, except that you're only 6 miles from downtown Juneau. Jay and Judy Urquhart built

Downtown Juneau

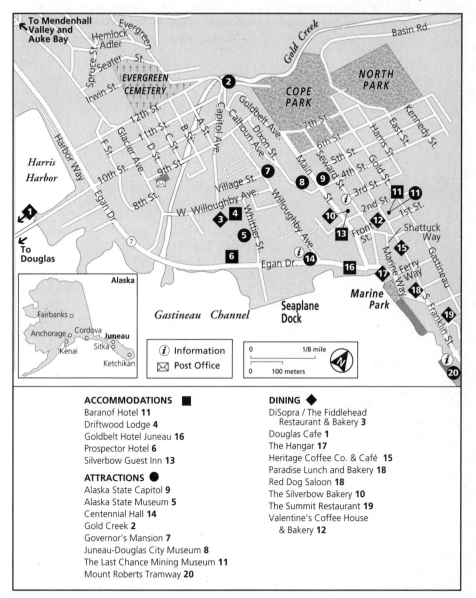

ACCOMMODATIONS ■
Baranof Hotel **11**
Driftwood Lodge **4**
Goldbelt Hotel Juneau **16**
Prospector Hotel **6**
Silverbow Guest Inn **13**

ATTRACTIONS ●
Alaska State Capitol **9**
Alaska State Museum **5**
Centennial Hall **14**
Gold Creek **2**
Governor's Mansion **7**
Juneau-Douglas City Museum **8**
The Last Chance Mining Museum **11**
Mount Roberts Tramway **20**

DINING ◆
DiSopra / The Fiddlehead
    Restaurant & Bakery **3**
Douglas Cafe **1**
The Hangar **17**
Heritage Coffee Co. & Café **15**
Paradise Lunch and Bakery **18**
Red Dog Saloon **18**
The Silverbow Bakery **10**
The Summit Restaurant **19**
Valentine's Coffee House
    & Bakery **12**

the spectacular log building themselves, looking out from the woods of Douglas Island onto an eagle's nest and the Gastineau Channel's Mendenhall Wetlands State Game Refuge. They keep a spotting scope in the living room and will lend you binoculars and rubber boots for an exploration down by the water. The five rooms are large, contemporary, and very clean, with rich colors that contrast with the huge logs of the walls, but they lack phones, TVs, or attached bathrooms. Being alone and entering without passing through the family's quarters are possible, but the general atmosphere is social, with two teenagers, two dogs, and a cat in residence. With all that activity and woods to play in, Blueberry Lodge is a good choice for families. Judy serves a big, fancy breakfast. You'll need to rent a car for the ten-minute drive to town.

9436 N. Douglas Hwy., Juneau, AK 99801. ☎ *and fax:* **907-463-5886.** *Internet:* www. blueberrylodge.com. *Rack rates: High season $105 double, low season $75 double; extra person older than 4 $15. Rates include full breakfast. AE, DISC, MC, V.*

The Driftwood Lodge
$–$$ **Downtown**

This motel next door to the State Museum is popular with families, and houses legislators and aides in winter in its apartment-like kitchenette suites. Although the building can't hide its cinderblock construction and old-fashioned motel exterior, small bathrooms, or lack of elevators, the rooms are remarkably comfortable and well kept. The management holds prices low while gradually improving the place, so adjoining rooms can have old shag carpeting or a brand new interior. For the price of a budget room elsewhere ($104), you can put four people in a two-bedroom suite with a full kitchen here. The round-the-clock courtesy van saves big money to the airport or ferry, and they rent bikes on site.

435 Willoughby Ave., Juneau, AK 99801. ☎ **800-544-2239** *or 907-586-2280. Fax: 907-586-1034. Internet:* www.driftwoodalaska.com. *Rack rates: High season $85 double, $93–$104 suite; low season $62 double, $89 suite; extra person $7. AE, DC, DISC, MC, V.*

Glacier Trail Bed & Breakfast
$$$ **Mendenhall Valley**

You wake up to an expansive view of the Mendenhall Glacier filling a picture window in a big, quiet, tastefully decorated room. Luke and Connie Nelson built the three-unit B&B with this moment in mind. Before beginning construction, they researched B&Bs all over the country, finding ideas for the amenities in the rooms and gaining inspiration for how to put the rooms together — not just as a bedroom with a lot of stuff in it, but as a cohesive, calming whole. A family apartment downstairs is perfect for large groups. The Nelsons also rent kayaks for outings on nearby Mendenhall Lake and they lend out bikes. Rooms all have refrigerators, microwave ovens, VCRs, and Jacuzzi tubs.

1081 Arctic Circle, Juneau, AK 99801. ☎ **907-789-5646.** *Fax: 907-789-5697. Internet:* www.juneaulodging.com. *Rack rates: High season $128–$153 double, low season $93–$108 double; extra person $20. Rates include full breakfast. AE, MC, V.*

Runner-Up Accommodations

Aspen Hotel Juneau

$$$ **Airport**   A comfortable hotel packed with amenities right on the airport grounds, this is both the closest and the best of the airport lodgings. *1800 Shell Simmons Dr., Juneau, AK 99801.* ☎ *888-559-9846 or 907-790-6435. Fax: 907-790-6621. Internet:* www.aspenhotelsak.com.

Goldbelt Hotel Juneau

$$$$ **Downtown**   Large bedrooms, with many amenities and either two full-size beds or one king-size bed, have bold colors and furniture in a dark cherry finish. They're noticeably quiet and immaculate. *51 W. Egan Dr., Juneau, AK 99801.* ☎ *888-478-6909 or 907-586-6900. Fax: 907-463-3567. Internet:* www.goldbelttours.com.

Prospector Hotel

$$$ **Downtown**   Newly remodeled rooms with waterfront views in a modern downtown hotel. *375 Whittier St., Juneau, AK 99801-1781.* ☎ *800-331-2711 or 907-586-3737. Fax: 907-586-1204. Internet:* www.prospectorhotel.com.

Silverbow Guest Inn

$$$ **Downtown**   A hip little inn in a historic building in the heart of downtown with proprietors who cultivate a local alternative scene in the restaurant, bar, and bakery. *120 Second St., Juneau, AK 99801.* ☎ *800-586-4146 or 907-586-4146. Fax: 907-586-4242. Internet:* www.silverbowinn.com.

Where to Dine in Juneau

After Anchorage, Juneau has the second-best dining scene in Alaska. It's the best stop in the region for a special meal with memorable, creative food. However, it's still a fairly small town, so choices are limited.

Chan's Thai Kitchen

$–$$ **Auke Bay**   **Thai**

The small, overlit dining room in the half-basement level of a steakhouse sees few tourists, but for a year after it opened, everyone I met would ask me, "Have you been to the Thai place yet?" When I finally went, I became a believer, too — the authentic Thai food is good, and the atmosphere, although lacking in polish, is conducive to a good time. Reservations are not accepted, and the restaurant does not have a liquor license. Waiting is uncomfortable, so think twice if you plan to go at a peak time.

11820 Glacier Hwy. (in Auke Bay, across the boat harbor). ☎ *907-789-9777. Main courses: $9–$13. MC, V. Open: Tues–Thurs 11 a.m. –2 p.m. and 5–8 p.m., Fri 11 a.m.– 2 p.m. and 5:00–8:30 p.m., Sat–Sun 4:30–8:30 p.m.*

Di Sopra/Fiddlehead Restaurant & Bakery
$–$$$ **Downtown** **Vegetarian/Seafood/Italian**

Two restaurants are under one roof. Upstairs, Di Sopra serves finely crafted northern Italian cuisine in a dining room with big windows, a mural, and solicitous service. The menu, which changes quarterly, presents the most sophisticated food available in town. Meanwhile, downstairs, the Fiddlehead has butcher-block tables, knotty pine paneling, and ferny stained glass. It serves from a long menu of flavorful food, with a great variety of ethnic influences, delicacies made into sandwiches, and many rice and vegetarian dishes. You can have lunch or dinner here for about $10, or more expensive dinner entrees, similar to those upstairs, of seafood, beef, or pasta.

429 W. Willoughby Ave. ☎ *907-586-3150. Internet:* www.alaska.net/~fiddle. *Reservations recommended for Di Sopra. Dinner main courses: $9–$25; lunch $8–$12. AE, DISC, MC, V. Open: Summer, Di Sopra daily 5–10 p.m.; Fiddlehead daily 7 a.m.–10 p.m.; winter, Di Sopra Tues–Sat 5–9 p.m.; Fiddlehead daily 7 a.m.–9 p.m.*

Douglas Café
$–$$ **Douglas** **Eclectic**

Finding a place like this hiding in the guise of an ordinary small-town burger joint is a real pleasure. The key, I'm convinced, is the two owners working in the kitchen, indistinguishable from the other young guys in baseball caps back there. They turn out wonderful seafood, meat, and vegetarian dinners, drawing on many world cuisines, and lunches that translate such food into sandwiches and a great array of burgers. The small dining room is lively, bright, and casual but somewhat cramped, with stacking chairs and wooden benches that can feel hard by the end of a meal. Weekend breakfasts are an event, filling the place with townspeople. Service is quick and casual. Craft brews are on tap.

916 Third St., Douglas (turn left after crossing the bridge from Juneau, then continue until you see the cafe on the left). ☎ *907-364-3307. Lunch items: $6.50–$9; dinner main courses: $8.25–$17. MC, V. Open: Tues–Fri 11:00 a.m.–8:30 p.m., Sat 9:00 a.m.–8:30 p.m., Sun 9:00 a.m.–1:30 p.m.; closed Tues in winter.*

The Hangar
$$–$$$ **Downtown** **Steak/Seafood/Pasta**

Situated in a converted airplane hangar on a wooden pier with large windows, this bar and grill has great views and a fun atmosphere. Even during the off season, it's packed. It's a fine place to drink beer (with 24 brews on tap), listen to live music, or play at one of the three pool

TIP

Sandwiches, picnics, coffee, and such

Sometimes you just want an inexpensive lunch, possibly in a box to take on an outing or a light breakfast in a friendly coffee joint. **Paradise Lunch and Bakery,** at 245 Marine Way, near the cruise-ship dock (☎ 907-586-2253), can do any of those things. **Valentine's Coffee House and Bakery,** 111 Seward St. (☎ 907-463-5144), serves light hot meals in an authentic old-fashioned storefront. **Heritage Coffee Co. and Café,** 174 S. Franklin St. (☎ 907-586-1087), also serves light meals and is a good people-watching place. **The Silverbow Bakery,** 120 Second St. (☎ 907-586-4146), serves hearty, healthy lunches, good bagels for breakfast, and baked goods to go.

tables. What's surprising is that the food is good, too. The seared ahi sashimi appetizer, like steak tartare, had a pleasant texture and taste, and the jambalaya, a huge portion for $12, was spicy but balanced — the shrimp didn't get smothered the way they often do.

2 Marine Way. ☎ *907-586-5018. Reservations recommended. Main courses: $12–$21. AE, DISC, MC, V. Open: Daily 11 a.m.–11 p.m.*

The Summit Restaurant
$$$–$$$$ **Downtown   Steak/Seafood**

A great place for a romantic meal. The dining room, with only ten tables, looks out over the cruise-ship dock from big windows. The formal service manifests an easy, world-weary elegance not easily faked, and the Summit is the only restaurant in Alaska that really has it. If you're lucky enough to get a reservation during the summer season, you'll find that the seafood and vegetables from the constantly changing, sometimes creative menu, are well prepared and occasionally truly inspired. An example is the halibut with spinach and Grand Marnier sauce on mashed potatoes. A little European-style hotel, the Inn at the Waterfront, is upstairs.

455 S. Franklin St. ☎ *907-586-2050. Reservations recommended. Main courses: $15–$28. AE, DC, DISC, MC, V. Open: Daily 5–11 p.m. Closed Oct.*

Exploring Juneau

Juneau is like a comfortable, well-loved living room: It's a town where you can settle in and get comfortable, walk around and make your own discoveries, and quickly feel like you belong there. Set aside some slow-paced time to walk to the attractions and enjoy the human-scale surroundings.

Exploring the top attractions

Alaska State Museum
Downtown

The museum contains a large collection of art and historical artifacts, but it doesn't seem like a storehouse at all because the presentation of the objects is based on their meaning, not their value. Come here to put the rest of your visit into context. A clan house in the Alaska Native Gallery contains authentic art that you'd really find in its functional place. The Lincoln Pole is here, carved by an artist who used a picture of the president as his model to represent his clan's first encounter with whites. Native cultures from around the state contributed superb artifacts that are presented in a way that explains the lifestyle of the people who made them. The ramp to the second floor wraps around the natural history display, with an eagle in a tree, and at the top a state history gallery uses significant pieces to tell Alaska's story. Exploring the entire museum takes several hours, but you can easily take in a bite-sized piece in an hour. The gift store carries authentic Native arts and crafts, plus books, maps, and so on.

395 Whittier St. ☎ *907-465-2901. Internet:* www.museums.state.ak.us. *Open: High season, daily 8:30 a.m.–5:30 p.m.; winter, Tues–Sat 10 a.m.–4 p.m. Admission: $5 adults, free for ages 18 and under; winter discount $3.*

Macaulay Salmon Hatchery
Glacier Highway

The hatchery, known by locals as DIPAC (Douglas Island Pink and Chum), was ingeniously designed to enable visitors to watch from outdoor decks the whole process of harvesting and fertilizing eggs. From mid-June to October, salmon swim up a 450-foot fish ladder, visible through a window, into a sorting mechanism and then are "unzipped" by workers who remove the eggs. Guides and exhibits explain what's happening. You can often see seals and other wildlife feeding on the returning salmon just offshore from the hatchery at these times. Inside, large saltwater aquariums show off the area's marine life the way it looks in its natural environment. The tour is less impressive in May and June, before the fish are running. Then you see the incubation area, where the fish eggs develop in racks of trays. The tours don't take long. All you need is 45 minutes for the entire visit.

2697 Channel Dr. (3 miles from downtown, turn left at the first group of buildings on Egan Dr.). ☎ *877-463-2486 or 907-463-4810. Internet:* www.dipac.net. *Open: Summer, Mon–Fri 10 a.m.–6 p.m., Sat–Sun 10 a.m.–5 p.m.; Sept 15–May 15, call ahead. Admission: $3 adults, $1 children ages 12 and younger.*

Mendenhall Glacier
Mendenhall Valley

The Mendenhall Glacier glows bluish white, looming above the suburbs like an Ice Age monster that missed the general extinction. Besides being a truly impressive sight, Mendenhall is the most easily accessible glacier in Alaska and the state's third-most visited attraction. The parking and an adjacent shelter have a great view across the lake to the glacier's face, and a wheelchair-accessible trail leads to the water's edge. The land near the parking lot shows signs of the glacier's recent passage, with little topsoil, stunted vegetation, and in many places, bare rock that shows the scratch marks of the glacier's movement. Atop a bedrock hill, reached by stairs, a ramp, or an elevator, the recently remodeled Forest Service visitor center contains a glacier museum with excellent explanatory models, computerized displays, and ranger talks. A terrific network of trails leads up each side of the glacier and around the visitor center area, where you can get advice and a handy guide brochure from the rangers. In late summer, you can watch red and silver salmon spawning in **Steep Creek,** just short of the visitor center on the road.

At the head of Glacier Spur Road (right from Egan Drive on Mendenhall Loop to Glacier Spur). Visitor center ☎ 907-789-0097. Visitor Center open: Summer, daily 8:00 a.m.–6:30 p.m.; winter, Thurs–Fri 10 a.m.–4 p.m., Sat–Sun 9 a.m.–4 p.m. Visitor center admission: $3 for adults, free for children younger than 12.

Mount Roberts Tramway
Downtown

The tram takes only six minutes to whisk passengers from tourist-clogged Franklin Street to the clear air and overwhelming views at the tree line (1,760 feet), a destination that used to require a day of huffing and puffing just to view. The tram can be crowded, but once you're up there, the beauty hits you. The Alaska Native owners seem to understand that, and they have done a good job of building a network of paths that take advantage of the views as you pass through a fascinating alpine ecosystem, and they've even carved artwork into the living trunks of some of the trees. If you're energetic, you can start a 6-mile round trip to Mount Roberts's summit (at 3,819 feet), or you can hike the 2½ miles back to downtown. Anyone can profitably spend an hour, or even half a day if you're of a mind, and kids love it. An auditorium at the top tram station shows a film about Tlingit culture and a multimedia performance about wildlife. A bar and grill serves three meals a day (I've heard decidedly mixed reviews). Don't bother with the tram on a day of fog or low overcast — it isn't worth the money without the view.

490 South Franklin St., at the waterfront near the cruise-ship dock. ☎ 888-461-8726 or 907-463-3412. Open: Daily 9 a.m.–9 p.m.; closed Oct–Apr. Admission: All-day pass $21.95 adults, $12.60 children 12 and younger, tax included.

Other cool things to see and do

These just-missed-the-top attractions are well worth a visit when you're in Juneau for more than a day or two:

- ✔ **Juneau-Douglas City Museum:** Find out about Juneau at this fun little museum about the town. It features a tiny shop stocked with handy information for your visit, such as walking-tour maps and historic trail guides. It's at the corner of Fourth and Main streets (☎ **907-586-3572;** Internet: www.juneau.lib.ak.us/parksrec/museum). Admission is $3 adults ($2 in winter), free for ages 18 and younger. Summer hours are Monday to Friday from 9 a.m. to 5 p.m., and Saturday and Sunday from 10 a.m. to 5 p.m.

- ✔ **Last Chance Mining Museum:** You can mine Juneau's industrial past at these old mining buildings on forested Gold Creek. You can see immense original equipment still intact before hiking the nearby Perseverance Trail (see "Hiking," later in this chapter). From downtown, take Gold Street to the top, then turn left onto Basin Road, continuing 1½ miles up the valley to the end of the road (☎ **907-586-5338**). Admission is $3, and the museum is open in summer daily from 9:30 a.m. to 12:30 p.m. and 3:30 to 6:30 p.m.

- ✔ **Glacier Gardens:** Tour the rain forest. For people with mobility problems, this horticultural exhibit provides a unique way into the forest, starting in greenhouses and formal gardens and then riding a vehicle similar to a golf-cart up a steep trail through woods landscaped with pools and plantings to an overlook. The gardens are located near the airport; take Glacier Highway to near the Fred Meyer store (☎ **907-790-3377;** Internet: www.glacier gardens.com). Admission is $17.95 adults, $12.95 ages 6–12 (not worth it unless it's your only way of getting into the woods). It's open in summer daily from 9 a.m. to 6 p.m.

- ✔ **Take a scenic drive "Out the Road:"** The 40-mile Glacier Highway doesn't go much of anywhere beyond the Mendenhall Valley, but it does go *through* some lovely country with views of islands floating on sun-dappled water. Stop at the moving **Shrine of St. Therese** (☎ **907-780-6112;** Internet: www.dioceseofjuneau.org), 9 miles beyond the ferry dock, a simple chapel of rounded beach stones on a tiny island reached by a foot-trail causeway. It's also a great place for examining tide pools, and sometimes you can see whales from shore there.

Shopping

The most popular shopping district is located on the streets surrounding the cruise-ship dock and on South Franklin Street. Many shops that you see here are entirely seasonal, while others also have a local clientele. Some worthy of your attention include **The Raven's Journey,** 439 S. Franklin (☎ **907-463-4686**), which shows Alaska Native fine art; **Taku Smokeries,** at 550 S. Franklin (☎ **907-463-3474;** Internet: www. takusmokeries.com), a place to buy expensive seafood delicacies and see them made behind glass; and **Ad Lib,** at 231 S. Franklin St. (☎ **907-463-3031**), a good gift store oriented to items made in Alaska.

Walking up the hill a bit, you get to more of the year-round businesses. Check out **Juneau Artists Gallery,** at 175 S. Franklin (☎ **907-586-9891;** Internet: www.juneauartistsgallery.com), which is an artists' co-op; the shop operated by **Bill Spear** (174 S. Franklin; ☎ **907-586-2209;** Internet: www.wmspear.com), who makes colored enamel pins; and **The Observatory,** at 200 N. Franklin St. (☎ **907-586-9676;** Internet: www.observatorybooks.com), which specializes in rare maps and books about Alaska. **Annie Kaill's** fine arts and crafts gallery is half a block off Franklin at 244 Front St. (☎ **907-586-2880**).

Nightlife

For a family night out, consider the **Gold Creek Salmon Bake.** It's a 30-year tradition of a picnic with marshmallow roasting, music, and other entertainment. The cost is $28 for adults, $19 for children. Call ☎ **907-789-0052** to arrange pickup by van.

I mention **The Hangar** under "Where to Dine in Juneau." Other popular drinking establishments include **The Red Dog Saloon,** at 278 S. Franklin St. (☎ **907-463-9954**), with a sawdust-strewn floor and frontier atmosphere. Nightly live music is free of cover charge. Or join the locals across the street at **The Alaskan Bar,** 167 S. Franklin (☎ **907-586-1000**), which occupies an authentic gold rush hotel with a two-story Victorian barroom. Boisterous parties and music go on there all year; the highlight is the Thursday night open mike, when crowds pack in for a wild, noisy evening.

Getting Outdoors in Juneau

Juneau has more to do outdoors than anywhere else I can think of. And thanks to the town's role as a top visitor destination, you can do most of it with a guide instead of on your own.

You'll find support for self-guided outings, too. **Juneau Outdoor Center,** in the Douglas boat harbor at 101 Dock St., or at the Auke Bay Harbor (☎ **907-586-8220;** Internet: www.juneaukayak.com), rents sea kayaks, camping gear, and skiffs with outboard motors, which you can use for fishing or exploring, and offers guidance in planning where and how to go.

Bear-viewing

Bear are quite common around Juneau; they become pests for residents who live near the woods. But to see many a brown bear, close up and behaving naturally, the best place to go is Admiralty Island and its **Kootznoowoo Wilderness** (*Kootznoowoo* means "fortress of bears" in Tlingit). The island's **Pack Creek Bear-viewing Area** has a platform for watching bears up close as they feed on salmon spawning in July and August, with peak viewing in the middle of that period. Only 25 miles from Juneau, Pack Creek is so popular that the Forest Service uses a permit system to keep it from being overrun during the day (from 9 p.m. to 9 a.m., no humans are allowed). The easiest way to go is with a tour operator who has permits; here are a couple of good choices:

- ✔ **Alaska Discovery,** 5310 Glacier Hwy. (☎ **800-586-1911** or 907-780-6226; Internet: www.akdiscovery.com), has many permits for sea kayak trips to see the bears. Their one-day excursion flies out and then paddles to the creek; no experience is necessary, but you must be physically capable of hiking and paddling. It costs $495 per person.

- ✔ **Alaska Fly 'N' Fish Charters,** 9604 Kelly Ct. (☎ **907-790-2120;** Internet: www.alaskabyair.com), also has permits for its naturalist-guided 5½-hour fly-in visits, which cost $475 per person, with everything you need included.

Fishing

You'll find terrific salmon fishing on the waters around Juneau, and plenty of boats to take you. You can also use a six-passenger boat for a whale-watching outing, or combine whale-watching and fishing. (Another whale-watching option is discussed later in this chapter.)

Juneau Sportfishing and Sightseeing, 2 Marine Way, Suite 230 (☎ **907-586-1887;** Internet: www.juneausportfishing.com), is one of the largest operators, and its rates are typical: $215 per person for a full day of fishing, $125 for 4 hours, or $95 for a 2½-hour whale-watching trip.

Flightseeing and dog mushing

More than 36 major glaciers around Juneau flow from a single ocean of ice behind the mountains, the 1,500-square-mile Juneau Ice Field. You can land on it in a helicopter just to touch the ice, or for a nature hike or dog-sled ride. On the flight, you survey the bizarre scenery of long, sinuous strands of flowing glacier ice. Then, when you land, you find yourself transported into winter during the middle of summer, surrounded by blindingly white, crusty snow. **Era Helicopters** (☎ **800-843-1947** or 907-586-2030; Internet: www.eraaviation.com) is among Alaska's oldest and most respected operators. Its one-hour glacier landing flight costs $210 per person. It also offers a program of dog-sled rides on the ice, a chance to ride behind a real team on real snow in the middle of summer. That excursion costs $349 per person.

One caveat: Poor or even overcast weather makes seeing the ice clearly difficult to do, but if you wait for a sunny morning, all seats will likely be booked. Era has a 48-hour cancellation policy, so you must gamble to some extent on good viewing conditions.

Hiking

Juneau's superb trail network offers choices ranging from easy strolls to leg-burners up those omnipresent mountains. I mention the trails at Mendenhall Glacier earlier in this chapter; here are some other highlights, in order of increasing difficulty:

- ✔ **Mount Roberts:** The trailhead is downtown (just follow the stairway from the top of Sixth Street). The summit is 4½ miles and 3,819 vertical feet away, but you see great views much sooner. At the 1,760-foot level, you come to the top of the Mount Roberts Tramway, which is mentioned earlier in this chapter. (Of course, taking the tram up and hiking down is easier.)

- ✔ **Outer Point Trail:** This lovely but sometimes crowded trail leads 1⅓ miles on a forest boardwalk to a beach with good tide-pooling, plenty of eagles, and possible whale sightings. To get there, drive over the bridge to Douglas, then right on North Douglas Highway 11½ miles to the trailhead.

- ✔ **Perseverance Trail:** A fairly level 3-mile trails leads up behind town to the Perseverance Mine, at the Silverbow Basin, a mining community from 1885 to 1921. The trailhead is about 1½ miles from downtown on Basin Road; check out the Last Chance Mining Museum there (see "Other cool things to see and do," earlier in this chapter).

- ✔ **The Treadwell Mine Historic Trail:** This is a fascinating hour's stroll through the ruins of a massive hard-rock mine complex that once employed and housed 2,000 men. It's been abandoned since 1922. Numbered posts match a historic guide available from the Juneau-Douglas City Museum (see "Other cool things to see and do," earlier in this chapter). To find the trailhead, take Third Street in Douglas, bearing left onto Savikko Street, which leads to Savikko Park (also known as Sandy Beach Park). The trail starts at the far end.

Sea kayaking

The protected waters around Juneau welcome sea kayaking, and the city is a popular hub for trips farther afield on the water. Besides the sublime scenery, you'll almost certainly see eagles, seabirds, and seals, and possibly humpback whales. Following are a couple of providers to contact to arrange guided adventures:

✔ **Auk Ta Shaa Discovery** (☎ 800-820-2628 or 907-586-8687) offers a sea-kayak day trip that starts from an unspoiled spot way out the road for $95 per person, $47.50 ages 12–16. The seven-hour trip includes five hours of kayaking and a beach picnic.

✔ If you want a greater challenge, **Alaska Discovery**, 5310 Glacier Hwy. (☎ 800-586-1911 or 907-780-6226; Internet: www.akdiscovery.com), offers sea kayaking expeditions near Juneau, among the whales near Glacier Bay, and other places. A three-day, two-night trip is $495 to $595 per person.

Choosing glaciers: Glacier Bay or Tracy Arm

I admit that Glacier Bay National Park is awesome with huge glaciers, sheer rock mountains, and whales leaping out of the water. But I don't recommend it for most visitors, especially the ones with limited time and money. That's because you can see the same types of sights in less time and for less money as a day trip from Juneau to Tracy Arm in the Tongass National Forest. If whales are your main objective, you can see more on a day trip from Juneau to Icy Strait, near Glacier Bay (see "Whale-watching," elsewhere in this chapter).

Glacier Bay is a marine park. To get to the glaciers, you have to take a boat ride that lasts nine hours and costs $159. And to get to where the boat ride starts costs roughly $150 more. Moreover, it seems ridiculous to do all that as a marathon day trip, but spending the night at Glacier Bay costs more again (a double room at the Glacier Bay Lodge is $169, not including meals and transfers). On the other hand, an all-day boat trip to Tracy Arm, which includes mile-high mountains that come right out of the sea, calving glaciers, and often whale sightings, costs $110 and takes only eight hours, right from the dock in Juneau.

Auk Nu Tours is the largest of several Tracy Arm boat-tour operators (☎ 800-820-2628 or 907-586-8687; Internet: www.goldbelttours.com). Its daylong trip operates Tuesday, Thursday, and Saturday at 9 a.m. in summer. Light meals and the use of binoculars are included in the price.

If, however, you choose Glacier Bay (and I admit that it is awesome), you can book everything through the park concessionaire, **Glacier Bay Cruiseline,** (☎ 800-451-5952; Internet: www.glacierbaycruiseline.com). Its one-day package is $346.50 from Juneau, or $481 for an overnight package that includes the Icy Strait whale watch (a much better deal).

Whale-watching

From Juneau, you can take a boat to the most reliable whale-watching waters in Alaska and be back by evening. The *Auk Nu,* a high-speed catamaran that serves Gustavus from Juneau as a passenger ferry (☎ **800-820-2628** or 907-586-8687), takes visitors to the waters of Icy Strait, near Gustavus, to watch the humpback whales gathering there to feed. The boat leaves Juneau from near the ferry terminal at 11 a.m. daily in summer and returns at 8 p.m., with light meals served onboard. The fare of $139 adults, $104 children, includes a money-back guarantee that you'll see whales (a safe bet for the company). Gustavus is gateway to Glacier Bay National Park, and if you take this whale watch, you can stay over in Gustavus for the same fare, but getting into the main part of the park requires another lengthy boat ride and an overnight stay (see the "Choosing glaciers: Glacier Bay or Tracy Arm" sidebar, elsewhere in this chapter). A less expensive but less assured whale-watching option can be found in the "Fishing" section earlier in this chapter.

Spending 1, 2, and 3 Days in Juneau

Whenever you go to Juneau, you must go outdoors, even if only in a car or helicopter. So these aren't just *seeing* itineraries, they're *doing* itineraries, too. Each element of the following itinerary is reviewed in more detail elsewhere in this chapter.

Day 1 in Juneau

Start the morning by boarding a helicopter bound for the **Juneau Ice Field** to see vast glaciers and the icy plateau they spring from; if you can afford it, add a dog-sled ride on the ice. For a lower-budget alternative, take the **Mount Roberts Tramway** for mountain views and a walk. Returning to Juneau, stroll downtown for shopping on **Franklin Street** or for simply viewing the modest public buildings of the state capital. Have lunch at the **Fiddlehead Restaurant and Bakery** before going next door to the **Alaska State Museum** for an orientation to Alaska's history and culture. If the weather's nice, finish the day by eating outdoors while listening to music at the **Gold Creek Salmon Bake.**

Day 2 in Juneau

Rent a car today. Your first stop is the **Mendenhall Glacier,** where you definitely need to check out the visitor center and, if you're of a mind, take a hike. Next explore the **Glacier Highway** (or head "Out the Road," as locals refer to it) to see the views and visit the **Shrine of St. Therese.** Take a picnic or get back to Auke Bay for lunch (except weekends) at **Chan's Thai Kitchen.** On the way back into town stop at the **Macaulay**

Salmon Hatchery for the tour and then cross the bridge to **Douglas for a hike.** You may have time for the historic Treadwell Mine Trail and the natural Outer Beach Trail. Dine at the **Douglas Café.**

Day 3 in Juneau

Spend one day on an **all-day outdoor expedition:** taking the boat to Tracy Arm, sea kayaking in Juneau, whale-watching in Icy Strait, or bear-watching on Admiralty Island. Dine at the **Hangar** on the waterfront.

Fast Facts: Juneau

Banks

Among many other banks and stores, **Wells Fargo,** at 123 Seward St. (☎ 907-586-3324), has an ATM.

Hospital

Bartlett Regional, at 3260 Hospital Dr. (☎ 907-586-2611), is 3 miles out the Glacier Highway.

Information

The **Juneau Convention and Visitors Bureau** has an information center in the Centennial Hall at 101 Egan Dr., near the State Museum (☎ 888-581-2201 or 907-586-2201; Fax: 907-586-6304; Internet: www.traveljuneau.com).

Internet Access

Uncle Arty's, 493 S. Franklin St., second floor (☎ 907-463-2543), is open summer daily from 8 a.m. to 11 p.m.

Police

At 6255 Alaway Ave., ☎ 907-586-0600 for nonemergencies.

Post Office

Downtown in the federal building, 709 W. Ninth St., and in the Mendenhall Valley at 9491 Vintage Blvd., by Carr's supermarket.

Taxes

Sales tax is 5%. You pay 12% tax on **rooms.**

Chapter 21

Skagway

. . . .

In This Chapter

▶ Experiencing Skagway's gold rush history

▶ Getting to and around Skagway

▶ Finding rest and food

▶ Seeing the gold rush sites

▶ Exploring the outdoors

▶ Checking out the nightlife

. . . .

The 1898 Klondike Gold Rush was the last gasp of the Wild West and the first breath of Alaska's modern history. Skagway was where it hit its wildest. Miners found the gold near Dawson City, Yukon Territory, and Canada's Mounties kept the stampede in relatively good order. But in Skagway, men crazed with greed knew no law at all. They disembarked their boats on Skagway's dock for a tough cross-country trek to Dawson City. One day the area was wilderness, the next a city of saloons and brothels. After the men came ashore, they played cards, lifted drinks, spent time (and money) with some very busy women, and got fleeced by the thousands. They settled arguments with guns, and the absence of sanitation caused epidemics, so the cemetery grew fast.

No wonder the governor came to town and asked one of the most popular local citizens to be the territorial marshal, marching with him in the Fourth of July parade. The plan may have worked, too, except that the man he chose, Soapy Smith, was the most dangerous con man and gang leader in town. Four days after the parade, in Skagway's greatest tale, vigilante Frank Reid killed Soapy Smith in a fair fight standing face-to-face on the docks. Reid later died himself of the wounds he sustained, but not before breaking the grip of Soapy's men on the town. The story also was one of the last great Wild West tales of Skagway history. The rush lasted less than two years, and soon Skagway was an ordinary town, but one with a brief and illustrious past.

If that history interests you, Skagway does a good job of presenting it with the Klondike Gold Rush National Historic Park, a collection of buildings and museums. You can spend a good day there. If you're not interested in the gold rush and Wild West, however, you can skip Skagway without hazard.

Gold rush primer

At a big wedding I attended in Anchorage, most of the wedding party came to Alaska and toured the state together before the festivities. They spent many hours in gold rush towns visiting museums and sites devoted to the gold rush. I asked one of the young men what he thought of it. He said he'd enjoyed Alaska and thought all the historic sites were interesting enough. However, he was left with one nagging question: "What's the gold rush?"

Because the gold rush is just about the only big thing that's ever happened in Alaska, we tend to forget it's not on everyone's mind.

The rush started in 1897 when a group of regular guys got off a boat in Seattle with a ton of gold stuffed in steamer trunks and gunnysacks. A sourdough prospector, George Carmack, and his Native partners, Tagish Charlie and Skookum Jim, found gold in the Klondike River in Canada's Yukon Territory the year before — gold so plentiful it looked like slabs of cheese in a sandwich. At the time, the nation was in the fourth year of a financial collapse. People were poor, and when the newspapers told them about a river up north with gold by the ton, they didn't have to be told twice. Some 100,000 — even the mayor of Seattle — quit whatever they were doing and headed north. This rush happened at a time when the total non-Native population of Alaska was counted at 4,000.

The cheapest and most popular route was by boat to Skagway, on foot over the tortuous Chilkoot Pass or White Pass, and then by handmade boat across Lake Bennett and down the ferocious Yukon River to the new town of Dawson City. Just to make it alive was an impressive accomplishment. But few of those who did found any gold — the mining claims had been staked and big companies were soon doing the mining. Some of the gold rush stampeders gave up, but others had too much pride or too much greed to go home, or they just liked it here. They populated Alaska, rushing from one gold find to another in a series of gold strikes. That's how many of Alaska's cities were founded, including Fairbanks and Nome.

Gold fever didn't give out until World War I, and it never died completely. Big-time companies still mine around Dawson City and Fairbanks. And small-time prospectors still scratch the hills across the state in hopes of a strike as big as the one George Carmack, Tagish Charlie, and Skookum Joe made more than 100 years ago.

Skagway is the most touristy community in Alaska, with as many as five cruise ships pulling into town at a time. That's in a town with fewer than 900 residents. All the cruise-ship passengers make for an awful mob, and they're tough to avoid. If you plan sightseeing early and late in the day, it may help, and weekends appear to be quieter than weekdays. And of course, the city is quieter during the cruising off-season (usually October through April).

Getting There

You can drive, fly, or take a boat to Skagway, but for most visitors, the water is the most practical way.

By boat

Most visitors get to Skagway on a cruise ship (see Chapter 8). The **Alaska Marine Highway System** (☎ **800-642-0066** or 907-983-2941 locally; Internet: www.alaska.gov/ferry) connects Skagway daily with Haines and Juneau. The fare is $37 to Juneau, $21 to Haines. **Alaska Fjordlines** (☎ **800-320-0146**; Internet: www.alaskafjordlines. com) carries passengers daily from Skagway to Juneau and back on a high-speed catamaran that takes about three hours between the cities, instead of 5½ hours on the ferry. If you choose to use the catamaran in the reverse direction, you have to spend the night in Skagway. The fare is $109 round-trip.

By road

Klondike Highway 2 connects Skagway with Whitehorse, Yukon Territory, 99 miles away over the White Pass. It's a high, rocky gold rush route, giving views as good as those on the excursion train that operates over the pass. The international border is at the top of the pass; a few facts about clearing customs are in Chapter 6. The highway meets the Alaska Highway and Klondike Highway in Whitehorse for drives to the rest of the state or northward to Dawson City.

By air

Small, prop-driven planes serve Skagway. **L.A.B. Flying Service** (☎ **907-983-2471**; Internet: www.labflying.com) has scheduled flights from Juneau for $150 round-trip.

Orienting Yourself in Skagway

Broadway is the main historic street. A simple grid spans a few blocks on either side (see the nearby "Skagway" map). The Klondike Highway leads north out of town at the end of the grid. The gold rush cemetery is just past town on the right.

Walking is the best way to explore Skagway. To get to sites on the outskirts, you can rent a bike from **Sockeye Cycle,** on Fifth Avenue off Broadway (☎ **907-983-2851**; Internet: www.cyclealaska.com). If you can't walk, you can rent a car from **Avis,** at Third Avenue and Spring Street (☎ **800-331-1212** or 907-983-2247; Internet: www.avis.com), or take the guided tour described in "Exploring Skagway," later in this chapter.

Where to Stay

Skagway has no high-quality, chain-style hotel, but you can find several charming and comfortable places. All listed hotels have courtesy vans available, though all are within walking distance to the historic sites (as is the whole town).

At The White House
$$ **Skagway**

The Tronrud family essentially rebuilt a burned 1902 gable-roofed inn, which has dormer and bow windows and two porticos with small Doric columns. They made the rooms comfortable and modern while retaining the style of the original owner, Lee Guthrie, a successful gambler and saloon owner of the gold rush years. The inn has hardwood floors and fine woodwork. Bedrooms vary in size, and all have quilts and other nice touches.

Corner of Eighth and Main streets (P.O. Box 41), Skagway, AK 99840-0041. ☎ *907-983-9000. Fax: 907-983-9010. Internet:* www.atthewhitehouse.com. *Rack rates: High season $108 double, low season $75 double; extra person $10. Rates include breakfast buffet. AE, DISC, MC, V. No smoking.*

Golden North Hotel
$–$$ **Skagway**

This big yellow landmark on Broadway was built in 1898 and is Alaska's oldest operating hotel, and a fun place to stay. New owners spent $1.6 million to restore the creaking wooden building while keeping its campy character intact, including the big claw-foot tubs and the placards in each room about different gold rush families. The owners strive to make it like sleeping in your own museum. Eight rooms only have showers, while three have shower-tub combinations, and the remainder only have tubs. Four rooms share bathrooms. Room 24 has a lovelorn gold rush ghost. A brewpub restaurant is downstairs.

Third Avenue and Broadway (P.O. Box 343), Skagway, AK 99840. ☎ *888-222-1898 or 907-983-2294. Fax: 907-983-2755. Internet:* www.goldennorthhotel.com. *Rack rates: $75 double with shared bathroom; $105–$120 double with private bathroom; extra person $10. AE, DC, DISC, MC, V.*

Skagway

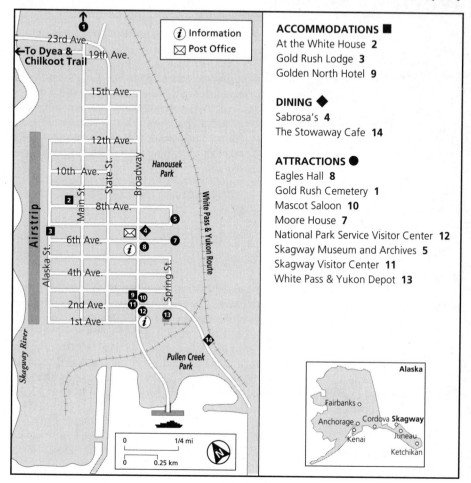

ACCOMMODATIONS ■
At the White House **2**
Gold Rush Lodge **3**
Golden North Hotel **9**

DINING ◆
Sabrosa's **4**
The Stowaway Cafe **14**

ATTRACTIONS ●
Eagles Hall **8**
Gold Rush Cemetery **1**
Mascot Saloon **10**
Moore House **7**
National Park Service Visitor Center **12**
Skagway Museum and Archives **5**
Skagway Visitor Center **11**
White Pass & Yukon Depot **13**

(i) Information
✉ Post Office

23rd Ave.
←To Dyea &
Chilkoot Trail
19th Ave.
15th Ave.
12th Ave.
Hanousek Park
10th Ave.
8th Ave.
6th Ave.
4th Ave.
2nd Ave.
1st Ave.
Airstrip
Main St.
State St.
Broadway
Alaska St.
Spring St.
White Pass & Yukon Route
Skagway River
Pullen Creek Park

Alaska
Fairbanks o
Anchorage o
Cordova **Skagway**
Kenai
Juneau
Ketchikan

0   1/4 mi
0   0.25 km
N

Gold Rush Lodge
$–$$ Skagway

This lodge is a clean, comfortable motel by the airstrip, three blocks from the historic district, with a grassy picnic area out back. The rooms are on the small side but modern and attractively decorated in light colors; they have VCRs, microwaves, refrigerators, and coffeemakers. Bathrooms have only shower stalls and no tubs. The hosts provide fruit, coffee, and cookies in the lobby, and write the guests' names and home-towns on an erasable board so that they can get to know each other.

Sixth Avenue and Alaska Street (P.O. Box 514), Skagway, AK 99840. ☎ 877-983-3509 or 907-983-2831. Fax: 907-983-2742. Internet: www.goldrushlodge.com. Rack rates: High season $80–$105 double, low season $60–$75 double; extra person $10. AE, DISC, MC, V. No smoking.

Where to Dine

Sabrosa's

$ Skagway   Deli/Vegetarian

This tiny sidewalk cafe down an alley across from the post office feeds locals. The tables are in a pleasant fenced area, a sort of patio arrangement (although not great in the rain). It's an island of intimacy out of the stream of the tourist rush. Our halibut, pasta salad, and vegetarian sandwich were tasty, wholesome, filling, and inexpensive — a rare combination in Skagway. Sabrosa's also serves Mexican specials and fresh baked goods. Service is quick and friendly.

Sixth Avenue and Broadway. ☎ *907-983-2469. All items: $3.50–$9. No credit cards. Open: Daily 7 a.m.–8 p.m. Closed winter.*

The Stowaway Café

$$–$$$$ Skagway   Seafood/Cajun

In a small, gray clapboard house overlooking the boat harbor, a five-minute walk from the historic sites, Jim and Kim Long's little restaurant is a labor of love — they met here when she hired him to fix it up and then married. Jim cooks the grilled and blackened salmon and halibut that anchor the menu; you also find beef, pasta, and all the usual waterfront restaurant items. Service is fast. The tiny dining room is decorated with a miscellaneous collection of knickknacks that keep your attention almost as well as the harbor view. The cafe has a beer and wine license and serves inexpensive lunches.

End of Congress Way near the small boat harbor. ☎ *907-983-3463. Reservations recommended. Dinner: $12.50–$28.50. V. Open: Daily 11 a.m.–10 p.m. Closed winter.*

Exploring Skagway

Skagway Streetcar Company, 270 Second Ave. (☎ **907-983-2908;** Internet: www.skagwaystreetcar.com), offers two-hour town tours using antique touring vehicles and costumed guides. The price is $36 for adults, half-price for kids, and advance reservations are needed.

The top attractions

Klondike Gold Rush National Historic Park

The historic park encompasses a collection of about 15 restored gold rush buildings on Broadway and nearby. A visit to Skagway focuses on a walk around these buildings. Start at the **museum** at the park's visitor center where you can also catch one of the frequent ranger-guided walk-ing tours. If you prefer to guide yourself, a handy brochure is available. Among the highlights are the **Mascot Saloon,** at Broadway and Third Avenue, where statues belly up to the bar. The saloon is open daily from 8 a.m. to 6 p.m. and admission is $2.

The Park Service offers free tours of the 1897 **Moore House,** near Fifth Avenue and Spring Street, 10 a.m. to 5 p.m. during the summer. Ten years before the gold rush, Captain William Moore brilliantly predicted it and homesteaded the land that would become Skagway. But when the rush hit, the stampeders simply ignored his property claims.

Visitor Center: Second Avenue and Broadway (P.O. Box 517), Skagway, AK 99840 ☎ *907-983-2921. Internet:* www.nps.gov/klgo. *Open May to September daily 8 a.m.–6 p.m., the rest of the year Mon–Fri 8 a.m.–5 p.m.*

The White Pass and Yukon Route

In 1900, after only two years of construction, workers completed this narrow-gauge railroad — an engineering marvel and a fun way to see spectacular, historic scenery. The summer-only excursion ride begins at a depot with the spine-tingling sound of a working steam engine's whistle. The steamer pulls the train a couple of miles, then diesels take the cars — some of them more than 100-year-old originals — up steep tracks that were chipped out of the mountains' side. The 40-mile round trip lasts a little over three hours. The trick is to go in clear weather. When the pass is socked in by weather, all you see are white clouds.

Tickets are expensive, and you have to reserve ahead. Take the gamble: Cancellation carries only a 10% penalty, and you can change dates for no charge. Also, try to go on a weekend, when fewer cruise-ship passengers are in town taking up the seats. You can book weekend trains as little as a week ahead, while you can reserve midweek excursions months ahead.

Second Avenue depot (P.O. Box 435, Dept. B), Skagway, AK 99840. ☎ *800-343-7373 or 907-983-2217. Internet:* www.whitepassrailroad.com. *Fare: $82–$156 adults, half price for children 3–12.*

Getting outdoors in Skagway

When you tire of mining for gold mine history, you can find a variety of outdoor activities to choose from during your stay in Skagway, whether in town or on the outskirts.

Biking

Sockeye Cycle, on Fifth Avenue off Broadway (☎ **907-983-2851;** Internet: www.cyclealaska.com), leads bike tours, including one that takes clients to the top of the White Pass in a van and coasts down on bikes;

the two-hour trip is $69. Sockeye Cycle also takes riders over in a van and then leads a bike tour of the quiet ghost town site of Dyea for $69. Or ride to Dyea on your own over a scenic, hilly, 10-mile coastal road, with a rented bike.

Flightseeing

Skagway is a good starting point to fly over Glacier Bay National Park, which is just to the west. **L.A.B. Flying Service (☎ 907-983-2471;** Internet: www.labflying.com) is one of several companies offering fixed-wing service. Expect to pay $150 with a two-person minimum. **Temsco Helicopters (☎ 907-983-2900;** Internet: www.temscoair.com) takes 55-minute tours over the Chilkoot Trail, including a 25-minute landing on a glacier (not in Glacier Bay); those flights cost $189. A helicopter and dog-sled tour on Denver Glacier is $329.

Hiking

You can take several good day hikes right from your hotel. An easy evening walk starts at the suspension footbridge at the north end of First Avenue, crossing the Skagway River to **Yakutania Point Park,** where pine trees grow from cracks in the rounded granite of the shoreline. Across the park is the **Skyline Trail and A.B. Mountain,** a strenuous climb to a 3,500-foot summit with great views. On the southern side of town, across the railroad tracks, a network of trails heads up from Spring Street between Third and Fourth avenues to a series of mountain lakes, the closest of which is **Lower Dewey Lake,** less than a mile up the trail. A *Skagway Trail Map* is available from the visitor center (see "Fast Facts: Skagway" at the end of this chapter).

If you want to hike the historic Chilkoot Trail, you have to allow several days and make arrangements for a special permit, gear, and transportation at the other end. For permit details, contact **Parks Canada,** 205–300 Main St., Whitehorse, Yukon Y1A 2B5 Canada (**☎ 800-661-0486;** Fax: 867-393-6701; Internet: http://parkscan.harbour.com/ct). You can rent equipment, get advice, or even arrange a guided hike with the **Mountain Shop,** at 355 Fourth Ave. (**☎ 907-983-2544;** Internet: www.packerexpeditions.com).

Other cool things to see and do

The **Skagway Museum and Archives,** Seventh Avenue and Spring Street (**☎ 907-983-2420;** E-mail: info@skagwaymuseum.org), rewards an hour of study in a dignified granite building at Seventh and Spring streets. Admission is $2 adults, $1 students, free for children 12 and under. The museum is open in summer 9 a.m. to 5 p.m. Monday through Friday and 1 to 5 p.m. Saturday and Sunday; winter hours vary, call ahead.

The graves of Soapy Smith and Frank Reid are the big attractions at the **Gold Rush Cemetery,** but don't miss the short walk up to crashing Reid Falls. The closely spaced dates on many of the cemetery's markers attest to the epidemics that swept through stampeders living in squalid conditions. The cemetery is 1½ miles from town, up State Street.

Nightlife

This tourist attraction is history itself: The *Days of '98 Show* has been staged every year since 1927 in the Fraternal Order of Eagles Hall No. 25, at Sixth Avenue and Broadway (☎ 907-983-2545). Imported actors from all over the United States perform three shows a day that include singing, cancan dancing, the story of the shooting of Soapy Smith, and a Robert Service reading. (Service arrived in the area in the early 1900s and witnessed the latter days of the gold rush era in his poetry.) Matinees are $14 and evening shows are $16. Children 15 and under are half price.

At the **Red Onion Saloon,** at Second Avenue and Broadway (☎ 907-983-2222), cruise-ship musicians often stretch out and jam on jazz tunes on their nights off. The place was a brothel originally and a mock madam offers tours. It's closed in winter.

Fast Facts: Skagway

Bank
Wells Fargo, at Broadway and Sixth Avenue, has an ATM.

Emergencies
Dial ☎ 911.

Hospital
The **Skagway Medical Clinic,** staffed by a physician's assistant, can be reached at ☎ 907-983-2255 during business hours, or ☎ 907-983-2418 after hours.

Information
Contact the **Skagway Convention and Visitors Bureau Center,** 245 Broadway (P.O. Box 1029), Skagway, AK 99840 (☎ 907-983-2854; Fax: 907-983-3854; Internet: www.skagway.org). The Web site contains

links to hotels, restaurants, and activities, or they'll send you the information on paper (order at ☎ 888-762-1898).

Internet Access
Alaska Cruiseship Services is at Third Avenue and Broadway (☎ 907-983-3398).

Police
For nonemergency business, call ☎ 907-983-2232.

Post Office
On Broadway between Sixth and Seventh avenues.

Taxes
Sales tax is 4%. The **bed tax** totals 8%.

Chapter 22

Sitka

Sitka has a combination of qualities you can't find anywhere else. It's the center of Russian–American history, with more to look at from that time than any other town. It's also the site of one of Native America's great battles: once a real battle of war against the Russians, and more recently, a successful on-going one — to keep Tlingit culture alive and accessible. And it's a town of irresistible charm in a wonderful natural setting — an island home of complex and kaleidoscopic beauty on waters rich with life. Altogether, Sitka is the best of Alaska. It's really worth taking the extra trouble just to get there.

Besides the fascinating historic and cultural places to visit, which can easily fill a day or two, make a point of getting outdoors in Sitka. The waters here are full of otters, whales, seabirds, and fish, and the town has some fine hiking trails.

Getting There

Sitka is on the west side of Baranof Island, accessible only by air or water. To get downtown from the airport or ferry dock, **Sitka Tours** charges $5 one-way, $7 round-trip on a bus. A ride with **Sitka Cab** (☎ 907-747-5001) is about $15.

By ferry

The ferries of the **Alaska Marine Highway System** (☎ 800-642-0066; Internet: www.alaska.gov/ferry) serve Sitka with large and smaller

Discovering Sitka's heritage

Here's the history you need to know to make sense of what you'll see on your visit to Sitka.

Two crucial historical events happened in Sitka: The Russians took over Southeast Alaska from the Native Tlingit population, and the Americans took over all of Alaska from the Russians. In 1799, the Russians had already conquered the coastal people west of here and were moving eastward in search of new sea otter hunting grounds (they sold the pelts in China for fabulous sums) when they set up a settlement near present-day Sitka. The Tlingit were a fierce and powerful people and they didn't accept the invasion: They massacred the Russian fort in 1802. In 1804, the Russians counterattacked. The battle lasted six days, but finally the Tlingit withdrew. That battlefield remains the heart of the Sitka National Historical Park, a peaceful and moving place under huge trees and totem poles.

After the battle, Sitka became the capital of Russian America, which at one time stretched all the way to California, and the best buildings from that era remain. But with bureaucratic management, the colony became a money loser, and in 1867, the Russian czar sold his claim to Alaska to the United States for $7 million, or 2 cents an acre. Even at that price, most Americans thought they'd been taken. When the Russian flag came down over Sitka's Castle Hill and the American flag went up, the United States didn't even bother to give the new territory a government. When gold discoveries provided Alaska with a white population, the capital moved to the gold town of Juneau.

vessels that must pass through the narrow and scenic Peril Straits. The fare from either Juneau (nine hours away) or Petersburg (ten hours) is $30. The ferry dock (☎ **907-747-3300**) is 7 miles out of town.

By air

Alaska Airlines (☎ **800-252-7522** or 907-966-2422 locally; Internet: www.alaskaair.com) links Sitka daily to Juneau and Ketchikan with flights that then continue nonstop to Seattle and Anchorage. The airport is on an island near downtown but is too far to walk.

Getting around Sitka

Sitka actually is on an island, so you can't drive far (see the nearby "Sitka" map). The **ferry terminal** is 7 miles out **Halibut Point Road.** The town faces Sitka Sound. Across Sitka Channel is **Japonski Island** and the **airport.**

Sitka

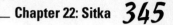

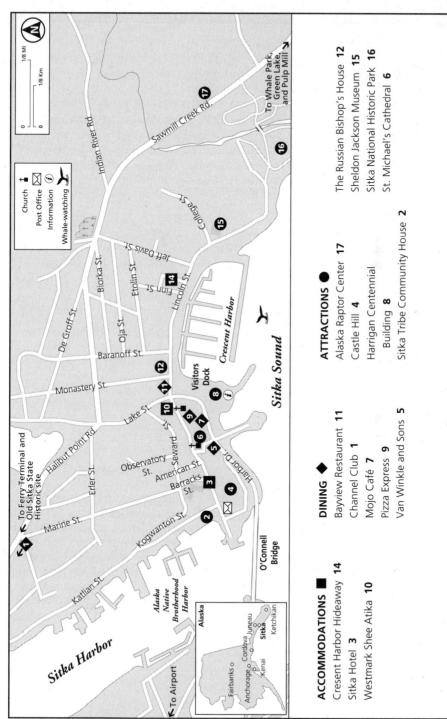

ACCOMMODATIONS ■

Cresent Harbor Hideaway **14**
Sitka Hotel **3**
Westmark Shee Atika **10**

DINING ◆

Bayview Restaurant **11**
Channel Club **1**
Mojo Café **7**
Pizza Express **9**
Van Winkle and Sons **5**

ATTRACTIONS ●

Alaska Raptor Center **17**
Castle Hill **4**
Harrigan Centennial
 Building **8**
Sitka Tribe Community House **2**

The Russian Bishop's House **12**
Sheldon Jackson Museum **15**
Sitka National Historic Park **16**
St. Michael's Cathedral **6**

You can easily manage Sitka on foot and with a visitor shuttle or taxi unless you choose lodging or take hikes out Halibut Point Road. All the accommodations listed in this chapter are within walking distance to the sites.

By bus

The Visitor Transit Bus operated by **Sitka Tribal Tours** at 200 Katlian St. (☎ **888-270-8687** or 907-747-7290; Internet: www.sitkatribal.com) makes a continuous circuit of the sites May through September, Monday to Friday, 12:30 to 4:30 p.m., with added morning hours when cruise ships are in. The fare is $7 all day, $3 one-way, and kids ride free. Guided town tours of various lengths also are offered.

By car

If you decide to rent a car for better access to trails or lodgings on Halibut Point Road, you can pick one up at the airport from **Avis** (☎ **800-331-1212** or 907-966-2404; Internet: www.avis.com) or **Allstar** (☎ **800-722-6927** or 907-966-2552; Internet: www.ptialaska. net/~rfahey).

Where to Stay

The **Sitka Convention and Visitors Bureau** (☎ **907-747-5940;** Internet: www.sitka.org) has links to many B&Bs on its Web site and can send you a printed list if you like.

Crescent Harbor Hideaway
$$–$$$ **Downtown**

This stately 1897 house, one of Sitka's oldest, stands across a quiet street from Crescent Harbor and the lovely park at the harbor's edge, with a glassed-in porch to watch the world go by. One unit is a large, one-bedroom apartment with a full kitchen and a private patio and phone line; it's the best unit I've seen in Sitka. The other nestles adorably under the eaves. The style is simple elegance, with antiques and colonial repro-ductions, Berber carpet, and attractive bathrooms. Everything is clean and fresh. Hostess Susan Stanford, an artist, enjoys her guests. Common areas are shared with an Australian shepherd named Lacy. Smoking is not permitted, even outside.

709 Lincoln St., Sitka, AK 99835. ☎ and Fax: 907-747-4900. Internet: www.
ptialaska.net/~bareis/B&B.htm. *Rack rates: High season $110–$145
double, low season $85–$115 double; extra person $25. Rates include continental
breakfast. No credit cards.*

Sitka Hotel
$ Downtown

This is a good, family-owned budget hotel. Each year, the proprietors take
on another improvement project in the 1939 building. Small rooms never
will be luxurious, and some have problems, such as poor heat regulation,
but the owners have put together many comfortable, quirky units and
keep them clean and well maintained. The location is prime, right across
from the Russian parade grounds. The rooms without a private bath are
about four to a bathroom, and the facilities are in good shape. **Victoria's
Restaurant,** with about a dozen tables in the storefront downstairs, tries,
like the hotel, for a high Victorian feel, but it's more a friendly small-town
diner, with hearty breakfasts and lunches in winter and an inexpensive
fine-dining dinner menu added in summer.

118 Lincoln St., Sitka, AK 99835. ☎ 907-747-3288. Fax: 907-747-8499. Internet: www.
sitkahotel.com. *Rack rates: $60 double with shared bathroom, $80 double with
private bathroom; extra person $7. AE, MC, V.*

Westmark Shee Atika
$$$ Downtown

The community's main upscale hotel, overlooking Crescent Harbor in the
heart of the historic district, falls short mostly because of the structure
itself, a brown, five-story wooden building with plywood siding, hanging
ceilings in the halls, and small rooms. The furniture, carpets, TVs, and
other amenities are up to date and the rooms well kept, but blah browns
and cramped spaces take away from the effect. The restaurant, lounge
(a local hangout), and most rooms have very good waterfront views;
harborside rooms are $10 more. The **Raven Dining Room** is everything
you'd expect from an upscale hotel cafe with a long menu of seafood and
beef in the evening.

*330 Seward St., Sitka, AK 99835-7523. ☎ 800-544-0970 for reservations or 907-747-
6241. Fax: 907-747-5486. Internet:* www.westmarkhotels.com. *Rack rates: High
season $149–$159 double, low season $139–$149 double; extra person older than 13
$15. AE, DC, DISC, MC, V.*

Where to Dine

The top restaurants

Bayview Restaurant

$–$$$$ Downtown   Burgers/Pasta/Seafood

The view of the boat harbor and good food make this small second-story restaurant popular year-round, although it's sometimes noisy and a bit cramped. Everything I've tried from the extensive menu has been well prepared and quickly served. The clam chowder sings, and people come back for the halibut and burgers. Some lunch items are priced a little high. My lunch of halibut fish and chips was tasty and done just right, but the portion and plate were quite small for $10. A BLT is $8. Dinner prices are more competitive. The wine list has a nice selection and reasonable prices. It's a great spot for breakfast.

407 Lincoln St. ☎ **907-747-5440.** *Main courses: $5.50–$27. AE, DISC, MC, V. Open: High season Mon–Sat 5 a.m.–10 p.m., Sun 5 a.m.–3 p.m.; winter, Mon–Thurs 7 a.m.–8 p.m., Fri–Sat 7 a.m.–9 p.m., Sun 7 a.m.–3 p.m.*

Channel Club

$$–$$$$$ Halibut Point Road   Steak/Seafood

The steaks have always been great here, and the salad bar, which comes with every meal, is legendary. It's really an appetizer bar, and the crab alone is worth the trip. The restaurant is in one big room, with a swordfish on one wall and the menu on another, and the dress code seems to be T-shirts and baseball caps. The service is as casual as in the greasiest greasy-spoon diner. That's all part of the manly club thing, and it works. The restaurant is several miles out Halibut Point Road, the only establishment I include that's outside of walking distance from the historic sites, because it offers a courtesy van to come get you and take you home at the end of the evening. They have a full bar.

2906 Halibut Point Rd. ☎ **907-747-9916.** *Reservations recommended. Main courses: $12–$41.50. AE, DC, MC, V. Open: Sun–Thurs 5–10 p.m., Fri–Sat 5–11 p.m.*

Runner-up restaurants

Mojo Café

$ Downtown   Coffee House   This spot is a cool hangout for a cold breakfast or for a lunch of soup, sandwiches, or specials. *203 Lincoln St.* ☎ **907-747-0667.** *All items under $10. Open: Daily 6:30 a.m.–2:00 p.m.*

Pizza Express

$–$$ **Downtown Mexican/Pizza** Come here for a filling, inexpensive meal in a light, pleasant dining room. Pizza Express also delivers good pizza. *236 Lincoln St., Ste. 106.* ☎ *907-966-2428. Main courses: $6–$13. MC, V. Open: Mon–Sat 11 a.m.–10 p.m., Sun noon to 10 p.m.; closes at 9 p.m. in winter.*

Van Winkle and Sons

$$–$$$ **Downtown Seafood/Pasta/Pizza** This is a good small-town family restaurant with a fine water view and booths. *205 Harbor Dr.* ☎ *907-747-7652. Reservations recommended. Lunch items: $6–$10.25; dinner main courses: $11–$24. AE, MC, V. Open: High season, Mon–Fri 11:30 a.m.–2:00 p.m., daily 5:00–9:30 p.m.; low season, Mon–Fri 11:30 a.m.–2:00 p.m., daily 5:00–8:30 p.m.*

Exploring Sitka

One full day is enough to see the highlights of Sitka's attractions, although you can spend an extra day here profitably. Getting the help of a visitor shuttle or guided tour is covered in the earlier "Getting around Sitka" section.

Exploring the top attractions

I've arranged these top attractions, starting with the Sitka National Historical Park, according to where you need to go first to get the context for the rest of what you're going to see. Following that, the attractions are arranged the way you encounter them geographically, starting on foot from the historical park.

Sitka National Historical Park

The park, designated in 1910, preserves the site of the 1804 Battle of Sitka, where Alaska's Russian invaders defeated the Tlingit and won control of the area (see the "Discovering Sitka's heritage" sidebar in this chapter). The park contains an extraordinary collection of early totem poles, with reproductions and contemporary originals displayed outside and ancient poles housed indoors in a new, 30-foot-high hall. The entire visitor center recently was remodeled, and curators did a great job with explanatory exhibits and workshops at which artisans from the Southeast Alaska Indian Cultural Center create traditional crafts of metal, wood, beads, textiles, and woven grass. Be sure to walk through the totem park and battle site. A free 12-minute video provides a good historical overview.

106 Metlakatla St. ☎ *907-747-6281. Internet:* www.nps.gov/sitk. *Visitor center open: Summer daily 8 a.m.–5 p.m.; winter, Mon–Fri 8 a.m.–5 p.m. Park open: Summer daily 6 a.m.–10 p.m., winter daily 7 a.m.–8 p.m. Admission: free.*

Sheldon Jackson Museum

Sheldon Jackson, a Presbyterian missionary with powerful friends in Washington, D.C., was Alaska's first General Agent for Education, a paternal guardian of the welfare, schooling, and spiritual lives of Alaska's Natives. On the side, he gathered an omnivorous collection of some 5,000 objects of Native art and culture from 1888 to 1898. That collection, the best in Alaska, has been displayed for more than a century in a concrete building on the college campus that bears Jackson's name. Despite the age of many of the pieces, they appear new, as if just made. Don't miss Katlian's raven-shaped helmet, which was worn by the Kiksadi clan's war leader in the Battle of Sitka in 1804. It's that rare piece of great history that's also great art. Native artists demonstrate their skills on summer days, and the gift shop offers almost exclusively authentic Native arts and crafts, with prices to match.

104 College Dr. ☎ 907-747-8981. Internet: www.museums.state.ak.us. *Open: Mid-May to mid-Sept, daily 9 a.m.–5 p.m.; mid-Sept to mid-May, Tues–Sat 10 a.m.– 4 p.m. Admission: $4 adults, free for ages 18 and younger.*

The Russian Bishop's House

In 1842, the Russian America Company retained Finnish shipbuilders to construct this extraordinary house for Bishop Innocent Veniaminov as a residence, school, and chapel. It survived many years of neglect in part because its huge beams fit together like those of a ship. Now beautifully restored, the building is the best of only four surviving from all of Russian America (one is in Kodiak, one in California, and one at 206 Lincoln Street in Sitka, occupied by Log Cache Gifts). The house is Alaska's most interesting historic site. Downstairs is a self-guided museum; upstairs, the bishop's quarters are furnished with original and period pieces. It's an extraordinary window into an alternate stream of American history, from a time before the founding of Seattle or San Francisco when Sitka was the most important city on North America's Pacific Coast.

Lincoln and Monastery streets. No phone; call Sitka National Historical Park Visitor Center (☎ 907-747-6281). Open: Summer daily 9 a.m.–5 p.m.; by appointment in winter. Admission: $3 per person or $10 per family.

St. Michael's Cathedral

The first Orthodox cathedral in the New World stands grandly in the middle of Sitka's principal street, where it was completed in 1848. The cathedral contains several miraculous icons, some dating from the 17th century. The original building burned down in a 1966 fire that started elsewhere and took much of Sitka's downtown, but almost all the contents were saved by a human chain in the 30 minutes before the building was destroyed. Orthodox Christians across the United States raised the money to rebuild the cathedral exactly as it had been, using a Russian architect who interpreted the original plans. It was completed in 1976.

A knowledgeable guide is on hand to answer questions or give talks when large groups congregate. Sunday services are sung in English, Slavonic, Tlingit, Aleut, and Yupik.

Lincoln and Cathedral streets. ☎ *907-747-8120. Open: Summer Mon–Fri 9 a.m.– 4 p.m., Sat–Sun varies. Call for winter hours. Donation requested: $2.*

Getting outdoors in Sitka

No wonder the Russians and the Tlingit fought for this place: It's absolutely gorgeous and full of wildlife and fish. See the historic sites, but also take the time to see the rich environment that lured the historic figures here — an environment that's still pretty much the way it was in those long-ago days.

Fishing

Many charter boats are available for salmon or halibut. The Sitka Convention and Visitors Bureau (☎ **907-747-5940;** Internet: www. sitka.org) keeps a detailed charter boat list, including rates, that goes on for pages. **Alaska Adventures Unlimited** (☎ **907-747-5576;** E-mail: akfish@gci.net) is a booking agent handling more than half the charter boats in the harbor.

Hiking

Sitka is a great hiking area. A dozen U.S. Forest Service hiking trails are accessible from the roads around town. A handy map, the *Outdoor Recreation Guide,* shows all the trails, including easy walks from downtown; pick up a copy from the town visitor center in the **Harrigan Centennial Hall** at 330 Harbor Dr., next to the Crescent Boat Harbor (☎ **907-747-3225**). Here are some favorites:

- ✔ **Indian River Trail:** From downtown, this is a 4.1-mile walk (one-way) through the rain forest, rising gradually up the river valley to a small waterfall. Take Indian River Road off Sawmill Creek Road just east of downtown.

- ✔ **Gavan Hill–Harbor Mountain Trail:** A steeper mountain-climbing trail to alpine terrain and great views. The trailhead is near the end of Baranof Street, which starts near the Russian Bishop's House. It gains 2,500 feet over 3 miles to the peak of Gavan Hill and then continues another 3 miles along a ridge to meet Harbor Mountain Road.

- ✔ **Starrigavan Recreation Area trails:** The recreation area is at the north end of Halibut Point Road, near the ferry dock, 7½ miles from downtown. On the right, the **Estuary Life Trail** and **Forest Muskeg Trail** total about a mile. Exquisitely developed and accessible to anyone, they circle a grassy estuary rich with birds and fish. The well-built **Mosquito Cove Trail** starts from the far end of the campground loop on the left, loops 1¼ miles along the shore to the secluded gravel beach of the cove, and returns over boardwalk steps through the old-growth forest.

Marine wildlife tours

Tour boats visit **St. Lazaria Island,** a bird rookery where you can expect to see puffins, murres, rhinoceros auklets, and other pelagic birds. Volcanic rock drops straight down into deep water, so even big boats pilot in close, but in rough weather even they won't go to this exposed location of the island. Even when you can't get to the island, you still have plenty to look at. Humpback whales show up in large groups in fall and often are seen by the half dozen in summer, and encounters with endearing sea otters are a near certainty.

The largest tour boat operation is the **Sitka Wildlife Quest,** operated by Allen Marine Tours (☎ **888-747-8101** or 907-747-8100; Internet: www.allenmarinetours.com), with well-trained naturalists to explain the wildlife. The two-hour cruise costs $49 adults, $30 children ages 3–12, and leaves from the Crescent Harbor Visitors Dock Tuesday and Thursday at 6 p.m. and Saturday and Sunday at 9 a.m. late May through August. Buy tickets onboard.

Sea Life Discovery Tours (☎ **877-966-2301** or 907-966-2301; Internet: www.sealifediscoverytours.com) offers an opportunity to see the rich underwater life in Sitka Sound from an extraordinary boat that has big windows four feet below the waterline; it's really cool. They charge $65 for a 90-minute tour; call for times.

Sea kayaking

Sitka's protected waters and intricate shorelines are perfect for sea kayaking. You're almost sure to come upon seals, sea otters, sea lions, and eagles, and you may see whales. Various companies offer guided trips. **Sitka Sound Ocean Adventures** (☎ **907-747-6375**; Internet: www.ssoceanadventures.com) offers small-group, two-hour trips that cost $50 per person, in addition to trips of up to three days. **Baidarka Boats** (☎ **907-747-8996**; Internet: www.kayaksite.com) offers trips of three hours or more, with time for beachcombing, tide pooling, and snacks. Competitive rates depend on the size of your group.

Tide pooling and shore walks

Halibut Point State Recreation Area, 4.4 miles north of town on Halibut Point Road, is a great place for a picnic, shore ramble, and tide pooling. The Mosquito Cove Trail (see "Hiking," earlier in this chapter) is also promising. Check a tide book to find out about the best low tides. They're available all over town. The best time to go is when the lowest tide is expected, arriving on the shore an hour before the low ebb. To identify the little creatures you'll see, buy a plastic-covered field guide at the National Park Service visitor center at the historical park.

What about Ketchikan?

When arriving by boat at the south end of the Southeast Alaska Panhandle, the first place you land is Ketchikan, Alaska's fourth largest city. Because of the location, Ketchikan is usually first in every Alaska guidebook. But I've neglected to include it at all here. It isn't an oversight. Ketchikan is a good town to visit. You'll find plenty to do there, with totem-pole viewing and fishing topping the list. But you can do those same activities and more in Sitka, and without struggling through the overwhelming cruise-ship crowds that gush out upon Ketchikan every summer morning. (Sitka gets cruise ships, too, but they can't dock; instead, they carry passengers ashore in launches. The impact on the town seems much less.)

My philosophy in this book is to send you to the best and forget the rest, and Sitka, unquestionably, is richer in history and wildlife and is Ketchikan's equal in totem poles and Tlingit heritage. If you still want to go to Ketchikan, get a copy of my more comprehensive book, *Frommer's Alaska* (Wiley, Inc.) or contact the **Ketchikan Visitors Bureau**, 131 Front St., Ketchikan, AK 99901 (☎ **800-770-3300** or 907-225-6166; Fax: 907-225-4250; Internet: www.visit-ketchikan.com).

More cool things to see and do

Sitka offers so much for so many, much of it inspired by its Native history and its proximity to wildlife habitat.

✔ **Attend a traditional Native dance performance.** The Sitka Tribe performs at the community house, 200 Katlian St. (☎ **888-270-8687** or 907-747-7290; Internet: www.sitkatribal.com), on the north side of the downtown parade ground. Performances last 30 minutes, including three dances and a story. It's entirely traditional and put on by members of the tribe. You can also sign up for tours and activities in the lobby. Admission is $6 adults, $3 children; call for times.

✔ **See eagles up close.** The nonprofit **Alaska Raptor Center**, 1101 Sawmill Creek Blvd. (☎ **907-747-8662**; Internet: www.alaskaraptor.org), takes in injured birds of prey (mainly bald eagles, but also owls, hawks, and other species) for veterinary treatment and release or, if too badly injured, for placement in a zoo or to join the collection of 25 that live on-site. Visitors get to see the impressive birds up close and learn about them from experts. The center is open in summer Sunday to Friday 8 a.m. to 4 p.m.; open in winter by appointment. Admission is $10 adults, $5 ages 12 and younger.

Shopping

Most of Sitka's best shops and galleries are on Lincoln and Harbor streets. Several are across the street from St. Michael's Cathedral, on the uphill side.

- ✔ **Impressions,** at 239 Lincoln St. (☎ **907-747-5502**), carries prints by many of Alaska's best contemporary artists.

- ✔ **Fairweather Prints,** at 209 Lincoln St. (☎ **907-747-8677**), has a fun, youthful feel; it is large and has a diverse selection, such as wearable art (including T-shirts), watercolors, prints, ceramics, and cute, inexpensive crafts.

- ✔ Continue west on Lincoln to **Old Harbor Books,** at 201 Lincoln St. (☎ **907-747-8808**), a good browsing store with an excellent selection of Alaska books. **The Backdoor** espresso shop inside is a great place for a break from your shopping labors.

- ✔ In the other direction, near the boat harbor, the **Sitka Rose Gallery** occupies a Victorian house at 419 Lincoln St. (☎ **888-236-1536** or 907-747-3030; Internet: www.sitkarosegallery.com), featuring higher-end work, mostly local: sculpture, original paintings, engraving, and jewelry.

- ✔ The **Sheldon Jackson Museum Gift Shop,** 104 College Dr. (☎ **907-747-6233**), is an excellent place to buy Alaska Native arts and crafts with assurance of their authenticity.

Fast Facts: Sitka

ATMs

Cash machines are at grocery stores and at banks at 300 and 318 Lincoln St.

Emergencies

Dial ☎ **911.**

Hospital

Sitka Community (☎ 907-747-3241) is at 209 Moller Dr.

Information

Get visitor information in advance of your trip from the **Sitka Convention and Visitors Bureau,** at P.O. Box 1226, Sitka, AK 99835 (☎ 907-747-5940; Fax: 907-747-3739). They maintain a very useful Web site at www.sitka.org.

Internet Access

Try **Highliner Coffee,** on Lake Street near Seward Street (☎ 907-747-4924), or at the downtown post office.

Police

Call ☎ 907-747-3245 for nonemergency business.

Post Office

At 338 Lincoln St.; it is open Saturday.

Taxes

Sales tax is 5%. The tax on **rooms** totals 11%.

Part VI

The End of the Road and Beyond: Bush Alaska

The 5th Wave   By Rich Tennant

"Martin, is this safe?"

In this part . . .

While reading adventure tales as children, some people develop an irresistible drive to go to Alaska. That drive has nothing to do with easy-to-reach towns or national parks on roads. They're looking for the Arctic, for remote bear country, for extreme places completely unlike anything they've experienced before. In short, they want to go to the bush. In this part, I deal with some of the best bush destinations: the ones with something to see and reasonable services to get you there and keep you comfortable. I cover the towns of the Arctic and the land of huge brown bears. Buckle your seat belts.

Chapter 23

The Arctic

● ●

In This Chapter

▶ Deciding whether you really want to go to the Arctic

▶ Picking an Arctic destination

▶ Taking in the Eskimo culture of Barrow

▶ Joining in the gold rush fun of Nome

● ●

*P*icturing the Arctic in your imagination is easy: in summer, flat green tundra without trees meeting a green ocean; in winter, flat white snow and ocean melding together into one. But you can't imagine the real beauty of the place until you go there. Under diffuse gray light, the land's watercolor tints and hues melt together with its stark shapes and shades. Under the beams of the low midnight sun, rich and yellow, the snow and sky are royal blue. A sense of incredible immensity always permeates; it's a feeling that can make you feel overwhelmingly tiny and vulnerable but also entirely free for the first time. The Arctic is a remote, unforgiving hell of harsh weather, but it's also a paradise.

All flowery writing aside, traveling to the Arctic definitely isn't for everyone. You can't go there cheaply. And, after you're there, you won't find much to do. The few communities that are in the Arctic are also tiny. Outdoor activities are rugged and cold. The towns have developed activities for visitors, but they're mostly designed for visitors on escorted tour packages and can be scripted and even dreary. If seeing the Arctic isn't a particular interest, you can find better ways to spend your time and money on an Alaskan trip.

If, on the other hand, you feel the drive to go way up north, fulfill your dream now. Just make sure to allow enough time for getting away from the tour bus so that you can have one of those strange, solitary moments that seem to happen only at the top of the world.

In this chapter, I cover in detail the two best towns to visit in the Arctic — Barrow and Nome — because each offers a different flavor to your visit. Although flying is the only way to get to Barrow and Nome, you can also reach the Arctic by driving the Dalton Highway north from Fairbanks. That very ambitious option is covered in Chapter 18.

Discovering the Arctic and Its Major Attractions

Because Barrow and Nome offer different activities that appeal to different interests, I describe the highlights of each in this section.

Barrow

This is the essential Arctic community. It's the farthest north of any mainland town in North America, lying on a point in the Arctic Ocean around which bowhead whales migrate. The Inupiat Eskimos here hunt the whales for their sustenance in a 1,000-year-old tradition. The town isn't much to look at: Modest plywood houses on pilings sit on flat green tundra along gravel roads. But it is a unique and potentially interesting place to visit, with some of the following highlights:

✔ The Inupiat Heritage Center, a living museum of Eskimo culture

✔ Bird-watching and polar bear-viewing tours

✔ Guided tour to discover more about the unusual town

Nome

Nome is a gold rush town, not a Native community like Barrow, and it isn't technically Arctic, lying below the Arctic Circle (although it looks like the Arctic). But in many ways, Nome is a better place for an independent traveler to visit, because you can do more on your own, including some of the following:

✔ Exploring the network of roads around Nome on your own or with a guide to see abundant wildlife

✔ Witnessing a gold rush town that still rocks, loaded with some of the best stories anywhere in Alaska

Beware the indoor pollution

Bush Alaska lags behind the rest of the country in many ways, few more startling than the prevalence of smoking in these remote little towns. It seems as if everyone smokes everywhere. Escape can be impossible. Restaurants usually are smoky, and lower-cost hotel rooms tend to smell smoky. If avoiding smoking is a high priority, stick to the most tourist-oriented (and most expensive) establishments.

> ✔ Watching the finish of the Iditarod Trail Sled Dog Race, Alaska's
> biggest annual sporting event

Reaching the Top of the World: Barrow

Barrow is an ancient Inupiat Native community, founded and still sustained by its access at this farthest north point to the migrating bowhead whale, which Eskimos hunt from small, open boats. It's also a modern town, rich in North Slope oil revenues, a center of scientific research about the Arctic, and home to Alaska's largest corporation, the Native-owned Arctic Slope Regional Corporation. If these seem like contradictions, they are, but they're like the ones that describe each person that you meet here: The chairman and the CEO of the corporation are also two of the region's most respected whalers. (Their hunt is not a threat to the bowhead whales' population, which is strong and growing.)

The town's Inupiat Heritage Center shows off this cultural mix. There you can view natural and cultural exhibits, see Inupiat dance, and meet Native people selling their crafts. The bus tour that most visitors take also shows off some of the town's interesting points, although it can't be described as a cultural immersion. You can also take a bird-watching tour and may be able to go out and see polar bears.

Beyond those formal activities, however, you won't find much else to do in Barrow. The town has only one main store and no trails to hike — the tundra tends to be swampy — yet it is possible to walk on the gravel beaches. Most visitors come up just for the day on the Alaska Airline Vacations–escorted package tour from Anchorage or Fairbanks, which is a good deal and gives you the highlights. If you want time on your own, you can spend the night and go back the next day. Few people want to spend more time here than that.

Getting there

The only way to get to Barrow is via **Alaska Airlines** (☎ 800-252-7522; Internet: www.alaskaair.com), which flies daily from Anchorage and Fairbanks, and offers one-day and overnight tour packages. The packages are good deals, competitive with stand-alone round-trip tickets from Anchorage, which range from $350 to $700. Book them through **Alaska Airlines Vacations** (☎ 800-468-2248). I explain more about that in "Exploring Barrow," later in this chapter.

Getting around

The Alaska Airlines Vacations package tours provide all your transportation. Otherwise, the easiest way to get around Barrow is in a taxicab, with several competing companies all charging the same flat rates ($5 per trip in town, plus $1 for each additional passenger). Try **Arcticab** (☎ 907-852-2227).

Where to stay

I list the best place to stay and the least expensive place to stay below. If you come on the Alaska Airlines Vacation package, you'll stay at the **Top of the World Hotel** (☎ 907-852-3900; Internet: www.topofthe worldhotel.com), which is also modern and comfortable.

Barrow Airport Inn

$$ Barrow

This is the most economical place to stay in Barrow. The rooms are worn and out of date but clean and perfectly comfortable, and you can cook in them: Nine units have full kitchens for the same price.

1815 Momegana St. (P.O. Box 933), Barrow, AK 99723. ☎ 907-852-2525. Fax: 907-852-2528. Rack rate: $115 double. Rates include continental breakfast. MC, V.

King Eider Inn

$$$$ Barrow

The best rooms in town are found in this like-new building near the airport. They're crisp and airy and so well kept up that it's as if no one has stayed there before. It probably helps that shoes are not allowed in the hotel — you have to take them off at the front door. Nor is smoking permitted, creating a rare nonsmokers' oasis in Barrow. The lobby is comfortable, with a stone fireplace. Bathrooms have showers only, not tubs.

1752 Ahkovak St. (P.O. Box 1283), Barrow, AK 99723. ☎ 907-852-4700. Fax: 907-852-2025. Internet: www.kingeider.net. Rack rates: Summer $195 double, winter $175 double; extra person $25. AE, MC, V.

Where to dine

On the Alaska Airlines Vacations package, you're taken to lunch at **Pepe's North of the Border** at 1204 Agvik St. (☎ 907-852-8200). It's an American-style Mexican restaurant of a kind that was popular two decades ago elsewhere.

Note: The sale of alcohol is illegal in Barrow, so you cannot buy a glass of wine or beer with your meal in any of the restaurants.

Arctic Pizza

$$–$$$ **Barrow**   **Steak/Seafood/Pizza**

The best fine dining in town is here (not too tough a competition), and you can obtain pizza and burgers, which are available everywhere. The menu is very diverse, with an Italian and Mexican section and steak and seafood; you can order almost anything. I've found everything surprisingly good, if not memorable. The same menu is served in the elegant upstairs dining room, which has a great view over ancient village ruins to the ocean, and in the downstairs dining room, where the TV is on and children and teens are allowed.

125 Apayauq St. ☎ 907-852-4222. Dinner main courses: $6.50–$19.50. MC, V. Open: Daily 11:30 a.m.–11:30 p.m.

Brower's Restaurant

$$–$$$ **Browerville**   **Diner/Down home**

The restaurant occupies an important historic structure, the whaling station that later became a store that was owned by Charles Brower, a Yankee whaler who became father of one of the community's largest and most successful Inupiaq families. The restaurant has booths with big windows right on the beach. Service is fast and respectful, and the diner food solid and tasty (although I'd steer clear of some of the fancier selections).

Off Hopson Street, at the west end of Browerville. ☎ 907-852-5800. Dinner main courses: $7.50–$26. MC, V. Open: Daily 11 a.m. to midnight.

Exploring Barrow

Barrow offers so few options in the pure attraction category that it's one of the few places where an escorted tour is the most logical offering. But you can also take in the Inupiat Heritage Center.

Basic Barrow: The Escorted Tour

Even if you hate package escorted tours, as I do, it makes all kinds of sense in Barrow. First, the package sold by Alaska Airlines saves money just about any way you cut it. The airline uses the program to fill seats that otherwise would be empty, so they sell the package cheap. Beyond the low cost, however, is the fact that Barrow is hard to figure out without a guide: It has no downtown, no shops, and few obviously public places. When you take the tour, you'll get a good six-hour orientation and some highlights. Then you can stay overnight to take your own measure of the place.

The tour drives around town, out the short roads beyond town, and visits the Inupiat Heritage Center, described in the next section, where visitors witness dancing and a blanket toss and can buy crafts direct from artists.

(To attend the dance program separate from the tour costs $15.) The day-trip tour is $399 from Anchorage; or for $450 per person, double occupancy, you can spend one night in Barrow at the Top of the World Hotel, giving you time on your own without the tour group; both prices include air fare. If you buy the tour separately, it's $65. A winter tour is also available for seeing the Aurora ($85 separately), but it does not include the cultural elements. The local business that operates the tour for Alaska Airlines Vacations is called **Tundra Tours** (☎ **800-882-8478** or 907-852-3900; Internet: www.tundratours.com).

Alaska Airlines Vacations. ☎ *800-468-2248. Internet:* www.alaskaair.com.

The Inupiat Heritage Center

This is the town's only real freestanding attraction. Completed in 1999, it is part museum, part gathering center, and part venue for living culture. Inside is a workshop for craftspeople and a performance space for storytellers and dancers. In the museum area, displays of Inupiat artifacts change regularly, while a permanent exhibit covers Eskimo whaling and the influence that Yankee whaling has had on it. The center is also the site of daily dancing, the blanket toss, and craft fairs put on for visitors on the Alaska Airlines Vacations package tour; independent travelers can view the dancing for $15.

Ahkovak and C streets. ☎ *907-852-5494. Open: May 15–Sept 15, Mon–Fri 8:30 a.m.–5:00 p.m.; winter, ask about admittance during business hours. Admission: $5 adults, $2 ages 6–17, free 5 or younger or older than 55.*

Getting outdoors in Barrow

Barrow is the only place in the United States with commercial **polar bear-viewing tours.** The bears are always around when the ice is close to shore (usually from October through June); they're dangerous, and people take real care to avoid them. Barrow and other North Slope communities have minimized contact by setting up sites outside of the villages to dispose of gut piles and other hunting waste. It's a way of bribing the bears to leave the town alone. In Barrow, heavy equipment hauls the leftovers from fall whale-butchering — bones and a few nonedible organs — out to the very end of the point. Recent controversy about bears coming into town caused the authorities to cancel bear-viewing at the point, but I can't believe that the service won't begin again. Check with one of the hotels listed above, or the mayor's office (see the "Fast Facts: Barrow" section, next). The company that operated in the past was called **Alaskan Arctic Adventures** (☎ **907-852-3800**). A business planning to offer bear-viewing and bird-watching without going to the point (thus avoiding the controversy) is **Arctic Photo Safaris** (☎ 907-852-2152).

Fast Facts: Barrow

Alcohol Legality

The sale of alcohol is illegal in stores or restaurants in Barrow, and importation for personal use in your luggage is limited and controlled by a permit system. If it's an issue, call ahead to the Barrow Alcohol Delivery Site (☎ 907-852-2337) or the Office of the Mayor (☎ 907-852-5211). Bootlegging is a serious crime. My advice: abstain while in Barrow.

ATMs

Wells Fargo at 1078 Kiogak St. has an ATM.

Emergencies

Dial ☎ **911.**

Hospital

Samuel Simmonds Memorial Hospital is at 1296 Agvik St. (☎ 907-852-4611).

Information

To obtain advance visitor information, contact the City of Barrow, Office of the Mayor, P.O. Box 629, Barrow, AK 99723 (☎ 907-852-5211; Fax: 907-852-5871; E-mail: barrow mayor@nuvuk.com); or call one of the hotels listed earlier in this chapter.

Internet Access

Free at the Tuzzy Library (☎ 907-852-1720) at the Inupiat Heritage Center.

Police

Contact the borough **Department of Public Safety** at 1068 Kiogak St. (☎ 907-852-6111).

Taxes

Barrow has no sales or bed tax.

Racing to Nome — by Dog Sled, Naturally

Compared to Barrow, Nome is not as far north, is not as rich in Alaska Native culture, and doesn't have a sizable museum or polar bear-viewing tours. But it does have one quality that may trump all of those in your planning: In Nome, you don't need a tour guide. Nome has shops, historic sites you can walk to, and, best of all, a long network of roads you can explore on your own to see wildlife and natural places. For an independent traveler, Nome is a place where you can get out on your own and have some fun. That, alone, may make it a better choice than Barrow.

Nome exploded into existence with gold finds around 1900. The beach sand in front of the community turned out to be full of gold. People poured in by steamship and built a boomtown powered by alcohol and gambling. At the Board of Trade Saloon, which still serves drinks on Front Street today, bettors set odds on sled mushers racing across the vast Seward Peninsula, their progress reported by telephone lines set up for the purpose.

The spirit of those days lives on, to some degree. Nome has more strange and funny community events than any other place I know, including the **Bering Sea Ice Golf Classic** in March and the **Memorial Day Polar Bear Swim,** which is scheduled June 21 (as early as the ice is likely to be clear enough for a dip). And, of course, Nome has the **Iditarod Trail Sled Dog Race.** The hoopla in March, when mushers arrive at the end of their 1,000-mile dash from Anchorage, is essential Nome.

Getting there

Flying is the only way to get to Nome. **Alaska Airlines** (☎ 800-252-7522; Internet: www.alaskaair.com) flies 90 minutes by jet either direct from Anchorage or with a brief hop from Kotzebue. Prices range from $350 to $600. Many visitors come on escorted tour packages sold by **Alaska Airlines Vacations** (☎ 800-468-2248); as a day trip, it costs $369. I don't think you need an escort to see Nome, but the price is hard to argue with.

Getting around

All taxis operate according to a standard price schedule. A ride to town from the airport is $5. Nome has three taxi companies, including **Nome Cab** (☎ 907-443-3030).

Unless you join a guided tour (see "Driving the tundra," later in this chapter), you need a car to explore the roads around Nome. **Stampede Rent-A-Car,** 302 E. Front St. (☎ 800-354-4606 or 907-443-3838), charges $80 a day for an SUV, $115 for a van. The same people operate the Aurora Inn (see "Where to stay," next).

Where to stay

Nome has many lodging options. Whenever you can't find a room at one of these top choices, get a referral from the **Nome Convention and Visitors Bureau,** Front and Division streets (P.O. Box 240), Nome, AK 99762 (☎ 907-443-6624; Internet: www.nomealaska.org/vc). Get the advice from a real person, either by phone or e-mail, to avoid stumbling into some of Nome's truly dreadful accommodations (one hotel has the slogan "Don't believe everything you hear" in its advertising).

Aurora Inn and Executive Suites
$$ Nome

Choose, at the same price, between these two comfortable buildings with different styles of accommodations under the same ownership. The new

Aurora Inn offers the best traditional hotel rooms in town in a mock country inn on the town's main street. The Executive Suites comprise a dozen apartment-like units, ranging from rooms with kitchenettes to two-bedroom apartments with full kitchens and living areas. That building, too, is only a couple of years old. Uniquely in town (see the "Beware the indoor pollution" sidebar, in this chapter), they have plenty of non-smoking rooms. Don't put too much faith in the rates listed here; instead, call and see what kind of deal you can work out.

Inn is located at 302 E. Front St.; Executive Suites are located at 226 W. D St. (P.O. Box 1008), Nome, AK 99762. ☎ 800-354-4606 or 907-443-3838. Fax: 907-443-6380. Internet: www.aurorainnome.com*. Rack rates: Summer $120 double, $175 suite; extra person older than 15 $10. AE, MC, V.*

Sweet Dreams B&B

$ Nome

It's the host who makes this place special; Nome Mayor, Leo Rasmussen, is a personable and funny man and a deep well of Nome history and local knowledge. The two-story house has a rustic, old-fashioned feel, with plenty of Alaskan memorabilia and a sunroom on top. The three units share bathroom facilities.

406 W. Fourth St. (P.O. Box 2), Nome, AK 99762. ☎ 907-443-2919. E-mail: leak nome@nook.net*. Rack rates: $85 double. Rates include full breakfast. MC, V.*

Where to dine

Milano's Pizzeria

$–$$$ Nome   Pizza/Japanese

In the style of small-town Alaska restaurants that stay alive through long winters by getting good at more than one thing, this place serves Italian and Japanese meals. The pizza comes highly recommended by the locals.

503 Front St. ☎ 907-443-2924. Main courses: $7.50–$26. MC, V. Open: Mon–Sat 11 a.m.–11 p.m., Sun 3–11 p.m.

Twin Dragons

$$ Nome   Chinese

The food here is probably the best you can reliably get in Nome. The specialty is Chinese cuisine (unlike the mixtures of ethnicities served elsewhere) in a fully decorated dining room.

Front Street near Steadman Street. ☎ 907-443-5552. Main courses: $12–$15. MC, V. Open Mon–Fri 11 a.m.–11 p.m., Sat noon to 11 p.m., Sun 3–11 p.m.

Exploring Nome

Taking a walk around Nome to see some of the surviving historic build-ings and other sites of interest is worth your time. Check out the gold rush–era Board of Trade Saloon, an old church, and a bust of Roald Amundsen, who landed near Nome, in Teller, after crossing the North Pole from Norway in a dirigible in 1926.

Below the library, at Front Street and Lanes Way, the small **Carrie M. McLain Memorial Museum** (☎ **907-443-6630**) contains an exhibit dedi-cated to the town's gold rush. The museum is free and is open in summer daily from noon to 8 p.m., and in winter Tuesday to Saturday from noon to 6 p.m.

In good weather, walk or take a taxi to the beach southeast of town, where you may see small-time miners still sifting the sand for gold. You can walk the beach for miles. The gold-digging **Swanberg Dredge** that you can see from here operated until the 1950s; a large dredge north of town worked into the mid-1990s.

Driving the tundra

Not exploring the extraordinary 250-mile road network that provides access to the tundra and mountains beyond the town during your visit to Nome would be a shame. Nowhere else is this kind of wilderness so easy to access. You're likely to see reindeer and musk oxen, and bird-watchers can add many exotic new entries to their life lists.

For instructions on the three routes there, check with the visitor center on Front Street or your car-rental agency. The best choice may be the **Nome-Council Road,** which heads 72 miles to the east, about half of that on the shoreline, before turning inland at the ghost town of Solomon, an old mining town with an abandoned railroad train known locally as the Last Train to Nowhere. The engines were originally used on the New York City elevated lines in 1881, and then were shipped to Alaska in 1903 to serve the miners along this line to Nome.

You can rent a car and drive the route on your own, or go with a tour guide such as Richard Beneville, a talented actor who performs as van driver for **Nome Discovery Tours** (☎ **907-443-2814;** E-mail: Discover@ nome.net). He picks you up and drives you anywhere in the area, shar-ing his quirky enthusiasm and extensive knowledge of the surroundings and culture. Besides wildlife and scenery on the roads out of town, he also visits an ivory carver and a working gold mine. Half days are $45 per person, full days $85.

Shopping

Nome is one of the best towns in Alaska to shop for ivory and other Eskimo artwork, with low prices and a variety of choices.

- ✔ Jim West has a legendary collection for sale, assembled in the barroom of the historic **Board of Trade Saloon,** which is attached to a shop on Front Street.

- ✔ The **Arctic Trading Post** (☎ 907-443-2686) is more of a traditional gift shop and has a good ivory collection.

- ✔ **Chukotka-Alaska,** at 514 Lomen St. (☎ 907-443-4128), is an importer of art and other goods from the Russian Far East and is really worth a look.

Alaska Native art that you find in Nome is likely to be authentic, but still you need to ask; check out the information concerning fake Native art in Chapter 11.

Fast Facts: Nome

Bank

Wells Fargo, with an ATM, is at 250 Front St.

Hospital

Norton Sound Regional is at Fifth Avenue and Bering Street (☎ 907-443-3311).

Information

Contact the **Nome Convention and Visitors Bureau,** Front and Division streets (P.O. Box 240), Nome, AK 99762 (☎ 907-443-6624; Internet: www.nomealaska.org/vc).

Internet Access

Nome Public Library is at 200 Front St. (☎ 907-443-6627).

Police

At Bering Street and Fourth Avenue (☎ 907-443-7766).

Post Office

At Front Street and Federal Way.

Taxes

The **sales tax** is 4%; tax on **rooms** totals 8%.

Chapter 24

Bear Country: Katmai National Park and Kodiak Island

● ●

In This Chapter

▶ Finding lots of big bears

▶ Choosing a bear-viewing destination

▶ Traveling to Katmai National Park

▶ Taking in the wonders of Kodiak Island

● ●

*W*here the moisture of the North Pacific Ocean runs into the mountains of Kodiak Island and the Alaska Peninsula, frequent snow and rain give rise to rivers full of salmon. During spawning season, brown bears catch as much of that rich, fatty food as they can. When the fish aren't spawning, bears still dine on seafood, using their huge claws to dig clams from the beaches. And to finish the feast, they can find abundant berries on limitless miles of green hills. Inland, the species is called the grizzly bear, growing to a few hundred pounds. Here, however, a big bear can weigh three-quarters of a ton and stand 9 feet tall. The Kodiak brown bear, the world's biggest, is an entire sub-species to itself.

Besides looking at bears, the region has other things to do. **Kodiak** is a fascinating little town on the huge island of the same name, with vestiges of Russian America and the Alaska Native culture that preceded and survived the Russian invasion of 250 years ago. **Katmai National Park** also contains the bizarre and spectacular **Valley of Ten Thousand Smokes,** where one of history's largest volcanic eruptions occurred. You can go salmon fishing at either place.

Bears remain the marquee attraction, and if bears are your main goal, you need to consider your options carefully. The cheapest way to see bears is from a bus at Denali National Park (see Chapter 19), but you won't see the great big ones and you may not see them close up. You can't get to big, coastal brown bear-viewing cheaply, but you can probably save money by taking a small plane from Anchorage or Homer (see Chapters 14 and 16). That may not get you to the absolute best bear-viewing sites, but in season, you can find brown bears. Admiralty Island near Juneau has a bear-viewing area with plenty of bears; if you reserve well ahead, you can count on seeing bears there (see Chapter 20).

Katmai is the ultimate bear-viewing destination, where visitors watch bears feeding from close up, but it's also expensive, and the limited facilities are crowded when bear-viewing is hot. From Kodiak, you can get to bears only by small plane; you have them to yourself when you find them, but you're less likely to see large numbers of bears close up.

Discovering Bear Country and Its Major Attractions

I call the two destinations in this chapter "Bear Country" because on Kodiak Island and at Katmai National Park bears rule the landscape. Not only are the bears much larger than the people, but they're also more numerous, the primary reason visitors trek to these remote locales.

Katmai National Park

Katmai is a remote, wilderness park far beyond the road network on the Alaska Peninsula southwest of Anchorage. Accommodations are only in wilderness lodges, but you can go for a day trip just to see the bears. And the region has a few other possibilities:

- ✔ Watching huge and abundant brown bear feeding in Brooks River
- ✔ Fishing for salmon
- ✔ Hiking in the Valley of Ten Thousand Smokes

Kodiak Island

The nation's second largest island (after Hawaii's Big Island) is almost entirely a part of an enormous bear refuge, a kingdom where big bears reign supreme. Besides tiny Alaska Native villages, the town of Kodiak is the only settlement, an unspoiled fishing port with several interesting sites and many outdoor opportunities, including the following:

- ✔ Watching brown-bear feeding areas accessed by floatplane
- ✔ Kayaking in the protected ocean waters of the Kodiak Archipelago
- ✔ Hiking and tide pooling on little-used trails and shorelines
- ✔ Fishing salmon in some of Alaska's most abundant streams

Bear-Gazing at Katmai National Park

Katmai National Park takes in a large section of the Alaska Peninsula, a wild, rugged, and sparsely visited land within which lies a hot ticket: **Brooks Camp,** a former fishing lodge and the site of an extraordinary congregation of large brown bears.

When fish are running in the Brooks River, in July and September (but not outside those times), bears come to catch them at a waterfall and feed to their hearts' content. Visitors are led by armed park rangers to elevated viewing platforms, where they can watch the bears in relative safety from quite close up.

The park became a park in 1918 after the most destructive volcanic eruption in the last 3,400 years blew up Novarupta Volcano here in 1914. A 40-square-mile area was buried as deep as 700 feet in ash. Named the **Valley of Ten Thousand Smokes,** the area continued steaming for decades. Now quiet, it remains a strange, unearthly wasteland, cut by erosion into precipitous gorges. To get to the valley, you first go to Brooks Camp and then take a bus.

Getting a room to stay overnight at Brooks Camp is prohibitively difficult: You must act far, far ahead of time. Even for day-trippers, the viewing platforms are crowded and you have to take turns. And getting there is costly. It's always so with a finite resource that's this desirable: The world's largest protected population of brown bears is here.

Getting there

You have one option to get to Katmai National Park's Brooks Camp: by plane. Most people first fly by jet from Anchorage to the village of **King Salmon,** which lies just west of the park, on **Alaska Airlines** (☎ 800-252-7522; Internet: www.alaskaair.com). Service is twice a day in summer for about $350 round-trip. Air taxis carry visitors the last leg from King Salmon to **Brooks Camp** for a fare of about $140 round-trip. **Katmai Air,** operated by park concessionaire Katmailand (☎ 800-544-0551 or 907-243-5448; Internet: www.bear-viewing.com), provides these flights and offers round-trip airfare packages from Anchorage that can save money and add simplicity to your planning.

Every visitor arriving at Brooks Camp is required to attend a 20-minute orientation called "The Brooks Camp School of Bear Etiquette," designed to train visitors (not bears) and keep them out of trouble.

Getting around

Brooks Camp is a place you get around on foot; don't go if you can't walk a mile or more over rough ground. To get to the Valley of Ten Thousand Smokes, you join a 23-mile bus tour by gravel road from the camp. The park concessionaire, **Katmailand,** charges $72 per person, round-trip, for the all-day excursion, plus $7 more for lunch.

Where to stay and dine

Brooks Camp Lodge
$$$$$ **Brooks Camp**

The park has 16 hotel rooms, and they're all at this lodge. Staying here, you can enjoy the bears close up, perhaps sipping a lemonade on the deck while they wander by. Otherwise, they're ordinary rooms with private bathrooms with shower stalls. The problem is, you have to reserve farther ahead than most people can manage. All peak dates (when the bears are around) book up six months out or earlier; for your choice, you have to call a year ahead. The reservation system opens 18 months ahead, January of the year before the visit. To save money, book the lodge rooms as packages with air travel.

The least expensive with airfare is a one-night visit for $673 per person, double occupancy, meals not included; three nights is $1,103. A double room without airfare is $412. Three buffet-style meals are served daily for guests and visitors who aren't staying in the lodge. Breakfast is $12, lunch $16, and dinner $22. For food only, they take MasterCard and Visa; everything else, you pay for in advance.

Katmailand, 4125 Aircraft Dr., Anchorage, AK 99502. ☎ *800-544-0551 or 907-243-5448. Fax: 907-243-0649. Internet:* www.bear-viewing.com.

Exploring Katmai National Park

You may have been to many national parks, but you've likely never been anywhere that's like Katmai. Read on to prepare for a unique experience.

The bears of the Brooks River

When the fish are running, in July especially, but also in September, 40 to 60 brown bear gather to feed at the falls on the Brooks River, half a mile from Brooks Camp. Visitors sign up for an hour on the viewing platforms, and then hike out with park rangers as guides to enjoy their viewing period. Make sure to bring binoculars and warm fleece or wool clothing and rain gear, because the region is cool and damp.

The number of day-trippers who can go is limited only by their ability to arrange the travel and pick up a park service permit, which costs $10 per person. Inquire about the permit when you reserve your travel; the permit is included when you reserve a room at the lodge. If you need to obtain your own permit, use the Park Service national reservation system (☎ **800-365-2267** or 301-722-1257; Internet: reservations. nps.gov). If you're using the phone reservation system, enter **KAT#** at the prompt.

The Valley of Ten Thousand Smokes

If you spend more than one day at Brooks Camp, you can take time to enjoy an outing to the Valley of Ten Thousand Smokes, ground zero of a volcanic eruption ten times more powerful than the 1980 eruption of Mount St. Helens. Although the smokes have stopped smoking, the area remains a dusty desert zone of strange landforms created by the erosion of the thick ash layer. For information about an all-day tour to the area, see "Getting around," earlier in this chapter.

Fishing

Katmai is a prime salmon and trout fishing area. **Katmailand** operates two fishing lodges in the park (☎ **800-544-0551** or 907-243-5448; Internet: www.katmailand.com).

Fast Facts: Katmai National Park

Bank

A **Wells Fargo** branch, with an ATM, is on King Salmon Highway.

Hospital

The **Camai Clinic,** in Naknek (☎ 907-246-6155), is open during normal business hours; after hours, calls to the number listed above go to emergency dispatchers.

Information

Reach **Katmai National Park Headquarters** at P.O. Box 7, King Salmon, AK 99613 (☎ 907-246-3305; Internet: www.nps.gov/katm).

Police

The park has no phones and no cellular service. In **King Salmon,** call ☎ 907-246-4222; elsewhere, call **Alaska State Troopers** at ☎ 907-246-3346 or 907-246-3464.

Venturing across to Kodiak Island

I've never seen a place as green as Kodiak. Flying over the island, vivid green hills of brush and meadow rise from intricate shorelines of black rock on green water. Huge spruce trees of dark green cast deep shadows over a forest floor of thick, bright green moss. The frequent rain helps the rich landscape, feeding the streams and plants that feed animals and fish. The people lucky enough to live here make their living from the fish, and they've built a town that reflects the island, too, with narrow, winding streets, curious old buildings, and a constant nearness to the sea.

Another part of Kodiak's charm lies in its undiscovered quality: You see few other tourists, and most businesses are locally owned and supported. The town is one of the oldest in Alaska and still has one of the best structures left behind by Russian America, in addition to a good museum owned by Alaska Natives still working to recover their culture from the Russian invasion of 250 years ago. But most of the attraction of Kodiak is in the outdoors, with its bear-viewing, sea kayaking, and fishing.

Getting there

Kodiak is easier to get to than other remote Alaska communities, reached by frequent air service from Anchorage or by ferry from Homer.

The flight by jet from Anchorage to Kodiak is an hour long on **Alaska Airlines** (☎ 800-252-7522; Internet: www.alaskaair.com). **ERA Aviation** (☎ 800-866-8394; Internet: www.eraaviation.com) also serves the route with prop-driven planes, adding a few minutes to your flight. A round-trip ticket from Anchorage costs $250 and up, depending on the deal you get. A **cab,** from **A and B Taxi** (☎ 907-486-4343), runs about $15 from the airport downtown.

The ferry *Tustumena,* of the **Alaska Marine Highway System** (☎ 800-642-0066 or 907-486-3800; Internet: www.alaska.gov/ferry), serves Kodiak from Homer and Seward. Homer, the closest port, is ten hours away. It's well worth traveling by ferry if you have the time, but the open ocean is often rough and passengers get seasick; take Dramamine *before* boarding. Booking a cabin is a good idea for an overnight run. The U.S. Fish and Wildlife Service staffs the trips with a naturalist. The adult passenger fare is $57, children half price; cabins range from $62 to $104. The Kodiak terminal is right downtown, in the same building as the visitor center (see "Fast Facts: Kodiak Island," at the end of this chapter).

Getting around

A rented car makes good sense in Kodiak, because the area has lovely remote roads to explore and the airport isn't close to downtown. You can rent from **Budget** (☎ 800-527-0700 or 907-487-2220; Internet: www.budget.com).

If it isn't raining, a bike is a great way to get around Kodiak, and strong riders will enjoy touring the roads out of town. Bikes are for rent at **Fifty-Eight Degrees North,** a full-service bike shop at 1231 Mill Bay Rd.

(☎ **907-486-6249**). Front-suspension mountain bikes rent for $30 for 24 hours.

Where to stay

Best Western Kodiak Inn
$$$ Downtown

This is the best hotel in downtown Kodiak, perched on the hill overlooking the boat harbor, right in the center of things. The attractive, up-to-date rooms in the wooden building vary in size and view, but all are acceptable standard units with refrigerators, microwave ovens, and other handy amenities. The courtesy van and central location can save you the cost of a taxi or rental car.

The **Chart Room** restaurant, specializing in seafood and with a great view of the water, is a good choice for a nice dinner out, with main courses in the $15 to $25 range.

236 W. Rezanof Dr., Kodiak, AK 99615. ☎ ***888-563-4254*** *or 907-486-5712. Fax: 907-486-3430. Internet:* www.kodiakinn.com. *Rack rates: High season $149 double, low season $99 double; extra person older than 12 $15. AE, DC, DISC, MC, V.*

Kodiak Bed and Breakfast
$$ Downtown

Hospitable and active, Mary Monroe runs this comfortable, homey place with a big, friendly golden retriever, Buffy. On sunny mornings, you can eat breakfast on a porch overlooking the harbor (fish is often on the morning menu). The location is convenient, right downtown, and the entry for the two small bedrooms, shared sitting room, and shared bathroom downstairs doesn't require you to walk through Monroe's own living quarters.

308 Cope St., Kodiak, AK 99615. ☎ ***907-486-5367***. *Fax: 907-486-6567. Internet:* www.ptialaska.net/~monroe. *Rack rate: $95 double. Rates include breakfast. MC, V.*

Where to dine

Eugene's Restaurant
$–$$$ Downtown   Chinese

This is a good, small-town family restaurant. The food is served in big portions by a pleasant family that works together. The dining room is comfortable, with booths with good views. We enjoyed the curry chicken and kung pao shrimp.

Upstairs at 202 E, Rezanof Dr. ☎ *907-486-2625. Main courses: $7–$23. AE, MC, V. Open: Mon–Thurs 11 a.m.–9 p.m., Fri–Sat 11 a.m.–10 p.m., Sun noon to 9 p.m.*

King's Diner
$ **Mill Bay Road**   **Diner**

This is a traditional Kodiak hangout, owned by the same family for many years. Although the fare is simple diner cuisine (try the sourdough pancakes), the place is clean and friendly and popular with families. The location is a drive from downtown.

4400 Mill Bay Rd. ☎ *907-486-4100. All items: $3.25–$13.50. MC, V. Open: Mon–Fri 5:30 a.m.–3:00 p.m., Sat–Sun 5:30 a.m.–4:00 p.m.*

Exploring Kodiak

Kodiak offers a few worthy stops for your visit, much of it relating to its Native heritage and its history with Russian settlers in the 1800s.

Alutiiq Museum

This exceptional museum, funded and governed by Natives, seeks to document and restore the Koniag Alutiiq people's culture, which the Russians virtually wiped out in the 18th century. Besides teaching about Alutiiq ways in a single gallery, the museum manages its own archaeological digs and repatriates Native remains and artifacts, which researchers removed by the thousands in the 1930s. The archaeological repository now includes 100,000 objects.

215 Mission Rd. ☎ *907-486-7004. Internet:* www.alutiiqmuseum.com. *Open: Summer, Mon–Fri 9 a.m.–5 p.m., Sat 10 a.m.–5 p.m.; winter, Tues–Fri 9 a.m.–5 p.m., Sat 10:30 a.m.–4:30 p.m. Admission: $2 adults, free for kids younger than 12.*

The Baranov Museum

The museum occupies the oldest Russian building of only four left standing in North America; it was built in 1808 by Alexander Baranov as a magazine and strong house for valuable sea otter pelts. It stands in a grassy park overlooking the water across from the ferry dock. Inside is a little museum rich with Russian and early Native artifacts. The guides know much about history and show 30 educational albums on various topics. The gift store is exceptional, selling antique Russian items and authentic Native crafts.

101 Marine Way. ☎ *907-486-5920. Internet:* www.ptialaska.net/~baranov. *Open: Summer, Mon–Sat 10 a.m.–4 p.m., Sun noon to 4 p.m.; winter, Mon–Wed and Fri–Sat 10 a.m.–3 p.m. Admission: $2 adults, free for children 12 and younger.*

Getting outdoors in Kodiak

Kodiak offers more than just brown bear-viewing — "just" may be an understated way of referring to these awesome creatures. You'll have opportunities outdoors for fishing, hiking, and sea kayaking.

Brown bear viewing

To see Kodiak's famous bears, you need to get out on a plane or boat. The easiest way is a Kodiak-based floatplane; expect to pay at least $400 per person, with a two- or three-person minimum (prices can fluctuate depending on the size of your party, the type of plane, how far you have to fly, and so on).

Landing on the water, you can sometimes watch from the safety of the plane's floats, although putting on rubber boots to walk for up to half an hour to get to where bears congregate often is necessary. Binoculars and telephoto camera lenses are essential, because no responsible guide will crowd Kodiak brown bears so closely that you don't need them (but the bears do sometimes choose to approach within 50 yards of you).

Bears congregate only when salmon are running, so the timing of your visit is critical. From early July through mid-August, you have a good chance of seeing bears fishing on Kodiak Island, and it's possible anytime from June to September, but calling ahead to the Kodiak National Wildlife Refuge (☎ 907-487-2600) is wise, because the refuge manages most of the island and knows that salmon runs and hot bear-viewing spots can vary from year to year. When flight services can't find bears feeding on salmon at an accessible spot, they fly over to the east coast of the Alaska Peninsula to watch bears digging clams from tidal flats.

The bear behavior is fascinating and the flight is spectacular, but it's a long way to go. If you're chartering, it can be expensive; however, some flight services charge their standard seat rate regardless of how far they have to fly to find the bears. Ask when you book. Several small flight services offer bear-viewing, including the following:

- **Highline Air** (☎ 866-486-5155 or 907-486-5155; Internet: www.highlineair.com)

- **Kodiak Air Service** (☎ 907-486-4446; Internet: www.kodiakair.com)

- **Sea Hawk Air** (☎ 800-770-4295 or 907-486-8282; Internet: www.seahawkair.com)

Fishing

The roads leading from the town of Kodiak offer access to terrific salmon and trout fishing. Get a list of where to fish and find help with contacting guides or charter boats for ocean fishing from the **Kodiak Island Convention and Visitors Bureau,** 100 Marine Way (☎ 907-486-4782; Internet: www.kodiak.org). To fish remote areas, you'll need to charter a plane, going for a day or staying at a remote cabin or wilderness lodge.

Hiking and tide pooling

Kodiak has some good, challenging day hikes and a wonderful seaside park with World War II ruins, easy walks, and tide pools for inspection. That's **Fort Abercrombie State Historical Park,** a couple of miles north of town on Rezanof Drive, where concrete ruins sit on coastal cliffs amid huge trees. Paths lead to beaches and tide pools, a swimming lake, and a number of other discoveries. The gun emplacements, bunkers, and other concrete buildings defended against the Japanese, who had seized islands in the outer Aleutians and were expected to come this way. One bunker has a volunteer museum that's open sporadically.

The **Division of State Parks** manages the area from its Kodiak District Office, 1400 Abercrombie Dr., Kodiak, AK 99615 (☎ 907-486-6339; Fax: 907-486-3320); stop there for a walking-tour brochure or, during the summer, join the Saturday-night interpretive program or a guided tide-pool walk, scheduled to coincide with the tides. The island's more challenging hikes are cataloged in the *Kodiak Hiking Guide,* available from the visitor center at 100 Marine Way.

Sea kayaking

The Kodiak Archipelago, with its many folded, rocky shorelines and abundant marine life, is a perfect place for sea kayaking. Kayaks were invented here and on the Aleutian Islands to the west. Several operators offer kayaking services and tours in and around Kodiak, and on the shore of Katmai National Park.

Mythos Expeditions (☎ 907-486-5536; Internet: www.mythos-expeditions.com) offers introductory paddles from the boat harbor — surprisingly complex and attractive waters for kayaking — starting at $40 per person. For a more ambitious trip — an expedition — they take kayakers along the coast of Katmai National Park for several days; guests paddle by day and sleep and eat aboard a converted commercial fishing boat.

Fast Facts: Kodiak Island

Banks

Several banks downtown have ATMs, including **Key Bank** on the mall at the waterfront.

Emergencies

Dial ☎ **911.**

Hospital

Providence Kodiak Island Medical Center is at 1915 E. Rezanof Dr. (☎ 907-486-3281).

Information

Check with the **Kodiak Island Convention and Visitors Bureau,** 100 Marine Way, Kodiak, AK 99615 (☎ 907-486-4782; Fax 907-486-6545; Internet: www.kodiak.org).

Internet Access

Office Express is at 202 Center St. (☎ 907-486-8780).

Police

Contact the **Kodiak Police Department** at ☎ 907-486-8000.

Post Office

Near Lower Mill Bay Road and Hemlock Street.

Taxes

Sales tax is 6% within city limits. The **room tax** inside the Kodiak city limits totals 11%, while outside the city it's 5%.

Part VII
The Part of Tens

The 5th Wave   By Rich Tennant

"It appears the fierce independent spirit of the Alaskan people is alive and well."

In this part . . .

Gee, going to Alaska on vacation sounds like a lot of work, doesn't it — all that planning, riding on airplanes, and paddling sea kayaks? Why not just stay at work, instead, and take an extra five minutes in the break room? If these thoughts have crossed your mind (and I'm sure they haven't), check out the info in this part and become inspired again about the incredible places you'll see, the interesting people you'll meet, and fascinating things you'll discover. Even if you're ready to go, the lists in this part are a safe bet for stoking your travel fire a bit more.

Chapter 25

Top Ten Walks and Hikes in Alaska

. . . .

In This Chapter

▶ Hiking Alaska's most spectacular trails

▶ Strolling Alaska's most interesting streets

▶ Walking Alaska's prettiest beaches

. . . .

*F*eet are wonderful things. They don't cost anything to use, and they can take you places where no other vehicle can. In Alaska, your feet are especially useful, because your hikes and walks transport you to places of inspiring beauty, often with very little company (except for the occasional moose or eagle).

You can easily get hiking information. Every town's visitor center has maps, handouts, and trail guidebooks. For strolls around small towns' historic downtown areas, you can frequently find a free walking-tour brochure. Information can enhance beach walks, too; you can usually find out where the tide pools are at public-land visitor centers or bookstores in coastal communities. In this chapter, I supply you with a head start to your information-gathering excursion by outlining ten great walks and hikes.

Bring good walking or hiking shoes to Alaska. You also need layers of warm clothing, good rain gear, snacks, and water. For beach walks or tide-pool explorations, shin-high rubber boots enhance the experience. You can find a pair for under $15 in any coastal town. While you're in Alaska, wear them everywhere you go and people will think you're a local. When you leave, take the boots home as a souvenir or, if you have no room in your bags, donate them to a charitable organization.

Glen Alps: Stepping from City to Mountain

The Glen Alps Trailhead in Chugach State Park, 2,000 feet above the city, is a sudden, magical portal between two worlds. On one side, Anchorage spreads out below you like a toy city. From the park, you can see how isolated the city really is — a mere splash of civilization on a much larger background of wild land. On the gateway's other side, wild land extends in every direction.

You can hike anywhere and in any style you like. Near the parking lot, take the paved overlook trail. Opposite the trail, climb steep Flattop Mountain. Up the valley, choose one of several trails through the mountains for hikes of up to a few days — you can camp anywhere along the trails. Or don't use a trail at all. Everything to see is above the tree line, and after you're past the brush near the parking lot, you can walk just about anywhere you want. Enjoy the other world — the total freedom beyond the city's edge. See Chapter 14.

Tony Knowles Coastal Trail: Exploring Urban Wilds

This coastal trail is the best of many paved multi-use trails that network through Anchorage like an alternative circulatory system. It starts downtown. Wander down to Elderberry Park. At the end of Sixth Avenue, pass through a tunnel, and find yourself face-to-face with the ocean and mudflat bird habitat. From there, the trail continues along the shore and in the wooded bluffs above the water for ten miles to Kincaid Park, the city's crown jewel of forest trails for cross-country skiing or mountain biking. At the trail's end, hikers commonly see moose and eagles, and you can see beluga whales in the nearby Knik Arm at any point along the trail. See Chapter 14.

Bird Ridge Trail: Taking a Spectacular Cardiac Test

About 25 miles south of Anchorage on the Glenn Highway, this Chugach State Park Trail mounts straight up a 3,500-foot mountain in just 2½ miles, with mind-expanding views all the way. (If you don't have the energy to make it to the top, you won't go home feeling disappointed.) You can see far along Turnagain Arm and into the series of mountains and valleys in the Chugach Range. If you have energy left, the ridge continues as an informal route, even higher and even farther into the heart of the mountains. See Chapter 15.

Alaska Center for Coastal Studies: Wading to a Tide-Pool Adventure

This nonprofit educational center in Homer takes visitors across Kachemak Bay, far beyond the reach of roads, to a lodge in the woods above a lovely, protected cove. From there, well-trained naturalists lead small groups to see the tiny animals in the tide pools of China Poot Bay, to discover the plants along the woodland paths, and to visit an archeological site where an ancient Native family once lived. Back at the lodge, you can use microscopes to inspect the plankton floating around tide-pool water and salt-water tanks and check out creatures you may not have seen in the wild. The best part? You don't have to hike more than a mile or two to see it all. See Chapter 16.

Granite Tors Trail: Touring Nature-Carved Monuments

This challenging hike to a strange destination leads you to a place called The Plain of Monuments where big granite monoliths stand up like abstract statues. The 15-mile looping route is in Chena River State Recreation Area, outside of Fairbanks on Chena Hot Springs Road. The trail slowly rises from the boreal forest to damp tundra, where you encounter the *tors,* naturally occurring towers of rock, standing at random spots upon the plateau without a sense of scale to orient their size. They were formed when softer material eroded from around granite that had oozed up from below. See Chapter 17.

Denali National Park: Finding Your Measure in the Backcountry

Denali National Park has few formal trails, and those that do exist have nothing on the places you can explore without a trail, setting out on your own on tundra or on a gravel river plain. Without trees to get in the way, you can walk anywhere you choose, keeping your common sense handy to remember your way back or to avoid other dangerous situations. Two of the best starting points are the Toklat River and the

Eielson Visitor Center; you can reach both only on the park's shuttle bus system. If you don't see wildlife on your hike, you'll probably see animals on the bus ride.

If you're not ready to head out on your own, join a ranger-guided Discovery Hike into the backcountry with a small group. See Chapter 19.

Outer Point Trail: Walking to Whale Waters

This trail, which leads from the North Douglas Highway near Juneau, is an easy walk of just 1⅓ miles. You take a boardwalk trail through mossy rainforest, over sunny wetlands, and out to a rocky beach looking across Stephens Passage, on the side of Douglas Island opposite the city, dotted with islets and frequented by whales. At low tide, you can explore the tide pools. The trail loops back through woods so pretty you have to remind yourself you're not in a botanical garden, but just a small slice of a huge forest. See Chapter 20.

The Streets of Juneau: Finding the Charm of Old Alaska

Start at the capitol building at Fourth and Main and walk uphill. You don't need a plan; every street is lined with charming, moss-roofed houses. You do need strong legs, however, as the streets climb insanely, sometimes quitting and becoming stairs, up to the ridge that is Seventh Street. Explore in any direction from Seventh Street: down the stairs that descend far down to Gold Creek, down Goldbelt Street to the Governor's Mansion, on Calhoun Street, or uphill toward the mountains along Seventh. You're just steps away from a hike into the rain forest that looms over the city. See Chapter 20.

Sitka National Historical Park: Picturing the War

The battlefield where the Russians and the Native Tlingit settled the ownership of Alaska in 1804 is reached along a quiet, seaside trail lined by big trees and priceless totem poles. The faces on the poles, so digni-fied and distant, seem laden with memories of the great events that happened here. You can imagine the Russian ship approaching the shore with its cannons blasting. And you can easily picture how the Tlingit warriors felt as they waited for the attack — hear the ravens call, see the waves on the shore, and smell the rain in the cedar trees — and understand why they fought so hard to hold onto this place. See Chapter 22.

Barrow's Arctic Ocean Beach: Standing at the World's Edge

You won't ever mistake the beach of pea-sized gravel where the land ends and the Arctic Ocean begins near Barrow for Waikiki, or even Bar Harbor, but it has its own desolate beauty. You're truly at the end of the world, and it feels and looks like it. Huge whale bones left over from Eskimo hunts lie on the beach in several places, especially near the Naval Arctic Research Laboratory (NARL) scientific facilities north of town. In the winter, the beach is a strange place — the frozen sea piles up into miniature mountain ranges. At those times, however, get local advice before walking to avoid the hazards of polar bears or dangerously cold weather. See Chapter 23.

Chapter 26

Ten Questions to Ask an Alaskan

I can say this because I'm an Alaskan and have been all my life: Alaskans tend to think they're better than people from other places. We've either got good self-esteem or delusions of grandeur — you can decide for yourself. One reason for this confidence is the mind-set that because Alaska is such a tough place, the people who live here must be tough, too. That's hooey. Another reason is that Alaska is such a wonderful place that Alaskans must be wonderful, too. More hooey. And yet another reason that actually begins to make a little sense: We love it here. Living here is a conscious decision for most of us, and we want to spread the word. Many Alaskans treat visitors as potential converts. As for you, well maybe, deep underneath, you're an Alaskan, too. You won't know for sure until it's time to get on the plane for home, but some good conversations on the way can give you an inkling. The questions in this chapter can help you get some of those good conversations started.

Where Are You from Originally?

In Alaska, the word Native means a member of an indigenous tribe and is always capitalized. Real Alaska Natives comprise about 15% of the population. Of the rest of the population, not many qualify to be called "Native" even by the ordinary meaning of the word, because the great majority came from somewhere else. Alaska is a young and growing state. It's still a place where people move to for a little adventure, knowing that they'll return to their previous home after a few years. Or at least that's what they think they'll do. My own parents came up for what they thought would be only three years. That was in 1966. They're still here; you do the math.

How Long Have You Lived Here?

Ask this question whenever you want to see someone light up with pride. When people get up to speak in public meetings in Alaska, they invariably start out by saying how many years they've lived here. Since gold rush days, it's been a rule that you can judge a resident's wisdom about the North by how many winters he or she has seen. Although people who don't enjoy winter sports can go stir crazy, these days, getting through the winter isn't really that tough. Instead, knowing how long a person has been here tells you how much they remember about the good old days. Alaska changes fast, and no matter how long you've been here, you think the real Alaska is what it was like when you arrived, not the pale copy that's here now.

Would You Tell Me about Your Boat?

This question is merely a template. You can insert all kinds of other items for the word *boat* at the end of the question — try *gun* or *snowmobile*. But save these questions for when you have plenty of time to kill. Guns, boats, and snowmobiles are essential tools for many people who spend time outdoors in Alaska. They're also subjects of intense interest, discussion, and even obsession. People — mostly guys, to be honest — can talk for hours about caliber, horsepower, and track length, discussing what they've owned, how well it worked, and what they dream of owning. Paying attention to the tools upon which your life depends makes sense when you're out in the wilderness. It's also quite fun to think about your toys.

What Do You Think of This New Land Management Plan?

Politics in Alaska — at least the interesting part that isn't just about money — is all about land, water, wildlife, and how they should be used or protected. Alaska is home to plenty of environmentalists, but plenty of other people here think that a good portion of the state's resources needs to be put to productive use. Because about 85% of the land is government owned (15% belongs to Alaska Natives and less than 1% is privately owned), almost anything anyone wants to do requires a public debate. Stating your own opinion isn't really a good idea until you find out the views of the person you're talking to. These are the kinds of issues that make people mad.

Is the Legislature Doing a Good Job?

No, the legislature is never doing a good job. In fact, you'll learn that the legislature is a bunch of self-dealing, bone-headed, free-spending buffoons who can't be trusted on a cakewalk at a penny carnival. Alaskans tend to get very worked up about state politics, and elections are often close and acrimonious. The reason for the poor results, despite the high interest, is because the population is a bunch of lazy, spoiled, latté-swilling newcomers (or ignorant, red-necked, pistol-toting old-timers) who want to lock up (or bulldoze) the most beautiful place on earth. (You'll have to guess which kind of Alaskan I am.)

Why Do You Need a Boat or a Plane to Get to the Capital?

Many people in Anchorage think the state capital should be in Anchorage, the largest city and the one with the best transportation network. Many people in Fairbanks think the capital shouldn't be in Juneau, but they'd like it even less if it were in Anchorage, a city they view kind of the way Canadians view the United States — big, arrogant, and unaware. In Juneau, everyone knows that keeping the capital means economic survival, and the town fights off, with all that it has within its powers, the referenda that surface every few years, seeking to move the capital (or some portion of it). They make many sensible arguments about the costs involved with such a move. And that's why the capital is still in Juneau.

Where Do You Like to Go in Summer?

Never ask, "Where's your favorite place to fish?" That's the best way to stop a conversation, not start one. Alaskans like to think they guard their favorite fishing spots better than the U.S. government guards the gold at Fort Knox. But you'll get the same information whenever you ask for favorite places to camp or to go to a cabin. Cities empty out on long summer weekends. Everyone goes somewhere. Living in Alaska and wasting those precious summer days would be nuts. And the places you go — on the ocean, on a river somewhere, or up in the mountains — are the places where you remember why you live in

Alaska and why you enjoy being alive on this earth. Some people may keep that sort of information — and hopefully those places — to themselves, but most love telling for the sheer joy of talking about their special places. Chances are, in their enthusiasm, they'll end up telling you about their favorite fishing hole, too.

Have You Ever Encountered a Bear?

While dining with my brother's family and his in-laws in New Jersey recently, I made the mistake of wondering out loud the best way to get to a certain address in Manhattan at rush hour the next morning. The topic stayed alive for 45 minutes. Bringing up the topic of bears at an Alaskan dinner table works about the same way. Two problems with the topic: One problem is that everyone wants to talk, because each thinks he or she has the best bear story (or five). The other problem is that, after the conversation, you'll be afraid to leave your room for the rest of your trip. Just remember that the information you receive this way has roughly the same accuracy that you'd expect whenever you ask, "Have you ever lost a really big fish?"

Here's My Itinerary: Do You Have Any Suggestions?

Some of my questions are silly, but this one is a good idea. No matter how much time you spend planning, as a visitor, you'll never be able to find out as much as someone who already lives here. They'll probably have their own little-known trails, restaurants, and shortcuts to suggest. Besides, many Alaskans are travel experts whether they want to be or not. When you live here, you get a lot of visitors.

Why Do You Live in Alaska?

In many other places, the answer might be, "This is where I was born," or "This is where my job is." But most people who live in Alaska have made a conscious decision to be here. They probably moved here from somewhere else, and living wherever they came from would probably be easier. But they're here, and they know why, and they're probably willing to tell you. It can come out as something prosaic such as, "I enjoy hunting," or "I love the snow." Or it can be as eloquent as a gesture toward a grand view of a white mountain range. After you hear those answers and after you see the place for yourself, you may find yourself asking, "Why don't *I* live in Alaska?"

Chapter 27

Ten Ways to Be an Alaska Know-It-All

● ●

In This Chapter

▶ Learning how big Alaska really is

▶ Finding out about mountains, earthquakes, and volcanoes

▶ Puzzling out Alaska's strange government finances

▶ Boning up on fish, fowl, and fur

● ●

*H*ere's your chance to lean over to your fellow passenger on a trip through Alaska and deliver a long stream of informational nuggets to amaze your listener that make you sound like a resident. Or more likely, to make your listener raise a hand and say, "Excuse me, can I switch seats?" Call it the Cliff Clavin chapter. (Remember, he was the know-it-all barfly on the TV series *Cheers* who bored everyone to death with his encyclopedic command of dubious factoids.)

How Big Is It?

Alaska is so big . . .

✔ . . . that if each of the roughly 600,000 residents were spaced evenly through the state, no one would be within a mile of anyone else.

✔ . . . that there are a million acres for every day of the year (365 million acres of land).

✔ . . . that if it were placed on top of the contiguous 48 states, it would span from coast to coast (if you include the Aleutian Islands).

✔ . . . that the span of north-south latitudes is the same as the distance from Miami, Florida, to Bangor, Maine.

✔ . . . that you can fit Germany, France, Italy, and the United Kingdom within its borders, and still have room left over for the state of Maine.

✔ . . . that if its shoreline of 34,000 miles were stretched out into a straight line, it would wrap all the way around the world, and then some.

That's a Lot of Park

In 1980, Congress protected a block of Alaskan parks and other conservation lands that combined are as large as the state of California, bringing the total protected area to roughly the size of Texas. Alaska contains 69% of all the national park lands in the United States, and 85% of the wildlife refuges. Alaska has 150 times more protected land than privately owned property. Wrangell–St. Elias National Park is the largest of all at 13.2 million acres, more than six times larger than Yellowstone. East of Wrangell–St. Elias is the Canadian border, where Canada's Kluane National Park begins, covering another 5.5 million acres. Between the two, that's almost as much park as the entire state of Maine. (Why do I keep picking on Maine?) This is why some Alaskans get irritated when people say the state needs to be protected from development.

Those Mountains Are Really Tall

The top of Mount McKinley is 20,320 feet above sea level. That's the tallest in Alaska, and about a mile taller than California's Mount Whitney, which is the tallest mountain in all the other states. Moreover, McKinley stands taller from its base to its top than any other mountain in the world. Sure, mountains on other continents are taller in total, but they all start off on higher ground to begin with. That's like my three-year-old saying he's taller than Daddy when he's sitting on his mother's shoulders. And, although McKinley is Alaska's star center, it also has a deep bench. The fact is that Mount Whitney is only the nation's 17th tallest mountain.

And They're Getting Bigger

You may think that Mount McKinley is big enough, which shows how much you underestimate the strong Alaskan spirit! In fact, McKinley is growing about an inch every three years. The state tourism board would like to take responsibility, but the real reason is that the Pacific *tectonic plate* (massive oceanic slabs of rock) is constantly crushing itself against Alaska's southern coast. The Alaska Range, of which McKinley is the star attraction, is basically a big dent caused by that massive collision. The mountains of Southeast Alaska are growing fast too, but for another reason. There the cause is the melting of immense sheets of ice from the last Ice Age. All that weight lifted off the land is enabling it to spring up like a sofa cushion — about 1½ inches a year in Glacier Bay.

A Whole Lot of Shaking . . .

Alaska averages 10 to 20 earthquakes *a day.* Of course, we don't feel that many (Alaska is very big and most of the earthquakes are small), but we do feel our share. To be precise, Alaska claims

✔ Eleven percent of the world's earthquakes

✔ Fifty-two percent of all earthquakes in the United States

✔ Three of the six largest earthquakes in recorded history

✔ Seven of the ten largest earthquakes in U.S. history

It's all thanks to those tectonic plates bashing into each other (see the preceding section), which is also why we have so many volcanoes. But that's another topic — the next one, in fact.

. . . And a Whole Lot of Spewing

Forty of Alaska's more than 100 volcanoes are active. That's 80% of the volcanoes in the United States, and 11% of all the volcanoes in the world. A look at a globe tells much of the story. The long arc of the Aleutian Islands, stretching across the North Pacific Ocean to Russia's Kamchatka Peninsula, is the northern edge of the Pacific's *Ring of Fire,* the zone where the collision of tectonic plates causes leaks of the earth's internal heat in the form of volcanic eruptions. Eruptions are like flares at the site of the collision. Or, maybe, they're bigger than flares. The 1912 eruption that created the Valley of Ten Thousand Smokes in Katmai National Park was the largest in the 20th century and was heard clearly in Juneau, more than 500 miles away. More recently, the 1989–90 eruptions of Mount Redoubt near Anchorage were the second most costly in U.S. history for their disruption of aviation and the oil industry.

Breathing for a Living

Yes, it's true: Every man, woman, and child gets a check from the state government just for living through the year. When the Prudhoe Bay oil field was developed in the 1970s (the biggest ever in North America; are you sick of the bragging yet?), it produced so much tax money for the state that, for at least a few years, the politicians in Juneau couldn't spend it fast enough. (You'll be relieved to hear that they've gotten over that problem.) The voters amended the state constitution and diverted a share of the tax money to a permanent investment account. Half the annual income from that account is passed out in annual checks, called Permanent Fund Dividends, which rose to about $2,000. However, with the recent tanking of the stock market, the checks began shrinking quickly (cue the violins).

If Alaska Is So Rich, Why Is the Campground Closed?

Yes, you may come across a campground that's inexplicably not in operation during your visit. Well, I'm sorry about that. I can refer you to the info about the stupidity of the legislature in Chapter 26, but it's more complicated than that. True, Alaska does have more than $20 billion in the bank, but it also has the Permanent Fund Dividend, and no one wants to give up that goody. And, no one wants to pay taxes. And, the oil that produces all the money is running out. So the state is cutting the budget. In the 2002–03 budget, the legislature cut some campground funding. Even though the campgrounds are more than self-sustaining with user fees. . . . I just realized this is making less sense as I go along. Maybe I better move on to another topic, but to be safe, try to stay at camping facilities that accept pre-booking.

Catching Politically Correct Fish

Alaska's biggest employer is the fishing industry, and the biggest catch is the plentiful wild Pacific salmon. A fact that is universally acknowledged and beyond dispute is that fresh Alaska salmon, properly prepared, is the tastiest and healthiest food on earth. You'll have plenty of opportunities to agree with that, because people will try to feed you salmon every time you turn around. Unfortunately, the salmon industry is in decline because of competition from fish farmers from other places (fish farming is illegal in Alaska) who pawn off mushy, less flavorful captive salmon (at lower prices) as fresh year round. Adding insult to

injury, farmed salmon, which fishermen consider an environmental out-
rage, can be certified organic, but wild salmon cannot. (In the warped
reasoning of the bureaucrats, no one knows exactly where the wild fish
have been.)

Stating the Facts

If you still have someone sitting next to you on the plane after spouting
all the knowledge you've gained from this chapter so far, don't give up
yet. It's time to pull out the heavy artillery:

- **State bird:** The willow ptarmigan, a grouse so dumb you can hunt
  it with a big rock.

- **State fish:** The king salmon, of which the biggest commercial
  catch (146 pounds) and biggest sport catch (97 pounds) both
  came from Alaska.

- **State flower:** The forget-me-not. Isn't that sweet?

- **State fossil:** The woolly mammoth. Quick, what's your state's
  official state fossil?

- **State insect:** The mosquito. No, that would be too honest. The real
  state insect is some kind of dragonfly (by vote of Alaskan school-
  children), an insect that at least eats mosquitoes.

- **State sport:** Dog mushing. But basketball is even more popular.

Appendix

Quick Concierge

• •

Sometimes when you need information, you need it right away. That's where the Quick Concierge helps out: These pages are here for you to look up handy phone numbers, Web sites, and other tidbits of information about how things work in Alaska.

Alaska A to Z: Facts at Your Fingertips

AAA

For roadside assistance, call ☎ 800-222-4357. For other services, call ☎ 800-391-4222 or 907-344-4310.

Banks and ATMs

You can find banks and automated teller machines (ATMs) in all but the tiniest towns. In larger towns, every gas station has an ATM.

Business Hours

In the larger cities, major grocery stores are open 24 hours a day (or almost 24 hours a day) and carry a wide range of products (even fishing gear) in addition to food.

At a minimum, **stores** are open Monday through Friday from 10 a.m. to 6 p.m., are open on Saturday afternoon, and are closed on Sunday, but many are open much longer hours, especially during summer.

Banks may close an hour earlier, and if open on Saturday, only in the morning.

Under state law, **bars** don't have to close until 5 a.m., but many communities have an earlier closing, generally around 2 a.m.

Cellular Phone Coverage

Most of the populated areas of the state, and some of the highways, have cellular coverage. Calling-area maps for the largest provider are online at www.acsalaska.com/wireless. Check roaming charges with your own cellphone provider before you leave home, so you can avoid getting fleeced.

Emergencies

Generally, you can call ☎ 911 for medical, police, or fire emergencies. Remote highways sometimes have gaps in 911 coverage, but dialing 0 generally connects you with an operator, who can connect you to emergency services.

Citizens Band channels 9 and 11 are monitored for emergencies on most highways, and so are channels 14 and 19 in some areas.

Holidays

Besides the normal national holidays, banks and state- and local-government offices close on two state holidays: **Seward's Day** (the last Monday in March) and **Alaska Day** (October 18, or the nearest Friday or Monday whenever the 18th falls on a weekend).

Hospitals

The location of local hospitals is listed in the "Fast Facts" sections in each city chapter or section.

Information

See "Where to Get More Information," later in this appendix.

Liquor Laws

The minimum drinking age in Alaska is 21. Most restaurants sell beer and wine, while a minority have full bars that also serve hard liquor. Packaged alcohol, beer, and wine are sold only in licensed stores, not in grocery stores, but these stores are common, and you'll find that they're open long hours every day, including Sunday.

More than 100 rural communities have laws that prohibit the importation and possession of alcohol (better known as being *dry*) or only the sale but not possession of alcohol (known as being *damp*). With a few exceptions, these are limited to tiny bush communities that are off the road network (urban areas are all *wet*). Of the communities featured in this book, Barrow is damp and the rest are wet. Before flying into a Native village with any alcohol, ask about the liquor law in that community — bootlegging is a serious crime (and serious bad manners) — or check a list online at www.abc. revenue.state.ak.us/local.htm.

Mail

The location of the local post office is listed in the "Fast Facts" sections in each city chapter or section.

Maps

You can buy street maps almost anywhere. For the outdoors, I recommend the excellent trail maps published by **Trails Illustrated** (☎ 800-962-1643; Internet: www.trails illustrated.com). They're available in sporting goods stores and public land visitor information centers. **The Maps Store,** in Anchorage at 601 W. 36th Ave. (☎ 907-562-7277), sells every Alaska map imaginable.

Newspapers

The state's dominant newspaper is the *Anchorage Daily News* (Internet: www.adn.com); it's available everywhere but isn't always easy to find in Southeast Alaska.

Seattle newspapers and *USA Today* often are available, and in Anchorage, you can get virtually any newspaper.

Restrooms

Don't expect interstate highway rest stops. When you find the infrequent public restrooms on Alaska's highways, they're usually outhouses. If you require plumbing, you'll have to wait for a roadhouse or town. On unpaved rural highways, you need to be ready to go in the bushes.

In the cities, it's usually easy to find a restroom in a hotel lobby, shopping center, or the like. Any business that serves food is required to have public restrooms.

Safety

You can find tips about rural highway safety in Chapter 7 and about outdoor safety in Chapter 9.

As for avoiding being a victim of crime, follow the same precautions you'd take anywhere else when traveling. Don't assume that small towns don't have crime. Although mugging is rare in Alaska, rape is much more common than it is nationally, and women need to be careful. Avoid rough bars and don't go out alone at night.

Smoking

In rural Alaska, smoking remains quite common and can be hard to get away from. Make a point of asking for an authentically nonsmoking room if you want one in a small town.

Anchorage is more in tune with the times, and smoking isn't allowed in public places except for bars.

Taxes

Alaska has no state sales tax, but most local governments have a sales tax and a bed tax on accommodations. The tax rates are listed in the "Fast Facts" sections for each town in the book.

Telephone

All of Alaska is in area code **907**. In the Yukon Territory, the area code is **867**. When placing a toll call within the state, you must dial 1, the area code, and the number.

I am assured that all major calling cards will work in Alaska, but that certainly hasn't been the case in the past. To make sure, contact your long-distance company, or buy a by-the-minute card.

Time Zone

Although the state geographically spans five time zones, in the 1980s, Alaska's middle time zone was stretched so that almost the entire state lies in one zone, known as Alaska time. It's one hour earlier than the U.S. West Coast's Pacific time, four hours earlier than Eastern time. Crossing over the border from Alaska to Canada adds an hour and puts you at the same time as the West Coast.

Like almost everywhere in the United States, daylight savings time is in effect from 1 a.m. on the first Sunday in April (turn your clocks ahead one hour) until 2 a.m. on the last Sunday in October (turn clocks back again).

Tipping

Follow the same guidelines that you'd use anywhere else in the United States. For information about tipping guides, fishing charters, and wilderness lodges, see Chapter 4.

Weather Updates

The most complete source of weather information is the Web site of the Alaska Region Headquarters of the National Weather Service (NWS), www.arh.noaa.gov.

The NWS also maintains a system using voice-mail technology that enables you to receive forecasts and other weather information (even sea ice conditions) for every part of the state with a telephone call. Within Alaska the toll-free number is ☎ 800-472-0391. From outside Alaska, you have to pay for the call at ☎ 907-266-5145 (also the local number in Anchorage).

Toll-Free Numbers and Web Sites

Major airlines serving Alaska

Air Canada
☎ 888-247-2262
www.aircanada.com

Alaska Airlines
☎ 800-252-7522
www.alaskaair.com

Continental Airlines
☎ 800-525-0280
www.continental.com

Delta Air Lines
☎ 800-221-1212
www.delta.com

Northwest Airlines
☎ 800-225-2525
www.nwa.com

United Airlines
☎ 800-241-6522
www.ual.com

Major cruise lines serving Alaska

American Safari Cruises
☎ 888-862-8881
www.amsafari.com

Carnival Cruise Lines
☎ 800-CARNIVAL
www.carnival.com

Celebrity Cruises
☎ 800-437-3111
www.celebritycruises.com

Clipper Cruise Line
☎ 800-325-0010
www.clippercruise.com

Cruise West
☎ 800-426-7702
www.cruisewest.com

Crystal Cruises
☎ 800-446-6620
www.crystalcruises.com

Glacier Bay Cruiseline
☎ 800-451-5952
www.glacierbaycruiseline.com

Holland America Line
☎ 800-426-0327
www.hollandamerica.com

Lindblad Expeditions
☎ 800-397-3348
www.expeditions.com

Norwegian Cruise Line
☎ 800-327-7030
www.ncl.com

Princess Cruises
☎ 800-LOVE-BOAT
www.princess.com

Radisson Seven Seas Cruises
☎ 800-285-1835
www.rssc.com

Royal Caribbean International
☎ 800-327-6700
www.rccl.com

World Explorer Cruises
☎ 800-854-3835
www.wecruise.com

Major car-rental agencies operating in Alaska

Alamo
☎ 800-462-5266
www.goalamo.com

Avis
☎ 800-230-4898, U.S.
☎ 800-272-5871, Canada
www.avis.com

Budget
☎ 800-527-0700
www.budget.com

Dollar
☎ 800-800-4000
www.dollar.com

Hertz
☎ 800-654-3131
www.hertz.com

National
☎ 800-CAR-RENT
www.nationalcar.com

Thrifty
☎ 800-847-4389
www.thrifty.com

Major hotel and motel chains in Alaska

Aspen Hotels
☎ 866-GUEST4U
www.aspenhotelsak.com

Best Western
☎ 800-780-7234
www.bestwestern.com

Choice Hotels International: Clarion Hotel, Comfort Inn, Quality Inn
☎ 877-424-6423
www.hotelchoice.com

Days Inn
☎ 800-329-7466
www.daysinn.com

Hilton Hotels: Hilton, Hilton Garden Inn, Hampton Inn & Suites
☎ 800-HILTONS
www.hilton.com

Holiday Inn
☎ 800-HOLIDAY
www.sixcontinentshotels.com

Marriott: Courtyard, Residence Inn, SpringHill Suites
☎ 888-236-2427
www.marriott.com

Microtel Inn & Suites
☎ 888-771-7171
www.microtelinn.com

Motel 6
☎ 800-4-MOTEL6
www.motel6.com

Red Lion Hotels & Inns
☎ 800-RED-LION
www.redlion.com

Sheraton Hotels
☎ 800-325-3535
www.sheraton.com

Super 8 Motels
☎ 800-800-8000
www.super8.com

WestCoast Hotels
☎ 800-325-4000
www.westcoasthotels.com

Westmark Hotels
☎ 800-544-0970
www.westmarkhotels.com

Where to Get More Information

Alaska's statewide visitor bureau is the **Alaska Travel Industry Association,** P.O. Box 143361, Anchorage, AK 99514-3361 (☎ **800-862-5275** or 907-929-2242; Internet: www.travelalaska.com). For information on outdoor recreation, the **Alaska Public Lands Information Centers** are centralized sources of information on all government lands, which include some 85% of the state. The centers, in Anchorage, Fairbanks, Ketchikan, and Tok, are operated cooperatively by many land agencies, including the National Park Service and the U.S. Forest Service. The Anchorage center is at 605 W. Fourth Ave., Suite 105, Anchorage, AK 99501 (☎ **907-271-2737;** Internet: www.nps.gov/aplic).

The following list provides contact information for tourism sources in individual towns:

- **Anchorage Convention and Visitors Bureau:** 524 W. Fourth Ave., Anchorage, AK 99501 (☎ **907-276-4118;** Internet: www.anchorage.net)

- **City of Barrow:** Office of the Mayor, P.O. Box 629, Barrow, AK 99723 (☎ **907-852-5211;** Fax: 907-852-5871; E-mail: barrowmayor@nuvuk.com)

- **Fairbanks Convention and Visitors Bureau:** 550 First Ave., Fairbanks, AK 99701 (☎ **800-327-5774** or 907-456-5774; Fax: 907-452-4190; Internet: www.explorefairbanks.com)

- **Homer Chamber of Commerce Visitor Information Center:** 201 Sterling Hwy. (P.O. Box 541), Homer, AK 99603 (☎ **907-235-7740;** Internet: www.homeralaska.org)

- **Juneau Convention and Visitors Bureau:** 101 Egan Dr., Juneau, AK 99801 (☎ **888-581-2201** or 907-586-2201; Fax: 907-586-6304; Internet: www.traveljuneau.com)

- **Kenai Visitors and Cultural Center:** 11471 Kenai Spur Hwy., Kenai, AK 99611 (☎ **907-283-1991;** Internet: www.visitkenai.com)

- **Nome Convention and Visitors Bureau:** Front and Division streets (P.O. Box 240), Nome, AK 99762 (☎ **907-443-6624;** Internet: www.nomealaska.org/vc)

- **Seward Chamber of Commerce:** P.O. Box 749, Seward, AK 99664 (☎ **907-224-8051;** Internet: www.sewardak.org)

- **Sitka Convention and Visitors Bureau:** P.O. Box 1226, Sitka, AK 99835 (☎ **907-747-5940;** Fax: 907-747-3739)

- **Skagway Convention and Visitors Bureau Center:** 245 Broadway (P.O. Box 1029), Skagway, AK 99840 (☎ **907-983-2854;** Fax: 907-983-3854; Internet: www.skagway.org)

- **Soldotna Visitor Information Center:** 44790 Sterling Hwy., Soldotna, AK 99669 (☎ **907-262-9814** or 907-262-1337; Internet: www.SoldotnaChamber.com)

Making Dollars and Sense of It

Expense	Daily cost	x	Number of days	=	Total
Airfare					
Local transportation					
Car rental					
Lodging (with tax)					
Parking					
Breakfast					
Lunch					
Dinner					
Snacks					
Entertainment					
Babysitting					
Attractions					
Gifts & souvenirs					
Tips					
Other					
Grand Total					

Fare Game: Choosing an Airline

When looking for the best airfare, you should cover all your bases — 1) consult a trusted travel agent; 2) contact the airline directly, via the airline's toll-free number and/or Web site; 3) check out one of the travel-planning Web sites, such as www.frommers.com.

Travel Agency_____ Phone_____
    Agent's Name_____ Quoted fare_____

Airline 1_____ Quoted fare_____
    Toll-free number/Internet_____

Airline 2_____ Quoted fare_____
    Toll-free number/Internet_____

Web site 1_____ Quoted fare_____

Web site 2_____ Quoted fare_____

Departure Schedule & Flight Information

Airline_____ Flight #_____ Confirmation #_____

Departs_____ Date_____ Time_____ a.m./p.m.

Arrives_____ Date_____ Time_____ a.m./p.m.

Connecting Flight (if any)

Amount of time between flights_____ hours/mins

Airline_____ Flight #_____ Confirmation #_____

Departs_____ Date_____ Time_____ a.m./p.m.

Arrives_____ Date_____ Time_____ a.m./p.m.

Return Trip Schedule & Flight Information

Airline_____ Flight #_____ Confirmation #_____

Departs_____ Date_____ Time_____ a.m./p.m.

Arrives_____ Date_____ Time_____ a.m./p.m.

Connecting Flight (if any)

Amount of time between flights_____ hours/mins

Airline_____ Flight #_____ Confirmation #_____

Departs_____ Date_____ Time_____ a.m./p.m.

Arrives_____ Date_____ Time_____ a.m./p.m.

All Aboard: Booking Your Train Travel

Travel Agency_____ Phone_____

Agent's Name_____

Web Site_____

Departure Schedule & Train Information

Train #_____ Confirmation #_____ Seat reservation #_____

Departs_____ Date_____ Time_____ a.m./p.m.

Arrives_____ Date_____ Time_____ a.m./p.m.

Quoted fare_____ First class _____ Second class

Departure Schedule & Train Information

Train #_____ Confirmation #_____ Seat reservation #_____

Departs_____ Date_____ Time_____ a.m./p.m.

Arrives_____ Date_____ Time_____ a.m./p.m.

Quoted fare_____ First class _____ Second class

Departure Schedule & Train Information

Train #_____ Confirmation #_____ Seat reservation #_____

Departs_____ Date_____ Time_____ a.m./p.m.

Arrives_____ Date_____ Time_____ a.m./p.m.

Quoted fare_____ First class _____ Second class

Departure Schedule & Train Information

Train #_____ Confirmation #_____ Seat reservation #_____

Departs_____ Date_____ Time_____ a.m./p.m.

Arrives_____ Date_____ Time_____ a.m./p.m.

Quoted fare_____ First class _____ Second class

Your Cruise & Ferry Schedule

Travel Agency_____ Phone_____

Agent's Name_____

Web Site_____

Cruise Information & Departure Schedule

Cruise Line_____ Ship Name_____

Port of Embarkation_____ Date_____

Boarding Time_____ a.m./p.m.   Departure Time_____ a.m./p.m.

Ports of Call_____

Return Cruise Information

Port_____ Date_____ Time_____ a.m./p.m.

Ferry Information & Departure Schedule

Ferry Line_____ Ship Name_____

Departure Port_____ Date_____

Boarding Time_____ a.m./p.m.   Quoted Fare_____

Departure Time_____ a.m./p.m.   Arrival Time_____ a.m./p.m.

Ferry Information & Departure Schedule

Ferry Line_____ Ship Name_____

Departure Port_____ Date_____

Boarding Time_____ a.m./p.m.   Quoted Fare_____

Departure Time_____ a.m./p.m.   Arrival Time_____ a.m./p.m.

Ferry Information & Departure Schedule

Ferry Line_____ Ship Name_____

Departure Port_____ Date_____

Boarding Time_____ a.m./p.m.   Quoted Fare_____

Departure Time_____ a.m./p.m.   Arrival Time_____ a.m./p.m.

Sweet Dreams: Choosing Your Hotel

Make a list of all the hotels where you'd like to stay and then check online and call the local and toll-free numbers to get the best price. You should also check with a travel agent, who may be able to get you a better rate.

Hotel & page	Location	Internet	Tel. (local)	Tel. (Toll-free)	Quoted rate

Hotel Checklist

Here's a checklist of things to inquire about when booking your room, depending on your needs and preferences.

- ❏ Smoking/smoke-free room
- ❏ Noise (if you prefer a quiet room, ask about proximity to elevator, bar/restaurant, pool, meeting facilities, renovations, and street)
- ❏ View
- ❏ Facilities for children (crib, roll-away cot, babysitting services)
- ❏ Facilities for travelers with disabilities
- ❏ Number and size of bed(s) (king, queen, double/full-size)
- ❏ Is breakfast included? (buffet, continental, or sit-down?)
- ❏ In-room amenities (hair dryer, iron/board, minibar, etc.)
- ❏ Other_____

Places to Go, People to See, Things to Do

Enter the attractions you would most like to see and decide how they'll fit into your schedule. Next, use the "Going My Way" worksheets that follow to sketch out your itinerary.

Attraction/activity	Page	Amount of time you expect to spend there	Best day and time to go

Going "My" Way

Day 1
Hotel_____ Tel._____

Morning_____

_____

Lunch_____ Tel._____

Afternoon_____

_____

Dinner_____ Tel._____

Evening_____

_____

Day 2
Hotel_____ Tel._____

Morning_____

_____

Lunch_____ Tel._____

Afternoon_____

_____

Dinner_____ Tel._____

Evening_____

_____

Day 3
Hotel_____ Tel._____

Morning_____

_____

Lunch_____ Tel._____

Afternoon_____

_____

Dinner_____ Tel._____

Evening_____

_____

Going "My" Way

Day 4

Hotel_____ Tel._____

Morning_____

_____

Lunch_____ Tel._____

Afternoon_____

_____

Dinner_____ Tel._____

Evening_____

_____

Day 5

Hotel_____ Tel._____

Morning_____

_____

Lunch_____ Tel._____

Afternoon_____

_____

Dinner_____ Tel._____

Evening_____

_____

Day 6

Hotel_____ Tel._____

Morning_____

_____

Lunch_____ Tel._____

Afternoon_____

_____

Dinner_____ Tel._____

Evening_____

_____

Index

• D •

Dall sheep, 117, 197
Dalton Highway, 286
Danny J, 249
Darwin's Theory, 187, 191
David Green Master Furrier, 189
Dawn, 100
Dawson City, 287, 288, 334
day hiking, 109–110
Days of '98 Show, 341
de Creeft, Bill (aviator), 251
Decker/Morris Gallery, 187
Delta Junction, 284
Denali Air, 304
Denali Bluffs Hotel, 306
Denali Crow's Nest Cabins, 308
Denali Highway, 287
Denali National Park
  accommodations, 306–308
  campgrounds, 308–309
  children and, 301
  description of, 17, 291–292
  Discovery Hikes, 110
  entrance fees, 294
  hiking and backpacking from bus,
    302–303, 385–386
  itinerary for, 27–28
  layout of, 296–298
  main entrance and visitor
    center, 298
  packing for, 294
  ranger programs, 305
  restaurants, 309–310
  shuttle bus, 299–302
  Talkeetna/Denali Visitor Center, 299
  weather, 20
  wildlife, 10
Denali Outdoor Center, 108, 111, 305
Denali River View Inn, 308
Denali Wear, 187
Denali West Lodge, 113
Depot Museum, 285
Diamond Princess, 100–101
Dianne's Restaurant, 164
dining. *See* restaurants
disability, traveler with, 45–46, 80

discounts
  finding, 39
  room rate, 125–127
  senior traveler, 44–45
Discovery Hikes, 302
Discovery riverboat, 267–268
Di Sopra, 26, 322
dog mushing. *See also* sled dog race
  Anchorage, 181–182
  Fairbanks, 270
  Girdwood, 201
  Juneau, 329
  overview of, 112–113
  Seward, 227
Double Musky Inn, 203
Doug Geeting Aviation, 305
Douglas, 316
Douglas Café, 27, 322
Downtown Deli and Café, 31, 168
Driftwood Inn, 244–245
The Driftwood Lodge, 320
drinking tainted water, 106–107
driving. *See also* car, renting
  to Alaska, 61
  in Anchorage, 152–153, 176
  to Anchorage, 150
  from Anchorage to Glennallen,
    283–284
  from Anchorage to Valdez, 280–281
  to Denali National Park, 294–295
  from Denali to Anchorage, 285
  drinking and, 152
  in Fairbanks, 257–258
  to Fairbanks, 256
  from Fairbanks to Denali, 285
  from Glennallen to Anchorage, 283
  from Glennallen to Fairbanks, 284
  gravel roads, 70
  in Homer, 250
  in Juneau, 316
  off pavement, 277, 286
  restrooms along highways, 400
  road conditions, 73, 288
  safety tips, 71–73
  Seward Highway, 195–199
  tundra, 366
  from Valdez to Glennallen, 282–283

FOR DUMMIES®

A world of resources to help you grow

TRAVEL

0-7645-5453-0

0-7645-5438-7

0-7645-5444-1

EDUCATION & TEST PREPARATION

0-7645-5194-9

0-7645-5325-9

0-7645-5249-X

HEALTH, SELF-HELP & SPIRITUALITY

0-7645-5154-X

0-7645-5302-X

0-7645-5418-2

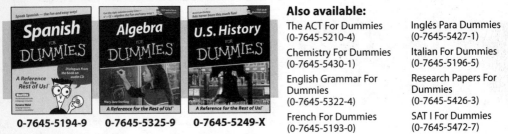

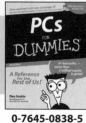